SD14: DIE GANZE GESCHICHTE

John Lingwood

SD14: DIE GANZE GESCHICHTE
John Lingwood

Eine Veröffentlichung von Ships in Focus

Erschienen 2005 in Großbritannien bei Ships in Focus Publications
18 Franklands, Longton
Preston PR4 5PD

© 2004 John Lingwood und Ships in Focus Publications

Deutsche Übersetzung durch C.Norbert Bellstedt

Druck: Amadeus Press Ltd., Cleckheaton, West Yorkshire
ISBN 1-901703-66-5

Schutzumschlag; vorn: *Bronte* (Southwick Werftnummer 1385) in Liverpool. *[Paul Boot]*
Schutzumschlag, hinten: Der erste und der letzte SD 14, die vom Stapel liefen: Bartram Werftnummer 410, wie sie zuletzt als *Wavecrest* im April 1985 auf Vlissingen Reede zu sehen war, und *North Islands* (Smith's Dock Werftnummer 1360) unmittelbar nach Stapellauf am 15. Oktober 1986. *[David Salisbury; Michael Green]*
Frontispiz: *Sunderland Venture*, der letzte in Sunderland gebaute SD 14, auf der Probefahrt (Southwick Werftnummer 1426). *[Sammlung John Clarkson]*
Titelseite: Eine großartige Aufnahme eines der frühen SD 14 von der Werft Southwick in klassischem Rahmen: *Syrie* (Werftnummer 853) in Kapstadt. *[Ken White, Sammlung Don Brown]*
Vorderes Vorsatzblatt: *Porto Alegre* in Kapstadt. (Southwick, Werftnummer 888) *[Sammlung V.H.Young und L.A.Sawyer]*
Hinteres Vorsatzblatt: *Ignacio Agramonte* in Vancouver (Austin & Pickersgill, South Dock, Werftnummer 453). *[Don Brown]*

EINFÜHRUNG

Nach meiner Erinnerung waren es nur acht Leute, die am Freitag, dem 21. Januar 1966 unter dem Vorsitz des Vorstandsvorsitzenden Ken Douglas am Tisch des Sitzungssaales von Austin & Pickersgill saßen. Wir hatten die Aufgabe, den Inhalt der Bauvorschrift festzulegen und die Entwurfskizze des Generalplans gutzuheißen, die das Konstruktionsbüro in aller Eile erarbeitet hatten. Sie waren die Grundlage einer Kostenschätzung, die meine Ingenieur-Kollegen und ich für etwas durchzuführen hatten, das seinerzeit in der Firma ziemlich abschätzig 'das Sparsamkeits-Schiff' genannt wurde. Ich betone 'in aller Eile', denn erst am späten Nachmittag des Vortages war der Aufsichtsratsvorsitzende der Gesellschaft, Charles Longbottom, nach dem Stapellaufempfang des 30.000 tdw Bulkcarriers *Margharita Chandris* erschienen und hatte die Mitteilung seines Schwiegervaters Basil Mavroleon (dem über seine Firma London & Overseas Freighters die Werft gehörte) überbracht, dieser würde zwei solcher 'Sparsamkeits-Schiffe' -bald unter der Bezeichnung Liberty Ship Replacement bekannt- bestellen, 'wenn der Preis stimmt'. Das war eine gute Nachricht für das kleine Konstruktionsteam, die schlechte Nachricht war, daß das offizielle Angebot innerhalb von zwei Wochen fertiggestellt werden mußte – daher die Eile.

Ich bin mir sicher, daß zu der Zeit keiner von uns die Bedeutung der Aufgabe erahnte, an der wir beteiligt wurden. In Southwick war der Bau von Standard-Bulkcarriern inzwischen normales Tagesgeschäft. Dabei wurde den Reedern die Auswahl aus einer Kollektion sehr unterschiedlicher Schiffe ermöglicht. Tatsächlich bot die Werft immer noch jeweils einmalige Schiffe an. Das neue Vorhaben hieß die Serienfertigung eines *einzigen Entwurfs*, verbunden mit allen Vorteilen der Techniken der Massenproduktion und des Masseneinkaufs, die andere Industriezweige bereits revolutioniert hatten. Damit dieses Konzept auch funktionieren konnte, mußte auch die Art der Auftragsvergabe für Schiffsneubauten geändert werden. Nun war die Werft gefordert, zum Reeder zu gehen und diesen davon zu überzeugen, daß der nun vorgelegte Entwurf von der Stange, der auf sorgfältigster Marktbeobachtung beruhte, zusammen mit einem günstigen Finanzierungspaket seinen Bedürfnissen vollständig entsprach. Ob das klappen würde ? Wären die Reeder bereit, diese radikale Veränderung der Art und Weise hinzunehmen, in der Schiffe fast immer bestellt und gebaut worden waren, außer vielleicht in Kriegszeiten ? Austin & Pickersgill hielten es bezeichnenderweise für klug, zu diesem Zeitpunkt nur ein anfängliches Bauprogramm von fünf Schiffen ins Auge zu fassen.

Auf den folgenden Seiten steht die Geschichte des phänomenalen Erfolges dieses Projekts. Erst 1984 sollte der 126ste und letzte in Sunderland gebaute SD14 fertiggestellt werden. Das letzte in Großbritannien erbaute Schiff dieses Entwurfs folgte zwei Jahre später von Smith's Dock in Middlesbrough, während 1988, also zwanzig Jahre nach Ablieferung der *Nicola*, des ersten Schiffs der Serie, die letzten beiden Exemplare dieses einfachen Trampschiffs ihre Bauwerft in Rio de Janeiro verließen und damit die Gesamtzahl der weltweit von den Schöpfern und ihren Lizenznehmern erbauten Schiffe auf 211 brachten. Es ist bedeutungsvoll und fällt zeitlich damit zusammen, daß im selben Jahr in Sunderland, 5.412 Meilen entfernt, sich ein ganzer Industriezweig verabschiedete. Widersprüchliche Pläne für das Ende des Schiffbaus in diesem Hafen entwickelten sich mit fast unanständiger Hast. Es schien, als würden die wenigen verbleibenden Werften und Schiffsmaschinenfabriken an den Ufern des Wear ohne viel Federlesen stillgelegt und damit das Erbe dessen ausgelöscht würde, was einstmals die größte Schiffbaustadt der Welt war. Nicht lange danach wiederholte sich diese Welle der Stillegungen in ganz Großbritannien. Es verbleiben nur noch eine Handvoll Werften mit Verbindungen zur Marine.

Auf der Southwick-Werft verbleiben heute nur noch der Ausrüstungskai und ein paar angrenzende Werkstätten mit diversen Leichtindustriebetrieben, bewacht von einem einzelnen, längst nicht mehr benutzen Kran. Sie bezeichnen die kurze aber bemerkenswerte Zeitspanne, in welcher der Bau des SD14 tatsächlich das war, was in der Unterzeile zu des Verfassers Buch aus dem Jahre 1976 so heißt: ‚Die große Erfolgsgeschichte des britischen Schiffbaus'.

John Lingwood   Sunderland 2004

ANMERKUNG DES VERLAGES

Es ist unmöglich, das Schlußwort über den SD 14 zu schreiben, bis nicht alle noch überlebenden Schiffe, bei Veröffentlichung immerhin mehr als 50, verschrottet wurden, verloren gingen, oder es eine Bestätigung über ihr Schicksal gibt. Statt bis dahin zu warten, haben sich Verfasser und Verlag entschlossen, die Geschichte jetzt zu erzählen. Zwecks Aktualisierung wird die Verlagszeitschrift ‚Ships in Focus Record' von Zeit zu Zeit Einzelheiten über die verbliebenen Schiffe veröffentlichen. Wir hoffen sehr, daß unsere Leser uns dabei durch Mitteilungen über etwaige Veränderungen helfen werden, auch mit Meldungen über SD 14, die noch in Fahrt sind oder schon nicht mehr existieren.

Das Veröffentlichungsteam, nämlich Paul Boot, John Clarkson und Roy Fenton, hat über jene hinaus, die in der Danksagung des Verfassers auf der gegenüberliegenden Seite erwähnt werden, Dank abzustatten an die vielen Photographen, die namentlich gewürdigt werden, besonders aber auch an die Nachstehenden, die uns ihre umfangreichen Sammlungen freigiebig zur Verfügung stellten und dadurch wesentlich dazu beitrugen, jeden SD 14 und Prinasa-121 abzubilden: David Salisbury, Nigel Jones, Roy Kittle, Don Brown, Trevor Jones, David Whiteside, Michael Green, Harold Appleyard und Ian Farquhar. Dank gebührt auch all jenen, die auch in letzter Minute Informationen zu noch in Fahrt befindlichen Schiffen lieferten. Dazu gehören einmal mehr Nigel Jones und Trevor Jones, besonders aber David Hazell und Simon Smith, die The Shipping Information Service betreiben und per e-Mail unter shipinform@aol.com zu erreichen sind. Paul Boot vor allem ist Nigel Bowker dankbar für seine Hilfe bei der Herstellung und Sinclair Marine Arts für die Mithilfe bei der Gestaltung des Umschlags.

INHALT

DANKSAGUNGEN

Zu den faszinierendsten Merkmalen des SD14-Programms zählt das Interesse, das es nicht nur bei 'Profis' sondern auch von Schiffahrt-Begeisterten aller Schichten hervorgerufen hat. Daraus entstand eine Anteilnahme, die in den allerersten Tagen begann, sich über fast 40 Jahre erhielt und immer noch nicht nachläßt, wie aus den Briefen, Fotografien und Informationen hervorgeht, die ich regelmäßig aus Quellen rund um die Welt bekomme. Weder die vorliegende Geschichte des SD14 noch 'SD14 – The Great British Shipbuilding Success Story', erschienen 1976 bei der World Ship Society, wären ohne diese Unterstützung geschrieben worden. Für die Hilfe dieser Freunde, und das sind sie, die alle in irgendeiner Weise zum Entstehen dieses Buchs beitrugen, bedanke ich mich hiermit bei:

Jack Appleton, David Aris, David Asprey, Tony Atkinson, Rod Baker, M.Beckett, Andrew Bell, Guilermo Berger (Buenos Aires), Markus Berger (Schweiz), David Burrell, Ian Buxton, J.K.Byass, Michael Cassar (Malta), Anne Cowne (Lloyd's Register), Malcolm Cranfield, Peter Crichton, David Crolley, Michael Crowdy, M.R.Dippy (Australien), Malcolm Donnelly, dem verstorbenen Alex Duncan, Ian Gilbert (Südafrika), Andy Goodson, Brent Hanson (Neuseeland), David Hazell, Paul Hood, David Hunt, Dennis Johnzon, Barbara Jones (Lloyd's Register), Nigel Jones, J.M.Kakebeeke (Niederlande), Michael Lennon, Zygmunt Lietka (Polen), Norman Middlemiss, dem verstorbenen Bill Mitchell, Kevin Moore (Südafrika), B.S.Nicholl, Kevin O'Donaghue, Jean M.Otten (Niederlande), Jim und Alice Prentice, Ivor Rooke, Selim San (Türkei), dem verstorbenen Len Sawyer, Oliver Sesemann (Deutschland), David Shackleton (Südafrika), John Sins (Niederlande), Alan Sparrow, Ian Tremlett (Südafrika), M.H.Turner, Stephen Woods, dem verstorbenen David Worthy, und der New Zealand Ship and Marine Society. Ich weiß, daß es noch viele weitere Kontakte gibt, deren Namen mir nur nicht einfallen. Bei ihnen entschuldige ich mich in aller Form dafür, sie nicht erwähnt zu haben.

Viele der oben Aufgeführten haben Fotografien geliefert. Auf deren Herkunft wurde an passender Stelle im Text dieser Veröffentlichung hingewiesen. Hier wird der Dank dafür wiederholt, zugleich auch an Turners (Photography) Ltd. und an Airfotos, die hauptsächlichen offiziellen Probefahrtsfotografen von Austin & Pickersgill in der Zeit des SD14-Bauprogramms. Auch Fotografien der Fotoabteilung der Werft wurden verwendet.

Der überwiegende Teil des Forschungsmaterials entstammt den persönlichen Aufzeichnungen des Verfassers. Die Lebensläufe der Schiffe wurden mit ,Lloyd's Register', ,Lloyd's Confidential Index', persönlichen Listen der oben Aufgeführten (vor allem von Kevin Moore) und ,Marine News', der Zeitschrift der World Ship Society verglichen, hauptsächlich von Roy Fenton. Ich danke dafür, die Einrichtungen der Guildhall-Bibliothek und von Lloyd's Register of Shipping benutzen zu dürfen. Besonderer Dank gilt dem Redaktionsteam von ,Ships in Focus', Roy Fenton, John Clarkson, Paul Boot, Heather Fenton und Marion Clarkson.

Besondere Anerkennung gebührt allen, die zum Erfolg des SD14-Programms durch ihre Arbeit in den Werften Southwick und South Dock und bei den Lizenznehmern, Herstellern der Hauptmaschinen und den Unterlieferanten beigetragen haben, und auch den Reedern und Maklern, von denen dieses ungewöhnliche Schiff betrieben und vermittelt wurde. Ihre Gesamtzahl müßte, gerechnet über die 20jährige Produktionszeit, bei mehreren Tausend liegen. Sie alle können stolz darauf sein, ein Teil der großen Erfolgsgeschichte des Schiffbaus im Zwanzigsten Jahrhundert gewesen zu sein.

SD14 – DIE GANZE GESCHICHTE

Austin & Pickersgill vor dem SD14

Austin & Pickersgill Ltd. (A&P) entstand 1954 aus der Fusion zweier alteingesessener Schiffbauunternehmen aus Sunderland, nämlich S.P.Austin & Sons Ltd. und William Pickersgill & Sons Ltd. 1826 hatte Peter Austin mit dem Schiffbau in North Sands begonnen, nahe der Mündung des Flusses Wear. Zwanzig Jahre später zog der Betrieb zur Wear Marinewerft am südlichen Flußufer um, gleich unterhalb der beiden Brücken, die heute die hauptsächlichen Straßen- und Bahnverbindungen über den Fluß bilden. Dort wurden Schiffe gebaut und repariert, bis der Betrieb 1964 geschlossen wurde. Die Familie Pickersgill begann den Schiffbau 1838 im North Dock nahe von North Sands und verlegte die Aktivitäten später in eine Werft etwa vier Meilen stromaufwärts nach Southwick. Nachkommen der Gründer behielten zwar Anteile an ihren jeweiligen Unternehmen bis zu deren Fusion im Jahre 1954, aber in beiden Firmen waren zwei führende einheimische Reederfamilien, die Westolls und die Adamsons, Mehrheitsaktionäre geworden. Sie waren auch die treibenden Kräfte der Fusion, die vermutlich dadurch entstand, daß beide Betriebe unter beengten räumlichen Bedingungen arbeiteten.

Während des Zweiten Weltkriegs ergab sich für Pickergill die Möglichkeit. zur Erweiterung ihres Betriebsgelände durch Wiedereröffnung der benachbarten Schiffswerft von Sir John Priestman. Diese war einige Jahre früher während der Wirtschaftskrise der dreißiger Jahre geschlossen worden. Jetzt wurden hier Fregatten und Landungsfahrzeuge für die Royal Navy gebaut. Nach Kriegsende nahm Pickersgill den Handelsschiffbau an beiden Standorten wieder auf, die durch eine große ungenutzte Fläche voneinander getrennt waren. In deren Mitte befand sich ein großer Hügel aus Ballastsand und Kies, hier angelandet von Kohleschiffen, die in der Zeit, als Wasser noch nicht als Ballast genutzt wurde, zum Kohleladen in den Hafen kamen. Die jeweiligen Geschäftsleitungen von Austin

und von Pickersgill betrachteten die beiden Werften und die ungenutzte Fläche als eine Grundlage für einen neuen Schiffbaubetrieb mit großen Fertigungs- und Montagehallen und für die Einführung des Baukastensystems und modernster Schiffbautechniken. Hier gab es die Möglichkeit, in Southwick Schiffe bis zu 40.000 tdw zu bauen statt der zuvor maximal 10.000 tdw, und das auf neuen Hellingen mit großzügiger Kranausrüstung in der früheren Priestman-Werft. Die Ausrüstung konnte dann in modernen Anlagen auf dem alten Pickersgill-Gelände stattfinden. Der letzte dort fertiggestellte Neubau (der 9.305 tdw Erzfrachter *Needles*) wurde im Mai 1958 abgeliefert.

Eine wesentliche Entwicklung trat 1957 ein, als die neue Gesellschaft von einem Konsortium erworben wurde, das aus der Londoner Griechen gehörenden Reederei London & Overseas Freighters Ltd. (LOF), der Reederei-, Versicherungs- und Schiffsmaklerfirma Lambert Brothers Ltd. und dem Bankhaus Philip Hill, Higginson Ltd. bestand. 1970 übernahm LOF die Anteile der anderen Partner und gewann damit die Kontrolle über A&P. Dabei blieb es, bis im Zuge der Verstaatlichung die Firma 1977 der British Shipbuilders Corporation eingegliedert wurde. In diesen fast zwanzig Jahren bauten Austin & Pickersgill 27 Schiffe für unmittelbar zu LOF gehörende Gesellschaften und führten Reparaturen an weiteren Schiffen durch.

Ebenfalls im Jahr 1838 hatte George Bartram, zusammen mit einem gewissen John Lister, in South Hylton angefangen, Schiffe zu bauen. Das war etwa dort, wo der Fluß Wear schiffbar wird, rund zwei Meilen flußaufwärts vom späteren Austin & Pickersgill Betriebsgelände. Nach verschiedenen Umzügen landete er schließlich am entgegengesetzten Extrem, in einer Werft an der Flußmündung innerhalb der South Docks, jedoch liefen die Schiffe, was einmalig war, direkt ins Meer vom Stapel. Seine Firma hieß anfänglich Bartram, Haswell & Company, später Bartram & Sons Ltd. Nach einem Abkommen aus dem Jahr 1965 führte die neu eingerichtete Maschinenausrüstungsabteilung von Austin & Pickersgill solche Arbeiten für

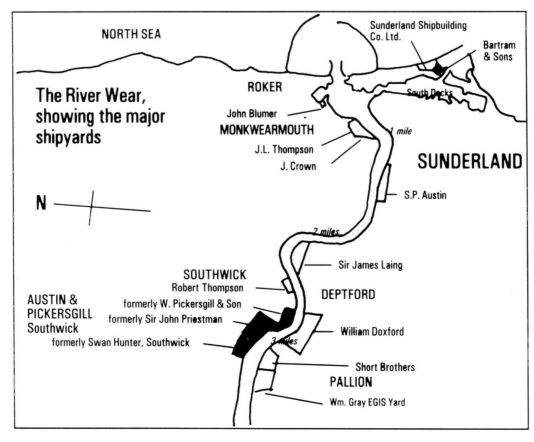

The River Wear, showing the major shipyards

Bartram durch. Diese Zusammenarbeit wurde 1966 erweitert, als Bartram begannen, SD14-Schiffe in Lizenz zu bauen. Zwei Jahre später fusionierten beide Unternehmen. Die Werft im South Dock wurde 1978 geschlossen und die Produktion in eine erst kurz zuvor erweiterte Werft in Southwick verlagert, wahrscheinlich die modernste Schiffswerft ihrer Zeit. Ihr Schicksal war es, nur weitere zehn Jahre zu bestehen, bis Regierungsmaßnahmen zum Ende des industriellen Handelsschiffbaus in Großbritannien führten. Das Werft wurde ziemlich rasch demontiert.

Ersatz für die Liberties

Während des Zweiten Weltkrieges wurden die Flotten der Alliierten um mehr als 3.000 Tramp-Frachtschiffe von etwa 10.000 tdw verstärkt. Großbritannien und Canada trugen zwar erheblich zu dieser Zahl bei (und nicht zu vergessen Hong Kong mit fünf Einheiten), aber die Vereinigten Staaten von Amerika lieferten mit 2.770 Schiffen den weitaus größten Teil. Die Mehrzahl davon waren Frachter, von der United States Maritime Commission mit EC2-S-C1 bezeichnet, später aber amtlich deshalb ‚Liberty Ship‘ genannt, um gegen die vielen herabsetzenden Namen anzugehen wie ‚Häßliches Entlein‘ oder ‚Seekuh‘, die ihnen von einer nicht sonderlich begeisterten amerikanischen Presse gegeben worden waren. Im weiteren Verlauf des Krieges setzte sich das ‚Liberty Ship‘ derartig stark durch, daß schließlich nahezu alle im Kriege gebauten Tramper dieser Größe ohne Ansehen ihrer Herkunft so genannt wurden. Das wiederum führte in den sechziger Jahren dazu, daß alle Schiffstypen, die sich in jener Zeit als Ersatz für die Frachtschiffsflotten der Welt in der Planung befanden, der Einfachheit halber unter der Bezeichnung Liberty Replacements liefen.

In der Mitte der sechziger Jahre gab es nach Schätzungen noch etwa 700 fahrende Liberty-Frachter und

Luftaufnahme der Southwick-Werft von Austin & Pickersgill aus dem Jahr 1978. Das Schiff am Ausrüstungskai links im Vordergrund ist die *Cluden* (Werftnummer 1378). Rechts neben dem Ausrüstungskai die Ausrüstungswerkstätten. Wiederum rechts davon ein Stahl-Vorratslager. Ein größeres ist weiter rechts davon zu sehen. Die leicht grau gehaltenen Schuppen direkt am Fluß in Bildmitte sind die 1976 errichteten Sektionsbau- und Montagehallen. Die dunkelgrauen Hallen etwas weiter vom Fluß entfernt stammen aus der Planung für die ‚neue‘ Werft 1955 . Der SD 14 am gegenüber liegenden Ufer des Flusses Wear ist wahrscheinlich die *Australind* (Werftnummer 464) bei der Ausrüstung am Pallion Quay, der früher Short Brothers gehörte und 1960 von Bartrams gekauft wurde. Das Schiff mit der grauen Außenhaut auf dem nördlichen konventionellen Helgen ist die *Aegira* (Werftnummer 1379) kurz vor dem Stapellauf, daneben die *Funing* (Werftnummer 1381) in einem frühen Bauzustand. Dahinter die Schiffbauhalle und die Heck- sowie die Sektionsbauhalle aus dem Jahr 1975. [Austin & Pickersgill Ltd.]

vermutlich weitere 800 in der US Marine-Reserveflotte. Auch die jüngsten dieser Einheiten waren zwanzig Jahre alt und näherten sich einer weiteren sehr teuren Klasseverlängerung. Nicht wenige wiesen Zeichen altersbedingter Mängel auf. Die Reeder hatten Schwierigkeiten, Versicherer zu finden, welche die Kasko- oder Ladungsrisiken ohne erhebliche Prämienaufschläge zu decken bereit waren und sahen sich deshalb gezwungen, diese Schiffe zu verschrotten. Für Reeder, die im Geschäft bleiben wollten, war das natürlich eine große Sorge, denn ihnen gehörten jetzt Schiffe, deren niedrige Verkaufserlöse nicht einmal zur Finanzierung gebrauchter Ersatztonnage reichten, und das in einem Markt, in dem Neubauten sehr und für die meisten von ihnen

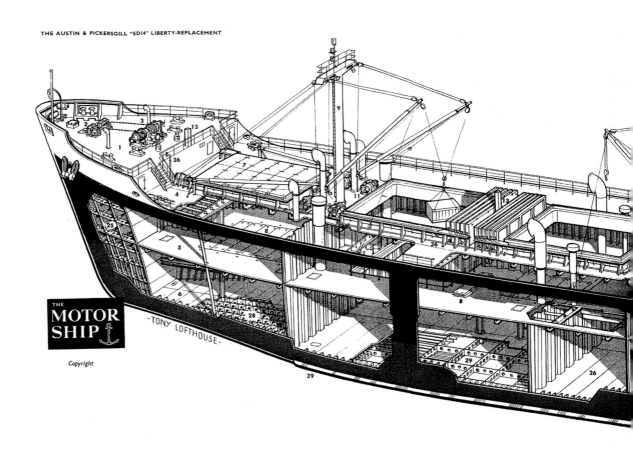

THE AUSTIN & PICKERSGILL "SD14" LIBERTY-REPLACEMENT

THE MOTOR SHIP ⚓

Copyright

-TONY LOFTHOUSE-

A BRITISH LIBERTY-REPLACEMENT SHIP
THE 'SD 14'

A 14 200 TON D.W., TWO-DECK, 14-KNOT, 22 TON/DAY
GENERAL PURPOSE SHIP DESIGNED AND BUILT BY
AUSTIN AND PICKERSGILL LTD., SUNDERLAND, U.K.
AND OFFERED BY OTHER BRITISH AND GREEK SHIPYARDS

	ft	in	metres		
Length, overall	462	6	140·97	Fuel capacity	969 tons
Length, b.p.	440	0	134·13	Diesel oil capacity	111 tons
Breadth, moulded	67	0	20·42	Fresh water capacity	126 tons
Depth, moulded	38	6	11·74	Water ballast	3 323 tons
Draught, loaded	28	6	8·69	Main machinery	Sulzer 5RD68-type
Gross register			8 800 tons	Service rating	5 500 bhp at 135 rev/min
Total d.w.			14 200 tons	Service speed	14 knots

Schnittzeichnung eines SD 14 aus 'The Motor Ship'. *[Veröffentlichung
mit freundlicher Genehmigung von 'The Motor Ship']*

8

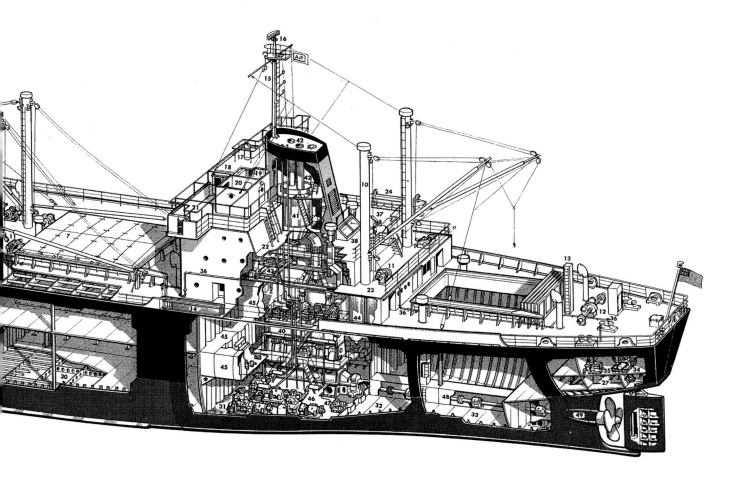

KEY TO THE PRINCIPAL FEATURES OF THE
AUSTIN AND PICKERSGILL BASIC SD 14 DESIGN

1.—Forecastle deck
2.—Bow stoppers
3.—Electric windlass
4.—Upper deck
5.—Second deck
6.—Tank top
7.—MacGregor single-pull hatch covers
8.—Portable pontoon hatch covers
9.—Unstayed mast
10.—Unstayed derrick posts
11.—Cargo/topping winches
12.—Electric warping winch
13.—Hatch stowage posts
14.—Accommodation ladder
15.—Signal mast
16.—Radar scanner

17.—Magnetic compass
18.—Wheelhouse top
19.—Wheelhouse/chartroom
20.—Radio room
21.—Navigating bridge deck
22.—Bridge deck
23.—Boat deck
24.—Glass fibre motor lifeboat stbd. (glass fibre oared lifeboat port)
25.—Forepeak tank
26.—No. 3 hold/deep tank
27.—Aft peak W.B. tank
28.—No. 1 D.B. W.B. tank
29.—No. 2 D.B. W.B. tank
30.—Nos. 3 and 4 D.B. fuel tanks
31.—No. 5 D.B. F.W. tanks, P. and S.
32.—No. 6 D.B. W.B. tank

33.—Tunnel escape
34.—Electro-hydraulic steering gear
35.—Emergency fire pump
36.—Fire/wash deck lines
37.—Spare propeller
38.—Removable skylight
39.—Bilge keel
40.—Sulzer 5RD68 main engine
41.—Composite boiler
42.—Main engine exhaust
43.—Engine-room crane
44.—Main air reservoirs
45.—Fuel and lub. oil tanks
46.—170 kW diesel alternator sets
47.—Main compressors
48.—Main shafting
49.—Stern bossing

Liberty und Liberty Replacement. Das noch erhaltene Liberty-Schiff *Jeremiah O'Brien* (7.176/1943) passiert den chinesischen SD 14 *Rong Jiang* (South Dock, Werftnummer 463) im Panamakanal im Jahre 1994. [David Aris]

unerreichbar teuer wurden. Wer über Neubauten nachdenken konnte stand vor der Frage: Womit ersetzen wir unsere Schiffe?

Auch die Schiffbauer waren besorgt. Viele hatten hohe Investitionen getätigt, um ihre Werften auf Serienfertigung von Standard-Schiffen einzurichten. Es war also wichtig, einen Einstieg in den bereits als lukrativ angesehenen Liberty Replacement-Markt zu finden. Sie mußten allerdings eine ähnliche Frage beantworten: Was bieten wir als Ersatz an? Für einige schien der Weg klar vorgezeichnet, sie sahen es als sicher an, daß die Zukunft bei den vor kurzem eingeführten Bulkern und/oder Containerschiffen lag. Andere, vor allem die Zielgruppe der potentiellen Kunden, die griechischen Reeder mit geringen Eigenmitteln, die den Großteil dieser alternden Libertyflotte besaßen oder sie betrieben, glaubten, es gebe immer noch einen Markt für Zwischendecker mit 14.000 bis 15.000 Tonnen Tragfähigkeit und einer Geschwindigkeit von etwa 15 Knoten, zum Preis von unter £ 1 Mio und, besonders wichtig, mit günstigen Krediten. Mit anderen Worten ein modernisierter Liberty, zuverlässig, ohne Kinkerlitzchen und von einem Typ, mit dem sie vertraut waren. Das wurde am Ende zur bevorzugten Richtung. Anfang 1966 kamen Werften aus aller Welt mit einigen dreißig Entwürfen für Liberty Ship Replacements auf den Markt, die alle mehr oder weniger den obigen Parametern entsprachen. Nur zwei davon sollten größere Erfolge verzeichnen: der SD14, von Austin & Pickersgill, Sunderland, entwickelt, und der Freedom, entworfen vom kanadischen Schiffbauberater G.T.R.Campbell, der sein Handwerk am Tyne erlernt hatte. Das Schiff wurde von Ishikawajima-Harima Heavy Industries (IHI) auf ihrer Werft in Tokyo gebaut sowie von einigen Lizenznehmern.

Eine Anzahl britischer Werften, darunter Austin & Pickersgill (A&P), erörterten erstmals während einer Sitzung im Februar 1965 in Edinburgh die Möglichkeit, einen einheitlichen britischen Liberty Replacement-Typ zu vermarkten, der unter Lizenz von mehreren britischen Werften gebaut werden könnte. Wie in den einleitenden Absätzen erläutert, waren A&P 1954 aus einer Fusion zweier kleinerer Schiffswerften aus Sunderland hervorgegangen und drei Jahre danach von einem Konsortium unter der Führung von London & Overseas Freighters Ltd (LOF) übernommen worden, ihrerseits ein Teil der Familien-Schiffahrtsgruppe Londoner Griechen, Rethymnis/Kulukundis/Mavroleon. A&P nahmen auf diese Sitzung einen Rat von Mr. B.M.Mavroleon von LOF mit, der selbst eine große Flotte hauptsächlich in Kanada gebauter Standardschiffe aus Kriegszeiten betrieb, wonach griechische Reeder den Preis für einen Liberty Replace-ment von um £800.000 für annehmbar hielten. Weil A&P die einzigen Sitzungsteilnehmer waren, deren Schätzpreis von etwa £ 900.000 auch nur entfernt in der Nähe dieses Zieles lag, konnte das Projekt nur aufgegeben werden.

Gemeinsam war die Frage des Liberty Ship Replacement nicht zu lösen, und dennoch ließen Austin & Pickersgill nicht von der Idee, hatten aber ihre Arbeiten an dem Entwurf fast ein Jahr lang zurückzustellen, weil andere feste Bauverträge Aufmerksamkeit verlangten.

Das Projekt erwachte plötzlich zu neuem Leben, als Anfang 1966 Mr. Mavroleon der Werft erklärte, er würde sofort zwei Zwischendecker mit 14.000 tdw und 14-15 Knoten, erbaut nach einem Liberty Ship Replacement-Entwurf, bestellen, „...wenn der Preis stimmt." Der richtige Preis, meinte er, seien maximal £ 900.000. Eine Gruppe von Konstrukteuren wurde zusammengestellt, darunter auch der Verfasser als Erster Kalkulator. Während einer Sitzung am 21. Januar 1966 unter der Leitung des damaligen Vorstandsvorsitzers Kenneth Douglas wurden Entwurf und Baubeschreibung der Schiffe festgelegt, und es begann die Arbeit an der Kostenschätzung. Die Arbeitsgruppe stand vor einem großen Problem: seit Kriegsende hatten viele teure Verfeinerungen Eingang in die Konstruktion derzeitiger Frachter dieser Größe gefunden, die dadurch deutlich mehr als £ 1 Mio kosteten und wegen der eingebauten Preissteigerungsklauseln noch teurer zu werden drohten. Um Mr. Mavroleon's Vorgabe zu erreichen, mußten jetzt aus der Bauvorschrift alle Positionen gestrichen werden, die für den wirtschaftlichen Betrieb des Schiffs verzichtbar waren.

Die Gruppe war der Meinung, daß einer der wesentlichen Faktoren für den Verkauf dieses Typs ein niedriger Preis war, meinte aber, es würde immer noch Reeder geben, die einige der gestrichenen Positionen für ihre Schiffe wünschten. Daraus entstand die Idee, eine Liste von Zusatzausrüstungen aufzustellen, die auf Wunsch lieferbar war. Die Liste sollte Änderungen zur Verbesserung des Basisentwurfs enthalten, welche die Werft vorzunehmen bereit war, und die darauf entfallenden Kosten. Der Käufer sollte also sehen, wieviel ihn das Schiff voraussichtlich kosten werde und konnte die Bankdarlehen und Kreditzusagen entsprechend aushandeln, ehe er das Schiff endgültig bestellte. Das war deshalb wichtig, weil nach Kontraktzeichnung vorgenommene Veränderung bar bezahlt werden mußten.

Viele der Positionen, die während der ersten Besprechung gestrichen wurden, betrafen die Maschineneinrichtung, in die in den letzten Jahren aus verständlichen Gründen mancherlei Reservevorrichtungen eingebaut worden waren, denn kein Reeder, und besonders kein technischer Inspektor, wollte sein Schiff wegen eines Maschinenschadens oder fehlender Ersatzteile nicht einsatzbereit in einem weit entfernten Hafen liegen sehen. Inzwischen hatte aber die rasche Entwicklung der Luftfracht dazu geführt, daß Ersatzteile oder ganze Ersatz-Baugruppen innerhalb von Tagen an jeden Platz der Erde geliefert werden konnten. Folglich beschlossen Austin & Pickersgill, teure Ersatzteile wie Propeller oder Schwanzwellen oder sonstige Standard-Ersatzteile zu streichen. Vielmehr wurde vorgesehen, daß die Lieferanten solche Ersatzteile vorhalten, um sie bei Bedarf an Schiffe zu liefern, die sie benötigten.

Die Wahl der Hauptmaschine wurde sehr sorgfältig überdacht. Die Maschine mußte sich unbedingt bewährt haben und von einfacher Konstruktion sein, um so weit wie möglich einen störungsfreien Betrieb und lange Laufzeiten zu gewähren. Diese Grundvoraussetzungen gaben einem langsam laufenden Diesel den Vorzug vor mittelschnell laufenden Anlagen mit Getriebe, die weit mehr bewegliche Teile aufwiesen, um diese Zeit aber auf den Markt kamen. Also wurde beschlossen, die erfolgreiche Fünfzylinder Sulzer 5RD68 Maschine einzubauen, die den Vorteil hatte, von vielen

Lizenznehmern gebaut zu werden und über eine weltweite Ersatzteile- und Serviceorganisation zu verfügen. Vor allem aber galt von Anfang an und über die gesamte Projektdauer hinweg das Leitmotiv, wonach das Schiff zwar preisgünstig sein soll, aber nie zu Lasten der Qualität. Paradoxerweise besaß das Konkurrenzschiff Freedom nicht nur eine mittelschnell laufende Pielstickmaschine, sondern hatte diese sehr unkonventionell nach Backbord versetzt angeordnet mit einer am vorderen Ende des Motors herausgeführten Antriebswelle. Diese war mit einem Untersetzungsgetriebe verbunden, aus dem dann die Propellerwelle auf Mitte Schiff austrat und damit das Drehmoment zum Propeller übertrug. Soweit bekannt, hat diese neue und, wie manche dachten, komplizierte Anordnung (sowie eine Menge anderer Neuerungen) zwar die Skeptiker verwirrt (das schloß A&P ein), aber weder den Schiffen noch deren Besatzungen betriebliche Schwierigkeiten verursacht.

Die Entwürfe und die Kostenkalkulationen waren wie erbeten am 4. Februar 1966 fertig. Die Kostenschätzung ergab einen Verkaufspreis von £ 915.000, welcher der Werft noch einen kleinen Gewinn ließ. Die beiden Schiffe wurden Mr. Mavroleon zu dem herabgesetzten Preis von £ 895.000 pro Einheit angeboten, der, da der Preis seiner Forderung entsprach, sofort Aufträge für zwei Liberia-Firmen erteilte, die im Management von Mavrolean Brothers Ltd., London, standen. Wir haben oben bereits die Bezeichnung SD14 gebraucht, aber offiziell wurde sie erst von diesem Stand der Entwicklung an benutzt. Austin & Pickersgill hatten schon seit einigen Jahren Standardschiffe gebaut, und zwar eine Reihe von Bulkcarriern, die bereits in Fahrt waren und für die folgende Bezeichnungen galten: **B** (für Bulker), gefolgt von einer Ziffer wie z.B. **26,** welche die Tragfähigkeit

Eine Bodenplatte wird ausgerichtet (oben), und eine Hauptmaschine wird abgesenkt (unten), beides im neuen Schiffbaukomplex in Southwick. Im oberen Bild ist der Rumpf eines Schiffs in fortgeschrittenerem Bauzustand zu sehen, dazwischen auch die Gleitschienen für Sektionen.

angab, beispielsweise 26.000 Tonnen. Für den Typ Liberty Ship Replacement lag auf der Hand, daß die Typenbezeichnung **SD** sein mußte (= shelter-deck) und **14** (14.000 tdw). Einzelheiten der wesentlichen Hauptdaten, eine kurze Bauvorschrift und ein Generalplan des Schiffs, so wie es entworfen wurde, befinden sich in diesem Buch, aber schon vor Baubeginn der ersten Schiffe nahm man Änderungen vor, und weitere folgten während der Dauer des SD14 Bauprogramms, als Folge-Serien des Entwurfs entwickelt wurden. Darauf wird in späteren Kapiteln Bezug genommen.

Der Anfang des SD14

Kurz ehe die Arbeiten am Entwurf für den SD14 begannen, im Januar 1966, hatten Austin & Pickersgill Verhandlungen mit einem anderen griechischen Reeder aufgenomme, George Papalios, dessen rasch wachsende Aegis Shipping Group neue Tonnage zum Ersatz einer Flotte von überwiegend im Kriege gebauten Standardschiffen suchte. Die Werft bot zunächst einen 16.000-Tonner mit 17 Knoten an, gestützt auf MS *Exning*, das im Jahr davor auf der Werft gebaut worden war, doch das Schiff erwies sich als zu groß und zu teuer. Als die Verhandlungen zu ihrem Ende kamen, wurde dem Reeder bedeutet, daß sich die Neuentwicklung mit 14.000 tdw besser eignen könne. Das war der Fall, und zwei Tage nach Unterzeichnung der Mavroleon-Verträge erteilte Aegis Aufträge für das zweite Schiffs-Paar. Die fünfte Einheit des ursprünglich von Austin & Pickersgill geplanten ersten Bauprogramms konnte kurz darauf an eine andere einflußreiche Londoner griechische Reederei, Lykiardopulo & Co., verkauft werden. Die Schiffe erhielten die Werftnummern 852 und 853, 854 und 855, sowie 856.

Diese fünf Aufträge, zusammen mit festen Anfragen anderer Reedereien und Aufträgen, die für Konkurrenzentwürfe weltweit vergeben wurden, waren der deutliche Beweis für das Potential des Konzepts Liberty Ship Replacement. Um zu verhindern, daß britische Werften diesen Markt durch unnötige Konkurrenz untereinander mit einer Vielzahl von Entwürfen verloren, regte die Shipbuilding Conference (der britische Schiffbauindustrie-Verband) an, den SD14 als British Liberty Replacement Design anzubieten. Der Verband berief zur Erörterung des Vorschlags im September 1966 eine Sitzung ein. Vierzehn britische Werften nahmen an einer Kostenkalkulation teil, die auf der Bauvorschrift von A&P beruhte. Die Absicht war, Vergleichspreise vorzulegen, aber es konnte keine preisliche Übereinkunft erreicht werden, auf deren Basis es einen gemeinsamen britischen Vorstoß in diesen Markt hätte geben können. Austin & Pickersgill fanden die Aktion besonders wertvoll, da sie klar aufzeigte, wo etwaige britische Konkurrenten zu finden waren. Tatsächlich gelangten nur vier Werften einigermaßen in die Nähe des Verkaufspreises von A&P. Zwar erarbeiteten eine oder zwei davon während der folgenden Monate Angebote für SD14-Schiffe, aber ohne Erfolg. In Anhang 3 findet sich eine Tabelle mit den Preisen der teilnehmenden Werften.

Tatsächlich muß hier gesagt werden, daß viele dieser Firmen ganz einfach an dem Projekt nicht interessiert waren. Das bewies ein Vertreter der Tyne-Werft Swan Hunter (damals unter dem Namen Associated Shipbuilders), der dem Verfasser während der Mittagspause sagte, ‚daß sie gerade einen hochentwickelten Linienfrachter für die Union-Castle Line fertigstellten und es ihrer Belegschaft wohl kaum zumuten könnten, sich auf das primitive Niveau für den Bau von SD14-Schiffen zurückzubegeben.' Andere Werften äußerten ähnliche Ansichten. Während der Sitzung wurden die Werftvertreter reihum gebeten, die Kosten zu nennen, die sie für Einzelpositionen der A&P-Bauvorschrift in ihre Kalkulationen eingesetzt hatten, etwa für Rettungsboote, Rudermaschine und verschiedene Lohnkosten. Gleich zu

Anfang dieser Umfrage schien es angezeigt zu sein, die berühmte Clyde-Werft von John Brown auszulassen, um sie nicht weiter in Verlegenheit zu bringen – so unglaublich hoch waren deren Kostenansätze.

Eine andere Werft aus Sunderland ließ echtes Interesse an dem Projekt erkennen, nämlich Bartram & Sons Ltd. Ihre Kostenschätzung kam jener von Austin & Pickersgill am nächsten. Über die Zusammenarbeit zwischen beiden Werften wurde bereits berichtet, wonach Bartrams auf den beim Nachbarn gebauten Schiffen die Maschineneinrichtung vornahmen und drei derartige Aufträge zufriedenstellend abgewickelt hatten. In einer Situation, in der sich A&P in der peinlichen Lage befand, wegen anderer Aufträge keine frühen Ablieferungsdaten für weitere SD14-Neubauten anbieten zu können, auf der anderen Seite aber Bartrams vermutlich vor der letzten Kiellegung standen, begrüßten beide Firmen die Gelegenheit, über ein Lizenzabkommen zu verhandeln. Diese Zusammenarbeit wurde 1970 auf eine dauerhafte Basis gestellt, nachdem Austin & Pickersgill die vollständige Kontrolle über die letzte familiengeführte Werft am Wear übernommen hatte.

Es war dies die erste einer Anzahl ähnlicher von Austin & Pickersgill geschlossener Vereinbarungen. Ein Gruppe von Verkäufern, darunter auch Vertreter von Bartrams, reiste im Januar 1967 nach Griechenland, um den SD14 bekanntzumachen und um Besprechungen mit der Hellenic Shipyards Company aufzunehmen in der Absicht, dieser Werft den Lizenzbau von SD14-Schiffen auf der ehemaligen Marinewerft in Skaramanga zu übertragen. Der Entschluß von A&P, die Neukonstruktion auch im Heimatland jener Reeder bauen zu lassen, die das hoffentlich größte Kundenpotential darstellten, war umstritten. Andererseits war man der Ansicht, daß eine derartige Vereinbarung das Vertrauen in die britische Konstruktion nur erhöhen könne, zumal einige dieser Reeder bereits mit Konkurrenzschiffen liebäugelten. Wie richtig der eingeschlagene Weg war, wurde in der Zukunft durch Neubauaufträge von sowohl Hellenic als auch Austin & Pickersgill bewiesen.

Ein weiterer Lizenzvertrag wurde 1971 unterschrieben, diesmal mit der brasilianischen Werft Companhia Comercio e Navegaçao, Rio de Janeiro. Ursprünglich galt die Vereinbarung nur für SD14-Neubauten für den heimischen Markt, aber spätere Aufträge wurden auch für chilenische und deutsche Reeder ausgeführt. Es war vermutlich nicht sehr weise von CCN, sich sehr rasch ein Auftragsvolumen für insgesamt 43 Schiffe aufzubauen, die über einen Zeitraum von zehn Jahren ausgeliefert werden sollten. Die Werft geriet durch übermäßig optimistische Produktionsvorhersagen und Lieferverzug bei Unterlieferanten unter Druck. Manche Besteller wollten wegen veränderter Märkte ihre Schiffe nicht abnehmen, so daß einige Neubauten, als sie dann schließlich ablieferungsbereit waren, unmittelbar nach Fertigstellung aufgelegt

werden mußten. Ohne wirkliche Absicht trug die Werft maßgeblich zur Geschichte des SD14 bei, denn zwei Schiffe (Werftnummern 143 und 160), die 1983 bereits verspätet vom Stapel liefen, wurden erst 1988 in Dienst gestellt. Sie waren somit die letzten abgelieferten Schiffe dieses Typs und verlängerten den Zeitraum, in dem nach diesen Entwürfen gebaut wurde, auf beachtliche 20 Jahre.

Zu einem späteren Zeitpunkt wurde das Lizenzabkommen mit CCN um eine Baureihe erweitert, die auf einem späteren Pickersgill-Konzept beruhte, nämlich dem SD15, von den Brasilianern als Prinasa-121 weiterentwickelt. Nach erfolgreicher Markteinführung des SD14 vermuteten A&P einen Bedarf für eine höherwertige Linienfrachterversion des Schiffs. Der Name SD15 bezog sich auf die Tragfähigkeit von 15.000 Tonnen (ehe man erkannte, daß der SD14 tatsächlich 15.000 Tonnen tragen kann). Verbesserte Schiffsformen und eine stärkere Hauptmaschine ergaben eine Dienstgeschwindigkeit von 16,5 Knoten. Austin & Pickersgill selbst bauten nur ein Schiff dieses Typs (Armadale, Werftnummer 866), aber CCN erwarben eine Lizenz zum Bau ihrer weiterentwickelten Version, von der sie insgesamt dreizehn Schiffe ablieferten. Anmerkung: die von CCN an A&P gezahlte Lizenzgebühr für die Nutzung der Konstruktionsunterlagen betrug lediglich £ 10.000 pro Einheit.

1971 gab es eine interessante Entwicklung: Austin & Pickersgill gründeten zusammen mit Court Line Ltd. eine Anzahl von Joint-Venture Beratungsfirmen unter dem Namen A&P Appledore (APA). Diese Firmen sollten die maritime Wirtschaft auf technischem, finanziellem und kaufmännischem Gebiet beraten. Auf diese Weise nahmen sie weltweit an der Planung und Verwirklichung neuer Werften teil und errangen rasch den Ruf globaler Marktführer dieses Sektors. Court Line wurde 1905 als Trampreederei gegründet, hatte aber wie viele andere auch in diesem Geschäft in den sechziger Jahren Schwierigkeiten. Eine neue, unternehmerisch denkende Geschäftsführung änderte den Kurs vollständig. Zwar wurde das Kerngebiet Schiffahrt noch eine kurze Zeit beibehalten, die Firma expandierte jedoch kräftig in das Touristikgeschäft und erwarb Flugzeuge und Hotels.

Im Jahre 1967 begann die Court Line, sich im Schiffbau zu betätigen, indem sie eine kleine Werft in Appledore, North Devon, kaufte, die sich in Liquidation befand, und nahm sofort ein Modernisierungsprogramm in Angriff, das 1970 abgeschlossen wurde. Dazu gehörte der Bau einer innovativen, vollständig überdachten

Panaghis Vergottis (Werftnummer 439) vor dem Stapellauf unmittelbar in die Nordsee in der South Dock Werft. [Sammlung John Lingwood]

Neubauwerft und der Einsatz modernster Schiffbaumethoden, von denen viele später in der Southwick-Werft von Austin & Pickersgill und auch anderswo genutzt wurden. Die Werft wurde zur Appledore Shipbuilders Ltd. umgegründet, und unter diesem Namen beteiligte sich die Court Line an der neuen Beratungsfirma. Mit dem Kauf von North East Coast Shiprepairers Ltd. an den Flüssen Tyne und Humber betrat Court Line im Jahre 1970 das Gebiet der Schiffsreparaturen. Die Werftaktivitäten erfuhren 1972 eine erhebliche Ausweitung durch Übernahme des sehr bedeutenden Unternehmens, das damals in Sunderland als Doxford and Sunderland arbeitete und zu dem so berühmte Schiffbauer-Namen gehörten wie J.L.Thompson, Sir James Laing und William Doxford. Das Touristikgeschäft mußte im Jahr 1973 massive Einbrüche hinnehmen, wodurch das Court Line-Imperium zusammenbrach. Die Schiffbau- und Reparaturaktivitäten wurden nur durch eine Regierungs-Intervention mit anschließendem vollständigen Ankauf vor dem so gut wie sicheren Untergang bewahrt.

Glücklicherweise konnten diese Geschäftszweige auch im Staatseigentum nahezu unverändert weiterarbeiten, bis im Jahre 1977 die vollständige Verstaatlichung der britischen Schiffbau-, Schiffsmaschinenbau- und Schiffsreparaturbetriebe zu deren Zusammenlegung unter dem Dach der British Shipbuilders Corporation führte. Die Geschäftsführer der am Tyne belegenen früheren Court Line-Schiffsreparaturfirmen, die inzwischen als Tyne Shiprepair firmierten, erhielten 1984 die Gelegenheit, der Staatsholding ihr Unternehmen abzukaufen. Der Beschluß der Regierung, im Jahr 1988 praktisch alle verbliebenen Schiffswerften im Rahmen des ‚Lame Duck'-Programms zu schließen, bedeutete das Ende einer der letzten Verbindungen zum früheren Court Line-Konzern. Doxford and Sunderland (inzwischen bekannt als Sunderland Shipbuilders) waren zwar erst kurz zuvor durch British Shipbuilders mit ihren Nachbarn Austin & Pickersgill und mit Smith's Dock am Tees zur neuen Gruppe North East Shipbuilders Ltd. zusammengelegt worden, stellten aber ihre Tätigkeit ein. Die Werft Appledore in Devon konnte diesmal noch die Schließung verhindern und wurde als bestehendes Unternehmen von Langham Industries erworben. Sie arbeitete noch bis Anfang 2004 im Schiffbau.

weiter. Im selben Jahr verkündete der Konkursverwalter, daß er mit Devonport Royal Dockyard über den Ankauf der Werft verhandele, was dem bahnbrechenden und während seiner kurzen Geschichte erfolgreichen Unternehmen hoffentlich ein neues Leben verheißt.

Die A&P Appledore Beratungsfirmen überlebten den Zusammenbruch der Court Line in 1973 ebenfalls, nachdem zunächst Austin & Pickersgill und deren Eigner, London & Overseas Freighters, ihre Anteile erhöhten, um den Wegfall der in Konkurs gefallenen Gesellschafter auszugleichen. Als dann 1977 die Schiffbauwirtschaft verstaatlicht wurde, gehörte APA nicht zu den Unternehmen, die übernommen werden sollten, obwohl sie ein Tochterunternehmen von Austin & Pickersgill war. Mit dem Ende der Beteiligung von A&P/LOF arbeitete das Unternehmen erfolgreich weiter und expandierte international, anfänglich unter den bisherigen Geschäftsführern. In den Folgejahren fanden verschiedene Management Buy-outs und sonstige Veränderungen statt. Einige davon führten zu vollständigen Kurswechseln und der Wiedervereinigung mit Teilen der früheren Court Line Schiffsreparaturbeteiligungen, die ursprünglich an die British Shipbuilders gefallen waren, mit der Folge, daß es auf diesem Gebiet den Namen A&P weiterhin gibt, als Bestandteil lokaler Firmen wie z.B. A&P Tyne Ltd.

Noch ein wenig früher im Jahre 1973 bewies A&P Appledore eine weitere Spielart ihrer Tüchtigkeit, indem sie noch ein SD14-Lizenzabkommen zustandebrachte, diesmal unter Einschluß von Caledon Shipbuilding & Engineering Co.Ltd. aus Dundee (später umbenannt in Robb Caledon Ltd.), d.h. eines derjenigen Unternehmen, die vor ein par Jahren wenigstens ein Minimum an Interesse an dem erfolglosen Versuch zeigten, aus dem SD14 einen British Liberty Replacement zu machen, ferner Astilleros y Fabricas Navales del Estado (AFNE) aus Ensenada bei Buenos Aires, sowie Doxford Engines Ltd. aus Sunderland, seinerzeit noch Teil der Court Line-Gruppe.

Salta, die erste SD 14-Variante, gebaut von Robb Caledon in Dundee (Werftnummer D568). Der den SD 14 von Austin & Pickersgill verpaßte Schornstein mit abgeplattetem Rücken erzeugte einiges Stirnrunzeln, aber diese Version ging noch einen Schritt weiter. [Don Brown]

Standard-Bulker im Angebot, doch wurden solche Schiffe im allgemeinen einzeln bestellt und erlangten somit die Vorteile einer Fließbandfertigung nicht. Das Liberty Ship Replacement-Programm bot nun die Möglichkeit, diese Methoden anzuwenden und das Potential der Werft voll auszunutzen.

Das Abkommen bezog sich auf die Lieferung von neun verbesserten SD14-Schiffen: drei gebaut in Dundee und sechs von AFNE, geliefert an die argentinische Staatsreederei Emprese Lineas Maritimas Argentinas (ELMA). Bei A&P Appledore lag die Verantwortung für technischen Beistand und für die Koordination des Arbeitsfortschritts, ferner für Kauf und Lieferung von benötigtem Material und von Anlagen, davon vieles geliefert von damaligen Court Line Tochterfirmen, einschließlich einer Doxford 67J4 Hauptmaschine. Leider erhielten Austin & Pickersgill keine finanziellen Zuwendungen von den Lizenznehmern, es profitierte allein APA.

Auf anderen als Sunderland-Werften entstanden zwischen 1982 und 1987 weitere sechs SD14-Neubauten, allerdings nicht als Ergebnis von Lizenzabkommen. Es wurde schon von der Verstaatlichung der britischen Schiffbauwirtschaft im Jahre 1977 berichtet, in deren Folge die betroffenen Unternehmen unter dem gemeinsamen Namen British Shipbuilders mit gewisser Selbständigkeit weiterarbeiteten. Später gab es dann ein etwas zentraleres Kontrollsystem. Als 1981 Austin & Pickersgill ein recht gut gefülltes Auftragsbuch hatten und über zwei weitere Aufträge verhandelten, wurden diese durch British Shipbuilders an Smith's Dock Ltd. in South Bank, Middlesborough vermittelt, da diese damals Aufträge benötigten. Es handelte sich um Schiffe der Vierten Serie (s.unten), aber mit manchen zusätzlichen Wünschen der Reeder. Darauf wurden vier weitere Aufträge für ähnliche Schiffe von British Shipbuilders an Smith's geleitet. Mit Ausnahme der beiden weiter oben erwähnten verspäteten Schiffen aus Brasilien waren dies nun die letzten SD14-Neubauten und bestimmt die letzten in Großbritannien gebauten.

Der Schiffsentwurf
Die Entscheidung von Austin & Pickersgill, sich ab 1966 im Liberty Ship Replacement-Markt zu betätigen, wurde durch das plötzliche breite Interesse an einem derartigen Schiffstyp ausgelöst und durch den Wunsch, im Wettlauf nicht zu unterliegen, in dem es um die Positionierung des SD14 als Marktführer ging. Schließlich war die Southwick Werft 1954/1955 besonders im Hinblick auf die Serienfertigung von Standardschiffen ausgelegt worden. Das Ziel wurde nie so recht erreicht. Das Unternehmen hatte zwar eine Anzahl von Entwürfen erfolgreicher

Auch wenn es nicht gelang, ein Serienbauprogramm durchzuhalten, hatten A&P ihre Fertigungsmethoden umgestellt, nicht zuletzt zur Abrundung der erheblichen Investitionen in einen automatisierten Maschinen- und Gerätepark in und um die ausgedehnten neuen Fabrikations- und Sektionsbauflächen. Soweit wie möglich wurden diese Veränderungen beim Bau aller Schiffe seit Inbetriebnahme der neuen Einrichtungen eingesetzt und mußten unbedingt bei der Konstruktion des SD14 genutzt werden, sollten die erforderlichen Kosteneinsparungen erreicht werden. Die erste Abweichung von der herkömmlichen Bauweise bestand darin, den parabolischen Decksprung und die Balkenbucht durch eine gerade Konstruktion zu ersetzen. Das geschah erstmals 1958 bei einer Serie von 10.450/ 11.950 tdw Frachtern mit dem Ziel, weniger Decksbalken aufwendig zu biegen und so viele gerade Seitenspanten wie möglich praktisch derselben Länge zu verwenden. Das Spiegelheck hatte die von Spezialisten auszuführende Beplattung des eleganten Kreuzerhecks verdrängt, aber die wahrscheinlich am meisten Widerspruch erregende Neuerung bei diesen Standardschiffen bestand, wenigstens aus Sicht der Ästheten, in der Konstruktion der Aufbauten. Rundungen, Schrägen, Überhänge, oftmals übertriebene Krümmungsradien und extravagante Niedergänge gab es nicht mehr, welche das Erscheinungsbild der Aufbauten von Nachkriegsschiffen in aller Welt geprägt hatten, darunter auch vieler gut aussehender neuzeitlicher Pickersgill-Schiffe. An ihre Stelle traten viele gerade Linien und als besonderer Stein des Anstoßes, seitlich gesickte und hinten versteifte Deckshäuser. Wenigstens deren Vorderseiten waren davon verschont geblieben. Ebenso wie bei der umstrittenen Einführung gesickter Haupt- und Mittellängsschotte vor fast einem Jahrzehnt rechtfertigten die Gewichtseinsparungen und die durch den Fortfall genieteter, später geschweißter Steifen verringerten Arbeitslöhne diese besondere Änderung vollen Umfangs.

In jenen frühen Nachkriegsjahren besaßen Austin & Pickersgill gegenüber ihren britischen Wettbewerbern einen wahrscheinlich einzigartigen Vorteil, nämlich weil sie so etwas wie eine ‚grüne Wiese' hatten, auf der sie eine neue Werft an der Stelle planen und bauen konnten, wo früher der Ballasthügel war. Alles überragten die großen Hallen für die Vorbereitung, Verarbeitung und Montage der Stahlteile. Wie bereits oben erwähnt, hatte die Werft im vergangenen Jahrzehnt ihre Arbeitsmethoden verändert, um die neuen Anlagen nutzen zu können, und das geschah nun auf vorteilhafte Weise beim Bau des SD14. In vielen Fällen brachten die Änderungen den Abschied von überlieferten Abläufen. So verlief beispielsweise der erste Arbeitsgang auf der Helling nicht mehr durch Legen der ganzen Länge der Kielplatte und des Mittelträgers, gefolgt vom Anbringen von Spanten, geformt aus Bodenwrangen, Seitenspanten und Decksbalken, an die Außenhaut- und Decksplatten Stück für Stück ‚angehängt' wurden. Stattdessen bestand das erste Bauteil eines SD14-Neubaus aus einer großen Sektion von in der Montagehalle fertiggestellten Mittschiffsbodenplatten, herangefahren auf einem traktorgezogenen Vielachsanhänger und von parallel zur Helling verfahrbaren Schwerlastkranen auf die Kielpallen abgesenkt. Weitere Bodenplatten wurden sodann vor und hinter der ersten installiert. Dem folgten der Doppelboden, die Außenhaut, Schotte, Decks usw. in einem Ablauf, in dem der Schiffskörper schließlich durch den Einbau der Bug- und Hecksektionen und die Errichtung der Deckshäuser und der Masten vervollständigt wurde.

Krananlagen an Hellingen wurden zwar schon seit Jahrzehnten in einigen Werften genutzt, aber erst im Kriege wurden sie allgemein in Großbritannien eingeführt, nachdem der Turmdrehkran Einzug gehalten hatte, der auf Schienen neben der Helling fährt und eine große Hubhöhe aufweist. Die wiedereröffnete Priestman-Werft war mit Unterstützung der Marineleitung mit derartigen Kranen ausgerüstet worden, ähnliche Einheiten waren für die Hellinge der ‚Werft von 1954' vorgesehen. Anfänglich hielt man eine Hebefähigkeit von 5 Tonnen für ausreichend, aber als das SD14-Programm in vollem Gange war, war der Kranpark in Southwick schon soweit verbessert worden, daß es auch Krane mit 60 Tonnen Hebefähigkeit gab, die im Verbund arbeiten konnten. Das ermöglichte den Bau von Schiffen aus Groß-Sektionen, die unter Dach vorgefertigt waren. Auch gestattete dies nun stets den Einbau der Hauptmaschine vor dem Stapellauf.

Insgesamt haben Austin & Pickersgill vier Serien der SD14-Konstruktion entwickelt. Die Erste Serie entsprach den Zeichnungen und der Bauvorschrift, die zum Zeitpunkt der Vermarktung der Konstruktion erstmals veröffentlicht wurden (wiedergegeben in Anhang 2). Allerdings brachten es die Änderungen, die schon während der Vertragsverhandlungen für die ersten Schiffe vorgenommen wurden mit sich, daß kein Schiff dem Original-Entwurf exakt entsprach. Der Grund war, daß die Reeder gegen Zahlung der Zusatzkosten die Luken 2, 3

und 4 von 22 auf 28 Fuß verbreitert haben wollten und statt der 3 x 170 kW Wechselstromgeneratoren 3 x 218 kW Leistung wünschten. Zufällig in dieser Zeit vorgenommene Änderungen der Internationalen Ladelinienbestimmungen führten zu einer Erhöhung des Sommer-Tiefgangs um 6 Zoll. Das entsprach einer zusätzlichen Tragfähigkeit von 400 Tonnen. Gleichzeitig änderten die Klassifikationsgesellschaften ihre Vorschriften, und nun konnte das Stahlgewicht verringert werden, wodurch sich die Tragfähigkeit um weitere 400 Tonnen erhöhte. Diese wurde nun mit 15.000 Tonnen angegeben, verglichen mit den ursprünglichen 14.200 Tonnen. Mit dem erhöhten Tiefgang wuchs die Länge zwischen den Loten auf 440'2" (134,16m). Hier sei gesagt, daß die Original-Konstruktion nach den Vorschriften der Klassifikationsgesellschaft Lloyd's Register of Shipping entstand. Als später einige Reeder ihre Schiffe von anderen Gesellschaften klassifizieren lassen wollten, übernahmen diese trotz gewisser Unterschiede zwischen ihren Vorschriften und denen von Lloyd's Register of Shipping die LR-Standards, damit A&P ihre standardisierten Zeichnungen nicht zu ändern brauchten.

Austin & Pickersgill betrachteten die veränderten Lukenabmessungen und Generatorleistungen als vorteilhaft für das SD14-Konzept und beschlossen folglich, diese und andere Zugabeveränderungen, die im vorherigen Absatz beschrieben wurden, in die Basis-Bauvorschrift des Typs aufzunehmen, der nun als Zweite Serie vermarktet wurde. Noch weiterreichende Veränderungen gingen in die Schiffe ein, die als Dritte Serie angeboten und ab 1970 abgeliefert wurden. Die wichtigste Veränderung bestand in der Verwendung der neuen Sulzer 5RND68 Hauptmaschine, die eine von 5500 PSe auf 7500 PSe erhöhte Maximal-Dauerleistung aufwies, wodurch die Dienstgeschwindigkeit auf 14,9 Knoten stieg. Sonstige Veränderungen bestanden darin, daß eine Reihe von Positionen, die aus Ersparnisgründen aus der ersten Bauvorschrift gestrichen worden waren, sich nun wieder darin befanden. Dazu gehörte beispielsweise der Ersatz des einen großen stählernen Lukendeckels über der flutbaren Luke 3 zwecks Erleichterung des Handlings durch zwei kleinere Deckel sowie die Vergrößerung des Fassungsvermögens der Proviantkühlräume. Man hatte festgestellt, daß zwar in den Unterkünften gestrichene Sperrholz- oder Spanfaserplatten als Schotte oder Verschalungen grundsätzlich vernünftig waren, aber beim Einbau leicht beschädigt wurden und kostspielig repariert und nachgestrichen werden mußten. Folglich wurden sie bald durch beständigere plastikbeschichtete Produkte ersetzt. Aus ästhetischen Gründen erhielten die Decken in den Kammern des Kapitäns und des Leitenden Ingenieurs sowie im Speiseraum und im Rauchsalon eine Verkleidung. Einige dieser Veränderungen zogen erhöhten Strombedarf nach sich, also wurde die Generatorleistung durch Einbau von drei Generatoren von je 280 kW erneut gesteigert.

Zwei SD 14, *Arrino* und *Westland* (Werftnummern 895 und 896) während der Ausrüstung in Southwick im Herbst 1974.
[Harold Appleyard]

Ganz allgemein haben A&P allen Versuchen widerstanden, vom Originalkonzept der SD14-Konstruktion abzuweichen, das darin bestand, ein einfaches, wirtschaftliches ‚Arbeitspferd' anzubieten. Das Konzept konnte durch zusätzliche Einbauten aus der werfteigenen Liste oder nach Wünschen der Besteller erweitert erden, aber immer unter der Voraussetzung, daß sie keine wesentlichen konstruktiven Veränderungen erforderten. Nur einmal wurde von dieser Politik abgewichen, als im Jahr 1969 Bartrams einen Auftrag der französischen Reederei Compagnie de Navigation Denis Frères, Paris, für zwei SD14-Schiffe für den Transport westafrikanischen Stammholzes erhielt. In diesem Sonderfall wurde von dem flutbaren Unterraum abgesehen, um die Stauung dieser schwierigen Ladung zu erleichtern. Außerdem gab es Raum für Kühlladung und verbessertes Schiffsgeschirr. Zur Erreichung einer Dienstgeschwindigkeit von 15 Knoten erhielt der erste der beiden Neubauten eine Sulzer 6RD68 Hauptmaschine mit 7.200 PSe. Während des Baus des zweiten Schiffs kam die neue, stärkere 5RND68 mit 7.500 PSe auf den Markt, vorgesehen für die Dritte Serie. Es ist bemerkenswert, daß Denis Frères einige Jahre danach diese beiden Schiffe durch Verlängerung und Einbau von Deckskranen noch weiter verändern ließen, um sie dem neuen Containerverkehr anzupassen.

Eine weit umfassendere Änderung der Bauvorschrift wurde 1976 vorgenommen. Sie schloß auch konstruktive Veränderungen ein und bedeutete gleichzeitig die Einführung der letzten Serie von Austin & Pickersgill SD14-Schiffen, genannt die Vierte Serie. Wiederum spielten Verbesserungen der Sulzer RD/RND-Baureihe dabei eine Rolle. Sulzer hatte die Leistungsabgabe pro Zylinder erhöht. Damit lieferte die neue RND68M mit vier Zylindern 7.600 PSe, verglichen mit 7.500 PSe aus fünf Zylindern der bisher eingebauten 5RND68. Vorangegangene Änderungen der Hauptmaschine hatten keine Änderungen der Schiffsform nach sich gezogen, aber jetzt wurde die Gelegenheit genutzt, die Vorschiffslinien durch Einbau eines Rammstevens zu verändern. Dieser sollte die selben Vorteile bieten wie der erst kürzlich entwickelte Wulstbug, war aber sehr viel einfacher zu bauen. Beim SD14 wurde diese spatenförmige Vergrößerung der Unterwasserform versteckt, um ein kompliziertes Konstruktionsproblem zu vermeiden in dem Bereich, in dem die Oberkante des Rammstevens mit dem ursprünglich ausfallenden Vorsteven an der Wasserlinie zusammentraf. Dies wurde dadurch erreicht, daß der

vorderste Teil des Rammstevens vertikal nach oben geführt wurde, bis er auf die normale Stevenlinie ein gutes Stück oberhalb der Freibordwasserlinie traf. Damit wurde der Eindruck eines Klipperbugs erzeugt. Diese Veränderungen erbrachten nur eine bescheidene Erhöhung der Geschwindigkeit, nämlich auf 15 Knoten, aber der Gesamtpropulsionswirkungsgrad verbesserte sich. Gleichzeitig konnte wegen der leichteren Hauptmaschine die Tragfähigkeit auf 15.025 Tonnen festgelegt werden. Als Folge der Veränderungen am Vorschiff betrug die Länge über alles der Vierten Serie nun 472,44 Fuß (144,0m) und die Länge zwischen den Loten 451,11 Fuß (127,50m).

Eigentlich war der SD14 als ein wirtschaftlicher Tramper konzipiert worden, empfahl sich aber mit steigender Beliebtheit des Typs auch anspruchsvolleren Kunden, und sogar Linienreedereien fanden es interessant, dieses Schiff zu besitzen oder zu chartern. Um den Bedürfnissen der jeweiligen Reeder zu entsprechen, gelangten immer mehr Positionen aus der Liste der auf Wunsch erhältlichen Sonderlieferungen in die Basis-Bauvorschrift. Deshalb wurde beschlossen, einige dieser Positionen in die Bauvorschrift der nun angebotenen Vierten Serie aufzunehmen. Die bedeutendsten Verbesserungen betrafen die Anordnung der Ladewinden auf den Deckshäusern zwischen den Luken und das Anheben der Tankdecke in Luke 5 auf Höhe des Wellentunnels, was den Laderaum einfacher zu bedienen machte und mehr Raum für Ballastwasser neben dem Wellentunnel schaffte. Klimaanlagen, beim Entwurf des ersten SD14 als Luxus angesehen, waren zum Standard geworden, ebenfalls die Verbesserung des Ladegeschirrs, das nun 10-Tonnen-Bäume bei den Luken 2, 3 und 4 aufwies.

In den etwa zehn Jahren, seit der SD14 erstmals auf den Markt kam, hatten sich die Anforderungen an die Unterkünfte als Folge internationaler Bestimmungen immer wieder geändert und wurden bei Bedarf berücksichtigt. Im Rahmen der Planung der Vierten Serie nahm man die Gelegenheit wahr, die gesamte Anordnung der Unterkünfte zu überprüfen. Das war deshalb nicht einfach, weil der ursprüngliche Entwurf nicht viel Spielraum für eine Vergrößerung der Deckshäuser ließ. Gleichwohl waren auf

Calixto Garcia, abgeliefert als *Ajana* (Southwick Werftnummer 904) im Eis auf dem St.Lorenz-Strom, 23. Dezember 1989. Sie hat einen 30-Tonnen-Velle-Baum bei Luke IV und einen 80-Tonnen Schwergutbaum Vorkante Luke II. *[René Beauchamp, Sammlung David Salisbury]*

Funing, aus der Vierten Serie SD 14, während der Ausrüstung in Southwick im Sommer 1982. Die Werftnummer 1381 zeigt deutlich die beginnend mit dieser Serie veränderten Linien des Vorstevens. *[Sammlung V.H.Young und L.A.Sawyer]*

Wunsch der Reeder und auch wegen des Einsatzes von Besatzungen unterschiedlicher Nationalität mancherlei attraktive und wohnliche Einrichtungen entstanden. Verbesserungen im Maschinenraum umfaßten die standardmäßige Lieferung von selbstreinigenden Ölreinigern, eine Abwasserentsorgungsanlage und einen Frischwassererzeuger höherer Leistung. Das alles wiederum ließ den Strombedarf steigen, so daß 3 x 350 kW Wechselstromgeneratoren vorgesehen wurden. Nachdem nun frühere Sonderlieferungen in die Basis-Bauvorschrift aufgenommen worden waren, entstand eine neue Liste solcher Lieferungen, welche die Werft auf Anfrage anbot. Darin enthalten waren ein Schwergutbaum bei Luke 2, Vorrichtungen für die Stauung von Holzladung an Deck, die sichere Stauung von Getreideladungen, die Einhaltung der Vorschriften für das Passieren des St.Lawrence Seaway, der Einbau von CO_2 Feuerlöschvorrichtungen in den Laderäumen und von künstlicher Lüftung in Unterräumen und Zwischendecks.

Im Maschinenbereich konnten nunmehr die Bedienung der Maschine von der Brücke aus und der unbemannte Maschinenraum in Betracht gezogen werden. Noch spätere Verbesserungen der Sulzer-Hauptmaschine brachte die RLB-Baureihe hervor, darunter die fünfzylindrige 5RLB56 mit 560 mm Bohrung, die für die Vierte Serie als am besten geeignet angesehen wurde. Diese Maschine lieferte 7.500 Pse bei 170 Upm. Sie wurde in das letzte Schiff dieses Typs eingebaut, der in Southwick entstand, und in die sechs von Smith's Dock gelieferten Neubauten.

Die in Griechenland und in Brasilien gebauten SD14-Schiffe kamen nicht als Serie auf den Markt, entsprachen aber im allgemeinen der ursprünglichen Basis-Bauvorschrift, mit Änderungen der Lukenabmessungen

und einer höheren Generatorleistung, wie schon bei den ersten fünf bei Austin und Pickersgill in Auftrag gegebenen Einheiten. Die Bauvorschriften berücksichtigten auch die von den neuen Tiefgangs-Bestimmungen und Klasse-Vorschriften ausgelösten konstruktiven Änderungen. Außerdem erhielten die von CCN gebauten Schiffe andere Hauptmaschinen, nämlich vom Typ MAN K6Z70/120E, mit 8.400 PSe viel leistungsstärker als die RD/RND-Reihe von Sulzer. Der Grund dafür lag hauptsächlich im Wunsch, von Mecapesa im Lande in Lizenz gebaute Maschinen zu verwenden. Die Mehrzahl dieser SD14-Neubauten waren für brasilianische Linienreedereien vorgesehen, so daß CCN häufiger Änderungen vornahm, welche die Schiffe für den Liniendienst verbesserten. Dazu gehörte geeigneteres Schiffsgeschirr wie etwa Deckskrane und der Einbau eines Zwischendecks in Luke 5. Damit konnte den Schiffen nach der kürzlich erfolgten Änderung der Vermessungsvorschriften eine Tonnagemarke zugewiesen werden. Schiffe mit dieser Bezeichnung können in den CCN-Neubaulisten dadurch erkannt werden, daß sie eine doppelte Vermessung aufweisen.

Hellenic Shipyards bauten außerhalb des Lizenzabkommens mit Austin & Pickersgill einen ‚Linien-SD14' und kamen damit den Wünschen der Hellenic Lines aus Piräus entgegen. Es wurden sechs dieser Schiffe gebaut, die zwar alle die Hauptmerkmale des SD14 beibehielten, aber einen Wulstbug erhielten und einen MAN R9V52/55 Mittelschnelläufer mit 8.220 PSe, der den Schiffen eine Dienstgeschwindigkeit von 16,5 Knoten verlieh. Die Schiffe bekamen ein zweites Deck in Luke 5 sowie 34.000 Kubikfuß Ladungskühlraum. Ferner wurden Tieftanks zum Transport pflanzlicher Öle eingebaut und das Schiffsgeschirr erheblich verbessert. Noch bedeutender mochte die Tatsache sein, daß die Schiffe 12 Passagiere befördern konnten.

Hellenic Champion (Skaramanga Werftnummer 1071), eine der sechs für Hellenic Lines Ltd. erbauten Linienfrachter-Versionen. Nach über 60 Betriebsjahren bewirkte der Konkurs der Reederei leider das rasche Auseinanderfallen dieser Serie. *[Trevor Jones, Sammlung David Salisbury]*

Auch die neun in Dundee und Buenos Aires für die ELMA gebauten Schiffe wurden, ebenso wie einige der von CCN gebauten Varianten, mit einem zweiten Deck in Luke 5 versehen, wenn auch ohne Zuflucht zur Tonnagemarke, mit Kühlladeraum von 45.000 Kubikfuß und mit etwa ähnlich großen Tieftanks für pflanzliche Öle in Luke 3. Zum Ladegeschirr gehörten fünf Schwingbäume von 22 Tonnen Hebefähigkeit für den Umschlag von 20-Fuß-Containern. Die Hauptmaschine war vom Typ Doxford 67J4 mit 8.000 PSe. Die Generatorleistung der Schiffe wurde auf 3 x 370 kW gesteigert.

Eine letzte Variante des SD14 erschien im Jahr 1984, aber weder unter dem Namen von Austin & Pickersgill noch mit der Bezeichnung SD14. Ganz allgemein gesagt hatten die zur Organisation der British Shipbuilders gehörenden Unternehmen seit der Verstaatlichung 1977 selbständig weiterarbeiten können. In den achtziger Jahren wurden Konstruktion, Marketing und Verkauf einer zentralen Gruppe des Managements unterstellt. Wohl in der Absicht, eine eigene Note zu setzen, stellte diese Gruppe unter der Bezeichnung ‚King'-Baureihe eine neue Kollektion von Entwürfen vor. Sie umfaßte ein 45.000 tdw Bulker/Container-Kombischiff, einen 22.000 tdw Mehrzwecklinienfrachter, ein 7.450 tdw RoRo-Frachtschiff sowie das SD King 15 Stückgutschiff. Letzteres stellte eine nur wenig veränderte Version der zu jener Zeit erbauten bzw. bei Smith's Dock im Bau befindlichen sechs SD14-Schiffe dar. Die Bezeichnung SD15 bedeutete nichts anderes als was seit 1968 klar war, nämlich daß die Tragfähigkeit des SD14 eher 15.000 als 14.000 Tonnen betrug.

Erneut beeinflußte eine weitere Änderung der Sulzer Hauptmaschine die Entscheidung, diese neue Variante vorzustellen. Die Schweizer Maschinenbauer boten jetzt eine als 5RTA48 bezeichnete Einheit an, die bei 154 UpM 7.400 PSe lieferte. Mit der Fünften Serie legte der SD14 endgültig den ihm bei seiner Einführung vor fast zwanzig Jahren von der volkstümlichen Presse des Landes angehängten Spitznamen ‚Plain Jane' ab und wurde zum richtigen Linienschiff. Es gab keine Niedrigpreis-Bauvorschrift mehr. Der SD15 King 15 verfügte immerhin über elektrische Ventilation der Laderäume mit sechsfachem Luftwechsel in der Stunde, CO_2 Feuerlösch-vorrichtungen und Rauchmelder in Unterräumen und Zwischendecks. Das Ladegeschirr umfaßte sechs 10-Tonnen und vier 5-Tonnen-Bäume sowie zusätzlich einen 30-Tonnen und einen 90-Tonnen-Schwergutbaum. Die gesamte Konstruktion war verstärkt worden. Auf den Lukenabdeckungen des Wetterdecks und des darunter liegenden Zwischendecks konnten 126 TEU gestaut werden und weitere 70 TEU auf der Tankdecke auf der Fläche unterhalb der Luken-abdeckungen. Wie weiter unten dargestellt, ließen es die Marktverhältnisse nicht zu, daß Schiffe dieses Typs jemals gebaut wurden.

In Fahrt

Bedenkt man das volle Auftragsbuch der Werft, hauptsächlich für die erfolgreichen Standard-Bulkcarrier, dann war das Jahr 1966 eindeutig nicht der ideale Zeitpunkt für Austin & Pickersgill, ein neues Projekt vorzustellen. Der abzuarbeitende Auftragsberg bedeutete, daß in Southwick der Kiel des ersten SD14 nicht vor dem 4. Oktober 1967 gelegt werden konnte, etwa zwanzig Monate nach Auftragsunterzeichnung. Der Bau zweier Bulkcarrier mußte irgendwie zwischen die Ablieferung der beiden ersten Paare von SD14-Neubauten eingepaßt werden. Glücklicherweise konnte das Interesse an dem Entwurf durch die oben beschriebenen, mit Bartram & Sons Ltd. ausgehandelten Lizenzabkommen am Leben erhalten werden, auch ein wenig durch den darauf folgenden Abschluß mit Hellenic Shipyards.

Im November 1966 wurden in Monte Carlo Verhandlungen über die ersten SD14-Aufträge für Bartrams geführt, die zum Ergebnis hatten, daß die Werft vier Schiffe für Gesellschaften der Onassis-Gruppe bauen sollte. Schwierigkeiten bei der Kreditbeschaffung und den Modalitäten der Kreditbürgschaften bedeuteten letztendlich, daß diese Schiffe nicht gebaut wurden. Beflügelt durch die Mitarbeit im SD14-Programm und von der Vorstellung, die Vorteile früher Lieferung zu nutzen, hatten Bartrams den Bau der Schiffe vorangetrieben, noch während die Finanzfragen verhandelt wurden. Angesichts der weit fortgeschrittenen Konstruktionsarbeiten und der fest bestellten Zulieferungen hätten die Auftragsstornierungen unter anderen Umständen die Werft in eine katastrophale Lage gebracht. Eine Teillösung trat durch die Übernahme von zwei Onassis-Kontrakten durch Aegis Shipping ein, welche zwei Folgeaufträge, über die mit Austin & Pickersgill verhandelt wurde, auf die Werft in South Dock übertrug. Der vierte Neubau wurde an einen anderen griechischen Reeder, A.Alafouzos, veräußert, aber das dritte Schiff blieb zunächst unverkauft.

Am 7. Juni 1967 wurde der erste SD14-Kiel für den ersten der beiden Aegis-Neubauten gestreckt, etwa vier Monate vor dem gleichen Ereignis in Southwick für den ersten SD14, die *Nicola*, für Rechnung von Mr. Mavroleon. Als dieses Schiff vom Stapel lief, waren drei Monate des Zeitvorsprungs von Bartrams bereits verschwunden. Richtig mulmig wurde es A&P, und weit mehr noch Mr. Mavroleon, erst dann, als man sich darüber klar wurde, daß das ‚eigene' Schiff nicht als erste Einheit dieses bedeutenden Entwurfs in Dienst gestellt werden könnte. Im Laufe der Zeit ging die Erinnerung daran verloren, wie die ‚Ehre' wiederhergestellt werden, die

Die *Nicola* von Basil Mavroleon, mit einem Tag Vorsprung der erste fertiggestellte und abgelieferte SD 14 (Southwick Werftnummer 852). [Ken White, Sammlung Don Brown]

Schöpfer des Entwurfs auch liefern und der Geldgeber des Ganzen dieses Schiff mit seinem überaus hohen Prestigewert übernehmen konnte. Hier sei nur gesagt, daß die *Nicola* am 14. Februar 1968 und die *Mimis M.Papalios* am Tage darauf abgeliefert wurden. Die Indienststellung der *Nicola* fand im Rahmen einer großangelegten PR- und Verkaufsveranstaltung statt. Das Schiff fuhr von Sunderland in den Hafen London, um dort von einer höchst eindrucksvollen Auswahl von Reedern, Schiffsmaklern und An-und-Verkaufsmaklern dieser Welt besichtigt zu werden, darunter vor allem Griechen. Der Verfasser entsinnt sich noch seiner Bestürzung, als er kurz vor Auslaufen des Schiffs nach London bei einem kurzen Rundgang die grauenvolle Unordnung an Bord erblickte, das Ergebnis der Hetze, um das Ablieferungsdatum zu halten. Aber ,have no fear, a Lascar crew is near', es geschahen Wunder, und offenbar war das Schiff in makellosem Zustand, als die ersten Käuferinteressenten an Bord kamen.

Der Mißerfolg mit den Onassis-Kontrakten spiegelte die damals von den Werften gehegten Befürchtungen deutlich wider. Zur Vermarktung des SD14-Programms gehörte ein mit Banken und Finanzierungsgesellschaften ausgehandelter, niedrig verzinster Kredit, verbürgt vom Export Credits Guarantee Department (ECDG) der britischen Regierung. Die Mehrzahl der von ausländischen Kunden eingehenden Anfragen erfolgte für Ein-Schiffs-Gesellschaften. Die ECDG ließ sich in keiner Weise von der Tatsache beeindrucken, daß der wirtschaftliche Eigentümer der Gesellschaft einer der wohlhabendsten Männer der Welt sein mochte. Sie sah nur darauf, daß die nominelle Reederei über geringe finanzielle Mittel und minimale zusätzliche Sicherheiten verfügte. Die ECGD prüfte die Anträge sehr sorgfältig und benötigte dafür oft viel Zeit, so daß, wie oben angemerkt, die Werften sich manchmal genötigt sahen, Arbeiten in Angriff zu nehmen, noch ehe Bauverträge und Finanzierungsabkommen unterschrieben waren.

Zum Glück verursachten nur die Onassis-'Aufträge' größere Verlegenheit. Als nämlich das SD14-Programm fortschritt, gab es im allgemeinen viele Reeder, die nur darauf warteten, in abgebrochene Vertragsverhandlungen einzusteigen. In den siebziger Jahren war die Nachfrage nach SD14-Schiffen derartig groß, daß systemimmanente Verzögerungen sich für einige Besteller vorteilhaft auswirkten: sie hatten zu den jeweils geltenden Bedingungen Schiffe bestellt, die Verträge dann aber, wenn sie unterschrieben werden sollten, an andere Reeder weiterverkauft. Damit ließen sich auch nur innerhalb weniger Monate, unter Einsatz nur geringer Kosten, gute Gewinne erzielen, denn die Anzahlung an die Werft wurde üblicherweise erst bei Kontraktzeichnung fällig. Austin & Pickersgill verloren auf diese Art viel Geld und setzten das Schlupfloch schließlich dicht, indem sie eine Abtretungsgebühr auf weitergegebene Verträge erhoben. Dadurch holten sie sich etwas von den Zusatzgewinnen zurück, die von Leuten eingestrichen wurden, die in Wahrheit nur Spekulanten waren.

In diesem Zusammenhang mag es von Interesse sein, die Hintergründe dieser ersten SD14-Aufträge zu beleuchten. Austin & Pickersgill hatten als Zielgruppe des Liberty Ship Replacement-Programms diejenigen griechischen

Schiffahrtsfirmen ausgemacht, die zu jener Zeit den größten Teil der noch fahrenden Liberty-Schiffe betrieben. Diese Reeder hatten ihre geschäftlichen Wurzeln in den Fahrtgebieten des Mittelmeers und des Schwarzen Meeres des achtzehnten Jahrhunderts und waren überwiegend auf einer der vielen griechischen Inseln zuhause. Ihren Wohlstand verdankten sie oft dem engen Zusammenhalt innerhalb der Familien und der Mitbewohner der Inseln. Typischerweise begann ein Mann seine Laufbahn ganz unten auf Schiffen, die in dieses enge Geflecht gehörten. Wenn er dann ausreichende Mittel und Erfahrungen gesammelt hatte, wurde er selbst zum Reeder. Gegen Ende des neunzehnten Jahrhunderts wanderten einige der erfolgreicheren Reeder/Händler nach London aus, wo sie sich nicht nur als Schiffseigner betätigten sondern auch als Agenten und Vermittler für die nachfolgende Generation der Familie oder anderweitig Nahestehender, die ihrerseits auf die beschriebene Weise in die Schiffahrt eintraten.

Die wohl einflußreichsten dieser sogenannten Londoner Griechen waren Rethymnis & Kulukundis Ltd. (R&K). Die Firma war von den fünf Brüdern Kulukundis, deren Vettern aus der Familie Rethymnis und einem weiteren Vetter, Basil Mavroleon (BM) gegründet worden. Zu einem späteren Zeitpunkt hielten sie alle, sowohl als Einzelpersonen und über den Ableger London & Overseas Freighters, größere oder kleinere Anteile an Austin & Pickersgill. Im allgemeinen galt jedoch stets BM als derjenige, der das Schiffbauunternehmen der Gruppe kontrollierte. R&K waren über lange Jahre hinweg für die Londoner Geschäfte der Verwandten und Freunde verantwortlich. Außerdem besaßen sie ihre eigene britische Tochterfirma, Counties Ship Management, unter deren Management nach dem Kriege über 40 Schiffahrtsfirmen standen, welche hauptsächlich Trampschiffe betrieb, die in Canada nach der gleichen Basiskonstruktion von J.L.Thompson gebaut waren wie die amerikanischen Liberty-Schiffe.

Es ist schon interessant, die Namen der Direktoren dieser überwiegend Ein-Schiffs-Firmen zu studieren. Fast immer erscheint ein Mavroleon oder Kulukundis in der Liste, daneben aber auch deren Schützlinge und die aufstrebenden Familienmitglieder und Freunde. Ohne Frage spielte die Erfahrung, die sie mit dem Betrieb dieser in Canada gebauten sogenannten ,Hill boats' (eine Sammelbezeichnung nach der Namensgebung für die Counties-Schiffe, z.B. *Lulworth Hill*) gemacht hatten, eine ganz große Rolle bei der Entwicklung des SD14. Der Einfluß der Rethymnis/Kulukundis/Mavroleon wirkte sich besonders auf den nachhaltigen Erfolg des Schiffstyps aus. Gar nicht selten, wenn das Auftragsbuch von A&P schwächelte, reichte ein Auftrag von Mr. Mavroleon (den er stets zu einem Niedrigpreis vergab) als Signal für weitere Aufträge anderer Griechen, die sich

Stapellauf der *Cosmostar* (Werftnummer 878) in Southwick, 27. April 1972. *[Turners (Photography) Ltd., Sammlung John Lingwood]*

19

sagten: ‚Wenn BM glaubt, daß man jetzt bestellen soll, können wir doch kaum etwas anderes tun.'

Nicht nur die Familie und andere Inselbewohner der R&K-Dynastie stützten zu Anfang das SD14-Programm. Die Schiffbaulisten von Austin & Pickersgill sowie Bartram weisen wiederholte Ablieferungen an Firmen auf, die von so Alteingesessenen wie Lykiardopulu, Lemos, Vergottis, Vlassopulos, Dracopoulos und Pateras kontrolliert wurden, um nur einige wenige zu nennen. Alle 27 von Hellenic Shipyards gebauten SD14-Schiffe entstanden für griechische Reeder, darunter so bekannte Namen wie Livanos, Yemelos und Tsavliris, aber auch für in jüngerer Zeit etablierte Mitglieder der griechischen Handelsschiffahrt, vornehmlich George Papalios, zu dessen Aegis-Flotte schließlich sechs bei Hellenic gebaute SD14 zählen sollten.

Griechische Reeder wurden eigentlich immer als Individualisten dargestellt, die, außer in den oben geschilderten Kreisen, in Schiffahrtsdingen nicht mit anderen Griechen zusammenarbeiteten. George Papalios war ein relativer Neuling unter den Reedern. Es ist überliefert, daß Mr. Mavroleon die Beziehungen zwischen A&P und Mr. Papalios ein wenig argwöhnisch betrachtete. Also mußte ein ‚zufälliges' Zusammentreffen der beiden in einem Londoner Hotel eingefädelt werden. Gottlob schwanden nach ein paar Drinks alle Zweifel, die BM gegenüber dem ‚unbekannten Fremden' gehegt hatte, und so erhielt Mr. Papalios zusammengenommen zehn SD14-Neubauten, einschließlich der oben erwähnten sechs.

Eine Pause trat in den Verhandlungen für weitere Verträge ein, als Southwick Aufträge über fünf SD14

verbucht hatte, und die Sorgen über die Finanzierung der ersten Bartram-Verträge endgültig überwunden waren. Dann aber verlieh einer der Kickstarts von Mr. Mavroleon dem Programm neuen Schwung, nämlich durch Aufträge für zwei weitere Schiffe. Sie wurden Anfang 1968 von Liberia-Gesellschaften erteilt, die zur Familie Mavroleon gehörten und im Management von Mavroleon Brothers Ltd. in London standen. Gleichzeitig traf ein dritter Auftrag für einen Nachbau von Lykiardopulo & Co. ein. Von besonderer Bedeutung war der nächste SD14-Auftrag, der erste für eine britische Reederei, den Southwick von Larrinaga Steamship Company, Liverpool, hereinnahm. Larrinaga machten von der erst kurz zuvor von der britischen Regierung eingeführten Finanzhilfe für britische Reeder Gebrauch und bestellten zwei Neubauten, später noch einen dritten. Zu diesem Zeitpunkt buchten A&P den Auftrag für zwei 26.000 Tonnen Bulkcarrier für Gesellschaften der Rethymnis & Kulukundis-Gruppe, welche die Finanzhilfe für Bulker nutzten. Das wirkte sich nachteilig auf das SD14-Programm in Sunderland aus. Bartrams kontrahierten den Bau eines 23.000 tdw Bulkcarriers mit einem geschätzten Kunden. Es wäre das größte von Bartrams gebaute Schiff geworden, doch wurde der Auftrag zu einem späteren Zeitpunkt auf Southwick übertragen, womit South Dock sich auf den Bau von SD14-Schiffen konzentrieren konnte. Dies geschah für weitere zehn Jahre, während derer in einer beachtlichen Folge insgesamt 54 Schiffe abgeliefert wurden.

Als A&P mit Australind Steam Shipping Ltd. den Vertrag zum Bau eines Schiffes vom oben beschriebenen Typ SD15 zeichneten, ging damit eine weitere Verlängerung der Unterbrechung des SD14-Programms in Southwick einher. Es sollte dies das einzige Schiff dieser Klasse werden, das in Sunderland gebaut wurde, obwohl Spekulaten aus Hong Kong 1973 den Auftrag für zwei von insgesamt sechs SD14-Neubauten erst in den Typ SD15 wandelten, dann aber zum SD14 zurückkehrten. Wie auch im Falle anderer Hong Kong-Abkommen jener Zeit gingen diese Bauverträge sodann mit beträchtlichem Gewinn an

Carina (Southwick Werftnummer 859), der dritte SD 14 für ein von der Familie Mavroleon kontrolliertes Unternehmen. Zwar in hervorragendem Pflegezustand, aber ohne das für viele Mavroleon-Schiffe typische weiße Rumpfband ("Dividendenstreifen"). Auffällig die kleinen Brückenhausfenster. Dafür wurden später größere Fenster mit erweiterter Sicht eingeführt. *[Sammlung David Hunter]*

den ursprünglichen ‚Reeder'. Da das Interesse am SD14 stieg, nahm die Southwick-Werft erneut nach dieser Pause von vier Einheiten den Bau von SD14-Schiffen auf und erfüllte 30 aufeinanderfolgende Verträge, bis sie sich 1975 wieder dem Bau von Bulkcarriern zuwandte.

    Linienreedereien betrachteten den SD14 inzwischen als sehr brauchbar für ihre regulären Frachtdienste und charterten folglich viele dieser eigentlich als Tramper gedachten Schiffe. Die gute Verwendbarkeit in Liniendiensten wurde durch die Aufträge für neun Schiffe unterstrichen, welche in den siebziger Jahren die Colocotronis-Gruppe zur Erfüllung von Zeitcharterverträgen mit den deutschen Linien Hamburg-Süd und DAL (Deutsche Afrika-Linien) erteilte. Nach diesem gelungenen Test fanden sich auch die Namen weiterer Linienreedereien in der Referenzliste der Werft, vornehmlich jener der Peninsular and Oriental (P&O Line). Diese begann mit Aufträgen im Jahre 1973, als sie in der geschilderten Form zwei Kontrakte von Auftraggebern aus Hong Kong kaufte, und erweiterte das Volumen durch vier zusätzliche, direkt bei der Werft bestellte Schiffe. Es dauerte nicht lange, und die Australind Steam Shipping Ltd., zusammen mit den Royal Mail Lines und Lamport & Holt (Blue Star Lines) folgten mit Aufträgen für Schiffe der Vierten Serie, während die Ellerman Lines einen der P&O-Kontrakte für eigene Zwecke übernahmen. Diese

hochangesehenen Gesellschaften taten den Schritt zum Eigentum an SD14-Schiffen leider etwas zu spät, denn die Dienste, für die sie vorgesehen waren, wurden containerisiert. Mit den chinesischen und cubanischen Staatsreedereien fanden sich jedoch rasch Abnehmer, die sich durch Ankäufe gebrauchter Schiffe und danach auch Aufträge für Neubauten sehr bald zu den größten Betreibern von SD14-Schiffen aller Zeiten gesellten.

    Inzwischen hatten die beiden Werften in Sunderland vollauf mit dem Bau von Schiffen zu tun, deren Auftraggeber noch anspruchsvollere Spezifikationen wünschten als selbst in den laufenden Serien vorgesehen. Wie im vorausgehenden Absatz geschildert, benötigten diese Reeder vor allem Verbesserungen des Ladegeschirrs und schrieben regelmäßig den Einbau von Schwergutbäumen mit Hebefähigkeiten von 20 bis 60 Tonnen vor. Zwar eignete sich der SD14 nicht besonders für den Transport von Containern, bot aber dennoch Stellplätze für die bescheidene Anzahl von fast 200 TEU. Eine ganze Anzahl von Schiffen wurde mit Schwingbäumen mit einer Hebefähigkeit von 22 Tonnen ausgestattet, völlig ausreichend für den Umschlag von damals gebräuchlichen 20-Fuß-Containern (TEU). Ein Mann kontrollierte drei Winden über einen Joystick und damit das Auftoppen, Schwenken und Heben mit diesem einen Baum. Das erwies sich als fast so leistungsfähig wie aber bestimmt als kostengünstiger als eine Ausrüstung mit Deckskranen. Solche wurden gleichwohl in verschiedenen Kombinationen auf einer Reihe von später von CCN gebauten Schiffen vorgesehen.

    Zweifelsfrei waren für Austin & Pickersgill die Siebziger

die erfolgreichsten Jahre der SD14-Ära. Zu der Zeit machten nur wenige britische Werften keine Verluste, geschweige denn Gewinne mit ihren Betrieben. Verglichen damit wies die Werft in Sunderland im Zeitraum 1971 bis 1977 folgende Überschüsse nach Steuern aus: £ 1,205 Mio; £ 1,259 Mio; £ 1,398 Mio; £ 2,254 Mio; £ 4,923 Mio und £ 2,506 Mio. London & Overseas Freighters, inzwischen die alleinigen Gesellschafter von Austin & Pickersgill, bezogen aus ihrer Investition eine jährliche Dividende von einer Million Pfund, und auch die Mitarbeiter freuten sich über gute Löhne, Bonuszahlungen und Arbeitsbedingungen. Im Anhang Nr. 4 und 5 werden die Gewinne aus einer Reihe einzelner Neubauverträge zusammen mit weiteren Finanzdaten zu den erbauten Schiffen aufgeschlüsselt.

Varianten

IHI gemeinsam mit ihren Konstruktions-Partnern G.T.R.Campbell ließen der Eigendynamik des ‚Freedom' Liberty Ship Replacement-Programms mit einer langen Folge unterschiedlicher Varianten der F-Klasse freien Lauf, etwa mit den Typen Freedom I, Fortune und Friendship, dagegen konnten Austin & Pickersgill mit der einzigen Variante des SD14, dem SD15, keine vergleichbaren Erfolge erzielen. Wie schon oben erwähnt, bauten sie davon auch nur ein Exemplar, die *Armadale*, die 1970 in Dienst gestellt wurde. Dafür hatten A&P zur Ergänzung des SD14-Programms einen weiteren Pfeil im Köcher, nämlich das umfangreiche Angebot an Bulkcarriern, das sich über viele Jahre als erfolgreich erwiesen hatte. Vor allem bestand immer Bedarf am Typ B26 (26.000 tdw). Später wurden auch Schiffe der Typen B30 (30.000 tdw) und B35 (35.000 tdw) geliefert.

Das Modell SD15 erfreute sich eines gewissen Zuspruchs, als die Werft CCN in Rio de Janeiro ihr SD14-Lizenzabkommen mit A&P um den Typ SD15 erweiterten, den sie in leicht veränderter Form als Prinasa-121 Frachter anboten. Von dieser Klasse bestellten hauptsächlich brasilianische Reeder dreizehn Einheiten. Bedauerlicherweise litten auch diese Schiffe unter den Produktionsschwierigkeiten, mit denen CCN in den späten siebziger Jahren zu kämpfen hatte. Die meisten davon wurden leider sofort aufgelegt, ehe sie weiterverkauft und von anderen Eignern in Dienst gestellt werden konnten.

Armadale der Australind Steam Ship Co. Ltd., das einzige Exemplar eines SD 15 (Southwick Werftnummer 86). *[Paul Boot]*

In ihrer äußeren Erscheinung ähnelten sich der SD14 und der SD15 stark, obwohl letzterer das größere Schiff mit nachstehenden Hauptabmessungen war:

Länge über alles	525'0"	160,020 m
Länge zwischen den Loten	500'0"	152,400 m
Breite auf Spanten	70'0"	21,336 m
Seitenhöhe bis zum Oberdeck	41'3"	12,573 m
Seitenhöhe bis zum zweiten Deck	31'3"	9,525 m
Ladetiefgang	30'2°"	9,209 m
Tragfähigkeit	15.150 metr. Tonnen	

Beide Schiffe wiesen fünf Luken auf. Die flutbare Luke wurde beim SD15 nach vorne zu Luke 2 verlagert und in zwei Abteilungen, 2A und 2B unterteilt. In allen Luken gab es nun Zwischendecks. Für die Dienstgeschwindigkeit von 16,5 Knoten war eine Sulzer-Hauptmaschine vom Typ 6RND68 mit 9.900 PSe höchster Dauerleistung bei 150 UpM vorgesehen. Den Wünschen des Reeders entsprechend erhielt die *Armandale* eine Doxford-Maschine vom Typ 76J4 von 10.000 PSe bei 119 UpM. Nach der Basis-Bauvorschrift für den SD15 umfaßte das Ladegeschirr 10 x 10-Tonnen konventionelle Ladebäume, für die *Armadale* jedoch wurde das in 2 x 16 Tonnen und 3 x 26 Tonnen Schwingbäume geändert. Wie schon oben angemerkt, wurde solches Geschirr zunehmend auch in nachfolgende SD14-Schiffe eingebaut. Die CCN-Version des SD15, Prinasa-121, unterschied sich nur unwesentlich vom A&P Typschiff, erhielt aber wegen des Wunsches nach lokalen Zulieferungen eine Mecapesa MAN K6SZ70/125A Hauptmaschine mit 8.385 kW, die eine Dienstgeschwindigkeit von 17 Knoten ermöglichte. Ebenso wie die SD14-Neubauten von CCN wurden einige der SD15-Schiffe mit Deckskranen und Ladungskühlräumen ausgestattet.

Seit den späten sechziger Jahren findet in zweijährigem Abstand in Piräus, dem Mittelpunkt der griechischen Schiffahrt, als wiederkehrende Veranstaltung der internationalen Schiffahrt die Poseidonia-Ausstellung statt. Für Austin & Pickersgill war das immer ein erfolgreiches Marketing-Ereignis. Man ergriff 1978 die Gelegenheit, eine neue Baureihe der Serie ‚SD' vorzustellen. Das kleinste Schiff der Reihe war der SD9, ein Shelterdecker mit Maschinenraum und Unterkünften ganz achtern und drei Ladeluken, 9.000 tdw und einer Dienstgeschwindigkeit von 14,25 Knoten. Der SD12 war dem in der Anordnung sehr ähnlich, hatte aber vier Ladeluken. Die Reeder fanden jedoch keinen Gefallen an den Entwürfen, und Aufträge konnten dafür nicht

Ein Schiff vom Typ Prinasa-121, paradoxerweise namens *Sunderland Endeavour*, obwohl in Rio de Janeiro gebaut (CCN Werftnummer 099), kräftig qualmend auslaufend Birkenhead am 8. April 1991. *[Paul Boot]*

verbucht werden, obwohl attraktive Schiffsmodelle im Sitzungssaal der Gesellschaft in Southwick und im vor kurzem eröffneten griechischen Verkaufsbüro zu besichtigen waren.

Nur geringer Erfolg war dem dritten der neuen Entwürfe beschieden, dem SD18. Den Vorstellungen der Zeit entsprechend als Mehrzweckschiff ausgelegt, sollte der Frachter der steigenden Nachfrage nach Schiffen mit angemessener Containerladefähigkeit ebenso entsprechen wie auch für Schüttgut und Stückgüter geeignet sein. Auch auf diesem Schiff war die Maschine achtern angeordnet. Die drei Einheiten dieses Typs, bestellt von der Pakistan National Shipping Corporation, die *Muree, Kaghan* und die *Ayubia*, wiesen vier Laderäume auf sowie zur Verbesserung des Ladungsumschlags Doppelluken mit Ausnahme von Luke 1. Die Typenbezeichnung verweist auf die Tragfähigkeit von 18.000 Tonnen, und es gab Containerstellplätze für fast 500 TEU. Bezeichnenderweise

erforderte dieser Auftrag beträchtliche Finanzhilfe aus den Entwicklungshilfeprogrammen, die regelmäßig von der britischen Regierung für überseeische Staaten aufgelegt wurden. Es war auch ein Hinweis auf die Art, in der zukünftige Neubauaufträge verhandelt werden würden. Die Lebensläufe dieser drei Schiffe wie auch jene der SD15 und Prinasa-121 finden sich an anderer Stelle in diesem Buch.

Keine Aufzählung der SD14-Varianten wäre vollständig, ohne den einzigen ‚Ausreißer' zu erwähnen, das Passagierschiff (ganz recht, das Passagierschiff !), das 1982 für die Postschiffslinie der St. Helena Shipping Company zwischen Großbritannien und Südafrika/ St.Helena entwickelt wurde, um das in die Jahre gekommene Postschiff *St.Helena* zu ersetzen. Andrew Bell, Geschäftsführer von Curnow Shipping, die damals das Management von SHS ausübten, hatte sich schon länger für den SD14 interessiert. Er regte an, die Konstruktion daran auszurichten, was seine Firma für die

Ayubia, dritter und letzter SD 18, vor Karachi (Southwick Werftnummer 1409). Auch dieses Schiff hat Velle-Geschirr. *[Nigel Jones]*

Ein faszinierender Blick auf die mögliche Entwicklung. So hätte, ohne Eingreifen der Bürokratie von British Shipbuilders und der Regierung, nach einem Modell von Andrew Bell ein SD 14(P) ausgesehen. *[John Lingwood]*

bemerkenswerten Zufall stammten A&P Appledore (Aberdeen) Ltd. natürlich direkt von den A&P Appledore-Firmen ab, die 1971 mit Beteiligung von Austin & Pickersgill gegründet wurden.

Fahrt voraus

A&P hielten, beflügelt von den Erfolgen der siebziger Jahre, die Zeit für gekommen, um eine verbesserte Version des SD14, die bereits beschriebene Vierte Serie, vorzustellen und den Werftbetrieb in Southwick zu modernisieren. In gewisser Weise wurde die zweite Entscheidung dadurch beeinflußt, daß der Pachtvertrag für die ehemalige Bartram-Werft in South Dock nur noch eine kurze Laufzeit hatte. Außerdem waren die Betriebseinrichtungen schon alt, und das Betriebsgelände eignete sich nicht für Verbesserungen. Am Ende langer Überlegungen stand der Entschluß, die Werft zu schließen und den zukünftigen Schiffbau im neuen Werftkomplex Southwick zusammenzufassen. Dazu gehörte auch die Erweiterung der im Zuge der Werftmodernisierung 1954/55 errichteten Stahlverarbeitungshallen und der Bau von zwei Schiffbauhallen. Die erste dieser Hallen sollte auf dem gerade erworbenen, unmittelbar benachbarten Gelände der ehemaligen Werft Swan, Hunter gebaut werden. Diese berühmte Gesellschaft hatte den Betrieb kurz vor dem Ersten Weltkrieg zur Unterstützung der Produktion ihrer Werften am Tyne errichtet. Der Betrieb wurde während der Depression der Dreißiger stillgelegt, aber 1942 unter der Regie der Shipbuilding Corporation als kriegsbedingte Notmaßnahme wieder eröffnet, bis er 1947 erneut schloß. Die zweite Schiffbauhalle sollte rechtwinklig zur ersten auf den damals genutzten konventionellen Hellingen angeordnet werden. Die Planungen sahen auch einen zusätzlichen Ausrüstungskai vor.

A&P Appledore Ltd., die technische Beratungsfirmentochter, erhielt den Auftrag zum Entwurf und zur Bauleitung. Die Arbeiten begannen im März 1975. Leider gefährdete ein niedriger als erwartet ausgefallenes Darlehen der Regierung zu den Investitionskosten das ganze Vorhaben. Eine Zeitlang sah es so aus, als würde die Schiffbauhalle nur eine Seitenwand und kein Dach (!) erhalten. Am Ende wurden die dafür benötigten Mittel jedoch aufgetrieben, aber erzwungen durch das mangelnde Kapital, mußten die zweite Halle

zukünftigen Bedürfnisse des einzig verbliebenen Königlichen Postdienstes hielt. Auf der Grundlage des Rumpfes der Vierten Serie wurden auf dem SD14(P) über dem Wetterdeck Aufbauten mit zwei Decks angeordnet, die sich vom Heck aus bis beinahe mittschiffs erstreckten. In diesem Aufbau und einem darüber befindlichen Deckshaus mit vier Decks befanden sich die Unterkünfte für 198 Passagiere und 86 Besatzungsangehörige. Die vier Laderäume vor den Aufbauten verfügten über einen 25-Tonnen- und einen 12,5-Tonnen-Kran. Die kleine Luke 5 ganz hinten im SD14 wurde in Vorratsräume umgewandelt. Die Passagierunterkünfte bestanden aus Zweibett-Suiten und Zwei- bzw. Dreibettkabinen, jeweils mit direktem Zugang zum Bad und umfaßten ferner einen Speisesaal, einen Gesellschaftsraum mit Tanzfläche, ein Schwimmbad und ein Ladengeschäft.

Leider teilten weder die Overseas Development Agency (ODA) der britischen Regierung, welche die Zeche zu bezahlen hatte, noch die damaligen beratenden Schiffbauingenieure die Begeisterung der Firma Curnow für diesen Entwurf. Neben sonstiger Kritik wurde gesagt, das Schiff basiere auf einer Konstruktion ‚aus den dreißiger Jahren'. Der Schätzpreis des SD14(P) betrug £ 16 Mio. Schließlich erhielt die Werft von Hall Russell in Aberdeen den Auftrag für ein kleineres Ersatzschiff, die heutige *St.Helena,* zum Preis von £ 19 Mio, der in Nachverhandlungen auf £ 24 Mio stieg. Die Bauwerft fiel in Konkurs und deren Geschäftsbetrieb wurde von A&P Appledore (Aberdeen) Ltd. übernommen, die das Schiff zu Gesamtkosten von £ 32,3 Mio fertigstellten. Die Ablieferung verspätete sich um acht Monate und fand etwa fünf Jahre nach der ersten Vorlage des SD14(P)-Entwurfs bei der ODA statt. Durch einen

Der Rumpf eines SD 18 im Bau im neuen Schiffbaukomplex in Southwick. Die Außenhaut besteht aus einzelnen, vertikal markierten Paneelen, die wiederum einzelne Platten enthielten, zusammengehalten durch horizontale Schweißnähte. *[Harold Appleyard]*

und der Ausrüstungskai in die zweite Bauphase verschoben werden und wurden tatsächlich nie verwirklicht.

Die sogenannten Schiffbauhalle enthielt ‚anderthalb' Bauhellinge. Das entsprach dem von Appledore Shipyard in North Devon entwickelten Konzept, nach dem das Achterschiff, üblicherweise mit der gesamten Maschineneinrichtung und dem Unterkünftemodul, auf der ‚halben' Helling gebaut wurde. Wenn das Achterschiff weit genug fertiggestellt war, wurde es auf die daneben gelegene ‚ganze' Helling geschoben, wo das Vorderschiff angefügt wurde. Während das geschah, begann mit dem Bau eines neuen Hinterschiffs eine weitere Fertigungssequenz auf der ‚halben' Helling.

Seit der weiter oben erwähnten Übernahme von Appledore durch die Court Line 1970 wurde hier nach diesem Verfahren gearbeitet, das auch gerade in der ehemaligen Doxford-Werft in Pallion am Wear, gegenüber von Austin & Pickersgill, eingeführt worden war. Bei diesen Werften befanden sich die Bauhellinge in einem Trockendock, das man flutete, wenn die eine Schiffshälfte schwimmend zur ‚ganzen' Helling verholt wurde, wo die Fortsetzung des Baus stattfand. Nach Fertigstellung ließ man das ganze Schiff einfach wie in einem normalen Reparaturdock aufschwimmen. In Southwick hatten die Bauhellinge die richtige Stapellaufbahnneigung und standen wie sonst üblich an Land, allerdings in der überdachten Schiffbaushalle. Hier wurde die Hinterschiffssektion mit hydraulischen Schubpressen über eine teflonbeschichtete Ablaufbahn von der halben zur ganzen Bauhelling hin verlagert. Nach Fertigstellung fand dann ein konventioneller Stapellauf statt. Theoretisch hätte das fertige Schiff gleich anschließend an Stapellauf/Aufschwimmen sofort auslaufen können. Ganz wichtig war die zeitliche Steuerung des Fertigungszyklus. Das nachfolgende ‚halbe' Schiff mußte bereit zum Hinüberschieben sein, sobald das ‚ganze' Schiff nebenan fertiggestellt war. Vor dem Aufschwimmen im Trockendock mußten beide Schiffshälften natürlich wasserdicht sein.

Mit Beginn der Arbeiten am neuen Werftkomplex im Jahr 1975 verarbeitete Southwick jährlich rund 23.000 Tonnen Stahl, und weitere 16.500 Tonnen in South Dock, gleichbedeutend einem Ausstoß von etwa 15 SD14-Neubauten. Auch ohne den zweiten Bauabschnitt waren ca. 52.000 Tonnen Stahl als Jahres-Verarbeitungsmenge angenommen worden, oder etwa 18 SD14-Neubauten. Marktforschungsdaten erlaubten den Schluß, daß die Nachfrage die Produktion auf überschaubare Zeit auf dieser Höhe halten würde. Diese Voraussage wurde durch den Auftragseingang bei der Werft im Jahr 1976 gestützt, in dem nicht weniger als zwanzig Bestellungen für SD14-Schiffe der Vierten Serie gebucht werden konnten. Als diese Schiffe zur Ablieferung heranstanden, hatte sich das Bild bereits geändert. Fünf der ersten sechs Schiffe aus dieser Liste wurden gleich nach Fertigstellung auf Zeit aufgelegt. Drei konnten schließlich gegen Preisnachlaß an andere Reeder verkauft werden, andere Verträge wurden storniert.

Das Auftragsbuch des Jahres 1976 konnte am Heiligabend mit der Unterzeichnung von Bauaufträgen für drei SD14 für Egon Oldendorff, Lübeck, abgeschlossen werden. Sie traten zu den sechs schon für diesen anspruchsvollen Reeder in Fahrt befindlichen Schiffen gleichen Typs hinzu. Oldendorff behielt die Schiffe fast während ihrer gesamten Dienstzeit in seiner Flotte und unterstrich damit zweifelsfrei die Stärke des SD14-Konzepts. Zu einem späteren Zeitpunkt bestellte Oldendorff mit zwei hochklassigen Mehrzwecklinienfrachtern von der Southwick-Werft von Austin & Pickersgill die letzten Hochseeschiffe, die hier vor der Stillegung des Betriebs gebaut wurden. 1988 bemühte sich Oldendorff intensiv aber erfolglos darum, die Werft zwecks Weiterführung des Betriebs zu erwerben.

Im 1976er Auftragsbuch standen auch die vier schon weiter oben erwähnten hochwertigen Schiffe für Lamport & Holt Line. Im Zweithandmarkt war die Volksrepublik China bereits als Käufer für eine Anzahl von SD14-Schiffe aufgetreten. Vier Jahre nach ihrer Fertigstellung gingen diese Schiffe denselben Weg. Der

Imme Oldendorff, einer der an Egon Oldendorff gelieferten SD 14, in dramatischer Beleuchtung am 23. August 1975 auf der Schelde. Die Oldendorff-Schiffe wiesen einige besondere Merkmale auf: Schwergutbäume bei Luken II und IV, was die Anordnung zweier Masten erforderte (später bei fast allen SD 14), während der Signalmast sich üblicherweise nicht auf der Mittellinie befand. *Imme Oldendorff*, Werftnummer 877 von Southwick. *[Roy Kittle]*

letzte Versuch der berühmten Linienreederei, konventionelle Stückgutdienste in ihren südamerikanischen Fahrtgebieten beizubehalten, mußte alsbald vor der Containerisierung kapitulieren. Nach diesen Ankäufen folgten zwei Aufträge direkt aus China sowie vier weitere als Ergebnis eines Joint Venture zwischen der Volksrepublik und World Wide Shipping aus Hong Kong.

Die letzten der insgesamt 72 SD14-Neubauten, die Austin & Pickersgill auf der Southwick-Werft fertigstellten, fast genau baugleich mit den vorerwähnten Schiffen aber mit dem Sulzer-Typ 5RLB56 als Hauptmaschine, wurden wiederum von einem Hong Kong-Reeder in Auftrag gegeben. Die Familie Chao kontrollierte Wah Kong Shipping. Frank Chao verband mit diesem Auftrag so etwas wie eine sentimentale Erinnerung, denn er hatte einige Jahre zuvor in Sunderland Schiffbau studiert, und deshalb sollte das Schiff auch *Sunderland Venture* genannt werden. Das ‚Venture' verlief leider nicht nach Plan, und auch dieses Schiff wurde als überschüssig erklärt. Etwas mehr als ein Jahr nach Ablieferung ging das Schiff in Bareboat-Charter einschließlich einer Kaufoption nach Cuba und wurde 1999 letztendlich ein Teil der cubanischen Handelsflotte.

Die cubanischen Staatsreedereien hatten ebenso wie die chinesischen seit Jahren regelmäßig gebrauchte SD14-Tonnage gekauft und darüber hinaus 1975/1976 vier Neubauten von der South Dock Werft bezogen. Zwischen 1983 und 1986 erwarben sie weitere sechs Neubauten, die bei Smith's Dock in South Bank, Midlesbrough, gebaut wurden. Die ersten beiden Schiffe wurden 1981 bestellt, zu einer Zeit, als Austin &

United Drive und *United Effort*, beide für World Wide Shipping (Werftnummern 1416 und 1417) bei der Ausrüstung in Southwick. Wegen der Ausrichtung der Schiffbauhallen kamen Schiffe von dort mit dem Kopf voraus an den Ausrüstungskai. Von den konventionellen Helligen wurden sie flußabwärts mit dem Heck voraus bugsiert. [Les Ring, Sammlung Nigel Jones]

Pickersgill über zwei Aufträge für SD14-Nachbauten der Vierten Serie mit Carrian Shipping, Hong Kong, verhandelten. Da aber A&P auf einem einigermaßen wohlgefüllten Auftragsbuch saß, verfügte die British Shipbuilders Corporation (BS), bei der die Kontrolle lag, die Vergabe der Aufträge an die Teeside-Werft, der die Arbeit auszugehen drohte. Carrian fielen jedoch vor Ablieferung dieser mit Sulzer-Maschinen vom Typ 5RLB56 ausgestatteten Neubauten in Konkurs. Nach einer Aufliegezeit handelte BS ein Lease/Charter-Abkommen aus, wodurch die Schiffe in cubanische Dienste gerieten. Als 1984 Smith abermals Arbeit benötigte, schloß BS einen weiteren Vertrag mit den Cubanern, und so wurden vier weitere Schwesterschiffe für auf Zypern registrierte Firmen gebaut, die von Havanna kontrolliert wurden.

Zwar begrüßten die Gewerkschaften, die Belegschaft und das zeitunglesende Publikum diese Aufträge enthusiastisch, aber in Wahrheit brachten nur wenige davon, wenn überhaupt nur einer, Austin & Pickersgill finanzielle Vorteile. Die Reeder waren verständlicherweise auf die bestmöglichen Konditionen für ihre Investitionen erpicht. Unter welch schwierigen Bedingungen damals verhandelt werden mußte, wird eindrucksvoll in einem Telex wiedergegeben, das der verzweifelte A&P Geschäftsführer Derek Kimber seinem Verhandlungspartner in Hong Kong schickte, der noch weitergehende Preisnachlässe forderte, und das im Original zitiert werden sollte: „You've had the shirt off my back, do you now want the skin?" Die Werft nahm immer noch ein paar Aufträge für Bulkcarrier herein und konnte auch drei Einheiten der SD18-Variante des SD14-Entwurfs, wieder ohne finanziellen Nutzen, an pakistanische Reeder verkaufen, Mehrzweckfrachter von 18.000 tdw Tragfähigkeit. Um die Auslastung der Werften zu erhalten, war es aber erforderlich, die schon im Bauprogramm fest eingeplanten SD14-Kontrakte zu verkaufen, welche die Reeder bereits storniert hatten oder ihrerseits verkaufen wollten. Auf diese Weise zustandegekommene Abschlüsse brachten die

SD 14 im Bau bei Smith's Dock, Middlesbrough Links die unglückliche *North Islands* (Werftnummer 1360) auf dem Helgen am 30. August 1986. Sie lief als letzter in Großbritannien erbauter SD 14 am 15. Oktober vom Stapel.

Unten die *West Islands* (Werftnummer 1358), beim Stapellauf am 26. März 1986. Mit Ausnahme der *North Islands*, die 1997 verlorenging, sind soweit bekannt alle übrigen SD 14 von Smith's Dock Mitte 2004 noch vorhanden. [Michael Green]

Staatsreedereien von Angola und Vietnam in das Auftragsbuch der Werft, bedeuteten für die Werft aber hohe Verluste. Es scheint fraglich zu sein, ob der volle Verkaufspreis von allen Käuferländern jemals hereingeholt werden konnte, wie aus einem Bericht in Lloyd's List aus dem Januar 1994 hervorgeht. Darin heißt es, daß ein Bankenkonsortium eine vietnamesische Bank wegen Zahlung von £ 38 Mio (£ 9 Mio Kreditsumme plus £ 29 Mio Zinsen) verklagte, herrührend aus offenen Forderungen für vier SD14-Neubauten, die Austin & Pickersgill vor zehn Jahren lieferten. Die Reederei hatte vorher lediglich eine Zahlung von £ 575.000 für die Schiffe geleistet. Wie aus der Sammlung der SD14-Schiffsbiographien an anderer Stelle hervorgeht, sorgten diese vietnamesischen Aufträge für erhebliches Durcheinander bei der Zuordnung von Werftnummern.

Auf Betreiben der britischen Regierung versuchten British Shipbuilders um diese Zeit, mittels verschiedener Strategien die Kosten zu senken und die sehr hohen Verluste zu drücken, die sämtliche unter ihrer Kontrolle stehenden Unternehmen erlitten, darunter auch

Austin & Pickersgill. Leider blieben sie alle erfolglos. Daraufhin wurde für den Bereich Handelsschiffbau beschlossen, die Marketingpolitik von BS zu ändern und nur noch ein gestrafftes Programm mit lediglich vier Entwürfen anzubieten. Wie schon oben ausgeführt, waren dies ein 45.000 tdw Kombifrachter für Schüttgut oder Container, ein 22.000 tdw Mehrzweckfrachter, ein 7.450 tdw RoRo-Frachter und der SD King 15 Frachter. Letzterer war nichts anderes als ein Nachbau der sechs SD-Neubauten von Smith's Dock, d.h. das Schiff der Vierten Serie mit einer umfassenden Liste von Zusatzeinrichtungen, die nun alle zum neuen SDKING-15 Entwurf gehörten.

Die über die Jahre an der ursprünglichen SD14-Bauvorschrift vorgenommenen Änderungen, besonders nach Markteinführung der Vierten Serie, hatten sich vom Anfangskonzept eines preiswerten, einfachen und wirtschaftlichen Frachters entfernt. Anhang 4 vermittelt einen Eindruck der sich daraus ergebenden Preiserhöhungen. Die Frachtraten waren damals noch ausreichend hoch, die Nachfrage nach

Zwischendeckfrachtern bestand fort, und neue Aufträge konnten weiterhin gebucht werden. Es wurde schon ausgeführt, daß sich die Marktverhältnisse bald verschlechtern sollten, und daß die Reeder deshalb darum baten, die Fertigstellungstermine hinauszuzögern. Andere Neubauverträge wurden mit Verlust weiterverkauft oder storniert. Die Markteinführung des SD King 15 hätte zu keinem ungünstigeren Termin stattfinden können, denn private Reeder konnten die Mehrkosten der verbesserten Entwürfe nicht mehr aufbringen. Folglich kamen keine Aufträge für die neue Version herein, und Anfragen auch nur tröpfchenweise, und das ausschließlich von Reedern aus der Dritten Welt, die zwar gern Neubauaufträge vergaben, aber so gut wie mittellos waren. Tatsächlich gab es hier nur dann Fortschritte, wenn die britische Regierung ausreichende Finanzhilfen bereitstellte, und das tat sie nicht.

Die Reihe der in Sunderland gebauten Schiffe endete am 15. Februar 1984 mit der Ablieferung der *Sunderland Venture*, sechzehn Jahre und einen Tag nach Übergabe des ersten SD14-Neubaus von der Werft in Southwick durch Austin & Pickersgill. Die *North Islands*, letztes in Großbritannien gebautes Schiff dieser Reihe, wurde am 12. Februar 1987 von Smith's Dock abgeliefert, zufällig fast genau am 19. Jahrestag der Übergabe der *Nicola*. Der inzwischen weltberühmte Schiffsentwurf widerlegte schließlich alle Kritiker und erreichte seinen zwanzigsten Geburtstag 1988, als die letzten beiden CCN-Lizenzbauten, *Leonor* und *Tucurui*, endlich die Werft verließen. Dem Verfasser erscheint es unglaublich, daß er dies sechsunddreißig Jahre nach Ablauf der *Nicola* schreibt und immer noch eine Anzahl von SD14-Schiffen fährt. Sie bestätigen des Verfassers Behauptung in der Unterzeile seiner Veröffentlichung des Jahres 1976, wonach dies in der Tat „Die größte Erfolgsgeschichte des britischen Schiffbaus" war.

A&P nach dem SD14
British Shipbuilders Corporation kündigte 1985 an, Sunderland Shipbuilders und Austin & Pickersgill am Wear mit Smith's Dock, Teeside, zur neuen Gesellschaft North East Shipbuilders Ltd. (NESL) mit Hauptsitz in der Pallion-Werft von Sunderland Shipbuilders zu fusionieren. Aus heutiger Sicht bestehen kaum Zweifel, daß es geheime Pläne gab, wonach mit Zustimmung der obersten Geschäftsleitung die Smith's Werft unmittelbar stillgelegt werden sollte, weshalb die Zusammenlegung dieser Werft mit den beiden anderen nordöstlichen Unternehmen auch nie durchgeführt wurde.

Mit der Gründung von NESL endete die ein halbes Jahrhundert während Geschichte von Austin & Pickersgill, oder, unter einem breiteren Blickwinkel, etwa 160 Jahre ununterbrochenen Schiffbaus in Sunderland durch mit A&P zusammenhängende Unternehmen. Es ist sehr bedauerlich, daß die Erfolge und das außerordentliche Ansehen, das die Firma weltweit in der kurzen Zeit ihrer Tätigkeit errungen hatte, ein Opfer der Probleme wurden, mit denen die britische Schiffbauindustrie fast während der ganzen nachkriegszeit kämpfen mußte und die während der achtziger Jahre, besonders unter öffentlicher Verwaltung, unüberwindlich wurden.

Zwischen Dezember 1978 und Dezember 1980 hatten Austin & Pickersgill in Southwick hintereinander 23 SD14-Neubauten abgeliefert, aber nur sieben weitere in den beiden Folgejahren, neben 14 verschiedenen Bulkcarriern. Vielleicht war das ein Beweis für den Anfang vom Ende des SD14. Der letzte Bauvertrag für einen SD14 wurde, wie schon erwähnt, im Mai 1981 unterschrieben und das Schiff als *Sunderland Venture* im Februar 1984 fertiggestellt. So groß war der Auftragsmangel der Southwick-Werft, wohl das modernsten Schiffbaukomplexes in Europa wenn nicht in der Welt, daß das Auftragsbuch Bauverträge für fünf antriebslose Flachdeck-Schleppkähne zum Einsatz in den Nordsee-Ölfeldern aufwies. Gerechterweise muß eingestanden werden, daß diese Fahrzeuge wegen ihres hohen Anteils an Stahlverarbeitung ideal für die Gegebenheiten des Unternehmens waren, aber selbst diese simplen Schiffe erbrachten der Werft hohe finanzielle Verluste.

Vier Aufträge für Linienfrachter kamen 1983 und 1985 zustande und bedeuteten die letzten von Austin & Pickersgill gebauten Hochseeschiffe. Die ersten beiden waren 10.500 tdw Mehrzweckschiffe für die Ethiopian Shipping Lines Corporation, die 1984 und 1985 als *Abyot* und *Abba Wonz* abgeliefert wurden. Egon Oldendorff kehrte im Februar 1985 zur Werft zurück und zeichnete Verträge für den Bau von zwei 22.800 tdw Mehrzwecklinienfrachtern. In der Flotte dieser Lübecker Reederei befanden sich schon neun SD14-Schiffe, wohl die am besten ausgerüsteten der gesamten Baureihe. Die Neubauten nun wiesen einen gleichhohen Standard auf und wurden zu den Vorbauten eines Mehrzweckschiffs, das Oldendorff ein wenig später über seine neuerworbene Werft Flensburger Schiffbau-Gesellschaft als den Typ ‚Ecobox' anbot. Wir werden nie erfahren, ob diese Serie A&P ein neues Leben verschafft hätte, wenn Oldendorff von der britischen Regierung und der Europäischen Union der Ankauf der Sunderland-Werften genehmigt worden wäre, als 1988 entschieden wurde, nicht nur diese Werften, sondern den größten Teil des britischen Handelsschiffbaus stillzulegen.

Ehe diese Schließung erfolgte, kam es noch zu einem allerletzten Akt. Für den Verfasser ist es von besonderem Interesse, daß er, der 1966 an der ersten SD14-Sitzung teilnahm, mit der auch diese Darstellung beginnt, zwanzig Jahre später von der Londoner Marketingabteilung von British Shipbuilders telefonisch informiert wurde, daß ein dänischer Unternehmer 24 kleine Fähren bestellen wolle. Aus einer Bauvorschrift per Telex von nur einem halben Dutzend Zeilen wurde ein Vertrag, der NESL Beschäftigung für fast drei Jahre sichern sollte. Es war vorgesehen, die Arbeit gleichmäßig zwischen den Werften in Southwick und Pallion aufzuteilen. Angesichts der Tatsache, daß die Bauvorschrift vom Reeder stammte, der die meisten Zulieferungen direkt von den Unterlieferanten bestellt hatte, war es schon etwas erstaunlich, daß er die ersten Einheiten als nicht der Bauvorschrift entsprechend ablehnte. Nach ausgedehnten rechtlichen und finanziellen Verhandlungen wurden nur fünfzehn Einheiten fertiggestellt, von denen der Besteller nur acht übernahm. Die übrigen sieben erduldeten eine lange Aufliegezeit im Fluß Wear, ehe sie an einen anderen dänischen Reeder verkauft wurden.

Dieser Auftrag nun galt den wirklich letzten Schiffen, die jemals von der früheren Austin & Pickersgill-Werft gebaut wurden, sogar überhaupt in Sunderland. Nur dreizehn der ursprünglich bestellten 24 ‚Superflex'-Fähren wurden in den Werften in Sunderland und in Pallion gebaut, eine in Lizenz von Appledore Shipbuilders. Erstere lieferte die letzte Einheit im Dezember 1988 aus. Damit endet die lange Geschichte des Schiffbaus der Firmen Austin, Pickersgill und der Unternehmen der Austin & Pickersgill-Gruppe, in späteren Jahren gemeinsam mit Bartram & Sons. Nur ein paar Tage nach dem Stapellauf der letzten Fähre in Southwick verkündeten British Shipbuilders die Schließung von NESL und im Jahre darauf die der verbleibenden Firmen von BS. Das Werftgelände von Southwick wurde mit fast unanständiger Eile geräumt und in einen Industrie- und Geschäftspark verwandelt. Auf dem Grundstück, auf dem seit der Mitte des neunzehnten Jahrhunderts die Werft von William Pickersgill gestanden hatte, verblieben nur noch der Ausrüstungskai, die reichlich verfallenen Gebäude, die einmal die am besten ausgestatteten Schiffsschreiner-, Rohrschlosser-, Schmiede- und Motorenschlosserwerkstätten der Welt beherbergten und ein einziger Turmdrehkran des Typs, der nach dem Kriege zur Grundausrüstung jeder britischen Werft gehörte.

Vermelha (Austin & Pickersgill, Southwick, Werftnummer 888). *[Sammlung V.H. Young und L.A. Sawyer]*

ANMERKUNGEN ZU DEN SCHIFFS-BIOGRAPHIEN

Die Schiffe sind nach Bauwerften aufgeführt, in der Reihenfolge der Werftnummern. Der einzige SD 15 und die drei SD 18 sind in der Southwick-Aufzählung nach Werftnummern enthalten. Dagegen erhielten die 13 Prinasa 121 eine eigene Reihe. Die Werftlisten stehen in der Reihenfolge, in der die jeweilige Werft ihren ersten SD 14 vom Stapel ließ.

Die erste Zeile jedes Eintrags beginnt mit der Werftnummer, gefolgt von dem Schiffsnamen, den das Schiff bei Indienststellung trug. Lief ein Schiff unter einem anderen Namen vom Stapel, erscheint dieser vorangestellt in Klammern..

In der zweiten Zeile steht die Lloyd's Register/IMO-Nummer. Die Nummern wurden ursprünglich von Lloyd's Register vergeben und später von der International Maritime Organisation im Zuge der internationalen Anstrengungen übernommen, einzelne Schiffe zu identifizieren. Inzwischen werden sie auch schon auf Schiffe aufgemalt. Viele SD14-Schiffe gingen verloren oder wurden verschrottet, ehe die IMO das System übernahm. Zur Wahrung der Einheitlichkeit wird deren LR-Nummer gezeigt.

Die dritte, vierte und fünfte Zeile zeigen die Werte der Brutto- und Nettotonnage und die Tragfähigkeit der ersten Vermessung bei Fertigstellung. Wenn das Schiff während seiner Lebensdauer wesentlich umgebaut wurde, wird das durch eine weitere Zahlenreihe mit Datum angezeigt.

Die sechste Zeile enthält einige Einzelheiten der eingebauten Hauptmaschine. Im Anhang 1 stehen weitere Einzelheiten, auch der Hauptmaschinen der SD14-Varianten. In diesem Anhang sind auch die Hauptabmessungen der verschiedenen Schiffstypen aufgeführt.

Weitere Zeilen beschreiben ausführlich das Leben und das Schicksal des Schiffes, wo möglich seit Beginn der Auftragsverhandlungen, einschließlich Wechsel von Reeder, Manager, Operator, Schiffsname und Flagge.

Von Register zu Register werden Einzelheiten der Reeder, Manager und Operators unterschiedlich erfaßt. Zur Wahrung einer gewissen Einheitlichkeit wurde beschlossen, sich an ‚Lloyd's Confidential Index' als die Quelle zu halten, welche die meisten Angaben zu jenen macht, die Kontrolle über die Schiffe ausüben. Weil solche Eintragungen drei bis vier Namen umfassen können, gilt nachfolgende Regel für deren Wiedergabe: Im allgemeinen zeigt der erste Eintrag den eingetragenen Schiffseigner, häufig eine Ein-Schiffs-GmbH, zusammen mit Heimathafen und Staat des Firmensitzes, sofern sich dieser von

jenem des wirklichen Eigners oder Managers unterscheidet. Darauf folgt (in Klammern) die kontrollierende Dachgesellschaft, die in der Praxis der wirkliche Eigner oder Manager sein kann. Zwischen ihnen ist in den Registereintragungen nur schwer zu unterscheiden. Wird eine Einzelperson aufgeführt als über die Firma Kontrolle ausübend, steht ihr oder sein Name in diesem Eintrag, wiederum in Klammern. Oftmals wird das Schiff die Schornsteinmarke dieser Gesellschaft oder der Einzelperson tragen. Wenn der eingetragene Eigner oder der wirkliche Eigner/ Manager einen identischen Firmensitz haben, steht das hinter der Klammer. Ein dritter Eintrag weist gewöhnlich darauf hin, daß der Manager oder Operator ein anderer ist als der wirkliche Eigner, z.B. wenn ein Schiff in Bareboatcharter ist. Angaben zur geführten Flagge finden sich nur dann, wenn sie eine andere ist als diejenige des Staates, in dem der eingetragene Eigner seinen Sitz hat.

Schiffe wechseln oft innerhalb einer Gruppe von einem Unternehmen zu einem anderen. Eignerwechsel werden deshalb wie folgt wiedergegeben: ‚Sold' (‚verkauft') bezeichnet ein Geschäft, bei dem das Schiff zwischen Unternehmen verschiedener Kontrolle wechselt. ‚Transferred' (‚übertragen') bedeutet den Wechsel eines Schiffes zwischen zwei Unternehmen, von denen angenommen wird, daß sie unter identischer Kontrolle stehen. ‚Owners became' (‚Eigner wurden') heißt, daß die Eignergesellschaft ihren Namen geändert hat.

Es werden Einzelheiten größerer Unfälle beschrieben, auch Vorkommnisse, sofern dokumentiert, die zur anschließenden Verschrottung des Schiffes führten.

Einzelangaben zu den Abwrackbetrieben sind so ausführlich wie möglich. Im Falle von Verschrottungen jüngeren Datums, besonders auf dem indischen Subkontinent und in der VR China, werden die Namen der Abwrackbetriebe und der Beginn der Verschrottung nicht mehr veröffentlicht.

‚Still listed by Lloyd's Register' (‚Noch in Lloyd's Register geführt') bedeutet, daß Lloyd's Register of Shipping annimmt, daß es das Schiff noch gibt, gleich ob in Fahrt oder aufgelegt. Das kann durch ‚existence must be in doubt' (‚Vorhandensein zweifelhaft') eingeschränkt sein und durch weitere Angaben, wonach das Schiff noch in Lloyd's Register geführt wird, aber letzthin keine Bewegungen bekannt wurden. Alle weiteren Informationen, die zu Schiffen dieser Kategorie ans Licht kommen, auch Aktualisierungen hinsichtlich noch existierender Einheiten, werden in Abständen in der Zeitschrift des Herausgebers, ‚Ships in Focus Record', erscheinen.

Vessels built by Austin and Pickersgill Ltd., Southwick Shipyard, Sunderland

852. NICOLA

L.R./I.M.O. Number 6806626
8,848g
6,123n
15,246d
Hawthorn-Sulzer 5RD68
4.10.1967: Keel laid.
29.12.1967: Launched for General Freighters Corporation, Monrovia, Liberia (Mavroleon Brothers Ltd., London).
14.2.1968: Completed. Liberian flag.
1973: Transferred to Nicola Shipping Corporation, Monrovia (Mavroleon Brothers Ltd., London).

1979: Transferred to General Freighters Corporation, Monrovia (Mavroleon Brothers Ltd., London) and renamed AVLAKI.
11.1979: Sold to Toyamal Marine Co. Ltd., Limassol, Cyprus (Richmond Shipping Co. Ltd. (Diotima Co. Naviera S.A.), Piraeus, Greece) and renamed GLASGOW.
1982: Controlling group became Richmond Maritime Corporation (Panagis Dallias), Piraeus.
1983: Placed under Philippine flag.
27.10.1986: Arrived Kaohsiung for breaking up by Sie Yung Steel Mill.

Above: *Nicola* at Cape Town, 28th January 1975. *[Ken White, Don Brown collection]*

Below: Towards the end of her career, the first SD14, now named *Glasgow* under Greek ownership and the Philippines flag, with no apparent connection with the Scottish city, prepares to enter Birkenhead Docks on 5th July 1984. The tugs assisting her are *Coburg, Huskisson* and *Collingwood*. Note the paintings of Disney cartoon characters on the superstructure front. *[Paul Boot]*

853. **SYRIE**

L.R./I.M.O. Number 6810029
9,024g
6,214n
14,885d
Hawthorn-Sulzer 5RD68
13.11.1967: Keel laid.
14.2.1968: Launched for General Freighters Corporation, Monrovia, Liberia (Mavroleon Brothers Ltd., London).
1.4.1968: Completed. Liberian flag.
1973: Transferred to Syrie Shipping Corporation, Monrovia (Mavroleon Brothers Ltd., London).
1973: Management transferred to Mavroleon Brothers (Ship Management) Co. Ltd., London.
1978: Renamed AKRI under the Greek flag.
1980: Sold to Mareduc Maritime Corporation, Monrovia, Liberia (Oceanmaid Shipping Co. S.A. (S.M. Ranis and J.P. Samatzis), Piraeus, Greece) and renamed ATHENA under the Greek flag.
10.6.1983: Abandoned by her crew after springing a leak about 650 miles south of Adak Island, USA during a voyage from Port Alfred, Canada, to Xingang, China. Reported sinking in position 42.28

Above: *Syrie* arriving Cape Town in 1977. *[Ken White, Don Brown collection]*

Below: *Athena* at Montreal, 9th June 1981. *[René Beauchamp, David Salisbury collection]*

north by 178.20 west.
10.7.1983: Sighted semi-submerged in position 43.50 north by 167.05 west. A search was made but abandoned after nothing was found. The vessel was assumed to have foundered shortly after the sighting. Insurers agreed a total loss.

854. DEGEDO

L.R./I.M.O. Number 6825531
9,079g
6,143n
15,363d
Vickers-Sulzer 5RD68
4.4.1968: Keel laid.
9.9.1968: Launched for Agenor Shipping Co. Ltd., Famagusta, Cyprus (Aegis Shipping Co. Ltd. (N.D. Papalios), Piraeus, Greece).
31.10.1968: Completed. Cypriot flag.
1976: Transferred to Gerenuk Shipping Corporation Ltd., Monrovia, Liberia (Aegis Shipping Co. Ltd. (N.D. Papalios), Piraeus) and renamed AEGIS ISLAND.
6.1980: Sold (together with ships 855/410/411 for $13.5m) to Good Patriot Inc., Panama (Good Faith Shipping Co. S.A. (Nikolaos Frangos and Nicholas G. Moundreas), Piraeus) and renamed GOOD PATRIOT.
1984: Transferred to Antwerp Shipping Co. S.A., Panama (Good Faith Shipping Co. S.A. (Nikolaos Frangos and Nicholas G. Moundreas), Piraeus) and renamed ANTWERP.
1986: Transferred to Number One S.A., Panama (Good Faith Shipping Co. S.A. (Nikolaos Frangos and Nicholas G. Moundreas), Piraeus).
1986: Transferred to Marine Hope S.A., Panama (Good Faith Shipping Co. S.A. (Nikolaos Frangos and Nicholas G. Moundreas), Piraeus) and renamed LIBERATOR A.
1988: Transferred to Anko Shipping and Trading S.A., Panama (Good Faith Shipping Co. S.A. (Nikolaos Frangos

Above: Aegis Shipping took the first SD14s built by Bartrams, and also had some of the early Southwick vessels, including *Degedo*, photographed in the New Waterway on 28th August 1972. The name was formed from the first two letters of the owner's children's names, Demetrios, George and Dora. *[Roy Kittle]*
Below: As *Lord Venkata* in the Ghent Canal at Terneuzen in May 1988, the low light picks out the previous name *Good Patriot* and shows the plating between the frames, a common side effect of welded construction *[David Salisbury]*

and Nicholas G. Moundreas), Piraeus) and renamed LORD VENKATA.
1989: Sold to Corona Navigation Co. Ltd., Limassol, Cyprus (Rialto Shipping Co. Ltd., Piraeus) and renamed CAPTAIN NIKOS A.
16.4.1992: Arrived Alang for breaking up by Crown Steel Co.

855. **VENTURER**

L.R./I.M.O. Number 6901921
9,070g
6,137n
15,363d
Vickers-Sulzer 5RD68
19.9.1968: Keel laid.
19.11.1968: Launched for Agenor
Shipping Co. Ltd., Famagusta (Aegis
Shipping Co. Ltd. (N.D. Papalios),
Piraeus, Greece).
20.12.1968: Completed. Cypriot flag.
1977: Transferred to Tragonnisi
Shipping Corporation Ltd. (Aegis
Shipping Co. Ltd. (N.D. Papalios),
Piraeus, Greece and renamed AEGIS

VENTURE.
6.1980: Sold (together with ships
854/410/411) for $13.5m to Good
Dolphin Inc, Panama (Good Faith
Shipping Co. S.A. (Nikolaos Frangos
and Nicholas G. Moundreas),
Piraeus) and renamed GOOD
DOLPHIN.
1984: Transferred to Princess Venus
Shipping S.A., Panama (Good Faith
Shipping Co. S.A. (Nikolaos Frangos
and Nicholas G. Moundreas),
Piraeus) and renamed PRINCESS.
1986: Owners recorded as Selma
Finance Inc. of Garden City.
1987: Sold to Seacrest Shipping Ltd.,

Limassol, Cyprus and renamed DIMI.
1988: Sold to Rialto Shipping Co.
Ltd., Piraeus and renamed NIKOS A
under the Cyprus flag.
5.6.1992: Laid up under arrest at
Apapa.
1994: Sold to Cyprus owners and
renamed EKIMOGUN STAR.
1995: Sold to Oriental Establishment
Ltd., Monrovia, Liberia and renamed
GHULAM under the flag of St.
Vincent and the Grenadines.
19.12.1996: Arrived Gadani Beach for
breaking up by Dewan Sons, having
been sold for $150 per lightweight ton.

Above: *Venturer* at Vancouver about 1974.
[S. Klassen, David Salisbury collection]

Below: The Papalios vessels gradually adopted
'Aegis' names, *Venturer* becoming *Aegis Venture* in
1977. She is seen deeply laden off Singapore on

27th May 1980. Note the minimal poop deck
house on this ship, providing access only to the
steering gear and stores. *[Nigel Jones]*

856. NICOLAOS D.L.

L.R./I.M.O. Number 6904454
9,038g
6,341n
15,291d
Vickers-Sulzer 5RD68

18.10.1968: Keel laid.
24.12.1968: Launched for Ionmar Compania Naviera S.A., Panama (Lykiardopulo and Co. Ltd., London).
22.2.1969: Completed. Greek flag.
8.1979: Sold to Palis Shipping Enterprises Corporation S.A., Panama (Syros Shipping Co. Ltd. (L.M. Valmas and Son Ltd.), London) for $3.35m and renamed KAPTAMICHALIS under the Greek flag.
1983: Managers deleted.
1984: Sold to Ansari Shipping Corporation, Monrovia, Liberia (Eurolines Contracting Co. S.A. (John Laliotis) Piraeus, Greece) and renamed EURCO BANNER under the Greek flag.
1986: Transferred to Banner Shipping Co. Ltd., Gzira, Malta (Seaworld Management and Trading Inc. (Constantinos Dedopoulos), Piraeus) and renamed BANNER.
1988: Transferred to Armonia Maritime Co. Ltd., Valletta, Malta (Seaworld Management and Trading Inc. (Constantinos Dedopoulos), Piraeus) and renamed ARMONIA.
1988: Sold to Queen Jane Shipping Inc., Panama and renamed LUCKY CARRIER.
1990: Sold to Roula Shipping, Valletta, Malta (Interuniversal Chartering S.A. (D. Kyriakopoulos), Piraeus) and renamed ARGO CARRIER.
25.1.1991: Anchored off Piraeus for repairs during a voyage from Calais to Mokha, Yemen with a cargo of sugar.
18.4.1991: Grounded off Psittalia Island near Piraeus after anchor chain parted in heavy weather. As a result vessel flooded and sank in shallow water. Lying semi-submerged,

the vessel was declared a constructive total loss, and the wreck placed under arrest.

857-858.
Berths reserved for proposed contracts with Korea United Lines, South Korea. Negotiations not proceeded with.

Top: *Nicolaos D.L.* on the Thames, 5th June 1973. *[Roy Kittle]*

Middle: *Kaptamichalis* on the New Waterway in July 1980 on charter to a Swedish-French consortium. *[David Salisbury]*

Bottom: In Piraeus Roads on 29th September 1990, the rusty *Argo Carrier* is approaching the end of her career, and looks it. *[Nigel Jones]*

859. CARINA

L.R./I.M.O. Number 6910025
9,072g
6,245n
15,281d
Hawthorn-Sulzer 5RD68
7.12.1968: Keel laid.
25.2.1969: Launched for Fairsail
Carriers Corporation, Monrovia,
Liberia (Mavroleon Brothers Ltd.,
London).
3.4.1969: Completed. Liberian flag.
1978: Renamed ALIOUSSA under the
Greek flag.
5.1980: Sold to Sunflower Maritime
Co. S.A., Panama (Sounion Shipping
Co. S.A. (D. Kraniotis), Piraeus,
Greece) for $4m and renamed IO
under the Greek flag.
1980: Management transferred to Niva
Shipping Ltd., Piraeus.
1981: Management transferred to
Sounion Shipping Co. S.A. (D.
Kraniotis), Piraeus, Greece.
1982: Management transferred to Dido
Shipping Co. S.A., Piraeus (S.
Kafandris and K. Vernier, Athens).
1983: Management transferred to
Sounion Shipping Co. S.A. (D.
Kraniotis), Piraeus.
1.7.1985: Sold by auction at Durban to
Adonis Shipping Co. (Palmyra Tsiris
Lines S.A. (Anastase and Alexander
Tsiris), Piraeus) for $400,000.
1.8.1985: Renamed HYMETUS under
the Lebanese flag.
16.11.1986: Abandoned by her crew
after flooding when her hull cracked in
heavy weather 180 miles south south
east of Hong Kong in position 21.50
north by 116.30 east whilst on a
voyage from Bourgas to Shanghai with
a cargo of steel.
17.11.1986: Sank in position 19.50
north by 115.52 east.

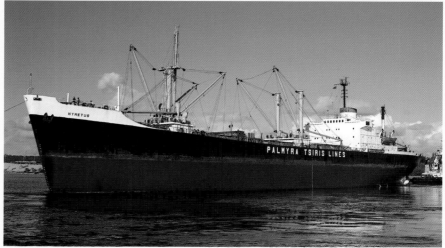

Top: The almost new *Carina* outward bound on
the River Thames, 18th June 1969. The owners
had opted for masthouses, the first time these
had appeared on an SD14. *[Roy Kittle]*
Upper middle: Sailing from Cape Town, she has
lost Mavroleon's white hull band. The basic
SD14 specification included a foremast to which
could be fitted a 25-ton derrick, and this
photograph confirms that *Carina* received such a
derrick during her career. *[Kevin Moore]*
Lower middle: *Io*, the shortest name carried by an
SD14. *[Rowley Weeks, David Salisbury collection]*
Bottom: *Hymetus* still looks smart at Durban in
1986. *[Trevor Jones, David Salisbury collection]*

Above: Lykiardopulo's *Ariadne* discharges grain in the East Float, Birkenhead on 6th January 1970. Before the opening of Seaforth Dock and its silo, much of Liverpool's grain came in 'tween deckers like her. *[Paul Boot]*

Below: *Pheasant* approaches Eastham with a hardwood cargo from Belem, on 7th March 1989, possibly the first SD14 in the Manchester Ship Canal. *[Paul Boot]*

860. ARIADNE

L.R./I.M.O. Number 6915843
9,038g
6,341n
15,291d
Clark-Sulzer 5RD68
20.1.1969: Keel laid.
16.4.1969: Launched for Libramar Compania Naviera S.A., Panama (Lykiardopulo and Co. Ltd., London).
28.5.1969: Completed. Greek flag.

1981: Sold to Buckingham Maritime S.A., Panama (Yama Maritime Inc, New York, USA) for $700,000 and renamed MICHELLE C.
1983: Transferred to Aniot Maritime Co. Inc., Panama (Yama Maritime Inc, New York).
1985: Sold to Pheasant Shipping Co. Ltd., Limassol, Cyprus (Vernicos Maritime Co. S.A., Piraeus, Greece) and renamed PHEASANT.
1989: Sold to Gisela Shipping Co.

Ltd., Limassol, Cyprus (Sea Justice S.A., Piraeus).
1993: Sold to Melinka Shipping Co. Ltd., Limassol, Cyprus (China Hainam Shuang Dao Shipping Corporation, Haikou, Hainan Island, People's Republic of China).
27.10.1993: Cypriot registry cancelled.
2004: Still listed in 'Lloyd's Register', but existence must be in doubt.

861. JANEY

L.R./I.M.O. Number 7000011
9,072g
6,245n
15,281d
Hawthorn-Sulzer 5RD68
17.3.1969: Keel laid.
29.5.1969: Launched for Seaspray Marine Corporation, Monrovia, Liberia (Mavroleon Brothers Ltd., London).
16.7.1969: Completed. Liberian flag.
1978: Renamed ARGOLIS under the Greek flag.
3.1980: Sold to Alkaios Compania Naviera S.A, Panama (Circe Shipping Enterprises Co. Ltd. (G.Z. Lanaras and Ion Paraschis), Piraeus, Greece) for $3.95m and renamed

ANAVISSOS under the Greek flag.
1983: Sold to Atlantic Crown Maritime Co. Ltd., Limassol, Cyprus (Vernicos Maritime Co. S.A., Piraeus, Greece) and renamed MARINER.
1986: Transferred to Zamora Navigation Co. Ltd., Limassol (Vernicos Maritime Co. S.A., Piraeus) and renamed PIGEON.
1990: Sold to Zante Navigation Co. Ltd., Limassol (Ancora Investment Trust Inc., Piraeus).
1990: Sold to Seapage Shipping Ltd., Nicosia, Cyprus (Sea Trade and Construction Ltd., Dhaka, Bangladesh) and renamed SUSAN SEA.
1991: Sold to Hyundai Sangsa Ltd., Cyprus (Hyundai International Inc., Seoul, South Korea) and renamed

VIVARI II.
1991: Sold to Crystal Shipping Co. Ltd., Limassol.
1992: Sold to Armas Shipping S.A., Singapore (Seamouth Shipping Ltd., Limassol) and renamed ARMAS.
1994: Sold to Marine Bulkship (Trans Overseas Co. Private Ltd., Singapore) and renamed CREST but believed not to have traded under this name.
31.1.1995: Arrived at Chittagong for demolition by J.L. Enterprises.

Top: *Janey. [V.H. Young and L.A. Sawyer collection]*

Bottom: *Anavissos*, another vessel retrofitted with a heavy derrick at number 2 hold. *[David Whiteside collection]*

862. RUPERT DE LARRINAGA

L.R./I.M.O. Number 6924002
9,268g
6,157n
15,241d
Hawthorn-Sulzer 5RD68
29.4.1969: Keel laid.
17.7.1969: Launched for Larrinaga Steamship Co. Ltd., Liverpool.
11.9.1969: Completed. British flag.
1974: Owners taken over by Vergocean Steamship Co. Ltd., London.
1975: Owners became Oceanverg Shipping Co. Ltd., London (Valiant Steamship Co. Ltd. (G. Vergottis), London) and renamed VERGRAY.
1977: Managers became Valiant Shipping Co. (London) Ltd.
1978: Transferred to Atheras Shipping Co. Ltd., Monrovia, Liberia

(Valiant Shipping Co. (London) Ltd. (G. Vergottis), London) and renamed ATHERAS under the Greek flag.
7.3.1982: Laid-up at Ithaki, surveys overdue.
1986: Sold to North View Shipping Corporation (Flandermar Shipping Co. S.A. (D. Agoudimos, G. Agoudimos and J. Meletis)), Piraeus, Greece and renamed AGIA EFYMIA.
1989: Managers became Bananeira Investment Trust Inc., Piraeus.
1991: Sold to Selini Shipping Co. Ltd., Valletta, Malta (Calais Shipping Inc., Piraeus) and renamed VIRGINIA.
11.12.1991: Stranded in the Black Sea at Kilyos, Turkey in heavy weather after engine trouble during a voyage from Piraeus to Kherson. Abandoned by her crew, she subsequently broke in two.

Top: The Larrinaga Steamship Co. Ltd. was the first British liner company to order SD14s, taking standard models rather than enhanced versions. Sadly, Larrinagas sold up after a few years, and photographs of their SD14s are rare. *Rupert de Larrinaga* is in almost pristine condition. Her boats have been raised to bridge deck level as her accommodation block was enlarged to accommodate a British crew. *[David Whiteside collection]*

Bottom: After her sale to Vergottis, she had several names, and is seen here at Durban as *Atheras*. *[V.H. Young and L.A. Sawyer collection]*

SD15 cargo vessel

866. ARMADALE

L.R./I.M.O Number 7022447
10,328/7,182g
6,184/4,086n
15,291/12,802d
Doxford 76J4
1969: Ordered by Australind Steam
Shipping Co. Ltd. (Trinder,
Anderson and Co. Ltd., managers),
London.
6.3.1970: Keel laid.
22.6.1970: Launched.
10.1970: Completed. British flag.
1.6.1979: Collided with and sank the
Cyprus-registered factory ship FRIO
KYKNOS (1,674/1968) which was at
anchor off Lagos.
1981: Sold to Odissea Shipping Co.,
Panama (Oceanmaid Shipping Co.
S.A., Piraeus, Greece) (J.P. Samartzis
Maritime Enterprises Co. S.A.,
Piraeus, managers) and renamed
DIDO under the Greek flag.
1985: Sold to Supertrans Navigation
Co. Ltd., Limassol, Cyprus (Mayfair
(Hellas) Co. Ltd. (Vas. Maltezos),
Piraeus, Greece) and renamed TETI.
31.3.1989: Abandoned by crew after
fire and explosion in position 33.49
north by 122.41 east whilst on a
voyage from China to Europe with a
cargo of groundnuts and minerals.
6.4.1989: Arrived Shanghai after
being taken in tow by the Chinese
tug which extinguished the fire.
1990: Broken up in China, having
been sold for $190 per lightweight
ton.

Top: *Armadale* sets up a tremendous bow wave,
exposing her mid-body. *[John Lingwood collection]*

Middle: *Armadale* sails up the New Waterway on
11th May 1973 whilst on charter to Arya

National Lines of Iran. *[Paul Boot]*

Bottom: Again in superb condition at
Singapore, March 1981. *[Roy Kittle, David
Salisbury collection]*

867. MIGUEL DE LARRINAGA

L.R./I.M.O. Number 7028398
9,247g
6,184n
15,180d
Hawthorn-Sulzer 5RND68
8.5.1970: Keel laid.
2.9.1970: Launched for Larrinaga Steamship Co. Ltd., Liverpool.
26.11.1970: Completed. British flag.
1974: Owners taken over by Vergocean Steam Ship Co. Ltd., London.
1975: Owners became Oceanverg Shipping Co. Ltd., London (Valiant Steamship Co. Ltd. (G. Vergottis), London) and renamed VERGSTAR.
1977: Managers became Valiant Shipping Co. (London) Ltd.
1978: Transferred to Maryland Corporation, Monrovia, Liberia (Valiant Shipping Co. (London) Ltd.

(G. Vergottis), London and renamed VARDIANI under the Greek flag.
7.12.1982: Laid-up at Argostoli.
1986: Transferred to Panmar Maritime S.A, Panama (Valiant Shipping Co. (London) Ltd. (G. Vergottis), London) and renamed ATROTOS under the Greek flag.
1.1987: Transferred to lay-up at Eleusis.
1987: Sold to Sea Mountain Maritime S.A., Monrovia, Liberia (Flandermar Shipping Co. S.A. (D. Agoudimos, G. Agoudimos and J. Meletis)), Piraeus, Greece and renamed NISSOS KEFFALONIA.
1987: Transferred to Emerald Seas Shipping Ltd., Valletta, Malta (Flandermar Shipping Co. S.A. (D. Agoudimos, G. Agoudimos and J. Meletis), Piraeus, Greece, managers).
1989: Managers became Bananeira Investment Trust Inc., Piraeus.

1989: Sold to SUS (Singapore) Private Ltd. (Sea-Pac Management (Private) Ltd.), Singapore and renamed HAE GUM GANG under the Maltese flag.
1993: Sold to Korea Undok Shipping Co. Ltd. (Government of the People's Republic of Korea), Pyongchang, North Korea.
1996: Sold to Citi Shipping Corporation (Citiglobal Shipping Co. Ltd.) and renamed CITI VENTURE under the St. Vincent and the Grenadines flag.
12.9.1996: Arrived Alang for demolition by Crosslink Shipbreakers (Private) Ltd.
1.10.1996: Work commenced.

Middle: *Miguel de Larrinaga* in charter markings. *[John Clarkson collection]*

Bottom: A weary looking *Nissos Keffalonia* leaves Liverpool by the Langton entrance on 23rd March 1989. *[Paul Boot]*

868. SAN GEORGE

L.R./I.M.O. Number 7033733
9,084g
6,403n
15,195d
Clark-Sulzer 5RND68
7.7.1970: Keel laid.
29.10.1970: Launched for Arka
Compania Naviera S.A., Panama
(Elpisaga Compania Naviera,
Piraeus, Greece) (M.J. Lemos Co.
Ltd., London).
22.1.1971: Completed. Greek flag.
1976: London management transferred
to M.J. Lemos and S.L. Houlis Ltd.

8.1983: Management transferred to
Ormos Compania Naviera S.A. (C.
Psaltis), Piraeus.
1988: Transferred to Algepsa
Shipping Co. Ltd., Limassol, Cyprus
(Ormos Compania Naviera S.A.,
Piraeus).
31.12.1991: Fire broke out in
numbers 2 and 3 holds whilst
anchored off Ko Sichang, Gulf of
Thailand during a voyage from
Cartagena, Spain to Bangkok with
cargo of fertiliser and copper
concentrates. Remaining cargo was
transhipped and vessel subsequently

Top: *Hae Gum Gang* ex *Miguel de Larrinaga* at
Singapore on 26th November 1989. *[Simon Olsen,
David Salisbury collection]*

declared a constructive total loss.
29.6.1992: Arrived Ryong, Thailand
in tow.
297.1992: Breaking up began by
Thai Hua Lee Co. Ltd.

Bottom: *San George* was the first Southwick-built
SD14 to have fully-plated bulwarks. Photographed
on the New Waterway, August 1974. *[David
Salisbury]*

869. NEFOS II

L.R./I.M.O. Number 7103019
9,083g
6,440n
15,195d
Hawthorn-Sulzer 5RND68
17.12.1970: Keel laid.
30.3.1971: Launched for Compania Naviera Zurubi S.A., Panama (Panchripol Ltd. (G.P. and G.A. Pateras), London).

17.5.1971: Completed. Greek flag.
11.1980: Sold to Ora Shipping Co. Ltd., Monrovia, Liberia (Krina Compania Naviera S.A., Piraeus, Greece) for $5.70m and renamed GIANNIS M under the Greek flag.
12.8.1985: Reported aground.
18.8.1985: Arrived Manila for repair.
1985: Managers became Mistral Shipping Agency (Nicholas J. Melis),

Piraeus and renamed SIMOON.
1987: Sold to Scarlet Shipping Co. Ltd., Limassol, Cyprus (Thesarco Shipping Co. S.A., Piraeus) and renamed TRINITY SIERRA.
1997: Sold to Nimbero Shipping Co. Ltd., Cyprus and renamed NIMBERO for delivery to breakers.
8.5.1997: Delivered to shipbreakers at Alang.

After completion, *Nefos II* had a head span beam fitted to her twin king posts, converting them into a goalpost structure to take a heavy derrick. The change is apparent from the top and middle photographs. *[V.H. Young and L.A. Sawyer collection; David Whiteside collection]*

Left *Nefos II* seen at Durban, still looking smart as *Trinity Sierra* [Trevor Jones, David Salisbury collection]

Top: *Belle Isle* at her home port, Port Louis, Mauritius on 7th April 1978. *[Michael Green]*

Right: *Belle Isle* was the first SD14 from Southwick with a high specification for cargo-liner work, including two extra sets of kingposts and winch houses. Seen first on the New Waterway in 1982, then at Cape Town on 1st June 1977. *[Wim van Noort, David Salisbury collection; Ian Shiffman, Roy Kittle collection]*

Bottom: *Belle Isle* as *Allma* at Terneuzen, inward bound for Antwerp at Terneuzen, May 1987. *[David Salisbury]*

870. **BELLE ISLE**

L.R./I.M.O. Number 7046209
9,327g
6,408n
15,139d
Clark-Sulzer 5RND68
6.11.1970: Keel laid.
20.1.1971: Launched for Mauritius Steam Navigation Co. Ltd. (Rogers and Co. Ltd., Port Louis, Mauritius).
31.3.1971: Completed. British flag.
1984: Sold to Sealord Investments Inc., Monrovia, Liberia (A.P. Madrigal Steamship Co. Inc., Manila, Philippines) and renamed SAINTE MARTHE under the Philippine flag.
1986: Sold to Prometheus Inc., Panama (Denholm Ship Management (Overseas) Ltd.) and renamed SARAH H.
1987: Sold to Grafford Shipping Ltd., Monrovia, Liberia (Citizen Shipping Ltd., Hong Kong) and renamed ALLMA under the Panama flag.
1988: Sold to Hakama Shipping Ltd., Monrovia, Liberia (Parakou Shipping Ltd., Hong Kong) and renamed BEIYUAN under the Panama flag.
1988: Sold to Qinhuangdao Shipping Co., Qinhuangdao, People's Republic of China and renamed YUAN GUANG.
1992: Sold to Vast Ocean Shipping S.A., Panama (Vastmetier Shipping

Co. Ltd., Hong Kong) and renamed VAST OCEAN.
9.2.1993: Left Vanino, Russia for Shanghai with a cargo of steel bars.
15.2.1993: After reporting from south west of Japan in position 34.00 north by 129.22 east nothing further was heard from the vessel. Searching failed to locate her, and it is presumed she sank shortly afterwards.

871. DUNELMIA (1)

L.R./I.M.O. Number 7038599
9,177g
6,071n
14,149d
Clark-Sulzer 5RND68
9.9.1970: Keel laid.
30.11.1970: Launched for Metcalfe Shipping Co. Ltd. (Metcalfe, Son and Co.), Hartlepool.
12.3.1971: Completed. British flag.
1976: Sold to West Hartlepool Steam Navigation Co. Ltd., Hartlepool and renamed ARDENHALL.
1981: Sold to Cross Point Steamship Corporation, Monrovia, Liberia (S.L. Sethia Liners Ltd., London) and renamed MOOLCHAND under the Panama flag.
1987: Managers became Nerofleet Ltd.
1989: Sold to Marsay Shipping Corporation, Monrovia, Liberia (Nerofleet Ltd., London) and

renamed MASCHO STAR under the Panama flag.
1992: Sold to Hasreen Maritime Ltd., Limassol, Cyprus (Delta One International, Dubai (Alva Corporation, London, managers) and renamed DELTA under the St. Vincent flag.
1992: Renamed DELTA II.
7.6.1993: Anchored off Bombay with

water entering engine room after encountering heavy weather on a voyage from Juball, Saudi Arabia to Madras with a cargo of sulphur. Sold to local shipbreakers and beached at Bombay.
22.9.1993: Demolition commenced.
31.3.1994: Demolition completed.

Top: *Dunelmia* was the first SD14 with a second mast in place of king posts. The masts served a 30-tonne heavy derrick at number 2 hatch and at number 4 a 60-tonne derrick, the heaviest fitted so far to an SD14 . She reverted to rails, rather than bulwarks, alongside her hatches.
[John Clarkson collection]

Middle: Built for charter to liner companies, *Dunelmia* is seen in Safmarine colours on the New Waterway, 30th March 1975. *[Paul Boot]*

Bottom: *Ardenhall* at Durban in 1978. *[Trevor Jones, David Salisbury collection]*

872. DORTHE OLDENDORFF

L.R./I.M.O. Number 7109037
9,079g
6,225n
15,017d
Hawthorn-Sulzer 5RND68
1969: Ordered by Half Moon
Shipping Corporation, Monrovia
(German principals).
1969: Contract purchased by Egon
Oldendorff, Lübeck, West Germany.
22.2.1971: Keel laid.
21.5.1971: Launched for Egon
Oldendorff, Lübeck.
22.7.1971: Completed. West
German flag.

3.8.1972: Transferred to Dorthe
Oldendorff K.G. (Egon Oldendorff,
manager), Lübeck.
4.9.1972: Transferred to Wursata
Shipping Corporation, Monrovia,
Liberia (Egon Oldendorff, Lübeck,
manager) under the Singapore flag.
1988: Sold to Sinzhong Lines Private
Ltd. (Unison Shipping (Private)
Ltd.), Singapore and renamed
SINFA.
30.5.1997: Reported attacked by
pirates and put back to Singapore.
30.11.2000: Arrived Surabaya.
2.2001: Reported sold to Chinese
breakers for $149 per lightweight ton.
13.12.2002: Sailed from Surabaya
for China.

Above: Lübeck shipowners Egon Oldendorff
proved excellent customers for SD14s, displaying
more faith in the Sunderland shipbuilders than
British politicians. Outward bound on the New
Waterway is *Dorthe Oldendorff.* Note the 30-
tonne and 60-tonne derricks, just two of the
additional features of Oldendorff ships. *[David
Salisbury]*

Below: *Sinfa* in Singapore Roads on 27th June
1998. The victim of piracy the previous year, she
may well be laid up awaiting sale to breakers.
The 'LH' funnel is that of Lin Huat Shipping Co.
(Private) Ltd., Singapore, a company which shares
an address and a managing director with Unison
Shipping, her registered managers. *[Nigel Jones]*

873. COSMONAUT

L.R./I.M.O. Number 7114721
9,234g
6,117n
15,103d
Clark-Sulzer 5RND68
4.5.1971: Keel laid.
8.7.1971: Launched for K.G. m.s. 'Cosmonaut' Felix Scheder-Beischen & Co. (O.H.G. Infrutra G.m.b.H. & Co.), Hamburg, West Germany.
27.9.1971: Completed. West German flag.
1972: Managers became K.G. Vineta Seereederei G.m.b.H. & Co. (O.H.G. Infrutra G.m.b.H. & Co.), Hamburg and put under Singapore flag.
1978: Managers became O.H.G. Vineta Seereederei G.m.b.H. & Co. (O.H.G. Infrutra G.m.b.H. & Co.), Hamburg.
3.1980: Sold to Seaward Marine Inc, Panama (Wallem Shipmanagement Ltd., Hong Kong) for $4.8m and renamed LADY ISABEL.
1985: Sold to Ultraocean S.A. (S.A. de Navegacion Cormoran), Buenos Aires, Argentina and renamed ISABEL MARIA.
1991: Sold to Dea Shipping Ltd., Malta (S.A. de Navegacion Cormoran, Buenos Aires, Argentina) and renamed DEA.
1992: Sold to Cromwell Shipping Ltd. (Brown Marine Services), Sunderland under the Maltese flag.
1994: Sold to Euston Shipping Co. Ltd., Valletta, Malta (Sougerka Maritime Co. Ltd. (G.D. Ventouris and I.S. Kouvelos), Piraeus, Greece) and renamed IDEA.

1995: Sold to Eastern Spirit S.A., Panama and renamed DORA.
1995: Sold to Lincoln Maritime Corporation, Monrovia, Liberia (Sany Shipping, Singapore) and renamed AMORE under the Panama flag.
25.5.1996: Demolition began at Chittagong by Mars Ship Breakers Ltd.

Above: The three German 'Cosmo-' SD14s were chartered to Naviera Alianca, a Brazilian company with strong German and Portuguese connections, as evidenced by the German national colours on the company's funnel. These are seen particularly well on the *Cosmonaut*, photographed from Penarth Head, South Wales in 1979. *[Bob Allen]*

Above: *Cosmokrat*, immediately after her launch from Southwick on 21st September 1971. The white marks painted on her hull at intervals were used to time the duration of the launch. A draughtsman was positioned at the end of the berth and clicked his stop watch as each mark passed him. *[Turners (Photography) Ltd., John Lingwood collection]*

Opposite top: *Cosmokrat* at Cardiff on a January evening in 1979. *[Nigel Jones]*

Opposite middle: Remaining under German control, but Liberian flagged, *Cosmokrat* is seen as *Durban Carrier* appropriately at Durban about 1981. The letters on her funnel are the initials of her owners, Maritime Carriers Schiffahrts. *[Trevor Jones, David Salisbury collection]*

Opposite bottom: *Avanti.* *[Malcolm Cranfield]*

874. COSMOKRAT

L.R./I.M.O. Number 7118973
9,248g
6,153n
15,103d
Clark-Sulzer 5RND68
15.6.1971: Keel laid.
21.9.1971: Launched for m.s. 'Cosmokrat' Felix Scheder-Bieschin & Co. K.G. (O.H.G. Infrutra G.m.b.H. & Co.), Hamburg, West Germany.
15.11.1971: Completed. West German flag.
1972: Management transferred to K.G. Vineta Seereederei G.m.b.H. & Co. (O.H.G. Infrutra G.m.b.H. & Co.), Hamburg and put under the Singapore flag.
1978: Managers became O.H.G. Vineta Seereederei G.m.b.H. & Co. (O.H.G. Infrutra G.m.b.H. & Co.), Hamburg.
12.1979: Transferred to Wave Shipping Inc., Monrovia, Liberia (Maritime Carrier Schiffahrts G.m.b.H. (O.H.G Infrutra G.m.b.H. & Co.), Hamburg) for $4.8m and renamed DURBAN CARRIER.

6.1981: Sold to Palsen Shipping Enterprises Corporation S.A., Panama (Syros Shipping Co. (L.M. Valmas and Son) Ltd., London) and renamed IRINI II under the Greek flag.
1983: Managers deleted.
1985: Sold to Northeast S.A., Panama (Capitol World Holdings S.A. (Nikolaos Frangos and Nicholas G. Moundreas), Piraeus, Greece) for $1.3m. and renamed AVANTI.
23.7.1998: Laid up at Piraeus.
20.2.1999: Arrived at Alang for demolition.

875. COSMOPOLIT

L.R./I.M.O. Number 7122467
9,241g
6,123n
15,158d
Clark-Sulzer 5RND68
25.8.1971: Keel laid.
2.11.1971: Launched for m.s.
'Cosmopolit' Felix Scheder-Bieschin & Co. K.G. (O.H.G. Infrutra G.m.b.H. & Co.), Hamburg, West Germany.
16.2.1972: Completed. West German flag.
1972: Managers became K.G. Vineta Seereederei G.m.b.H. & Co., Hamburg and transferred to Singapore flag.
1974: Sold to St. Clement Navigation Co. Ltd. (Hanseatic Shipmanagement Ltd. (H. Schoeller and P. Tsanos), managers), Limassol, Cyprus (Bernard Schulte, Hamburg).
1975: Managers became Hanseatic Shipping Co. Ltd. (H. Schoeller and Chr. Demetriades), Limassol.
1976: Renamed HEINRICH ARNOLD SCHULTE.
1977: Renamed PARANA STAR.
1978: Renamed HEINRICH ARNOLD SCHULTE.
1983: Sold to St. Francis Maritime Co. Ltd. (Hanseatic Shipping Co. Ltd., managers), Limassol, Cyprus (Bernard Schulte, Hamburg).
1988: Sold to Eastcross Transport Inc., Panama (Gleneagle Ship Management Co. Inc., Houston USA, managers) (Denholm Shipmanagement (Holdings) Ltd., Glasgow) for $1.85m and renamed LAKE HURON.
1989: Owners became Eastcross Navigation S.A., Panama (Gleneagle Ship Management Co. Inc., Houston USA, managers) (Denholm Shipmanagement (Holdings) Ltd., Glasgow).

1990: Sold to Decamar Shipping Corporation, Panama (Marlborough Shipping Co. Ltd. (G.P., J. and P.G. Margaronis), London) and renamed AGIOS MARKOS.
1991: Renamed KOS.
1992: Sold to Silver Dignity Shipping Co. Ltd., Nicosia, Cyprus (Silver Carriers S.A., Piraeus, Greece) (Bonyad Marine Services Inc., Athens, Greece, managers) and renamed KONARAK.
1993: Transferred to Abode Maritime Ltd., Cyprus (Silver Carriers S.A., Piraeus) (Bonyad Marine Services Inc., Athens, managers).

Top: *Cosmopolit. [Ships in Focus collection]*
Middle: At Durban in 1985 as *Heinrich Arnold Schulte* in the colours of Hanseatic Shipping. *[Trevor Jones, Davis Salisbury collection]*
Bottom: *Lake Huron* at Vancouver, 10th June 1988. *[Marc Piché, David Salisbury collection]*

1993: Sold to Yue Yang Shipping Co. Ltd., Kingstown, St. Vincent (People's Republic of China) and renamed YUE YANG.
2004: Still listed by 'Lloyd's Register' but continued existence must be in doubt, as no movements reported since July 1995, and registration cancelled in June 1996.

876. RAMON DE LARRINAGA

L.R./I.M.O. Number 7128734
9,181g
6,145n
15,180d
Hawthorn-Sulzer 5RND68
4.10.1971: Keel laid.
22.11.1971: Launched for Larrinaga Steamship Co. Ltd., Liverpool.
24.4.1972: Completed. British flag.
1972: Sold to Jade Bay Shipping Co. Ltd., Monrovia, Liberia (Valiant Steamship Co. Ltd. (G. Vergottis), London) and renamed JADE BAY under the Greek flag.

1977: Managers restyled Valiant Shipping Co. (London) Ltd.
1994: Sold to Great Eastern Shipping Co. (London) Ltd., London (Great Eastern Shipping Co. Ltd., Bombay, India) and renamed SANGITA under the Bahamas flag.
4.8.1994: Grounded when entering Cochin, India from Poland.
6.8.1994: Refloated and berthed. It was subsequently discovered that rudder stock and steering gear had been damaged.
26.9.1994: Sold to Haryana Steel Company, Delhi for breaking up.
31.10.1994: Arrived Alang.
18.11.1994: Demolition commenced.

Above: *Ramon de Larrinaga* is seen during her few months of service for Larrinaga. Note the elegant yellow line on her hull. Concessions to the liner trade included a Velle swinging derrick at number 2 hold, probably for handling containers. Operated like a crane by a single joystick, the modified cross tree on her fore mast was needed to suit the rigging for the hoisting, slewing and luffing motions. Conventional derricks have been fitted at the same mast to serve number 1 hold.
[V.H. Young and L.A. Sawyer collection]

Below: Later in 1972 she was sold to the long-established London-Greek Vergottis family. As *Jade Bay* under the Greek flag at Durban about 1990 she looks rather down at heel. The modified foremast is clearly seen is this view.
[Trevor Jones, David Salisbury collection]

877. IMME OLDENDORFF

L.R./I.M.O. Number 7207425
9,077g
6,347n
15,017d
Clark-Sulzer 5RND68
1969: Ordered by Babitonga Shipping Corporation, Monrovia, Liberia (German principals).
1970: Contract purchased by Egon Oldendorff, Lübeck, West Germany.
24.11.1971: Keel laid.
15.3.1972: Launched for Egon Oldendorff, Lübeck.
4.5.1972: Completed for a Kommanditgesellschaft (Egon Oldendorff, Lübeck, manager).
13.10.1972: Transferred to a Partenreederei (Egon Oldendorff, Lübeck, manager).
1973: Transferred to Holsatia Shipping Corporation, Monrovia (Egon Oldendorff, Lübeck, manager) under Singapore flag.
1987: Sold to Skyriver Maritime Ltd. (John McRink and Co. Ltd.), Hong Kong and renamed LADY ARYETTE.
1992: Sold to Paloma Enterprise S.A., Panama (Everett Steamship Corporation, Tokyo, Japan) (Everett-Orient Line Inc., Monrovia, managers) and renamed IVYEVERETT.
1994: Sold to D.M.S. Navigation S.A. (D.M.S. Marine Service Private Ltd., managers), Singapore and renamed TECHMAT PIONEER under the Panama flag.
1997: Sold to Naseer Rachid Lootah Group, United Arab Emirates (O.S.A Agencies (Singapore) Private Ltd., Singapore, managers) and renamed BIN LOOTAH under the Equatorial

Top: *Imme Oldendorff* on the New Waterway, June 1974. *[David Salisbury]*
Middle: *Imme Oldendorff* again, off Greenock in 1972. Note the offset signal mast characteristic of the Oldendorff SD14s. *[Malcolm Donnelly]*

Below: *Lady Aryette* at Durban about 1990. *[Trevor Jones, David Salisbury collection]*

Guinea flag.
1998: For the latter part of this year vessel was at Singapore under arrest.
2.1999: Reported sold by Sheriff to Bangladesh breakers.

10.6.1998: Arrived Chittagong Roads in tow of Canadian tug OCEAN GOLF (152/1959).
about 19.7.1999: Arrived Chittagong for demolition.

878. COSMOSTAR

L.R./I.M.O. Number 7213250
9,281g
6,171n
15,139d
Clark-Sulzer 5RND68
20.1.1972: Keel laid.
27.4.1972: Launched for m.s.
'Cosmostar' Felix Scheder-Bieschin
& Co. K.G., Hamburg (O.H.G.
Infrutra G.m.b.H. & Co. Hamburg,
West Germany).
14.6.1972: Completed.
1972: Manager became K.G. Vineta
Seereederei G.m.b.H & Co.,
Hamburg, under the Liberian flag.
1974: Sold to Blue Star Shipping
Co. Ltd., Vaduz, Liechtenstein
(Interislands Shipping Co. Ltd.,
Hong Kong) (Government of Cuba,
Havana, Cuba) and renamed STAR
under the Somali flag.
1975: Transferred to Toyo Islands
Shipping Co. Ltd., Vaduz, Liechten-
stein (Interislands Shipping Co. Ltd.,
Hong Kong) (Government of Cuba,
Havana, Cuba).
1976: Transferred to Campe S.A.,
Panama (Nippon Caribbean Ship-
ping Co., Tokyo, Japan, managers)
and renamed STAR I.
1982: Owners became Canipel S.A.,
Panama (Nippon Caribbean Ship-
ping Co., Tokyo, managers).
1988: Transferred to Empresa
Navegacion Mambisa, Havana,
Cuba and renamed STAR.
1991: Transferred to Good Hope
Shipping Co. Ltd., Valletta, Malta
(Nordstrand Maritimas) (Empresa
Navegacion Caribe, Havana, opera-
tors) and renamed CEDAR HILL.
1992: Sold to Cormorant Ltd., Malta
(Seabirds Management Inc, Piraeus,
Greece) and renamed
CORMORANT.
2.6.2000: Demolition began at
Alang by Triveni Shipping
Corporation.

Top: *Cosmostar* under the Liberian flag and in Alianca colours at Maassluis on the New Waterway on 19th June 1972. *[Roy Kittle]*

Middle: The Cuban Government were keen buyers of SD14s, taking new and secondhand examples, and putting them under a variety of nominal owning companies and flags. Seen at Vancouver about 1978, *Star 1* would have been under the Panama flag and managed by a joint Cuban-Japanese enterprise. Notwithstanding these polyglot connections, she is in excellent external condition. *[Don Brown, David Salisbury collection]*

Bottom: Nearing the end of her life, *Cormorant* at Durban about 1999. She was one of several elderly SD14s run by Seabirds Management: note the appropriate funnel marking. *[Trevor Jones, David Salisbury collection]*

879. NATAL

L.R./I.M.O. Number 7218644
8,849g
5,994n
15,139d
Clarl-Sulzer 5RND68
Name originally proposed
ARCADIAN PRIDE
17.3.1972: Keel laid.
14.6.1972: Launched for Hidalgo
Atlantico Navegacion S.A., Panama
(Colocotronis Ltd., London).
21.7.1972: Completed. Greek flag.
1974: Management transferred to
Colocotronis (Greece) S.A. (E.M.
Colocotronis), Piraeus, Greece.
1976: Sold with owning company to
Bouboulina Shipping S.A. (Jenny
Pournaras), Piraeus.

1977: Renamed JOCASTA.
1978: Sold to Ocean Bridge Bulk
Carriers S.A., Panama (Transocean
Liners (Pty.) Ltd. (John T. Essberger),
Hamburg, Germany) and renamed
TIBATI under the Singapore flag.
1981: Manager became Transocean
Lines Reederei G.m.b.H. (John T.
Essberger), Hamburg.
1984: Renamed TOPEGA under the
Panama flag.
1985: Sold to Raynville Shipping
Corporation S.A., Panama
(Bamaodah Ahmed Abdul Qawi,
Jeddah, Saudi Arabia) (Holbud Ltd.
Ship Management Division, London,
managers) and renamed
ALIADRIKNI.
7.10.1989: Sustained hull damage
and taken in tow in position 08.04

Top: *Natal* in Deutsche Afrika Linie colours passes
Maassluis on the New Waterway, 21st May
1976. Superstructure arrangements involving wide
or narrow second tiers were now commonplace,
the choice depending on the the number and
nationality of the crew. The Greek-flagged *Natal*
has the narrow arrangement. [Paul Boot]

Bottom: *Aliadrikni* at Singapore, 12th June 1981.
[Simon Olsen, David Salisbury collection]

south by 120.12 east during a voyage
from Point Lisas to Surabaya.
1995: Sold to Blue Horizon Shipping
Co. Ltd., Valletta, Malta (Harmony
Shipping L.L.C, Dubai) and renamed
HARMONY BREEZE.
21.5.1997: Arrived Alang for
demolition by Kalthia and Co. R.L.
23.5.1997: Demolition began.

880. HILLE OLDENDORFF

L.R./I.M.O. Number 7224849
9,077g
6,347n
15,017d
Hawthorn-Sulzer 5RND68
1969: Ordered by Copacabana Shipping Corporation, Monrovia, Liberia (German principals).
1970: Contract purchased by Egon Oldendorff, Lübeck, West Germany.
4.5.1972: Keel laid.
11.8.1972: Launched for E.L. Oldendorff & Co. G.m.b.H., Lübeck.
29.9.1972: Completed. West German flag.
5.7.1973: Transferred to Partenreederei m.s. 'Hille Oldendorff' (Egon Oldendorff, manager), Lübeck.
15.8.1973: Transferred to Singapore flag.
1979: Transferred to Westfalia Shipping Corporation, Monrovia (Egon Oldendorff, Lübeck, manager) under Singapore flag.
1987: Sold to Linksail Maritime Ltd. (John McRink and Co. Ltd.), Hong Kong and renamed LADY TRUDE.
1988: Sold to Chepo Ltd., Hong Kong (Gleneagle Ship Management Co. Inc., Houston, USA) (Denholm Ship Management (Holdings) Ltd., Glasgow, managers) and renamed LAKE TAHOE.
24.11.1990: Arrested at St. Anna Bay, Curacao.
1991: Sold to Laserway Shipping Ltd., Limassol, Cyprus (Ilios Shipping Co. S.A. (C.P. Eliopoulos), Piraeus, Greece) and renamed PANTOCRATOR CORFU.
1993: Transferred to Navalplanet

Top: *Hille Oldenforff. [David Whiteside collection].*
Middle: *Lake Tahoe* in the Welland Canal, 1st October 1988. *[D. Kohl, David Salisbury collection]*
Bottom: *Genesis Pioneer. [Russell Priest]*

Shipping Ltd., Limassol, Cyprus (Ilios Shipping Co. S.A. (C.P. Eliopoulos), Piraeus, Greece) and renamed FEAX.
1996: Sold to Open Skies Shipping Co. Ltd., Valletta, Malta and renamed SYBILLE.
1996: Sold to Genesis Worldwide Shipping and Trading Co. Ltd., Panama and renamed GENESIS PIONEER.
1997: Owners now at Apapa/Lagos, Nigeria and transferred to Nigerian flag.
13.11.1998: Under arrest at Mumbai.
6.2.1999: Arrived at shipbreaker's yard at Mumbai.

881. SACHA

L.R./I.M.O. Number 7232391
9,072g
6,245n
15,017d
Hawthorn-Sulzer 5RND68
16.8.1972: Keel laid.
7.11.1972: Launched for Northern Star Navigation Corporation, Monrovia, Liberia (Mavroleon Brothers Ltd., London).
5.1.1973: Completed. Liberian flag.
1979: Renamed ERMIONI under the Greek flag.
6.1982: Sold to Antares Shipping Co., Panama (Yama Maritime Inc., New York, USA) for $4.15m and renamed LORI R.
1984: Sold to Fonderane Overseas Inc., Panama (Seama International Shipping Ltd., London) and renamed SAFIR.
12.9.1989: Grounded on a reef near Tiran Island in position 27.59 north by 34.26 east whilst on a voyage from Aqaba to Bombay with a cargo of rock phosphate.
19.9.1989: Refloated but subsequently sank in position 27.47 north by 34.24 east.

Top: Another Mavroleon ship, *Sacha* is in pristine condition. Most of her hatch covers are raised and stowed. *[David Whiteside collection]*

Bottom: Under her last name, *Safir*, she looks distinctly less cared for. Note the addition of a pole mast forward. *[David Whiteside collection]*

882. TANGANYIKA

L.R./I.M.O. Number 7228259
8,927g
6,195n
15,139d
Clark-Sulzer 5RND68
Name originally proposed
ARCADIAN WARRIOR
22.6.1972: Keel laid.
4.10.1972: Launched for Mares
Nortenos Armadora S.A., Panama
(Colocotronis Ltd., London).
17.11.1972: Completed. Greek flag.
1974: Management transferred to
Joseph Colocotronis S.A. (J.
Colocotronis), Piraeus.
1976: Sold together with owning
company to Bouboulina Shipping
S.A. (Jenny Pournaras), Piraeus.

1977: Renamed JUVENTUS.
1978: Sold to Nigerian Green Lines
Ltd., Lagos, Nigeria (Edward
Nannini and Co. Ltd., London) and
renamed NIGER BASIN.
8.1981: Sold to Goodwood Shipping
Co., Monrovia, Liberia (Overseas
Shipping Co., Monrovia) (Navarino
Shipping and Transport Co. Ltd.,
Piraeus) for $4.75m and renamed
INTEGRITY II.
1983: Sold to Ranger International
Shipping Inc., Monrovia, Liberia
(Y.C. Cheng, Hamilton, Bermuda)
and renamed CONCORDIA I under
the Panama flag.
1985: Managers became Astro
Marine Inc. (Calvin Cheng),
Eaglewood Cliffs, New Jersey, USA.

1986: Sold to Oceanflash Shipping
Ltd., Limassol, Cyprus and renamed
DAMAAS.
1987: Sold to Geliper Shipping Co.
Ltd., Limassol, Cyprus (Perosea
Shipping Co. S.A., Piraeus) for
$850,000 and renamed LIA P.
24.11.1994: Arrived Colombo Outer
Anchorage and detained following
dispute over cargo damage.
3.2.1997: Sold at auction for breaking up for $157 per lightweight ton.
9.5.1997: Left under tow of the
Belize-registered tug SILK ROUTE
SUPPLIER (316/1975) for Alang.
28.5.1997: Arrived for breaking up
by Rajendra Ship Breakers (Private)
Ltd.
9.6.1997: Demolition commenced.

Top: *Tanganyika* at Durban about 1976. Since completion she had worn the funnel colours of Arcadia Reederei G.m.b.H. & Co. [*Trevor Jones, David Salisbury collection*]

Right: With a maximum upper deck loading of only 0.15 tons per square foot for early SD14s, *Niger Basin* is probably carrying empty containers. [*David Whiteside collection*]

883. **TOGO**

L.R./I.M.O. Number 7300796
8,927g
6,195n
15,139d
Clark-Sulzer 5RND68
Name originally proposed
ARCADIAN VALOUR
5.10.1972: Keel laid.
20.12.1972: Launched for Tropica
Ultramar S.A., Panama (Colocotronis
Ltd., London).
14.2.1973: Completed. Greek flag.
1974: Managers became Joseph
Colocotronis S.A. (J. Colocotronis),
Piraeus, Greece.
1976: Sold to Clarendon Shipping
Corporation, Monrovia, Liberia

(Devonia Shipping Agency Ltd.,
London) (Rocador Shipping Ltd.,
Hong Kong) and renamed CAPE
PRIDE under the Greek flag.
1980: Sold to Epimenidis Shipping
Co. S.A., Panama (N.J. Andriopoulos
Shipping & Commercial Enterprises
S.A., Piraeus) and renamed
EPIMENIDIS under the Greek flag.
1984: Sold at auction for $1m to
Express Ocean Transports Corpora-
tion, Monrovia, Liberia (Paramount
Ship Management Ltd., Nassau,
Bahamas) (Theodoros Giavridis
Brothers S.A., Piraeus) and renamed
EXPEDIENT under the Panama flag.
1996: Sold to Join Cheung Shipping
S.A., Hong Kong and renamed JOIN

Top: *Togo* in Deutsche Afrika Linie colours on the
New Waterway, 31st July 1973. *[Roy Kittle]*

Bottom: *Expedient* at Durban about 1989. *[Trevor
Jones, David Salisbury collection]*

CHEUNG under the Panama flag.
1998: Owners became Qingdao
Ocean Shipping Co. (COSCO
Qingdao), Qingdao, People's
Republic of China.
1.1999: Sold to Triveni Shipping
Corporation for $110 per lightweight ton.
6.1.1999: Arrived Alang and
demolition commenced same day.

884. SANTA CLIO

L.R./I.M.O. Number 7305423
8,849g
5,994n
15,139d
Clark-Sulzer 5RND68
Names originally proposed
ARCADIAN CHIVALRY and
SANTA SOPHIA
9.11.1972: Keel laid.
15.2.1973: Launched for Imperia
Delmar S.A., Panama (Colocotronis
Ltd., London).
30.3.1973: Completed. Greek flag.
1974: Management transferred to
Colocotronis (Greece) S.A., (E.M.
Colocotronis), Piraeus, Greece.
1976: Sold to Holstenbek Shipping
Corporation Inc., Monrovia, Liberia

(Reederei Claus-Peter Offen, Hamburg, West Germany) and renamed
HOLSTENBEK.
1979: Sold to Skipper Maritime
Corporation, Monrovia, Liberia (M.J.
Lemos and S.L. Houlis Ltd., London)
for $4.3million and renamed TIGER
BAY under Greek flag.
1982: Sold to Toro Shipping Corporation, Monrovia, Liberia (M.J.
Lemos and S.L. Houlis Ltd., London)
and renamed TOROS BAY under the
Panama flag.
22.11.1986: Grounded near Guam in
position 13.15 north by 144.38 east
during a voyage from Moji to Anewa
Bay, Solomon Islands with a cargo
including tyres, machinery and
ammonium nitrate.

Top: *Santa Clio.* The nine vessels ordered from
Sunderland by the Colocotronis brothers were
split between the two when the group operation
broke up in 1974. The closeness of the launch
and delivery dates of *Santa Clio* suggest some
outfitting was done before launch, perhaps
including the installation of her engine. *[V.H.
Young and L.A.Sawyer collection]*

Bottom: *Holstenbek* arriving Durban, 22nd
March1979. *[Trevor Jones]*

2.1.1987: Refloated with severe
damage to hull and steering gear and
declared beyond economical repair.
Sold to Chi Hsiang Steel Enterprises
Co. Ltd. for breaking up.
13.4.1987: Arrived Kaohsiung.
19.4.1987: Demolition commenced.

885. **WELSH TRIDENT**

L.R./I.M.O. Number 7310272
9,201g
6,085n
15,180d
Hawthorn-Sulzer 5RND68
22.12.1972: Keel laid.
22.3.1973: Launched for Welsh Ore Carriers Ltd. (Gibbs and Co. (Ship Management) Ltd., managers), Newport.
10.5.1973: Completed. British flag.
1978: Owners became Welsh Overseas Freighters Ltd.
1978: Sold to Agate Maritime S.A., Panama (Seiwa Kaiun K.K., Tokyo, Japan, managers) for $4.1m and renamed AGATE.
11.1981: Management transferred to Golden Star Shipping Ltd., Hong Kong (Government of the Socialist republic of Vietnam, Hanoi, Vietnam).
1989: Management transferred to Vietnam Ocean Shipping Co., Haiphong, Vietnam (Government of the Socialist Republic of Vietnam, Hanoi, Vietnam).
1991: Management transferred to Vicub Shipping Co. Ltd., London (Government of the Socialist Republic of Vietnam, Hanoi) and renamed AGATE I under the Malta flag.
1992: Management transferred to Vietnam Sea Transport and Chartering Co. (Vitranschart) (Cong Ty Van Tai Bien Va Thue Tau) Ho Chi Minh City, Vietnam and renamed SAIGON 2.
2001: Sold with yard number 886 to Chinese breakers.
5.6.2001: Arrived Xinhui.

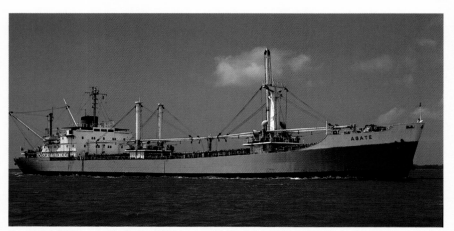

Top: *Welsh Trident*, one of only three SD14s owned in the South Wales ports classically associated with the tramp ship. *[Ian Shiffman]*

Middle: The two Southwick-built Gibbs SD14s remained together under subsequent ownership. This is *Agate* off Singapore in February 1983; her sister became *Quartz*. [Don Brown, David Salisbury collection]

Bottom: *Saigon 2* had recently been acquired by Vietnam when photographed, also off Singapore, in 1992. [Simon Olsen, David Salisbury collection]

886. WELSH ENDEAVOUR

L.R./I.M.O. Number 7314890
9,201g
6,085n
15,180d
Hawthorn-Sulzer 5RND68
Name originally proposed was WELSH PIONEER, but changed to avoid confusion with LONDON PIONEER of the associated London and Overseas Freighters fleet.
16.2.1973: Keel laid.
4.5.1973: Launched for Welsh Ore Carriers Ltd. (Gibbs and Co. (Ship Management) Ltd., managers), Newport.

29.6.1973: Completed. British flag.
1978: Owners became Welsh Overseas Freighters Ltd.
1978: Sold to Quartz Maritime S.A, Panama (Seiwa Kaiun K.K., Tokyo, Japan, managers) for $4.1m and renamed QUARTZ.
11.1981: Management transferred to Golden Star Shipping Ltd., Hong Kong (Government of the Socialist Republic of Vietnam, Hanoi, Vietnam).
1989: Management transferred to Vietnam Ocean Shipping Co., Haiphong, Vietnam (Government of the Socialist Republic of Vietnam, Hanoi).
1991: Management transferred to Vicub Shipping Co. Ltd., London

(Government of the Socialist Republic of Vietnam, Hanoi) under the Maltese flag.
1992: Management transferred to Vietnam Sea Transport and Chartering Co. (Vitranschart) (Cong Ty Van Tai Bien Va Thue Tau), Ho Chi Min City, Vietnam and renamed SAIGON 1.
7.8.1999: Damaged during a collision in Chittagong Outer Anchorage with the Cypriot flag motor ship FONTANA (9,077/1978), whilst inward bound with a cargo of 12,000 tonnes of cement.
2001: Sold with yard number 885 to Chinese breakers.
16.6.2001: Arrived Xinhui.

Top: *Welsh Endeavour* berthed in Barry Docks on 12th June 1978. *[Nigel Jones]*

Left: Although renamed *Quartz*, her original name is actually more prominent, as the bead welding collects rust whilst anchored off Singapore about 1982. *[Don Brown, David Salisbury collection]*

887. PATRICIA M

L.R./I.M.O. Number 7324106
8,957g
6,212n
15,251d
Hawthorn-Sulzer 5RND68
1971: Berth reserved for contract negotiating with Pacific Sealanes Corporation (M.A. Karageorgis S.A., Piraeus). Not proceeded with, and option taken over by Mavroleon Brothers Ltd., London.
24.3.1973: Keel laid.

29.6.1973: Launched for Marine Lanes Transport Corporation, Monrovia, Liberia (Mavroleon Brothers Ltd., London).
3.9.1973: Completed. Liberian flag.
1979: Renamed MAKRA under the Greek flag.
22.10.1982: Laid-up at Piraeus.
1985: Sold to Selatan Shipping Co. Ltd., Limassol, Cyprus (Baru Seri Inc., Piraeus, Greece) and renamed SELATAN..
1995: Sold to Nika II Shipping Co. Ltd., Valletta, Malta (Unit Maritime

Inc., Piraeus) and renamed NIKA II under the Cyprus flag.
14.2.1997: Ran aground in strong winds three miles off Boca del Rio breakwater, Vera Cruz, Mexico whilst inward bound to load sugar for Algeria.
8.3.1997: Refloated and towed to anchorage.
26.4.1997: Arrived at Tuxpan, Mexico to be broken up by Desguaces y Demeresa.
27.4.1997: Demolition began.
30.8.1997: Demolition completed.

Above: *Patricia M.* All Mavroleon S14s were named after female family members. *[Trevor Jones]*

Below: *Selatan* in the St. Lawrence Seaway, 14th July 1991. *[René Beauchamp, David Salisbury collection]*

888. BABITONGA

L.R./I.M.O. Number 7329508
9,290g
6,364n
15,124d
Clark-Sulzer 5RND68

1971: Berth reserved for contract negotiating with Oceanic Sealanes Corporation (M.A. Karageorgis S.A., Piraeus, Greece). Not proceeded with. Option taken over by Colocotronis Ltd., London and later transferred to Babitonga Shipping Corporation.
8.5.1973: Keel laid.
11.9.1973: Launched for Babitonga Shipping Corporation, Monrovia (W. Bruns, Bremen, West Germany).
13.10.1973: Completed. Management

transferred to Nautconsult Shipping Co. Ltd., London. Singapore flag.
1974: Renamed VERMELHA under the Greek flag.
1974: Renamed PORTO ALEGRE. Owners registered as Babitonga Shipping Corporation of Liberia, Monrovia, Liberia (Nautconsult Shipping Co. Ltd., London) under the Singapore flag.
1979: Sold to Aureola Shipping Corporation, Monrovia (Aegeus Shipping S.A., Piraeus (Fafalios Ltd., London)) for $4.6m and renamed GIORGIS under the Greek flag.
2.1.1983: Laid up at Stylis.
1989: Sold to Kingsford Lines II Ltd., Valletta, Malta (Norbulk Shipping Agencies S.A., London,

managers) and renamed LISSE.
1991: Sold to Tricolor Ltd., Monrovia, Liberia (Norbulk Shipping U.K. Ltd., Glasgow, managers) and renamed TRIXIE
1993: Sold to Disciple Shipping Ltd., Monrovia (Maritime Financial Services S.A., Geneva, Switzerland) (Norbulk Shipping U.K. Ltd., Glasgow, managers) and renamed OCEAN PILGRIM.
1995: Sold to Panda Marine Ltd., Nicosia, Cyprus (Bonyad Marine Services Inc., Athens, Greece and renamed PANDA FAGET.
1.1997: Managers became Seabon Holding Corporation, Athens.
29.1.1999: Arrived at Alang to be broken up by Kathiarwar Steels.

Above: *Babitonga* on trials. The funnel colours are those of Nautconsult Shipping Co. Ltd., London. *[Turners (Photography) Ltd., John Lingwood collection]*

Below: *Trixie. [Trevor Jones, David Salisbury collection]*

889. BELLE ROSE

L.R./I.M.O. Number 7340693
8,327g
6,408n
15,143d
Clark-Sulzer 5RND68
3.7.1973: Keel laid.
9.10.1973: Launched for Mauritius Steam Navigation Co. Ltd. (Rogers and Co. Ltd.), Port Louis.
31.1.1974: Completed. British flag, registered Port Louis.
1983: Sold to Panoriente Armadores S.A., Panama (Marlborough Shipping Co. Ltd. (G.P., J. and P.G. Margaronis), London) and renamed BELLE.
1991: Sold to Pylos Holding Inc., Vanuatu (Dalex Shipping Co. S.A. (G. Dalacouras), Piraeus, Greece) and

renamed KATERINA.

1993: Sold to Korea Daesong Trading Corporation, Pyongyang, North Korea (Samer & Co. Shipping S.r.L., Trieste, Italy, managers) and renamed OCEAN HO under the Honduras flag.

1995: Transferred to Typhoon Maritime Ltd., Monrovia (Government of North Korea, Pyongyang) under the Honduran flag (Samer & Co. Shipping S.r.L., Trieste, Italy, managers).

1999: Transferred to Korea Jan Dae San Shipping Co., Pyongyang and renamed JANGDAESAN.

22.7.1999: Grounded off Karachi in position 23.35.45 north by 67.55.30 east whilst on a voyage from Singapore to Karachi with a cargo of steel and green beans.

24.8.1999: Salvage operations terminated due to monsoon swell. Crew taken off. Subsequently reported to have sunk.

From opposite top, at each stage of her career:

Belle Rose fitting out at Southwick. Her lifeboats are carried higher than usual. *[Harold Appleyard]*

Belle Rose in Mauritius Steam Navigation's colours on the New Waterway, August 1976. *[David Salisbury]*

Belle, New Waterway 1984. *[Rowley Weeks, David Salisbury collection]*

Katerina. [David Whiteside collection]

Ocean Ho. [Ian Farquhar]

Jangdaesan, after removal of the forward pair of kingposts. Note the particularly wide fore mast crosstree. The name on her stern is *Jan Dae San. [Ian Farquhar/Nigel Kirby]*

890. **ATHANASSIA**

L.R. /I.M.O. No. 7340708
8,915g
6,177n
15,241d
Clark-Sulzer 5RND68
12.9.1973: Keel laid.
6.2.1974: Launched for Verde
Shipping Co. Ltd., Panama
(Condellis family, Athens) (Glafki
Shipping Company S.A. (A.
Alafouzos), Athens, Greece).
29.3.1974: Completed. Greek flag.
1985: Renamed LESVOS.
1986: Sold to Mammouth Shipping
Co. Ltd., Limassol, Cyprus (Saint
Michael Shipping Co. Ltd., Piraeus,
Greece) and renamed VRISSI.
1996: Sold to Gannet Shipping Ltd.,
Hamilton, Bermuda (Anglo Eastern
Ship Management Ltd., Hong Kong)
(Seabirds Management Inc., Piraeus,
managers) and renamed GANNET
under the Maltese flag.
12.5.2000: Arrived at Alang
23.5.2000: Demolition began by
Famous Shipbreaking Industries.

Top: *Athanassia*, another SD14 with
reduced size superstructure suitable for a
complement of 33 in single and double berth
cabins and a minimum of private toilets.
Seen on the New Waterway in March 1974.
[V.H. Young and L.A. Sawyer]

Middle: *Vrissi. [Ian Farquhar/Louis
Bosschaart]*

Bottom: A rust-streaked *Gannet* contrasts
with the colours of Durban harbour. *[Trevor
Jones]*

891. ANNA DRACOPOULOS

L.R./I.M.O. Number 7341867
8,915g
6,177n
15,241d
Hawthorn-Sulzer 5RND68
11.10.1973: Keel laid.
23.3.1974: Launched for Tricampion Compania Naviera S.A., Panama (Empros Lines Shipping Company Special S.A. (George Dracopoulos), Piraeus, Greece).
15.10.1974: Completed. Greek flag.
1979: Management transferred to Eurotraders Shipping Agencies Ltd. (C.C. Kokkinos and B. Logothetis), Piraeus.
1987: Transferred to Starlight Shipping Co. Ltd., Valletta, Malta (Eurotraders Shipping Agencies Ltd., Piraeus) (Empros Lines Shipping Company Special S.A. (George Dracopoulos), Piraeus, Greece) and renamed AVANCE.
1988: Sold to Kingsford Line Ltd., Valletta (Norbulk Shipping Agencies Ltd., Glasgow) and renamed ADVANCE.
1991: Sold to Denver Shipping Ltd., Monrovia, Liberia (World-Wide Ship Management Ltd., Valparaiso, Chile).
1993: Sold and renamed OONC WINNER for one day then resold to Yuan Hua Technical and Supply Corporation, Lyndhurst, New Jersey, USA (Shen Zhen Yiyang Shipping and Engineering Co. Ltd., Shenzhen, People's Republic of China) and

Above: *Anna Dracopoulos* leaves the New Waterway in classic Greek-tramp trim, with very little ballast and her propellor only partly submerged. She is probaby only on a short coasting voyage, but note that her derricks are all correctly stowed, in keeping with her very neat appearance. *[Paul Boot]*

Below: In complete contrast as *Bright Sea* she is down to her marks, and with a travel-stained hull. Note the tarpaulins over her hatches, which are clearly no longer watertight. *[Russell Priest]*

renamed FLOATING MOUNTAIN under the Panama flag.
1995: Owners became Floating Mountain Shipping Ltd., Hong Kong, under the Panama flag.
1998: Owners became Qingdao Ocean Shipping Co. (COSCO Qingdao), Qingdao, People's Republic of China

1998: Sold to Sun Bright Shipping Ltd., Hong Kong and renamed SUN BRIGHT under the Panama flag.
2000: Sold to Mellum Maritime S.A., St. Vincent and the Grenadines (Marine Fleet Management (Private) Ltd.) and renamed BRIGHT SEA.
15.12.2001: Arrived Mumbai to be broken up.

892. HINRICH OLDENDORFF

L.R./I.M.O. Number 7341879
9,067g
6,334n
15,018d
Clark-Sulzer 5RND68
7.2.1974: Keel laid.
8.5.1974: Launched for Holsatia Shipping Corporation, Monrovia (Egon Oldendorff, Lübeck, West Germany).

28.6.1974: Completed. Singapore flag.
1980: Egon Oldendorff management ceased.
1981: Renamed HAPPY CHANCE.
12.1991: Sold to Martin Maritime Co. Ltd., Valletta, Malta (Meadway Shipping and Trading Inc., Piraeus, Greece) and renamed MARTIN.
3.1995: Sold to Nika Shipping Ltd., Valletta (Unit Maritime Inc., Piraeus) for $1.5m and renamed NIKA.
Previous to 31.5.1999: Arrived Kolkata for demolition.

Top: *Hinrich Oldendorff* in the New Waterway, August 1976. The Oldendorff ships were built with, or quickly given, extensions to the exhaust pipes. *[David Salisbury]*

Bottom: Under her last name, *Nika* at Durban about 1996. Oldendorff's trademark offset signal mast is again apparent, probably arranged thus to minimise interference on the radar from the heavy profile masts and derricks. *[Trevor Jones, David Salisbury collection]*

893. EIBE OLDENDORFF

L.R./I.M.O. Number 7341881
9,070g
6,334n
15,018d
23.3.1974: Keel laid.
21.6.1974: Launched for Arabella Shipping Company S.A., Panama (Egon Oldendorff, Lübeck, West Germany).
30.8.1974: Completed. Singapore flag.
1979: Transferred to Holsatia Shipping Corporation, Monrovia. Liberia (Egon Oldendorff, Lübeck).
1981: Renamed FAIR SPIRIT under the Liberian flag.
1992: Transferred to Westfalia Shipping Corporation, Monrovia (Egon Oldendorff, Lübeck).
1994: Sold to Half Moon Shipping Co., Monrovia. (Egon Oldendorff, Lübeck).
1995: Sold to 'Coreck' Maritime G.m.b.H., Hamburg.
1995: Sold to Wealth Carriers Navigation Ltd., Hamburg, Germany and, after 1996, Monrovia (Lubeca Marine Management (HK) Ltd., Hong Kong, managers) under the Liberian flag.
1999: Sold to Global Shipping and General Trading Ltd. (Corner Stone General Trading) under the Liberian flag.
1.12.2002: Arrived at Mumbai for demolition.
11.12.2002: Work began.

Top: *Eibe Oldendorff* photographed in the River Scheldt on 24th May 1975. *[Roy Kittle]*

Middle: Change of name, but not of disponent owner, sees the ship as *Fair Spirit* on 12th July

1983. The funnel colours have been amended, the 'EO' of Egon Oldendorff giving way to 'H' for subsidiary, Holsatia Shipping. *[J. Wiltshire collection]*

Bottom: Still as *Fair Spirit* in 1996, but funnel colours have changed again. *[Russell Priest]*

894. CATHARINA OLDENDORFF

L.R./I.M.O. Number 7341893
9,070g
6,343n
15,081d
Clark-Sulzer 5RND68
9.5.1974: Keel laid.

20.8.1974: Launched for Westfalia Shipping Corporation, Monrovia, Liberia (Egon Oldendorff, Lübeck, West Germany.
11.10.1974: Completed. Singapore flag.
10.1981: Renamed SPLENDID FORTUNE.
9.1991: Sold to Delight Glory Shipping Ltd., Monrovia (Parakou

Shipping Ltd., Hong Kong, managers) and renamed DELIGHT GLORY under the Panama flag.
1993: Managers became Yue Hai Shipping Co. Ltd., Hong Kong.
1999: Sold to Indian breakers for $113 per lightweight ton.
12.9.1999: Arrived Calcutta for breaking up.

Above: *Catharina Oldendorff* is seen moored at Swanscombe on the River Thames in April 1977 on charter to Lauritzen. *[Roy Kittle]*

Below: Still with Oldendorff, but now as *Splendid Fortune* and in the funnel colours of subsidiary Westfalia Shipping, on the St. Lawrence on 22nd

July 1982. *[René Beauchamp, David Salisbury collection]*

895. **ARRINO**

L.R./I.M.O. Number 7341908
9,279g
6,346n
15,139d
Hawthorn-Sulzer 5RND68
21.6.1974: Keel laid.
30.9.1974: Launched for Australind
Steam Shipping Co. Ltd. (Trinder,
Anderson and Co. Ltd., managers),
London.
28.11.1974: Completed. British flag.
1978: Sold to Prekookeanska
Plovida, Bar, Yugoslavia for $4.5m
and renamed RUMIJA.
1992: Owners became Lovcen
Overseas Shipping Ltd. (Rigel
Shipmanagement Ltd., managers),
Valletta, Malta.
1993: Sold to Prudent International
Shipping and Trading Ltd., Nassau,
Bahamas (Fouladi General Trading Co.,
Dubai) and renamed PRUDENT
VENTURER under the St. Vincent flag.
16.5.1995-3.10.1995: Under arrest at
Apapa/Lagos.
1995: Sold to Guardian Shipping
Ltd., British Virgin Islands (Mary-
land Maritime Services Private Ltd.,
Mumbai, India) and renamed
GUARDIAN ANGEL under the St.
Vincent and Grenadines flag.
10.2.1998: Arrived at Alang for
demolition by Nagarseth
Shipbreakers.

Top: *Arrino* at Durban in 1976. She wears the
funnel colours of Compania Sud-Americana de
Vapores, Valparaiso, to whom she was on
charter throughout her career with Australind.
[Trevor Jones]

Middle   *Rumija,* Liverpool, 22nd September
1986. *[Paul Boot]*

Bottom: *Guardian Angel. [Ian Farquhar/Nigel
Kirby]*

896. WESTLAND

L.R./I.M.O. Number 7341910
8,936g
6,420n
15,099d
Hawthorn-Sulzer 5RND68
1973: Contract placed by United Faith Transport Inc., Monrovia, Liberia (P.S. Li, Hong Kong).
1973: Sold to N.V. tot Voorzetting van de Koninklijke Hollandsche Lloyd, Amsterdam, Netherlands.
21.8.1974: Keel laid.
14.11.1974: Launched.
3.2.1975: Completed. Netherlands flag.

1982: Transferred to Nedlloyd Lijnen B.V. and renamed NEDLLOYD WESTLAND.
1983: Renamed WESTLAND.
1983: Sold to Pamit C Shipping Co. Ltd., Limassol, Cyprus (Government of Cuba, Havana, Cuba) and renamed PAMIT C.
1991: Sold to Tephys Shipping Co. Ltd., Limassol, Cyprus (Nordstrand Maritime and Trading Co. Ltd., Piraeus) and renamed TEPHYS.
1994: Operators became Empresa Navegacion Mambisa, Havana.
2004: Still listed in 'Lloyd's Register' but

continued existence must be in doubt as her registration was cancelled in May 2000 and no movements have been reported since November 2000.

Top: *Westland* is assisted by the tug *Langton* in the Mersey on 16th July 1975. She is on charter to Safmarine, and possibly just completing her maiden voyage. Her enhanced cargo gear is similar to that on the *Belle Isle* and *Belle Rose* (yard numbers 870 and 889), although there are no winch houses to the kingposts abaft of number 4 hatch. The mast ahead of this hatch has the combination of conventional and swinging derricks seen on yard number 876, but this time the Velle derrick serves hatches number 4 and 5. The two masts are therefore of different designs. The square-section foremast is that usually fitted by Austin & Pickersgill when heavy derricks were required. The tubular-section mast was that designed and supplied for the Velle derrick by a subsidiary of Clydeside shipbuilders George Brown Ltd. *[Paul Boot]*

Bottom: As the Cuban owned *Pamit C* on an icy St. Lawrence, 30th December 1983. *[M. Piché, David Salisbury collection]*

70

904. AJANA

L.R./I.M.O. Number 7393377
9,006g
6,421n
14,822d
Hawthorn-Sulzer 5RND68
21.11.1973: Contract signed.
5.3.1976: Keel laid.
28.6.1976: Launched for Australind
Steam Shipping Co. Ltd. (Trinder,
Anderson and Co. Ltd., managers),
London.
15.10.1976: Completed. British flag.
6.1980: Sold together with
AUSTRALIND (yard number 464)

to Empresa Navegacion Mambisa,
Havana, Cuba for a total of $7.4m and
renamed CALIXTO GARCIA.
1995: Transferred to Pan Pacific
Shipping and Trading S.A., Hong
Kong (Government of Cuba, Havana) and renamed CALIX under the
Belize flag.
1997: Sold to Union Maritime and
Ports, Shanghai, People's Republic of
China, under the Belize flag.
1998: Sold to Adecon Shipping Inc.,
Mississagua, Ontario, Canada and
renamed CANADIAN CHALLENGER
under the Belize flag.

1999: Transferred to Roxford Enterprises (Adecon Shipmanagement),
Mississagua, Ontario.
6.2004: Still listed in 'Lloyd's
Register' but continued existence
must be in doubt, as no movements
have been reported since June 1999,
and her Belize registration was
cancelled in January 2002.

Top: *Ajana* anchored off Singapore in February 1980. On the bridge front can be seen the ladders fitted to British-registered SD14s to give access to the stowage fittings for derricks. These were necessary if the owner required the derricks to be stowed horizontally, or if deck cargo was to be carried regularly. Note also the substantial square foremast required for the 80-ton derrick, and the wide crosstree for the swinging Velle derrick. *[David Berg, David Salisbury collection]*

Left: *Canadian Challenger*, appropriately at Montreal on 13th November 1998. *[Marc Piché, David Salisbury collection]*

905. ANAX

L.R./I.M.O. Number 7393389
8,792g
6,516n
15,000d
Hawthorn-Sulzer 5RND68
3.12.1973: Contract signed.
13.5.1976: Keel laid.
26.8.1976: Launched for Maureen
Corporation, Panama (V. Tricoglu,
Piraeus, Greece).
26.11.1976: Completed. Greek flag.
1978: Sold to Linhas Maritimas de
Angola (Angonave), Luanda, Angola
for £2.9m and renamed HOJI YA
HENDA.
15.2.1994: Laid-up and under arrest at
Lisbon.
2003: Broken up at Lisbon.

Top: *Anax*, flying light on the Scheldt on 4th
August 1978. Note the letter 'T' for Tricoglu on
her funnel. *[Roy Kittle]*

Middle: Soon after the top photograph was taken,
Anax was sold to Angola as *Hoji Ya Henda*, seen
again on the New Waterway in June 1985. From
the funnel colours, it is not hard to guess the
political persuasion of Angola's rulers. *[Roy Kittle]*

Bottom: After almost ten years under arrest, *Hoji
Ya Henda* makes a sad sight in the Irmaos &
Batista scrapyard at Lisbon during October
2000. Alongside her is *Ebo*. *[Trevor Jones]*

906. ORMOS

L.R./I.M.O. Number 7393391
8,792g
6,516n
15,000d
Hawthorn-Sulzer 5RND68
3.12.1973: Contract signed.
29.6.1976: Keel laid.
6.10.1976: Launched for Mina Corporation, Panama (V. Tricoglu, Piraeus, Greece).
7.1.1977: Completed. Greek flag.

1978: Sold to China Ocean Shipping Company, Shanghai, People's Republic of China for $5.875m and renamed MEI JIANG.
1991: Owners became Guangzhou Ocean Shipping Co. (COSCO Guangzhou), Guangzhou, People's Republic of China.
1998: Sold to Linghai Marine Shipping Ltd., Dalian, People's Republic of China and renamed LING HAI 18. Subsequently renamed BAI AN 2 and JIN

Top: *Ormos* underway in the Maydon Channel, Durban. *[Trevor Jones]*

Bottom: *Mei Jiang* anchored off Singapore, 26th April 1987. *[Simon Olsen, David Salisbury collection]*

DA HAI, both under the Chinese flag.
12.7.2002: Class transferred to a non-IACS society. Last reported detained at Havana.

911. EUROPEAN EXPRESS

L.R./I.M.O. Number 7422831
9,120g
6,316n
15,210d
Clark-Sulzer 5RND68
27.9.1974: Contract signed with AB
Vasa Shipping oy, Vasa, Finland.
2.6.1976: Sold to Vroon B.V. Trading
& Shipping Company, Breskens,
Netherlands.

Subsequently transferred to Cargo
Express Navigation Co. Inc.,
Monrovia, Liberia and to Motorship
'European Express' B.V. (Vroon B.V.
Trading & Shipping Company,
Breskens).
3.5.1978: Keel laid.
28.9.1978: Launched.
18.12.1978: Completed. Netherlands flag.
1984: Sold to China Ocean Shipping
Company, Shanghai, People's Republic
of China and renamed AN LU JIANG.
1991: Owners became Guangzhou

Ocean Shipping Co. (COSCO
Guangzhou), Guangzhou, People's
Republic of China.
13.5.2004: Sustained cracks to deck on
stranding after drifting in area of
Anowara Thana, Chittagong Outer
Anchorage whilst on a voyage from
Chittagong Roads to Bangladesh with
a cargo of fertiliser.
15.5.2004: Towed out to sea and sank
10.5 miles off Patenga Lighthouse,
Chittagong in position 22.08 north and
91.37 east.

Top: *European Express* was the first of the Fourth
Series SD14s to be ordered; note the modified
stem. Like her sister yard number 912, she was
built out of sequence in the shipyard programme.
Two masts were now standard, the fore mast being
considerably thicker. The increased length of the
Fourth Series meant that the distance from the
forecastle head to the fore mast exceeded the
regulation distance for fixing the fore mast light,
so it was necessary to fit an extra mast to carry
this light. At Cape Town, 14th May 1982. *[Ken
White, Don Brown collection]*
Bottom: *An Lu Jiang* at New Orleans, 18th
October 1991. *[René Beauchamp, David
Salisbury]*

74

912. **AFRICAN EXPRESS**

L.R./I.M.O. Number 7422843
9,120g
6,316n
15,210d
Clark-Sulzer 5RND68
27.9.1974: Contract signed with AB
Vasa Shipping oy, Vasa, Finland.
2.6.1976: Sold to Vroon B.V. Trading
& Shipping Company, Breskens,
Netherlands.
Subsequently transferred to Cargo
Express Navigation Co. Inc.,
Monrovia and to Motorschip 'African
Express' B.V. (Vroon B.V. Trading &
Shipping Company), Breskens.
7.8.1978: Keel laid.
12.12.1978: Launched.
19.4.1979: Completed. Netherlands
flag.
1984: Sold to China Ocean Shipping
Company, Shanghai, People's Republic
of China and renamed AN SAI JIANG.
1991: Owners became Guangzhou
Ocean Shipping Co. (COSCO
Guangzhou), Guangzhou, People's
Republic of China.
1999: Sold to Xiamen Cheng Yi
Shipping Co., Xiamen, People's
Republic of China and renamed YU JIA.
12.8.2003: Sank after flooding in heavy
weather in the Bay of Bengal in position
16.08 north by 91.31 east whilst on a
voyage from India to China with a cargo
of chrome ore. 28 members of the crew
were rescued by the Panamanian motor
vessel CHIEFTAIN 2 (19,210/1978).

*At this point in Austin and Pickersgill
history the former Bartram's shipyard
was scheduled for closure and
subsequent hull numbers were
allocated by adding together the
numbers of the last vessels then
building at Southwick and South
Dock, i.e. 912 + 464 = 1376. The next
vessel to be built by the company was
therefore allocated the number 1377.*

Top: *African Express* anchored off Singapore in
February 1980. *[David Berg, David Salisbury
collection]*

Middle: *An Sai Jiang* at Hong Kong soon after her
sale to China in 1984. *[David Salisbury collection]*

Bottom: After change of name, registered owner
and application of the new COSCO funnel colours,
Yu Jia at Singapore on 31st March 2002.
[Nigel Jones]

1377. (EMPROS)

This vessel was ordered to the 'Third Series' design, however, the owner insisted that he should be allowed to change this to the new 'Fourth Series' configuration, then on the point of being introduced, and this was eventually agreed, except for the main engine, which was already on order.
L.R./I.M.O. Number 7610062
8,889g
6,405n
15,220d
Hawthorn-Sulzer 5RND68
29.3.1976: Contract signed.
15.6.1977: Keel laid.
10.11.1977: Launched un-named because of a dispute with the owner.

1.2.1978: Ran trials without owners present then laid-up in River Tyne pending completion and delivery.
25.5.1978: Ran official sea trials.
20.7.1978: Completed for Elm Company Ltd., Monrovia, Liberia (Eurotraders Shipping Agencies Ltd. (Empros Lines Shipping Co. Special S.A. (George Dracopoulos), Piraeus, Greece) (C. Kokkinos and B. Logothetis), Piraeus, managers). as EMPROS. Greek flag.
26.10.1979: Collided whilst outward bound in the River Scheldt with the cargo vessel MARIANN GEM (3,731/ 1960) which subsequently sank.
7.2003: Sold to W.V.P. Shipping S.A., Panama (Admiral Shipmanagement

S.a.r.l, Hazmieh, Lebanon and renamed TANIA under the Georgian flag.
7.2004: Still listed by 'Lloyd's Register'.

Top: *Empros* inward bound on the New Waterway on 7th August 1993. A Fourth Series SD14, compared with *European Express* she has only a short length of bulwark amidships. *[Clive Guthrie]*

Bottom: Unusually for a vessel of her size, *Empros* spent most of her life in the Dracopoulos fleet operating in her owners Empros Lines services from the UK and Continent to the Eastern Mediterranean. At Terneuzen on 31st July 2000, *Empros* is still very smart but her hull and masts colours have been changed. *[David Salisbury]*

1378. **CLUDEN (2)**

Because ships 911 and 912 were built out of sequence in the shipyard programme, this was the first Fourth Series SD14 to be completed.
L.R./I.M.O. Number 7611559
9,326g
6,165n
15,290d
Clark-Sulzer 4RND68M
29.4.1976: Contract signed.
19.9.1977: Keel laid.
10.1.1978: Launched for Matheson and Co. Ltd., London.
7.4.1978: Laid-up in River Tyne at owner's request pending delivery.
22.9.1978: Completed. British flag.
5.1982: Sold to China Ocean Shipping Company, Shanghai, People's Republic of China for $7.5m and renamed QING JIANG.
1991: Owners became Guangzhou Ocean Shipping Co. (COSCO Guangzhou), Guangzhou, People's Republic of China.
7.2004: Still listed by 'Lloyd's Register'.

Above: Matheson's simple but classic colours are seen to good effect in this aerial view of *Cluden*. She carries a Velle swinging derrick at the fore mast. *[David Whiiteside collection]*

Below: After a brief career under the Red Ensign, *Cluden* was sold to China as *Qing Jiang*, and was still in service in 2004. She was photographed in the Suez Canal on 19th September 1994. Note her short, midships bulwarks, designed to protect the air pipes to the floodable number 3 hold. *[Nigel Jones]*

1379. (AEGIRA) LUNDOGE

L.R./I.M.O. Number 7610074
8,889g
6,411n
15,290d
Clark-Sulzer 4RND68M
12.4.1976: Contract signed.
15.11.1977: Keel laid.
7.4.1978: Launched for Aegira Shipping Corporation, Monrovia, Liberia (Condellis family, Piraeus)

(Glafki Shipping Company S.A. (A. Alafouzos), Athens, Greece).
10.7.1978: Completed and laid-up in the River Tyne pending sale.
1978: Sale reported to Royal Nepal Shipping Corporation, Kathmandu but negotiations collapsed.
6.7.1979: Sold to Linhas Maritimas de Angola U.E.E. (Angonave), Luanda, Angola and renamed LUNDOGE.
28.7.1984: Damaged when a mine exploded against her hull whilst lying

Top: *Aegira* with *Cluden* inboard laid up on the River Tyne during 1978. *[Nigel Cutts]*

at Luanda, since when vessel has laid idle with mechanical problems and generators out of order.
7.2004: Still listed by 'Lloyd's Register'. Last reported laid up at Luanda in September 1999.

Bottom: *Aegira* as the *Lundoge* during her short operational career. *[David Whiteside collection]*

1380. (DALWORTH) SONG DÜONG

L.R./I.M.O. Number 7611561
9,173g
6,321n
15,210d
Hawthorn-Sulzer 4RND68
28.6.1976: Contract signed by R.S. Dalgleish Ltd., Newcastle-upon- Tyne.
24.2.1978: Keel laid.
14.7.1978: Launched as

DALWORTH in the presence of Dalgleish representatives, but name was removed immediately after launch as Dalgleish, who had been experiencing financial difficulties in the months prior to the launch, did not really own the vessel and negotiations for its possible sale to Vietnam had been proceeding for some time.
6.10.1978: Sold to Maritime Transportation Department of the

Socialist Republic of Vietnam.
3.11.1978: Laid-up in River Tyne pending finalisation of sale.
15.2.1979: Contract with R.S. Dalgleish terminated.
22.2.1979: Completed for Vietnam Ocean Shipping Co., Haiphong, Vietnam as SONG DÜONG. Vietnamese flag.
6.2004: Still listed by 'Lloyd's Register'.

1381. **FUNING**

L.R./I.M.O. Number 7607481
9,118g
6,386n
15,300d
Scott-Sulzer 4RND68M

30.1.1976: Order placed by Taikoo Chinese Navigation Co. Ltd., Hong Kong (John Swire and Sons Ltd., London).

5.4.1976: Contract signed with Taikoo Navigation Co. Ltd., Hong Kong (John Swire and Sons Ltd., London).

16.1.1978: Keel laid.

23.5.1978: Launched.

1.9.1978: Completed. Hong Kong (British) flag.

1982: Sold to China Ocean Shipping Co. Ltd., Shanghai, People's Republic of China for $8.2m and renamed PING JIANG.

1991: Owners became Guangzhou Ocean Shipping Co. (COSCO Guangzhou), Guangzhou, People's Republic of China.

6.2004: Still listed by 'Lloyd's Register'.

Top: *Dalworth* was the first ship built in the new shipbuilding complex at Southwick. The financial difficulties of Dalgleish meant her name was removed immediately after launch. She is seen fitting out whilst negotiations for her sale took place. *[V.H. Young and L.A. Sawyer collection]*

Middle: *Dalworth* entered service as the Vietnamese *Song Düong*, seen at Singapore, March 1983. *[Nigel Jones]*

Bottom: Swire's *Funing* anchored off Singapore in March 1979. *[Don Brown, David Salisbury collection]*

1382. (SEA HAWK) KIFANGONDO

L.R./I.M.O. Number 7610086
8,889g
6,411n
15,290d
Hawthorn-Sulzer 4RND68M
31.3.1976: Contract signed.
19.4.1978: Keel laid.
31.8.1978: Launched for Myral Shipping Corporation, Monrovia, Liberia (Glafki Shipping Company S.A. (A. Alafouzos) Athens, Greece).
26.11.1978: All work completed.
23.1.1979: Laid-up at Deptford Quay, Sunderland pending sale.
24.4.1979. Laid-up in River Tyne.
6.7.1979: Sold to Linhas Maritimas de Angola U.E.E. (Angonave), Luanda, Angola and renamed KIFANGONDO.
28.1.1994-to 1999/2000: At Le Havre with propulsion and generator problems. Owners unable to pay for repairs and vessel seized by several creditors.
6.1999: Sold by auction to Tango Shipping Co. Ltd., Malta and renamed TANGO D.
2001: Sold to Topaz Enterprises Inc., Panama and renamed ARGO STAR.
2001: Sold to Bangladesh breakers for $167 per lightweight ton.
About 28.8.2001: Arrived Chittagong.
9.9.2001: Arrived Gadani Beach having been resold to Pakistani breakers.

Left: *Sea Hawk* never entered service as such, but went into straight into lay up awaiting sale. She is seen on the Wear with *Bronte* (yard number 1385) inboard of her. *[Harold Appleyard]*

Below: *Sea Hawk* entered service as the Angolan *Kifangondo* seen on the New Waterway in July 1983. The career of this unfortunate ship both started and ended badly, as she spent most of the nineties laid up, under arrest, at Le Havre. *[David Salisbury]*

1383. GRAND FAITH

L.R./I.M.O. Number 7607493
8,926g
6,723n
15,250d
Scott-Sulzer 4RND68
20.4.1976: Contract signed.
22.6.1979: Keel laid.
5.12.1979: Launched for Grand
Kingdom Inc. (United Venture
Management Inc., managers),
Monrovia, Liberia (P.S. Li and Co.
Ltd., Hong Kong).
25.4.1980: Completed. Liberian flag.
1981: Owning company acquired by
Carrian Group Ltd. (United Fair
Agencies Ltd.), Hong Kong.
1983: Management transferred to
Univan Ship Management Ltd., Hong
Kong.
1983: Carrian Group liquidated and
ownership vested in the liquidators,
who were the shareholders.
6.1984: Sold to China Ocean Ship-
ping Co. Ltd., Shanghai, People's
Republic of China and renamed AN
YANG JIANG.
1991: Owners became Guangzhou
Ocean Shipping Co. (COSCO
Guangzhou), Guangzhou, People's
Republic of China.
6.2004: Still
listed by 'Lloyd's
Register'.

Above: *Grand Faith* in splendid condition, New
Waterway, July 1981. *[David Salisbury]*

*A confusing switch of certain ship
numbers occurred at this time,
resulting from the protracted
negotiations then being held with
Vietnam and which had begun in
1977. The Vietnamese had insisted
on actual ship numbers being
allocated to the vessels on offer,
although this would not normally be
done until the contract signing stage
had been reached. Yard numbers
1380, 1384, 1388 and 1390 were,
therefore, included in the documents
then being considered. However, as
a long time had elapsed with no
guarantee that these contracts
would ever be signed, Austin &
Pickersgill later decided to use these
numbers for contracts definitely
placed by other owners in the
meantime. When the Vietnamese
were ready to sign their contracts
they insisted that the numbers
originally declared must be retained
and the yard had to juggle a lot of
numbers around to suit.*

1384. THAI-BINH

L.R./I.M.O. Number 7611573
9,123g
6,342n
15,240d
Clark-Sulzer 4RND68M
21.7.1976: Contract signed by
Kardamada Compania Naviera S.A.,
Panama (Liberty Maritime Agency
Ltd., London).
19.12.1978: Contract terminated.
6.10.1978: Sold to Maritime Transport
Department of the Socialist Republic
of Vietnam, Haiphong, taking over
contact number 1388, already allocated
for Transcontinental Carriers, which
was then renumbered 1384 to conform
with earlier negotiations. The
Transcontinental vessel was renumbered 1397.
7.6.1979: Keel laid.
18.10.1979: Launched.
10.3.1980: Completed for Vietnam
Ocean Shipping Co., Haiphong,
Vietnam. Vietnamese flag.
6.2004: Still listed by 'Lloyd's
Register'.

Right: *Thai-Binh* on the
New Waterway, 9th
July 1988. She is an
unusual example of an
SD14 with one owner
throughout her life, at
least so far. *[Bernard
Morton, David
Salisbury collection]*

1385. **BRONTE**

L.R./I.M.O. Number 7614719
9,324g
6,150n
15,160d
Hawthorn-Sulzer 4RND68M
14.5.1976: Order placed by Sirta Ltd.
(Vestey Group), London.
11.10.1976: Contract signed by Bronte
Navigation Co. Ltd. (Lamport and Holt
Line Ltd.), Liverpool.
24.5.1978: Keel laid.
31.10.1978: Launched for Lamport
and Holt Line Ltd., Liverpool.
2.2.1979: Completed. British flag.
1983: Sold to Government of People's
Republic of China (China Ocean
Shipping Co. Ltd.), Shanghai and
renamed AN DONG JIANG.
1990: Transferred to Fortunate Star
Marine Ltd., Valletta, Malta (COSCO
Guangzhou) and renamed SAFE STAR.
2001: Transferred to Hainan Shipping
and Enterprises Co. Ltd. Haikou,
Hainan Island, People's Republic of
China and renamed AN DONG
JIANG.
6.2004: Still listed by 'Lloyd's
Register'.

Top: *Bronte*, first of the SD14s for Lamport & Holt,
entering her home port of Liverpool via the Gladstone
entrance on 15th May 1980. Note the tall funnel: a
Vestey group trademark. *[Paul Boot]*

Middle: After only four years service under the British
flag, she was sold to China as *An Dong Jiang*, as seen
on the New Waterway in June 1985. *[Roy Kittle,
David Salisbury collection]]*

Bottom: In 1990 she was put under the Maltese flag
as *Safe Star*, seen in the Suez Canal, 28th May 1996.
[Nigel Jones]

1386. **DERWENT**

L.R./I.M.O. Number 7614721
9,167g
6,469n
15,230d
Hawthorn-Sulzer 4RND68M
21.9.1976: Contract signed.
16.10.1978: Keel laid.
28.2.1979: Launched for Welldeck
Shipping Co. Ltd. (Houlder Brothers
and Co. Ltd.), London.
Ownership later transferred to Shaw,
Savill and Albion Co. Ltd. (Houlder
Brothers and Co. Ltd.), London.
30.5.1979: Completed. British flag.
1981: Transferred to Dee Navigation
Ltd. (Shaw, Savill and Albion Co. Ltd.,
managers), London.
1982: Transferred to Shaw, Savill and
Albion Co. Ltd. (Furness, Withy
(Shipping) Ltd., managers), London.
8.1982: Sold to Pioneer Atlantic
Navigation S.A., Panama (Toko Kaiun
K.K., Kobe, Japan) for $8m and
renamed MOUNTAIN AZALEA.
1988: Sold to Polestar S.A, Panama (E.
Pothitos, Athens, Greece) and renamed
EVPO AGSIMONE.
1991: Sold to Hanbonn Shipping Ltd.,
Hong Kong and renamed HANBONN
CONCORD under the St. Vincent and
Grenadines flag.
1994: Transferred to SCIT (Ship
Management) Ltd. (Shougang Concord
International Transportation Ltd.),
Hong Kong.
1995: Sold to Blue Sierra Shipping Co.
Ltd., Limassol, Cyprus (Thesarco
Shipping Co. S.A., Piraeus, Greece)
and renamed ALBA SIERRA.
1997: Sold to Neretva Shipping Co.
Ltd., Limassol, Cyprus (Argosy
Shipmanagement Inc., Piraeus).
12.11.2002: Delivered to Shri Ram
Shipbreakers, Alang for demolition.
21.11.2002: Work began.

Top: *Derwent* in Royal Mail's rather plain livery. As she is riding very light, the containers on deck are presumably empty. The 50-tonne swinging derrick at number 2 hold and the 22-tonne at number 4 were of a different design to those fitted to all other SD14s. There are also conventional derricks on the masts. *[David Whiteside collection]*

Middle: *Mountain Azalea* outward bound from Antwerp, in April 1986. *[David Salisbury]*

Bottom: Light ship again, and with her propellor only partly submerged, *Alba Sierra* in the St. Lawrence on 28th August 1999. *[Marc Piche, David Salisbury collection]*

1387. BROWNING

L.R./I.M.O. Number 7614733
9,324g
6,150n
15,160d
Hawthorn-Sulzer 4RND68M
14.5.1976: Order placed by Berioln
Ltd. (Vestey Group), London.
11.10.1976: Contract signed by
Browning Shipping Co. Ltd.
(Lamport and Holt Line Ltd.),
Liverpool.
1.9.1978: Keel laid.
26.1.1979: Launched for Lamport
and Holt Line Ltd., Liverpool.
9.4.1979: Completed. British flag.
11.1983: Sold to Government of
People's Republic of China (China
Ocean Shipping Co. Ltd.), Shanghai
for $6m and renamed AN FU JIANG.
1990: Transferred to Fortunate Star
Marine Ltd., Valletta, Malta
(COSCO Guangzhou) and renamed
FORTUNATE STAR.
1999: Transferred to Ocean Join
Shipping Inc., Hong Kong and
renamed OCEAN JOIN.
2004: Transferred to Good Future
Shipping S.A. Panama (Shangdong
Province Marine Shipping Co,
Qingdao, Shangdong Province,
People's Republic of China) and
renamed EVER BRIGHT.
6.2004: Still listed by 'Lloyd's
Register'.

Top: *Browning. [David Whiteside collection]*

Middle: *An Fu Jiang* at Cardiff, 18th March 1985.
[Nigel Jones]

Bottom: After service under the Chinese flag, she
was transferred to a Maltese company, still
controlled by China, as *Fortunate Star*, seen at
Singapore Roads, 26th June 1993. *[Nigel Jones]*

On the Lamport & Holt SD14s

A master's memories
Captain A.W. Kinghorn

The Falklands Conflict was drawing to its close when I joined Lamport & Holt's SD14 *Browning* in Liverpool on 7th June 1982. British ships had ceased visiting Argentina for the duration but trade with Brazil was booming.

Having completed unloading and secured for sea, we sailed for Glasgow on 11th June, arriving next day. Since I had last sailed up the Clyde fourteen years previously, unbelievable changes had taken place and now grass and trees grew where mighty ships had once been built. Apart from Yarrows where considerable naval construction was in hand, the river presented a truly rural appearance. We were the only cargo ship in King George V Dock, where blackberry bushes encroached all around and rabbits came out to play in the evenings on what had once been a busy quay.

For the next two weeks we loaded bagged malt for Brazil's Brahma Brewery, general cargo and cased whisky for Recife and Salvador. The pace was leisurely, no overtime being worked, and there was time for my wife and me to visit old friends in the city and walk the famous banks of Loch Lomond, especially bonny in the bloom of summer.

The *Browning,* built in 1979, was one of four sisters owned by Lamport and Holt, the last ships built for this old Liverpool company. Her class sisters *Belloc, Bronte* and *Boswell* were identical but by mid-1982 *Belloc* had already been sold abroad and it seemed only a matter of time before the others were also displaced by fully cellular container ships. As we sailed from Glasgow on 25th June, despite a gloomy wet evening with even gloomier weather forecast, we all felt a sense of relief induced by the Argentine surrender in the Falklands.

The *Browning's* funnel was not quite authentic according to the company's ancient rules which stated that colours must be 'blue for three sevenths of its lower part, white and black for two sevenths each above the blue'. But as the mate remarked, 'Those rules were probably made for coal-burners with woodbine funnels' and ours certainly looked fine, one seventh black over three sevenths white over regulation three sevenths blue. There was no doubting her proud ownership and she was maintained like a yacht - our Liverpool bosun saw to that! We carried the Lamport & Holt badge on our stem and always flew the City of Liverpool coat of arms flag as a stem jack in port. The British crew of thirty were keen as mustard. Predominantly Liverpudlian as befitted her port of registry, they came also from St. Albans and South Africa, Glasgow and Sunderland, York and Salford, Birmingham and Yarmouth, Barry and Lambeth, Chester, Darlington and North Shields - a good mixture! We came complete with one of those hardy Poles who became British during the Second World War, in the engine room.

Main engine was a Sulzer - a quaint little motor in the eyes of those accustomed to the power of larger vessels but quite capable of driving her along at 16.3 knots over a passage on a mean daily consumption of 24.2 tons of heavy oil. She was able to manoeuvre on heavy oil into and out of port and was the first ship to have the company-designed Star Blender, an invention which enabled heavy oil to be mixed with the lighter diesel oil on demand, for the ship's auxiliary engines thus contributing greatly to fuel cost savings. Heavy weather from ahead, I found, tended to cause her to slow down without being asked but her overall performance compared well with the turbine steamer *Dunedin Star* of similar size in which I had sailed as chief officer twenty years previously and which burned 46 tons of the same fuel per day for slightly less speed. The *Browning* also

evaporated ample fresh water for her daily need of ten tons per day though of course this facility was not employed in coastal waters where pollution exists, organic if invisible.

Navigation equipment included gyro compass and radar but lacked that modern marvel, a satellite navigator, so distance steamed was measured on a Walker's Patent Log - an age-old device which streams a 65-fathom line astern, at the end of which is a bronze 18-inch long streamlined rotator with curved fins so designed that its revolutions caused by the ship's way through the water measure distance travelled. Read on a special clock fitted to the taff rail, this transmits electrically to a similar clock in the chartroom, on the bridge. Nineteenth century sailing ships carried similar equipment and I was delighted to find that *Browning's* was as accurate a measure of our progress through the water as could be desired. And the absence of 'satnav' brought us back to basics, using the sextant whenever a sighting of the heavenly bodies coinciding with a sharp horizon made astronavigation possible.

The *Browning's* accommodation, though below the best of modern standards (juniors shared a bathroom between two for instance, and there were no baths, only showers) was far above that in the basic SD14, tastefully appointed and nicely finished. As with cars, you get what you pay for, if you're lucky.

For carrying cargo she was right up to date, with a total capacity of 689,278 cubic feet in five holds, the forward four of which, before the bridge, had 'tween decks, with sliding steel hatch covers and Velle swinging derricks, one to each hatch. The biggest, with a safe working load of 26 tonnes, was at number 2 hatch; numbers one, three and four had 22-tonners, while number 5 was served by a pair of 5-tonne derricks in union purchase. A handy vessel!

Crossing the Atlantic from north east to south west showed the SD14 to be a great roller - she rolled all the way and the first trippers - once they got used to the motion - insisted that 'this one would roll on damp grass' (as first trippers always do).

We experienced more heavy weather whilst sailing between Salvador and Rio Grande do Sul, over 1,400 miles to the south. South westerly gales up to force 10 combined with a heavy swell to force us well out into the South Atlantic. She seemed to want to head for the Falklands rather than coastwise to Rio Grande - and for the first time for forty years I was unable to make my ship go in the required direction. Speed had to be reduced to avoid pounding - the slamming of a ship's forefoot onto the sea which can cause untold structural damage if allowed. At five knots we were making more leeway than headway - rolling of course! - sliding sideways out to sea. Potted plants shot in all directions depositing soil and foliage freely across my carpet and furniture, but at first light on 14th July the cloud lifted and the chief officer, keeping the 4-8 watch, got good star sights. We were forty miles off course. As the sun rose in splendour over a tumultuous sea, wind and swell moderated to allow us to head in - only a day late - to find that, after all, we had to anchor for another 36 hours awaiting our berth. The tugs here had Lamport & Holt funnels and to an imaginative observer we must have resembled a duck with her brood of ducklings as we came alongside the quay. The chief engineer and I went down on to the quay to inspect the propeller, while a junior engineer turned it slowly from within on the electric turning gear. It pays to inspect your prop frequently on this coast as plenty of huge logs washed down the rivers present hidden hazards, floating awash as they do. But this time all was well - no sign of cracks or damage.

We left Brazil on 4th August with compliments ringing in our ears. The chief officer had run a particularly efficient cargo operation and we had committed none of those disastrously accidental crimes caused by pumping oil into the harbour or smoke from our funnel into Brazil's clear air. We counted our blessings and with our little ship fully laden, looking a picture of smartness, sailed for home.

Still rolling she crossed the Atlantic in 14 days, passing the curiously lop-sided mountain on the island of Fernando de Noronha, once a Brazilian penal settlement, now - we were told - a holiday paradise. Another sunny afternoon saw us passing through Gladstone Lock Entrance into the Royal Seaforth Dock on 18th August. We seemed to be the only working ship in the port. Our two remaining sisters, *Boswell* and *Bronte* were laid up - forlorn ships awaiting sale in a forlorn setting. We felt the docks somehow resembled England as it had been fifteen hundred years before, after the Romans left with elegant buildings and complex systems falling into ugly desuetude.

After a few more voyages *Browning* herself was sold to the Chinese, having filled her intended purpose of bridging the gap between the old, break bulk cargo ships and the fully containerised 'mode'.

I saw her last year at Shanghai, now named *Fortunate Star* and she must still have a good bosun - she looked immaculate!

[Adapted with the author's permission from 'Away to Sea: Life in Blue Star and Golden Line']

Lamport and Holt's *Boswell* at Swansea, about 1980. *[Des Harris, David Salisbury collection]*

A mate's notebook
Captain Bill Houghton Boreham

For anyone who had served as mate on container vessels, after an earlier career on general cargo vessels as I did myself, Lamport & Holts's SD14s provided a welcome return to conventional cargo stowage and derricks. Built as a stop-gap measure to bridge between the ageing general cargo ships then owned by the company and full containership operations, Lamport's *Bronte*, *Browning*, *Boswell* and *Belloc* were a pleasure to serve on in many ways.

Belloc, the ship on which I served the longest, was the last of the litter and as such was not fitted with the heated deep tanks that her other sisters had at the after end of number 3 hatch. Instead there was a single deep tank usable for dry cargo or ballast. The huge deep tank lid, when in the raised (open) position prevented the MacGregor maindeck covers being closed until the deep tank lid was closed: not an ideal situation when working cargo in showery weather.

Like her sisters, *Belloc* began life on the traditional Lamport & Holt liner service running from Glasgow, Liverpool and sometimes South Wales to a range of South American ports which included Recife, Salvador, Rio De Janeiro, Santos, Paranagua, Itajai, Rio Grande do Sul, Montevideo and Buenos Aires. Homeward, the vessels loaded for Liverpool and often Dublin with occasional calls at Belfast with Brazilian tobacco for Gallaghers' factory there.

The UK-South America lines at the time were trading under the abbreviation BHLR which stood for Blue Star, Houlder Brothers, Lamport & Holt and Royal Mail.

Cargoes homeward consisted of timber, tobacco and a range of manufactured goods from leatherware and shoes to cased engine blocks and Volkswagen parts. The vessels were fitted with container deck sockets on the hatch tops and main decks and containers could be stowed up from the lower holds in hatches 1, 2 and 4 through the 'tween decks with patent adjustable tomming bars to prevent the stow collapsing in heavy weather. 'Tween deck pontoons were stowed and lashed in the wings, often underneath the cargo.

Loading information for the mate came from the Santos office telex to the agent and consisted of all commodities with tonnage and quantity run together in endless lines and needed to be re-written to be comprehensible. Frequent changes kept the mate busy with a tape measure and a block of cargo allocation plans every day whilst in the southern ports.

Outward cargoes were often light due to the ban by the Brazilian government on the import of any product that was produced in Brazil itself. Scotch whisky and bagged barley were two exceptions, the latter for the Bramah Chop beer breweries. The number of containers increased almost voyage by voyage and various ingenious 'off slots' stowage positions had to be found with some very non-conventional derrick operations to get them into position. The 'tween deck wings continued to be stowed with general cargo which in turn had to be well lashed to prevent its almost pathological tendency to lurch into an empty hatch square. By the time the vessel left Brazil for the homeward run, the hatches were a mass of crossed container lashings and wires/bottle screws resembling a spider's web.

As the volumes of cargo carried dwindled on the outward voyages, the service itself became difficult to sustain and the *Belloc* was the first to be chartered out. One charter, with Hapag Lloyd to the Red Sea, was of short duration, but the ship was chartered to the Chilean CSAV Line for a number of voyages, trading between north continent and ports in Ecuador, Peru and Chile. It was on the latter run that I came to appreciate the flexibility of the ship's design.

On one occasion we had loaded copper bars in San Antonio and Valparaiso together with a number of containers, but were to proceed to Arica, in northern

Chile, to load 3,000 tons of bulk fishmeal for Brake on the Weser and proceed thence via Ilo (more copper bars) to Callao where we were to load 1,000 tons of zinc ore for Rotterdam. The trick was to finish loading 'on our marks' and on an even keel. After manual calculations on an almost hourly basis (there was no loading computer onboard) and several nightmares about excessive head trims and unacceptable bending moments, I was pleasantly surprised to find that the ship could not only take the planned loading with ease, but behaved like a lady on the return across the North Atlantic!

At a lighter draft, the SD14 floated on the water rather than in it and rolled viciously in bad weather. My son, then two years old, still has a slight nick on the edge of his left ear caused when he tottered against the cabin coffee table during a gale off the River Plate.

The Lamport SD14s carried a full UK crew and generally speaking they were a happy crowd. The reasonable overtime and the regular run to Liverpool (home port for many) probably helped. There was a pride in the appearance of the ship, which was 'painted round' once a voyage with a 'half day' for the bosun and the deck crew if the job was finished before Santos northbound. The Lamport white line around the hull was a bone of contention between Lamport's management and the superintendents, the latter seeing it as a 'waste of time and money'. It was, however, a subject close to the Liverpool bosun's heart and a call of 'watch out for the white line, John!' could usually be heard from the forecastle to the fender-toting shore gang as the ship entered Liverpool's Gladstone Lock at the end of another voyage from South America.

1388. LUC-NAM

L.R./I.M.O. Number 7614745
9,123g
6,342n
15,300d
Clark-Sulzer 4RND68M
22.9.1976: Contract signed by Transcontinental Carriers Ltd., Monrovia, Liberia (Kisinchand Chelleram (Hong Kong) Ltd., Hong Kong) and allocated yard number 1388.
6.10.1978: Contract sold to the Maritime Transportation Department

of the Socialist Republic of Vietnam, Haiphong and renumbered 1384 to conform with earlier negotiations, with the Transcontinental vessel re-numbered 1397. Contract number 1390 was then re-numbered 1388 and built as follows for Maritime Transport Department of the Socialist Republic of Vietnam.
30.8.1979: Keel laid.
18.12.1979: Launched.
20.6.1980: Completed for Vietnam Ocean Shipping Co., Haiphong, Vietnam. Vietnamese flag.

One of the few SD14s to have carried just one name throughout its life, *Luc Nam* anchored at Ko Sichang, 28th March 2001, not long before her last voyage. *[Nigel Jones]*

10.7.2001: Sank near Sandheads, Bay of Bengal after taking in water during a voyage from China to Haldia with 13,000 tonnes bagged fertiliser. The crew of 30 was evacuated.

1389. BOSWELL

L.R./I.M.O. Number 7614757
9,324g
6,150n
15,160d
Clark-Sulzer 4RND68M
14.5.1976: Order placed by
Balkermount Ltd. (Vestey Group),
London.
11.10.1976: Contract signed by
Boswell Shipping Co. Ltd. (Lamport
and Holt Line Ltd.), Liverpool.
1.11.1978: Keel laid.
11.4.1979: Launched.
2.7.1979: Completed. British flag.
8.1983: Sold to Chinese-Tanzanian
Joint Shipping Co., Dar-es-Salaam,
Tanzania and renamed SHUN YI
under the Chinese flag.
2002: Renamed XI RUN.
6.2004: Still listed by 'Lloyd's
Register' but existence in doubt as no
movements reported since 2001.

1390. TÔ-LICH

L.R./I.M.O. Number 7714769
9,123g
6,342n
15,300d
Hawthorn-Sulzer 4RND68M
21.10.1976: Contract signed by
Kourion Corporation Ltd., Monrovia,
Liberia (Alassia Steamship Co. Ltd.
(V. Hajioannou), Piraeus, Greece)
and allocated yard number 1390.
19.12.1978: Contract terminated.
6.10.1978: Sold to the Maritime
Transport Department of the Socialist
Republic of Vietnam, Haiphong.
Renumbered 1388 to conform with
earlier negotiations. Contract number
1392 was then renumbered 1390 and
built as follows for Maritime Transport
Department of Socialist Republic of
Vietnam, Haiphong.
19.9.1979: Keel laid.

Top: *Boswell*, like other Lamport and Holt SD14s,
permanently carried containers of spares,
prominently labelled with the ship's name. *[David
Whiteside collection]*

14.2.1980: Launched.
17.7.1980: Completed for Vietnam
Ocean Shipping Co., Haiphong,
Vietnam. Vietnamese flag.
2003: Reported to have been
renamed STURDY FALCON.
6.2004: Still listed by 'Lloyd's
Register' as TÔ-LICH.

Bottom: *Tô-Lich* anchored off Singapore in
December 1992. *[Simon Olsen, David Salisbury
collection]*

1391. BELLOC

L.R./I.M.O. Number 7614771
9,324g
6,150n
15,160d
Clark-Sulzer 4RND68M
14.5.1976: Order placed by
Gallduck Ltd. (Vestey Group),
London.
11.10.1976: Contract signed by
Belloc Shipping Co. Ltd. (Lamport
& Holt Line Ltd.), Liverpool.
11.1.1979: Keel laid.
10.5.1979: Launched.
1979: Vessel laid-up at Deptford
Quay, Sunderland until late 1979
whilst equipment was delivered for
modified cargo gear and hatch
covers.
1.2.1980: Completed. British flag.
11.1981: Sold to Montenegro
Overseas Navigation Ltd. Inc.,
Panama (Prekookeanska Plovidba,
Bar, Yugoslavia) and renamed PIVA.
1986: Transferred to
Prekookeanska Plovidba, Bar,
Yugoslavia.
1992: Sold to Bar Overseas Shipping Ltd. (Rigel Shipmanagement
Ltd.) (Lovcen Overseas Shipping
Ltd., managers), Valletta, Malta and
renamed RIO B.
1997: Transferred to Domino
Shipping Co. Ltd., Valletta, Malta
(Prekookeanska Plovidba, Bar).
2000: Sold to Yong Shun Shipping
Private Ltd., Singapore (Chinese-
Tanzanian Joint Shipping Co., Dar-
es-Sallam, Tanzania) and renamed
PANGANI.
6.2004: Still listed in 'Lloyd's
Register'.

1392.

No vessel built with this number
22.10.1976: Provisional order
placed by Seymour Shipping Ltd.,
London (Surrendra Overseas Ltd.,
Calcutta, India). Negotiations
discontinued.
6.10.1978 Sold to Maritime Transportation Department of Socialist
Republic of Vietnam, Haiphong.

Renumbered 1390 to conform with
earlier negotiations.

1393.

No vessel built with this number
Number allocated to vessel under
negotiation with C. Michalos and Co.
Ltd., London. Negotiations discontinued.

Top: *Belloc* in the River Mersey, 19th April 1980.
[Paul Boot]

Middle: As *Piva* in Swansea Bay on 5th August
1990. *[Nigel Jones]*

Bottom: This was the only one of the Lamport
and Holt SD14s not to go under the Chinese flag,
but there were Chinese connections, as she was
managed by a joint Chinese-Tanzanian company.
Seen as *Pangani* off Singapore in May 2002.
[Simon Olsen, David Salisbury collection]

1394. GOOD FAITH

L.R./I.M.O. Number 7640354
9,187g
6,424n
15,080d
Clark-Sulzer 4RND68M
24.12.1976: Contract signed by Westfalia Shipping Corporation, Singapore (Egon Oldendorff, Lübeck, West Germany). Subsequently transferred to Arabella Shipping Co. S.A., Panama then to Rhenania Shipping Corporation, Monrovia, Liberia (both Egon Oldendorff, Lübeck).
29.1.1979: Keel laid.
21.6.1979: Launched.
28.9.1979: Completed. Liberian flag.
1994: Transferred to Halfmoon Shipping Corporation, Monrovia (Egon Oldendorff, Lübeck).
1996: Transferred to Oldendorff Asia Private, Singapore (Egon Oldendorff, Lübeck).
1998: Renamed SECIL KIAAT.
7.2.1999: Renamed GOOD FAITH.
1999: Sold to Kudu Shipping Private Ltd. (ASP Ship Management Singapore), Singapore and renamed REEDBUCK.
2002: Renamed SPRINGBOK.
27.2.2003: In collision with Panamanian LPG carrier GAS ROMAN (44,690/1980) 16 miles north east of Horsburgh Lighthouse, Singapore whilst on a voyage from Durban to Malaysia with a cargo of timber products.
10.3.2003: Tugs separated the two vessels.
2003: Resumed trading as SPRING.
2.2004: Still in existence.

Opposite top: *Good Faith.* The last series of Oldendorff ships carried the largest heavy derricks yet fitted to the SD14s, with a lift of 100 tons. Somewhat surprisingly, they served number 4 hatch rather than the more accessible number 2. The former was served by a 30-ton derrick. *[Roy Fenton collection]*

Opposite middle: *Reedbuck* in the Maydon Channel, Durban. *[Trevor Jones]*

Opposite bottom: *Springbok*, also at Durban. *[Trevor Jones]*
This page: The effect of a 45,000 ton gas carrier on an SD14 hull: *Gas Roman* imbedded in

the *Springbok*, February 2003. One shudders to think of the outcome if the impact had been 20 feet further aft. Remarkably, the SD14 was repaired and returned to service as *Spring*. *[Both: Semco Towage and Salvage, courtesy Simon Smith]*

1395. FUTURE HOPE

L.R./I.M.O. Number 7640366
9,187g
6,424n
15,080d
Clark-Sulzer 4RND68M
24.12.1976: Contract signed by Westfalia Shipping Corporation, Singapore (Egon Oldendorff, Lübeck, West Germany). Subsequently transferred to Rhenania Shipping Corporation, Monrovia (Egon Oldendorff, Lübeck).
26.3.1979: Keel laid.
9.8.1979: Launched.
20.11.1979: Completed. Liberian flag.
1982: Transferred to Holsatia Shipping Corporation, Monrovia, Liberia (Egon Oldendorff, Lübeck).
1.1993: Sold to Crossdale Investment

Inc. (Reederei 'Nord' Klaus E. Oldendorff Ltd., manager.), Limassol, Cyprus. Intended to be renamed NORD HOPE, but not carried out.
26.1.1993: Beached one mile off Tomakomai West Breakwater after leaking water in numbers 2 and 4 holds whilst on a voyage from Dalian to Tomakomai in ballast.
15.3.1993: Reported sold to Fukada Kaji K.K. for scrapping.
24.5.1993: Refloated by her owner and moved to Tomato, East Tomakomai. Later declared a constructive total loss,
4.7.1993: Left Tomakomai as NORD HOPE under tow for Shanghai to be scrapped.
1995: Sold to Hainan Brother Maritime

Top: Oldendorff gave their flag-of-convenience ships meaningless names, *Future Hope* being amongst the worst. *[Roy Fenton collection]*

Bottom: *Globe Trader* at St. Nazaire in 1997. The posts at the ship's sides assisted the slewing of the 10-ton derricks which were rigged in a special arrangement specified by Oldendorff. Note also the 'verandah' behind the superstructure. *[Patrick Blaise, David Salisbury collection]*

Co. Ltd., Haikou, Hainan Island, People's Republic of China and returned to service as LIAN NONG.
1997: Renamed DONG FANG 66.
6.2004: Still listed by 'Lloyd's Register' but continued existence must be in doubt, as no movement reported since March 1995, and her class was withdrawn at owner's request in August 2002.

1396. GLOBE TRADER

L.R./I.M.O. Number 7640378
9,187g
6,424n
15,080d
Clark-Sulzer 4RND68M
24.12.1976: Contract signed by
Westfalia Shipping Corporation,
Singapore (Egon Oldendorff, Lübeck,
West Germany).
18.4.1979: Keel laid.
18.9.1979: Launched.
18.1.1980: Completed. Liberian flag.
1995: Transferred to Oldendorff Asia
Private Ltd., Singapore (Egon
Oldendorff, Lübeck).
1999: Sold to Impala Shipping
(Private) Ltd. (ASP Ship Management Singapore), Singapore.
2000: Renamed IMPALA.
20.2.2004: Sold to Taedonggang
Sonbak Co. Ltd., Pyongyang, North
Korea and renamed RYONG GANG 2
6.2004: Still listed by 'Lloyd's
Register'.

Above: *Impala*, formerly *Globe Trader*, on one of
her frequent visits to Durban. *[Trevor Jones,
David Salisbury collection]*

Below: *Darya Lok* at Durban about 1989.
[Trevor Jones, David Salisbury collection]

1397. DARYA LOK

L.R./I.M.O. Number 7628423
9,296g
6,143n
15,260d
Hawthorn-Sulzer 4RND68M
21.10.1976: Contract signed by
Paphos Corporation Ltd., Monrovia,
Liberia (Alassia Steamship Co. Ltd.
(V. Hajioannou), Piraeus, Greece).
19.12.1978: Contract terminated.
Contract number 1388 was then renumbered 1397 and built as follows
for Transcontinental Carriers Ltd.,
Monrovia, Liberia (Kischinchand
Chelleram (Hong Kong) Ltd.).
27.11.1979: Keel laid.
18.3.1990: Launched.
22.8.1980: Ownership transferred to

Citron Shipping Ltd. (Tolani Ltd.,
Bombay, India) (Kischinchand
Chelleram (Hong Kong) Ltd.,
managers), Hong Kong.
12.9.1980: Completed. Hong Kong flag.
2.1981: Transferred to Citron
Shipping Ltd. (Patt, Manfield and
Co. Ltd., managers), Hong Kong.
1.1982: Management transferred to
Kishinchand Chelleram (Hong Kong)
Ltd. Hong Kong.
1991: Sold to Hanbonn Shipping Ltd.,
Monrovia, Liberia and Hainan Haiyan
Shipping Enterprises Co. Ltd.,
Haikou, Hainan Province, People's
Republic of China (Hanbonn Ship-
ping Ltd., Hong Kong) and renamed
HANBONN BROTHER under the St.
Vincent flag.

1994: Owners became Far Full Ltd.,
Monrovia, Liberia (SCIT (Ship
Management) Ltd., Hong Kong,
managers) (Shougang Concord
International Transport Ltd., Hong
Kong) under the flag of St. Vincent
and the Grenadines.
1999: Sold to Eastern Bright Mari-
time Ltd., St. Vincent and the
Grenadines (Tianjin Eastern Ship-
ping Co. Ltd., Tianjin, People's
Republic of China) and renamed
EASTERN BRIGHT.
5.2001: Sold to Wonder Harvest
International Shipping Ltd., Hong
Kong.
2003: Renamed SHUN YUAN 6
6.2004: Still listed in 'Lloyd's
Register'.

1400. JADE II

L.R./I.M.O. Number 7822380
8,940g
6,455n
15,100d
Hawthorn-Sulzer 4RND68M
23.7.1978: Yard number allocated to
vessel agreed to be built for Royal
Nepal Shipping Corporation,
Kathmandu.
1979: Negotiations suspended and
19.7.1979: Contract signed with
Katerina I Compania Maritima S.A.,
Panama (Thomas H. Demseris,
Piraeus, Greece).
18.1.1980: Keel laid.
15.5.1980: Launched.
14.11.1980: Completed. Managers
Fereniki Lines S.A. (Thomas H.
Demseris), Piraeus, Greece. Greek flag.
1987: Sold to Ideal Maritime
Corporation, Manila, Phillipines
(Vroon B.V., Breskens, Netherlands)
and renamed SCOTIAN EXPRESS.
1990: Transferred to Scotian
International Navigation Inc.,
Valletta, Malta (Vroon B.V.,

Breskens).
1993: Sold to Vietnam Sea Transport
and Chartering Co., Ho Chi Minh
City, Vietnam and renamed SAIGON
3 under the Maltese flag.
1995: Transferred to Lunar Trading
Corporation, Majuro, Marshall
Islands (Vietnam Sea Transport and
Chartering Co., Ho Chi Minh City).
6.2004: Still listed by 'Lloyd's
Register'.

Top: *Jade II* as *Scotian Express* at Singapore1992
in Vroon ownership, but not their funnel colours.
[Simon Olsen, David Salisbury collection]

Middle: *Jade II* in the Kiel Canal. *[Michael Green]*

1401. JADE III

L.R./I.M.O. Number 7628411
8,940g
6,455n
15,100d
Clark-Hawthorn Sulzer 4RND68M
21.10.1976: Contract signed by Soloi
Corporation Ltd., Monrovia, Liberia
(Alassia Steamship Co. Ltd. (V.
Hajioannou), Piraeus, Greece).
19.12.1978: Contract terminated.
19.7.1979: Contract signed with
Katerina Delta Maritima S.A., Panama
(Thomas H. Demseris, Piraeus).
21.1.1980: Keel laid.

12.6.1980: Launched.
12.12.1980: Completed. Managers
Fereniki Lines S.A. (Thomas H.
Demseris), Piraeus. Greek flag.
1987: Sold to Ideal Maritime Corporation,
Manila, Phillipines (Vroon B.V,
Breskens, Netherlands) and renamed
SCANDINAVIAN EXPRESS.
1996: Sold to November International
Navigation, Monrovia, Liberia (Vroon
B.V, Breskens) and renamed SEAWAY
under the Vanuatu flag.
6.9.1997: Attacked by Nigerian Air
Force plane whilst discharging rice at
Freetown, Sierra Leone. Two bombs

reported to have hit forward part of
ship. Nigerians claimed vessel was
breaking an economic embargo.
1.1998: Reported at Rostock.
1998: Sold to Ship Traders International
Inc., Monrovia, Liberia (Vietnam Sea
Transport and Chartering Co., Ho
Chi Minh City, Vietnam) and
renamed SAIGON 5 under the
Vanuatu flag.
26.4.2002: Class suspended, surveys
overdue.
6.2004: Still listed by 'Lloyd's
Register'.

Opposite bottom: *Jade III* in her original owner's colours at Durban about 1993. *[Trevor Jones, David Salisbury collection]*

Above: *Jade III* as *Scandinavian Express* in Vroon colours at Montreal on 9th June 1992. *[Marc Piche, David Salisbury collection]*

Below: *Saigon 5* with an interesting variant on the standard Vietnamese funnel colours. *[Russell Priest]*

95

1403. HUN JIANG

L.R./I.M.O. Number 8000159
9,296g
6,153n
15,200d
Clark-Hawthorn Sulzer 4RND68M
1979: Ship number allocated to contract being negotiated with Egyptian Navigation Company, Alexandria. Negotiations discontinued.
2.11.1979: Ship number allocated to vessel to be built against an agreement negotiated with Mahonia Shipping Corporation, Monrovia (Eureka Shipping G.m.b.H., Hamburg, West Germany).
2.1980: Negotiations discontinued.
25.2.1980: Ship number allocated to vessel to be built against an agreement negotiated with China Merchants Steam Navigation Co. Ltd., Hong Kong.
21.5.1980: Contract signed.
12.6.1980: Keel laid.
9.10.1980: Launched.
6.2.1981: Completed for Guangzhou Ocean Shipping Company (China Ocean Shipping Company), Guangzhou, People's Republic of China. Chinese flag.
6.2004: Still listed by 'Lloyd's Register'.

1404/1405/1406.

 No vessels built with these numbers.
1979: Numbers allocated to SD14 vessels negotiating with Egyptian Navigation Company, Alexandria. Negotiations discontinued.

SD18 cargo vessel

1407. MURREE

L.R./I.M.O. Number 8000161
11,940/7,923g
7,170/4,724n
18,050d
Clark-Hawthorn Sulzer 6RND68M
1979: Ordered by the Pakistan National Shipping Corporation, Karachi, Pakistan.
19.6.1980: Keel laid.
18.12.1980: Launched.
22.4.1981: Completed. Pakistan flag.

Hun Jiang in the Welland Canal during May 1994. *[Dave Kohl, David Salisbury collection].*

28.10.1989: Abandoned and sank 20 miles off Devon in position 49.58 north by 03.14 west after containers broke loose in hurricane-force winds, causing damage which allowed water to enter her forward hold. She was on a voyage from Antwerp and London to Karachi with containers. Her crew was rescued.

Sailing from the Manchester Ship Canal in April 1983 was the unfortunate *Murree*, which foundered off Devon in 1989. *[Paul Boot]*

96

SD18 cargo vessel

1408. **KAGHAN**
L.R./I.M.O. Number 8000173
11,940/7,923g
7,179/4,740n
18,050d
Clark-Hawthorn Sulzer 6RND68M
1979: Ordered by the Pakistan
National Shipping Corporation,

Karachi, Pakistan.
17.10.1980: Keel laid.
20.3.1981: Launched.
15.7.1981: Completed. Pakistan
flag.
20.1.2004: Arrived Gadani Beach to
be demolished, having been laid up
at Karachi since October 2003.

Top: *Murree* on trials. The SD18s had a complete outfit of Velle swinging derricks, four of 25-tonne and two of 35 tonne. The two types were capable of being linked with a lifting boom to handle 55-tonne loads. The hulls were double-skinned, and with ballast tanks at the side this made box-shaped holds. The twin hatches gave access to virtually the entire hold, so containers could be simply dropped in. *[Airfotos, John Lingwood collection]*

Bottom: *Kaghan* passes Zeedorp on the Scheldt, 20th July 1996. *[David Salisbury]*

SD18 cargo vessel

1409. **AYUBIA**

L.R./I.M.O. Number 8000185
11,940/7,923g
7,179/4,740n
18,050d
Clark-Hawthorn Sulzer 6RND68M
1979: Ordered by the Pakistan
National Shipping Corporation,
Karachi, Pakistan.
23.12.1980: Keel laid.
19.6.1981: Launched.
10.11.1981: Completed. Pakistan
flag.
13.11.2000: Laid up at Karachi.
5.2001: Arrived at Gadani Beach to
be broken up by Dewan Scrap
(Private) Ltd., Pakistan.

1414. **YUAN JIANG**

L.R./I.M.O. Number 80011768
9,296g
6,143n
15,200d
Clark-Hawthorn Sulzer 4RND68M
25.2.1980: Agreement signed with
China Merchants Steam Navigation
Co. Ltd., Hong Kong.
21.5.1980: Contract signed.
9.10.1980: Keel laid.
6.2.1981: Launched.
21.5.1981: Completed for
Guangzhou Ocean Shipping Company (China Ocean Shipping Company), Guangzhou, People's Republic of China. Chinese flag.
6.2004: Still listed by 'Lloyd's
Register'.

This page top: *Ayubia* in Karachi outer
anchorage on Christmas Day, 2000. *[Nigel
Jones]*

Opposite top: *United Enterprise* at Vancouver in
July 1984. *[Don Brown, David Salisbury
collection]*

Opposite bottom: A well-kept *Fareast Beauty* at
Singapore on 16th November 1988. For once
both registers and whoever painted the name on
her stern agree that the first element of her name
should be one word. Note the 'cages' at the top
of the derrick posts, to enable crew to handle
cargo blocks in safety. *[Simon Olsen, David
Salisbury collection]*

This page bottom: *Yuan Jiang* off Singapore, 20th
March 1989. *[Simon Olsen, Roy Kittle collection]*

1415. **UNITED ENTERPRISE**

L.R./I.M.O. Number 8102086
9,282g
6,128n
15,171d
Clark-Hawthorn Sulzer 4RND68M
22.5.1980: Ship number allocated to contract signed for B26 bulk carrier with Blantyre Shipping Corporation, Panama (Wheelock, Marden Chartering Ltd., Hong Kong.).
7.1980: Negotiations terminated.
12.1980: Ship number re-allocated to SD14 negotiating with International United Shipping and Investment Co. Ltd. (World Wide (Shipping) Ltd.,

Hong Kong, a joint venture between World Wide and the People's Republic of China.
14.4.1981: Contract signed with World Clipper Shipping Ltd. (World Wide Shipping Agency Ltd.), Hong Kong.
23.7.1981: Keel laid.
27.11.1981: Launched.
8.3.1982: Completed. Hong Kong flag.
1983: Managers became International United Shipping and Investment Co. Ltd., Hong Kong.
1987: Sold to Trade Fair Maritime Corporation, Monrovia, Liberia (Parakou Shipping Ltd., Hong Kong) and renamed TRADE FAIR.

1988: Sold to Fareast Beauty Maritime Inc., Monrovia, Liberia (Wah Tung Shipping Agency Ltd., Hong Kong) and renamed FAREAST BEAUTY.
1992: Sold to Brightway Navigation Inc., Monrovia, Liberia (Vietnam Sea Transport and Chartering Co., Ho Chi Minh City, Vietnam) (Government of the Socialist Republic of Vietnam) and renamed FAR EAST under the Bahamas flag.
2000: Transferred to Vietnam Sea Transport and Chartering Co., Ho Chi Minh City.
1.12.2001: Class suspended at owner's request.
6.2004: Still listed by 'Lloyd's Register'.

1416. **UNITED EFFORT**

L.R./I.M.O. Number 8102098
9,282g
6,128n
15,175d
Clark-Hawthorn Sulzer 4RND68M
22.5.1980: Ship number allocated to contract signed for B26 bulk carrier with Pimbra Shipping Corporation, Panama (Wheelock, Marden Chartering Ltd., Hong Kong).
7.1980: Negotiations terminated.
12.1980: Ship number re-allocated to SD14 negotiating with International United Shipping & Investment Co. Ltd., Hong Kong (World Wide (Shipping) Ltd., Hong Kong, a joint venture between World Wide and the People's Republic of China.

14.4.1981: Contract signed with World Denver Shipping Ltd. (World Wide Shipping Agency Ltd.), Hong Kong.
27.11.1981: Keel laid.
12.3.1982: Launch postponed due to high winds. Named by Prime Minister Margaret Thatcher.
16.3.1982: Launched.
22.6.1982: Completed. Hong Kong flag.
1983: Managers became International United Shipping and Investment Co. Ltd., Hong Kong.
1987: Sold to Atlantic Light Corporation, Panama (Kent Trading Corporation, Piraeus, Greece) and renamed ATLANTIC III.
13.2.1990: Involved in incident off

Malta when refused permission to enter harbour. Vessel had loaded military equipment, including ammunition, at Aqaba six months previously for discharge in Lebanon and had sailed around the Eastern Mediterranean during this time awaiting an opportunity to unload. Crew had not been paid and provisions, fuel and stores had been consumed

Top: *United Effort* at Vancouver, January 1984. *[Don Brown, David Salisbury collection]*

Bottom: *Atlantic III* passing Terneuzen inward bound for Antwerp in April 1988. *[David Salisbury]*

but no port would grant access due to the dangerous cargo. Vessel eventually allowed to berth at Jounieh, Lebanon around 26.2.1990.
1990: Transferred to New Forum Marine Ltd., Limassol, Cyprus (Kent Trading Corporation, Piraeus, Greece) and renamed IVORY.
1990: Renamed IVORY K.
26.8.1990: Abandoned and sank off Porto Amboin in position 10.24 south by 11.31 east during a loaded voyage from Pointe Noire, Congo to Port Louis, Mauritius after water entered the engine room.

1417. UNITED DRIVE
L.R./I.M.O. Number 8102103
9,282g
6,128n
15,175d
Clark-Hawthorn Sulzer 4RND68M
6.1980: Ship number allocated to B26 bulk carrier negotiating with Sally Shipping Ltd., Panama (Nobleza Naviera S.A., Panama) (Universal Chartering Corporation, New York, USA).
7.1980: Negotiations terminated.
7.7.1980: Ship number allocated to contract signed for SD14 with Pharaonic Shipping Company (SAE), Alexandria, Egypt.
12.1980: Negotiations terminated.
12.1980: Ship number re-allocated to SD14 negotiating with International United Shipping and Investment Co. Ltd. (World Wide (Shipping) Ltd., Hong Kong) a joint venture between World Wide and the People's

Republic of China.
14.4.1981: Contract signed with World Hector Shipping Ltd. (World Wide Shipping Agency Ltd., Hong Kong).
23.11.1961: Keel laid.
6.4.1982: Launched by HRH Princess Margaret.
14.7.1982: Completed. Hong Kong flag.
1983: Managers became International United Shipping and Investment Co. Ltd., Hong Kong.
1987: Sold to Atlantic Winner Corporation, Panama (Kent Trading Corporation, Piraeus, Greece) and renamed ATLANTIC IV.
1989: Sold to Pal Bay Maritime Co. Ltd. (Square Ltd.), Piraeus and renamed PAL BAY.
1994: Sold to Manisti Shipping Co. Ltd., Limassol, Cyprus (Evangelos P. Nomikos Corporation, Piraeus) and renamed PETRA WAVE.
1995: Management transferred to Moss Marine Management S.A., Piraeus, Greece.
1996: Renamed CHIAN WAVE.
1997: Management transferred to Levant Maritime International.
1999: Sold to Chang Shun Shipping (Private) Ltd., Singapore (Chinese-Tanzanian Joint Shipping Co., Dar-es-Salaam, Tanzania) and renamed CHANG PING.
5.2004: Still listed by 'Lloyd's Register'.

Above: *United Drive* fitting out at Southwick in the summer of 1982. Ships launched from the covered berths had their sterns pointing downriver, and were berthed starboard side to the fitting out quay. *[Harold Appleyard]*

Below: *United Drive* at Vancouver in March 1985. *[Don Brown, David Salisbury collection]*

101

Above: *United Spirit. [V.H. Young and L.A. Sawyer collection]*

Below: *Naval Lady*. The 'NS' on her funnel stands for 'Nikolakis Shipping.' *[David Whiteside collection]*

1418. **UNITED SPIRIT**

L.R./I.M.O. Number 8102115
9,282g
6,128n
15,175d
Clark-Hawthorn Sulzer 4RND68M
6.1980: Ship number allocated to B26 bulk carrier negotiating with Lao Shipping Co. Inc. (Nobleza Naviera S.A.), Panama (Universal Chartering Corporation, New York, USA).
7.1980: Negotiations terminated.
7.7.1980: Ship number allocated to contract signed for SD14 with Pharaonic Shipping Company (SAE), Alexandria, Egypt.
12.1980: Negotiations terminated.
12.1980: Ship number re-allocated to SD14 negotiating with International United Shipping and Investment Co. Ltd., Hong Kong, (World Wide (Shipping) Ltd., Hong Kong, a joint venture between World Wide and the People's Republic of China.
14.4.1981: Contract signed with World Select Shipping Ltd. (World Wide Shipping Agency Ltd.), Hong Kong).
12.2.1982: Keel laid.
24.5.1982: Launched.
3.9.1982: Completed. Hong Kong flag.
1983: Managers became International United Shipping and Investment Co. Ltd., Hong Kong.
1987: Sold to Trade Freedom Maritime Corporation, Monrovia, Liberia (Parakou Shipping Ltd., Hong Kong) and renamed TRADE FREEDOM
1988: Sold to Fareast Cheer Maritime Inc., Monrovia, Liberia (Wah Tung Shipping Agency Co. Ltd., Hong Kong) and renamed FAREAST CHEER.
1991: Transferred to Sea Coral Marine S.A., Panama (Wah Tung Shipping Agency Co. Ltd., Hong Kong) and renamed SEA CORAL.
1995: Sold to Naval Lady Marine Ltd., Valletta, Malta (Nikolakis Shipping S.A., Athens, Greece) and renamed NAVAL LADY.
2001: Sold to Chang Shun Shipping (Private) Ltd., Singapore (Chinese-Tanzanian Joint Shipping Co., Dar-es-Salaam, Tanzania) and renamed CHAO YANG.
2003: Sold to Government of the People's Republic of Korea, Pyongyang, North Korea and re-named HYANG RO BONG.
5.2004: Still listed by 'Lloyd's Register'.

Opposite top: *Sunderland Venture*, the last Sunderland-built SD14, ran under this name for less than a year. *[Ships in Focus collection]*

Opposite middle: Sunderland Venture awaiting launch. *[Michael Green]*

Opposite bottom: A wintry shot: *Odelis*, now officially Cuban owned, photographed from Battery Point, Portishead on 18th February 2000. *[Nigel Jones]*

1426. **SUNDERLAND VENTURE**

Last SD14 to be launched at Sunderland; the 126th from there and the 207th worldwide.

L.R./I.M.O. Number 8207953
8,996g
6,238n
15,025d
Clark-Hawthorn Sulzer 5RLB56.
28.5.1981: Contract signed with Wynmouth Ltd. (Wah Kwong and Co. (Hong Kong) Ltd.), Hong Kong.
20.5.1983: Keel laid.
4.11.1983: Vessel named. Launch delayed because of unavailability of a fitting out berth.
17.11.1983: Launched.

1.1984: Flag changed to Panama.
15.2.1984: Completed for Shipley Shipping Corporation, Panama (Wah Kwong Shipping Agency Co. Ltd., Hong Kong). Panama flag.
4.4.1985: Bareboat chartered to Empresa Navegacion Mambisa, Havana, Cuba and renamed ROSE ISLANDS, remaining under the Panama flag.
1992: Management transferred to Venture Shipping (Managers) Inc.
1999: Sold to Rosario Shipping Inc, Panama (Naviera Poseidon, Havana, Cuba) and renamed ODELIS.
15.5.2002: Class suspended and later advertised for sale for $1.8m at Havana.
11.2004: Reported sold to breakers.

Vessels built by Bartram and Sons Ltd., South Dock, Sunderland

410. MIMIS N. PAPALIOS

L.R./I.M.O. Number 6803117
9,069g
6,133n
15,363d
Vickers-Sulzer 5RD68
1966: Ordered by Deko Trading S.A., Panama (Onassis Group).
1967: Negotiations cancelled.
7.6.1967: Keel laid.
1.12.1967: Launched for Marguardia Compania Naviera S.A., Panama (Aegis Shipping Co. Ltd. (N.D. Papalios), Athens, Greece).
15.2.1968: Completed. Greek flag.
1970: Transferred to Agenor Shipping Co. Ltd., Famagusta, Cyprus (Aegis Shipping Co. Ltd. (N.D. Papalios), Athens).
1976: Transferred to Olympos Shipping Enterprises, Monrovia, Liberia (Aegis Shipping Co. Ltd. (N.D. Papalios), Piraeus) under the Greek flag.
1976: Transferred to Parnis Shipping Enterprises Co. Ltd., Monrovia, Liberia (Aegis Shipping Co. Ltd. (N.D. Papalios), Athens).

6.1980: Sold to Good Sun Navigation Inc., Panama (Good Faith Shipping Co. S.A. (Nikolaos Frangos and Nicholas G. Moundreas), Piraeus) and renamed GOOD SUN under the Greek flag.
1984: Transferred to Wave Crest Shipping S.A., Panama (Good Faith Shipping Co. S.A. (Nikolaos Frangos and Nicholas G. Moundreas), Piraeus) and renamed WAVE CREST. The total sale price for ships 410, 411, 854, and 855 was $13.5m.
20.12.1994: Arrived Alang.
1.1.1995: Beached and subsequently scrapped at Alang by Sanjay Trade Corporation.

411. GEORGE N. PAPALIOS

L.R./I.M.O. Number 6811164
9,071g
6,136n
15,363d
Vickers-Sulzer 5RD68
1966: Ordered by Deko Trading S.A., Panama (Onassis Group).
1967: Negotiations cancelled.

23.8.1967: Keel laid.
29.2.1968: Launched for Marguardia Compania Naviera S.A., Panama (Aegis Shipping Co. Ltd. (N.D. Papalios), Athens, Greece).
30.4.1968: Completed. Greek flag.
1969: Transferred to Agenor Shipping Co. Ltd., Famagusta, Cyprus (Aegis Shipping Co. Ltd. (N.D. Papalios), Athens).
1975: Transferred to Olympos Shipping Enterprises, Monrovia, Liberia (Aegis Shipping Co. Ltd. (N.D. Papalios), Athens) under the Greek flag.
6.1980: Sold to Good Lord Inc., Panama (Good Faith Shipping Co S.A. (Nikolaos Frangos and Nicholas G. Moundreas), Piraeus) and renamed GOOD LORD under the Greek flag.
25.10.1984: Struck by a missile in the Khor Musa Channel whilst on a voyage from Banda Khomeini, Iran. Later that month arrived Bushire and declared a constructive total loss. Later towed to Karachi for demolition under the name WEHSIEN, Cyprus flag.
29.4.1985: Rajab Ali & Co. began demolition at Gadani Beach.

412.

No ship built with this number

1966: Ordered by Deko Trading S.A., Panama (Onassis Group).
1967: Negotiations cancelled.
1967: Option taken up by Aegis Shipping Co. Ltd., Piraeus but not finalised. Instead the contract was placed by mutual agreement with Hellenic Shipyards following signing of a licensing agreement, in order to get that yard's participation in the SD14 programme under way.

413. CAPETAN GIANNIS

L.R./I.M.O. Number 6822010
9,031g
6,337n
15,230d
Clark-Sulzer 5RD68
1966: Ordered by Deko Trading S.A., Panama (Onassis Group).
1967: Negotiations cancelled.
25.1.1968: Keel laid.
4.1968: Contract signed with Alafouzos Shipping Co. Ltd., Piraeus, Greece (Glafki Shipping Co. S.A. (A. Alafouzos) Athens, Greece).

9.7.1968: Launched.
30.9.1968: Completed. Greek flag.
1979: Sold to Evelpis Shipping Corporation, Monrovia, Liberia (Sigma Shipping Ltd. (A.S. Lemos, D.G. and G.D. Skinitis), London) and renamed AGIA SKEPI under the Greek flag.
23.2.1984-1.1988: Laid up at Piraeus.
1990: Sold to Greencoast Shipping and Trading Inc. (Hussein Kamel Aly Hassan Said Fanaki), Alexandria, Egypt and renamed GIGI F under the Panama flag.
1992: Renamed FAROS.
22.7.1993: Arrived Alang to be broken up by Kwality Steel Supplies.

Opposite top: Bartram's first SD14, *Mimis N. Papalios*, New Waterway on 2nd May 1974. *[Roy Kittle]*

Opposite bottom: Although founded in 1949, it was not until the early sixties that Aegis Shipping began a rapid expansion by acquiring a varied collection of second hand cargo liners, tramps and tankers. *Mimis N. Papalios* and *George N. Papalios*, the latter seen here at Cape Town, were the company's first newbuildings. *[Ken White, Roy Kittle collection]*

This page top: *Capetan Giannis* on the New Waterway, 30th May 1964. She was the first SD14 to mount a heavy derrick, of 30-tons capacity at number 2 hatch. *[Paul Boot]*

This page bottom: *Agia Skepi*. *[David Whiteside collection]*

414. ITHAKI

L.R./I.M.O. Number 6828193
9,066g
6,378n
15,251d
Clark-Sulzer 5RD68
29.4.1968: Keel laid.
24.9.1968: Launched for Ulysses Shipping Enterprises Special Shipping S.A., Piraeus, Greece (N. and J. Vlassopulos Ltd., London).
2.12.1968: Completed. Greek flag.
2.1981: Sold to Baruca (Panama) S.A., Panama (Bradford Shipping Inc. (J. Apostolakis and C. Miral), New York, USA) for $4.25m and renamed DANIELLA.
1985: Sold to Heliopolis Shipping Co. Ltd. (Cargo Carriers Co. Ltd.), Piraeus for $535,000 and renamed HELIOPOLIS under the Maltese flag.
1986: Transferred to Victoria Navigation Co. Ltd., Valletta, Malta (Cargo Carriers Co. Ltd., Piraeus) and renamed PALAWAN under the Philippine flag.
10.5.1986: Arrived Gadani Beach for demolition by Jamal Enterprises.

Top: Vlassopoulos, one of the longest-established London-Greeks, helped to ensure a good start to the SD14 programme by ordering four on behalf of his clients beginning with *Ithaki*, photographed on the New Waterway in 1974. She was the first SD14 with winch platforms, and the first to be broken up. *[John Phillips, David Salisbury collection]*

Middle: *Ithaki* is seen again on the New Waterway in 1974 in dramatic light.*[Paul Boot]*
Bottom: *Daniella. [Roy Fenton collection]*

415. CAPETAN MANOLIS

L.R./I.M.O. Number 6911067
9,044g
6,361n
15,291d
Clark-Sulzer 5RD68
14.10.1968: Keel laid.
17.2.1969: Launched for Sea Eagle
Shipping Co. Ltd. (Glafki Shipping
Company S.A. (A. Alafouzos)),
Athens, Greece as CAPETAN
MANOLIS.
25.4.1969: Completed. Greek flag,
registered at Piraeus.
1973: Management transferred to
Mornos Shipping Co., Panama (G.
Hasapodimos, Athens) remaining under
the Greek flag.
1978: Sold to Thakur Shipping Co.
Ltd., Bombay, India and renamed
VARUNA KACHHAPI.
5.1985 - 7.1985: Laid up at Bombay.
6.7.1988: Delivered to Bombay
shipbreakers, and gradually broken up.
Remains were still visible in December
1999, but had gone by March 2003.

Top: *Daniella*, St. Lawrence Seaway, 20th August
1982. *[René Beauchamp, David Salisbury collection]*

Middle: *Capetan Manolis* at Avonmouth, May 1971.
[Des Harris, David Salisbury collection]

Bottom: The remains of *Varuna Kachhapi*, ex *Capetan
Manolis*, at Mumbai, 29th December 1999. Her
hull looks very distorted, perhaps as the result of
an accident. It seems unlikely that, as reported,
she had been serving as a storage hulk. *[Nigel
Jones]*

416. CORFU ISLAND

L.R./I.M.O. Number 6904492
9,045g
6,225n
15,352d
Clark-Sulzer 5RD68
19.7.1968: Keel laid.
5.12.1968: Launched for Naxos
Shipping Corporation, Monrovia
(Transmarine Shipping Agencies Ltd.,
London) (Thrasybule Voyazides,
Athens, Greece).
14.2.1969: Completed. Liberian flag.
1974: Sold to Loyalty Shipping Co.
S.A., Panama (Navarino Shipping and
Transport Co. (M.P Tsikopoulos),
Piraeus, Greece) and renamed
LOYALTY under the Greek flag.
24.9.1980: Arrived Basrah, from Duluth,
USA with severe missile damage
sustained during the Iran/Iraq conflict and
subsequently trapped in port.
13.8.1993: Towed from Basrah and
sold to Pakistani shipbreakers.
22.9.1993: Arrived Gadani Beach.
23.9.1993: Demolition commenced at
Gadani Beach by Iqbal Javed and Co.

417. SKLERION

L.R./I.M.O. Number 6915910
9,057g
6,378n
15,246d
Clark-Sulzer 5RD68
10.12.1968: Keel laid.
15.4.1969: Launched for Cardamylian
Shipping Company Ltd. (N. and J.
Vlassopoulos Ltd., London), Piraeus,
Greece.
20.2.1969: Completed for Kardamylian
Special Shipping Co. Ltd. (N.C.
Halkias, Piraeus) (N. and J.
Vlassopoulos Ltd., London, managers).
Greek flag.
1978: Transferred to Baronet Compania
Naviera S.A., Panama (S.C. Halkias,
Piraeus) (Kardamylian Development
Corporation S.A. (Stylianos C. and
Nicholas S. Halkias), Piraeus, managers)
under the Greek flag.
1983: Reported to have been renamed
TEXEL LIGHT, but then reverted to
SKLERION.
1984: Reported class withdrawn due to
defects.

Top: *Corfu Island* in Canadian waters, 1st
September 1970. *[Roy Kittle collection]*

Bottom: *Sklerion*, with her multi-coloured hull, and
Halkias funnel colours, on the New Waterway in
August 1976. *[David Salisbury]*

Opposite top: Although 20 years old, the Egyptian
Salem Nine looks in superb external condition. *[Roy
Fenton collection]*

1985: Sold to Maunland Navigation
Inc., Manila, Phillipines (Vroon B.V.,
Bresken, Netherlands) for $500,000
and renamed SAMAR EXPRESS.
1988: Sold to Samatour Shipping and
Export Co. (Abdel Razzak Salem),
Alexandria, Egypt and renamed
SALEM NINE.
29.4.1994: Arrived Chittagong Roads
and later beached for breaking up.
5.1994: Demolition commenced by
Kabir Steel Ltd.

418. **PRODROMOS**

L.R./I.M.O. Number 6924038
9,073g
6,374n
15,266d
Clark-Sulzer 5RD68
24.2.1979: Keel laid.
30.5.1969: Launched for Sampsa
Compania Naviera S.A., Panama
(M.J. Lemos Co. Ltd., London) as
PRODROMOS.
19.9.1969: Completed. Greek flag.
1971: Sold to Mardinamico
Compania Naviera S.A., Panama
(Elpisaga Compania Naviera,
Piraeus, Greece) (M.J. Lemos Co.
Ltd., London) and renamed
IOANNIS S under the Greek flag.

1975: Sold to North Seal S.A.,
Panama (Kardamylian Development
Corporation S.A. (Stylianos C. and
Nicholas S. Halkias), Piraeus,
managers) and renamed JUANITA
HALKIAS under the Greek flag.
1982: Renamed RECALADA
LIGHT under the Panama flag.
1985: Sold to Weekend Navigation
Ltd., Nicosia, Cyprus (Lagousses
Shipping Co. S.A. (Argyrios and
Efstratios Saliarelis), Piraeus) and
renamed SAFARI III.
1987: Sold to Chi Hsiang Steel
Enterprises.
25.5.1987: Arrived Kaohsiung.
2.6.1987: Demolition commenced.

*Yard number 418 was originally
allocated to a 23,000d bulk carrier
for Oregon Steamship Co. Ltd.,
London. Following merger with
Austin and Pickersgill Ltd., this
contract was transferred to their
yard at Southwick and was built as
yard number 863, and yard number
418 was re-allocated as above.*

Below: *Juanita Halkias.* Note the tie bars on the aftermost set of kingposts, a feature almost certainly unique amongst SD14s. *[Trevor Jones]*

419. VIRTUS

L.R./I.M.O. Number 6928254
8,938g
6,224n
15,266d
Hawthorn-Sulzer 5RD68
6.6.1969: Keel laid.
27.8.1969: Launched for
International Navigation
Corporation, Monrovia., Liberia
(Tidewater Commercial Co. Inc.,
Baltimore, USA) (Industria
Armamento Societa per Azioni
(Albert Ravano), Genoa, Italy,

managers) as VIRTUS.
6.11.1969: Completed. Liberian flag.
1981: Sold to Intermarine Inc., New
York for $5m and renamed
POMONA under the Panama flag.
1981: Sold to Soto Grande Shipping
Corporation S.A., Panama (Y.C.
Cheng, Hamilton, Bermuda).
1985: Sold to New Seas Navigation
Corporation (Government of the
People's Republic of China),
Shanghai, People's Republic of
China and renamed XIN HAI TENG.
7.2004: Still listed in Lloyd's

Top: *Virtus* at Vancouver, 12th June 1971. *[Don Brown]*

Bottom: *Pomona* sails from Cape Town. As she is owned in the USA, it is more likely she is named after the town in California than the docks in Manchester. *[Trevor Jones]*

Register but vessel's continued existence must be in doubt, as no movement reported since June 1986 and her Chinese Registration closed in 1991.

420. SAINT FRANCOIS

L.R./I.M.O. Number 7002631

	1978:
9,107g	12,390g
6,151n	8,689n
15,241d	17,693d

1978: 167.70 (LBP) x 20.43 x 11.74m/ 8.486 metres

Hawthorn-Sulzer 6RD68

26.6.1969: Keel laid.

23.10.1969: Launched for Compagnie de Navigation Denis Frères, Paris, France.

18.2.1970: Completed. French flag.

1978: Lengthened and converted into 410teu container vessel by Estaleiros

Navals de Lisboa (Lisnave), Lisbon, Portugal.

1984: Sold to Sud Pacifique Navigation S.A. (Societe Francaise de Navigation S.a.r.L.), Noumea, New Caledonia and renamed CAPITAINE KERMADEC III under the French flag, registered at Matu Utu.

1987: Sold to Thoresen and Co. (Bangkok) Ltd., Bangkok, Thailand (Arne Teigen, Oslo, Norway) and renamed HAI HING.

28.9.1994: Sold to Ashwin Corporation and anchored off Alang.

7.10.1994: Beached for demolition.

19.10.1994: Demolition began.

Before and after photographs taken on the New Waterway show the alterations made when *Saint Francois* was lengthened and converted for container carrying in 1978. Even in her original configuration, she carried a substantial array of cargo gear with 22-ton Velle derricks at numbers 3 and 4 hatches, conventional derricks at numbers 1, 2, 4 and 5, and a 30-ton derrick at number 2. A pair of electric cranes also served numbers 2 and 3 hatches. On conversion a 25-ton container crane was added, one of the original 5-ton cranes was moved ahead of number 1 hatch. The superstructure was raised by an additional deck and a new bridge added. *[Top: Roy Kittle; bottom: Paul Boot, 13th May 1982]*

111

421. **SEA MOON**

L.R./I.M.O. Number 7006156
9,085g
6,173n
15,317d
Hawthorn-Sulzer 5RD68
16.9.1969: Keel laid.
23.12.1969: Launched for Vergocean Steamship Co. Ltd., London (Valiant Steamship Co. Ltd. (George Vergottis), London) as SEA MOON.
3.1970: Completed. British flag.
1977: Managers became Valiant Shipping Co. (London) Ltd.
1978: Transferred to Myrtos Shipping Co. Ltd., Monrovia, Liberia (Valiant Shipping Co. (London) Ltd. (George Vergottis), London) and

renamed MYRTOS under the Greek flag.
1986: Reported sold (together with ships 862/867) to Greek owners with name ANDRIOS, but this may have been only a temporary arrangement for one-day only before name AGIOS GERASSIMOS was taken up by Amelia Maritime Inc., Monrovia, Liberia (Flandermar Shipping Co. S.A. (D. and G. Agoudimos and J. Meletis), Piraeus, Greece) under the Greek flag.
1988: Transferred to Atlantic Shipping Inc., Valletta, Malta (Flanmare Shipping Inc. (D. Agoudimos), Piraeus).
1993: Transferred to Marnie

Top: George Vergottis was another of the old school of London-Greek shipowners to operate SD14s, both in his British and flag-of-convenience fleets. This is his *Sea Moon. [V.H. Young and L.A. Sawyer collection]*

Bottom: On transfer to the Liberian flag in 1978, *Sea Moon* was renamed *Myrtos* by Vergottis. She is seen leaving Durban. *[Trevor Jones]*

Shipping Inc., Monrovia (Flanmare Shipping Inc. (D. Agoudimos), Piraeus) under the St. Vincent flag.
20.7.1996: Arrived at Alang for breaking up by Deep Shipbreaking Industrial, having been sold for a reported $216 per light ton.
7.8.1996: Work commenced.

422. CARREL

L.R./I.M.O. Number 7012648
9,244g
6,013n
15,241d
Clark-Sulzer 5RD68
5.11.1969: Keel laid.
6.3.1970: Launched for Matheson and Co. Ltd., London.
14.5.1970: Completed. British flag.
1976: Sold to Nigerian Green Lines Ltd., Lagos, Nigeria (Edward Nannini and Co. Ltd., London) and renamed NIGER VALLEY.
8.1981: Sold to Mercantile Shipping Co., Panama (Navarino Shipping and Trading Co. S.A., Panama) (M.P. Tsikopoulos, Piraeus, Greece) for $3.4m and renamed HONESTY II.
1984: Sold to General Leasing and Financing Inc., Monrovia, Liberia (Overseas Shipping Co., Piraeus)

and renamed URANIA under the Greek flag.
1986: Sold to Cyprus owners and renamed THUNDER.
23.12.1986: Arrived Gadani Beach to be broken up by S.Z. Enterprises Ltd.

423. COLLIN

L.R./I.M.O. Number 7017741
9,256g
6,087n
15,241d
Clark-Sulzer 5RD68
21.1.1970: Keel laid.
20.5.1970: Launched for Matheson and Co. Ltd., London.
10.7.1970: Completed. British flag.
1976: Sold to Armadora Naviera Proestos S.A., Panama (Mediterranean Shipping Enterprises Ltd (M.P. Xilas), Piraeus, Greece) and renamed GIANNIS XILAS under the Greek flag.

Top: *Carrell* began a close relationship between builder and owner. *[David Hunt collection]*

1983: Management transferred to Nava Maritime (F.N. and N.C. Fafalios), London and renamed BROTHER.
1986: Sold to Blanchard Shipping Corporation S.A., Panama (Ahmed Abdul Qawi Bamaodam, Jeddah, Saudi Arabia) (Holbud Ltd., London) and renamed AL HAFIZU.
1996: Management transferred to SNP Shipping Services Private Ltd., Mumbai, India.
4.1.1999: Arrived at Mumbai for demolition.

Al Hafizu, ex *Collin*, off Singapore, March 1987 with the funnel colours of Holbud Ltd. *[Roy Kittle, David Salisbury collection]*

424. SAINT PAUL

L.R./I.M.O. Number 7025621

	1978:
9,126g	12,356g
6,152n	8,705n
14,730d	17,693d,

1978: 167.00 (LBP) x 20.43 x11.74/8.486 metres
Clark-Sulzer 5RND68
23.3.1970: Keel laid.
21.1.1970: Launched for Compagnie de Navegation Denis Frères, Paris, France.
16.10.1970: Completed. French flag.
1978: Lengthened and converted into 410 teu container vessel by Estaleiros Navals de Lisboa, Lisbon, Portugal.
1984: Sold to Sofrana New Guinea Line S.A. (Societe Francais de Navigation S.a.r.L), Noumea, New Caledonia and renamed CAPITAINE COOK III, under the French flag, registered at Matu Utu.
1987: Sold to Thoresen & Co. (Bangkok) Ltd., Bangkok, Thailand (Arne Teigen, Oslo, Norway) and renamed HAI MENG.
20.10.1994: Arrived Alang.
30.10.1994: Demolition commenced by Ship Trade Corporation.

Top: *Saint Paul* in as built condition on the New Waterway, 10th June 1971. [Roy Kittle]

Bottom: Some 13 years later, a rebuilt *Saint Paul*, now renamed *Capitaine Cook III*, is seen again on the New Waterway. Conversion to a container ship was along the lines described for yard number 420, *Saint Francois*. Comparison of the views emphasises how the superstructure has been enlarged. [Wim Van Noort, David Salisbury collection]

Opposite top: *Saint Paul* in her final guise as the Norwegian-owned, Thai-registered *Hai Meng*. [David Whiteside collection]

425. **MARIA**

L.R./I.M.O. Number 6505961
9,101g
6,431n
15,195d
Clark-Sulzer 5RND68
2.6.1970: Keel laid.
30.9.1970: Launched for Laertis

Shipping Enterprises Special
Shipping S.A. (N. and J.
Vlassopoulos Ltd., London).
11.12.1970: Completed. Greek flag.
1983: Sold to Maritime Courrier S.A.,
Panama (Good Faith Shipping Co
S.A. (Nikolaos Frangos and Nicholas
G. Moundreas), Piraeus, Greece) and

renamed MAR COURRIER.
1984: Management transferred to
Capitol World Holdings S.A., Piraeus.
1999: Sold to Alfa Shipping Ltd.,
Panama and renamed IGENMOON.
26.8.1999: Arrived Mumbai for
demolition by Sanjay Steel Corporation,
which began the same day.

Middle: *Maria,*
anchored off
Limassol about
1983. The bow
crest of the
owners
incorporates the
Greek letter
beta.
*[Alistair
Paterson, David
Salisbury
collection]*

Bottom: *Mar
Courrier* at
Durban about
1991. *[Trevor
Jones, David
Salisbury
collection]*

Above: *Erawan* at Vancouver in May 1971. Swire's smart but subdued colours are marred by abrasion marks on the hull. The basic SD14 fit of 10-ton derricks is clearly seen in this view. *[Steve Klassen, David Salisbury collection]*

Right upper: Seen again from Prospect Point, Vancouver, *Erawan* shows the damage resulting from a collision with the Japanese motor vessel *Sun Diamond* (7,300/1972). The date is 28th September 1973. *[Don Brown]*

Right lower: Anangel Shipping were major customers for rival Liberty replacements built in Japan, but had the SD14 *Anangel Champion*, possibly for comparison. Photographed on the St Lawrence, 25th May 1990. *[René Beauchamp, David Salisbury collection]*

426. **ERAWAN**

L.R./I.M.O. Number 7038604
9,229g
6,088n
15,190d
Hawthorn-Sulzer 5RND68
24.7.1970: Keel laid.
10.12.1970: Launched for John Swire and Sons (Shipping) Ltd., London.
19.2.1971: Completed. British flag.
1978: Ownership transferred to China Navigation Co. Ltd., Hong Kong.
1979: Sold to Rion Maritime Corporation, Monrovia, Liberia (Pegasus Ocean Services Ltd., London) for $3.35m and renamed CAPE RION under the Greek flag.
1981: Sold to Matthew Ship Chartering Ltd. (Matthew Shipping Co. Ltd.), Montreal, Canada (Denholm Ship Management Ltd. Glasgow, managers) for $5.8m and renamed TORTUGAS under the British (Cayman Islands) flag, registered Georgetown.
1981: Sold to Anangel Champion Compania Naviera S.A., Panama (Anangel Shipping Enterprises S.A. (A. Angelicoussis and G. Pateras), Piraeus, Greece) and renamed

ANANGEL CHAMPION under the Greek flag.
1992: Management transferred to Adelfia Shipping Enterprises S.A., Piraeus.
1993: Sold to Safehaven Shipping Corporation, Monrovia, Liberia (Alva Investment Corporation, London) and renamed RANA under the St. Vincent and Grenadines flag.
1994: Sold to Starglow Shipping

Corporation, Monrovia, Liberia (Austin Navigation Inc., London) and renamed MANTIS under the St. Vincent and Grenadines flag.
1997: Transferred to Lucky Marite Enterprises Ltd., Monrovia, Liberia (Austin Navigation Inc., London), and renamed MARTINA under the St.Vincent and Grenadines flag.
About 24.4.2000: Arrived Chittagong to be broken up.

427. MOLDOVA
L.R./I.M.O. Number 7048099
9,101g
6,431n
15,282d
Clark-Sulzer 5RND68
12.10.1970: Keel laid.
10.2.1971: Launched for Amazon Shipping Corporation, Monrovia, Liberia (Federal Motorship Corporation (Torrey Mosvold), New York, USA) (N.& J. Vlassopulos Ltd. London, agents).
26.4.1971: Completed. Greek flag.
1976: Sold to Scindia Steam Navigation Co. Ltd., Bombay, India and renamed JALAPUTRA.
20.2.1987: Laid up at Bombay.
1989: Sold to J.M. Industries for demolition.
2.2.1989: Beached at Bombay.

Top: *Moldova* anchored off Hong Kong, 2nd April 1974. Seen in Vlassopulos colours, she was built for time charter to Torrey Mosvold. Her name is a link with her owner's origins in the Black Sea trade. *[V.H. Young and L.A. Sawyer collection]*

Bottom: In Scindia ownership, *Jalaputra* sails from Liverpool with a full deck cargo of earth-moving equipment on 6th August 1983. *[Paul Boot]*

428. SANTA VASSILIKI
Name originally proposed
ARCADIAN SPLENDOR
L.R./I.M.O. Number 7104180
9,038g
6,338n
15,139d
Clark-Sulzer 5RND68
17.12.1970: Keel laid.
7.4.1971: Launched for Leyenda
Oceanica Navegacion S.A., Panama
(Colocotronis Ltd., London).
18.6.1971: Completed. Greek flag.
1974: Greek management transferred
to Joseph Colocotronis S.A. (J.
Colocotronis), Piraeus.
1976: Sold to Josef Roth Reederei,
Hamburg, West Germany and
renamed JOSEF ROTH under the

Panama flag.
1982: Transferred to Josef Roth
(Cyprus) Shipping Co. Ltd.,
Limassol, Cyprus (Josef Roth
Reederei, Hamburg).
1984: Transferred to Josef Roth
Reederei, Hamburg, retaining Cyprus
flag.
7.1985: Sold to Rive Navigation
Corporation, Monrovia, Liberia
(European Navigation Inc. (Captain
S. Karnessis and Mrs. D. Vlassakis),
Piraeus) for $650,000 and renamed
LILY under the Panama flag.
6.1989: Sold to China Ocean
Shipping Co. (COSCO), Beijing,
People's Republic of China and
renamed LIAN FENG.
1992: Transferred to Dalian

*Top: Santa Vassiliki sails from Cape Town. [V.H.
Young and L.A. Sawyer collection]*

*Bottom: Josef Roth leaving Durban. [Trevor
Jones, David Salisbury collection]*

Container Steam Shipping Co., Dalian,
People's Republic of China.
1993: Renamed SHU DE, although
according to 'Lloyd's Register' this
renaming occurred only in 2003.
7.2004: Still listed in 'Lloyd's
Register'.

429. SANTA KATERINA

Name originally proposed
ARCADIAN GLORY
L.R./I.M.O. Number 7112395
9,038g
6,388n
15,139d
Clark-Sulzer 5RND68
24.2.1971: Keel laid.
22.6.1971: Launched for
Transego Oceanica
Navegacion S.A.,
Panama (Colocotronis
Ltd., London).
27.8.1971: Completed.
Greek flag.
1974: Management
transferred to
Colocotronis (Greece)
S.A. (E.M. Colocotronis),
Piraeus.
1975: Sold to Josef Roth
Reederei, Hamburg and
renamed THOMAS
ROTH under the Panama
flag.
1984: Sold to Golden
Harvest Shipping Co.
S.A., Panama (Good
Harvest Maritime Co.
Ltd., Taipei, Taiwan) and
renamed GOLDEN
ANTWERP.
1987: Sold to Pleasance
Shipping Co. Ltd., Panama
(Kingstar Shipping Ltd.,
Hong Kong) and renamed
RAINBOW PRIDE
1992: Sold to Merrytrans
Shipping Ltd., Kingstown,
St. Vincent (Dalian Haida

Shipping Co. Ltd., Dalian, People's
Republic of China and renamed
MERRYTRANS.)
1994: Management transferred to
Shenzhen Hai Da Shipping Co. Ltd.,
Shenzhen, People's Republic of China.
1997: Management transferred to
Yangzhou Yuyang Shipping Co.

Ltd., Nanjing, People's Republic of
China and renamed MANDARIN
OCEAN.
7.1.1998: Demolition commenced at
Calcutta by M.J. Scrap Ltd. In October
1997 the ship had been reported sold to
Bangladesh breakers for $1.67m ($174
per lightweight ton).

Top: *Santa Katerina* at San
Francisco. *[George Lamuth, David
Salisbury collection]*

Middle: *Thomas Roth. [Roy Fenton
collection]*

Bottom: *Mandarin Ocean* at Penang,
25th June 1967. *[Nigel Jones]*

430. SANTA ARTEMIS
Name originally proposed
ARCADIAN CHALLENGER
L.R./I.M.O. Number 7118985
9,038g
6,388n
15,139d
Clark-Sulzer 5RND68
30.4.1971: Keel laid.
20.9.1971: Launched for Panmares
Armadora S.A., Panama
(Colocotronis Ltd., London).
8.11.1971: Completed. Greek flag.
7.1.1972: Sank about 35 miles off
Cape St. Francis, South Africa, in
position 34.26 south by 24.25 east
after colliding in fog with the Pakistan
motor vessel SHALMAR (8,942/
1970) whilst on her maiden voyage
from San Nicolaos, Argentina to
Kaohsiung with a cargo of maize.
Five crew members were lost.

Possibly the only colour photograph taken of the
ill-fated *Santa Artemis*, on trials 3rd November
1971. She was lost on her maiden voyage.
*[Turners (Photography) Ltd., John Lingwood
collection]*

431. SANTA MAJA
Names originally proposed
ARCADIAN FAME and SANTA
AMALIA, whilst between launch
and completion the alternative
spelling SANTA MAYA was
considered.
L.R./I.M.O. Number 7124702
9,038g
6,388n
15,139d
Clark-Sulzer 5RND68
30.1.1971: Keel laid.
15.11.1971: Launched for Tridente
Galante Navegacion S.A. Panama
(Colocotronis Ltd., London).

9.3.1972: Completed. Greek flag.
1974: Management transferred to
Colocotronis (Greece) S.A. (E.M.
Colocotronis), Piraeus, Greece.
1976: Sold to Josef Roth Reederei,
Hamburg, West Germany and
renamed CLAUDIA KOGEL under
the Panamanian flag.
1980: Owners restyled Kogel & Roth
Schiffahrts K.G. (Josef Roth
Reederei), Hamburg.
1985: Sold to Raynville Shipping
Corporation S.A., Panama (Holbud
Ship Management Ltd., London) and
renamed AL JOHFFA.
1989: Transferred to Ruxpin
International Corporation, Panama
(SNP Shipping Services Private Ltd.,
Bombay, India) (Holbud Ship
Management Ltd., London).
12.2.1996: Struck rocks in the Bay of
Santos after dragging anchor in
heavy weather whilst on a voyage
from Mombasa to Santos. Hull
cracked and water penetrated holds.
Subsequently refloated and towed
out to sea.
25.3.1996: Scuttled about 120 miles
off Santos.

Left: *Santa Maja* in London Docks, 15th April
1978. *[Roy Kittle]*

Opposite top: *Claudia Kogel* in the New
Waterway, July 1982. *[David Salisbury]*

Opposite middle: *Al Johffa* in Holbud colours.
[Roy Fenton collection]

Opposite bottom: Two views of the wreck of *Al
Johffa* taken in the Bay of Santos on 19th
March 1996. *[Walter Freitag, Markus Berger
collection]*

432. **LONDON GRENADIER**

L.R./I.M.O. Number 7205805
9,210g
6,091n
15,139d
Hawthorn-Sulzer 5RND68
24.9.1971: Keel laid.
17.2.1972: Launched for London and Overseas Freighters Ltd. London.
28.4.1972: Completed. British flag.
1979: Sold to Clyde Maritime Ltd., Limassol, Cyprus (Abdul Lalif Jameel Establishment, Jeddah, Saudi Arabia)(Acomarit Services Maritime S.A., Geneva, Switzerland, managers), and renamed FIRST JAY.
1982: Transferred to First Jay Shipping Ltd., Limassol, Cyprus (Abdul Latif Jameel Establishment, Jeddah, Saudi Arabia).
1986: Sold with yard number 442 to Maunland Navigation Inc., Manila, Philippines (Vroon B.V., Breskens, Netherlands) for a reported $1.5m each and renamed SIMARA EXPRESS.
20.9.1993: A few days after leaving Cape Town on passage Durban to Valparaiso, sent out a distress signal from position 39.47 south by 35.42 west, on direct route for Magellan Straits, stating that cargo in number 1 hold had exploded and there was a fire on board. Two days later master signalled that he was proceeding to River Plate with the outbreak under control.
26.9.1993: At Montevideo vessel

was kept out of port until surveyor's inspection was completed. Blast and fire had destroyed much of the cargo forward, including containers, and extensive damage was caused during extinguishing operations. Her shell structure had also buckled. Declared a constructive total loss but surveyors authorised canvas covers on hatches and approved the vessel to sail through Magellan Straits to Valparaiso for permanent repairs.
8.10.1993: Left Montevideo.
1994: Sold to Tian Fu Shipping Ltd., Kingstown, St. Vincent and Grenadines (An Da Shipping Inc, Hong Kong) and renamed TIAN YUAN XING under the Belize flag.
1996: Transferred to An Da Shipping Inc., Hong Kong and renamed AN

SHUN under the Belize flag.
1997: Renamed AN TAI.
23.11.1997: Started listing due to cracking in her hull alongside number 3 hatch whilst alongside at Port Klang Management Wharf discharging 8,485 tonnes of fertiliser loaded at Xingang, and sank early following morning. Salvors appointed.
4-6.1998: Initial attempts at refloating abandoned. Operations delayed because Kelang Port Authorities were awaiting treasury funds to pay for the task which was expected to take two months.
31.7.2000: Salvage recommenced.
2.2001: Vessel cut in two and stern refloated.

433. LONDON FUSILIER

L.R./I.M.O. Number 7213187
9,210g
6,091n
15,139d
Hawthorn-Sulzer 5RND68
30.11.1971: Keel laid.
26.4.1972: Launched for London and Overseas Freighters Ltd., London.
16.6.1972: Completed. British flag.
1979: Sold to Chian Chiao Shipping (Private) Ltd. (Sin Chiao Shipping (Private) Ltd.), Singapore for $4m and renamed NEW WHALE.
1985: Sold to Well World Navigation S.A., Panama (Wah Tung Shipping Agency Co. Ltd., Hong Kong) and renamed HER LOONG.
11.5.1987: Sustained extensive damage when fire broke out in number 5 hold while discharging at Hamburg following voyage from Shanghai with general cargo including peppermint oil and menthol crystals. Found to be beyond economical repair and declared a constructive total loss. Sold to Aquilar Y Peris S.L., Spain.
2.7.1987: Left Hamburg in tow.
14.7.1987: Arrived Valencia.
4.8.1987: Demolition began.

Above: *London Fusilier* with a deck cargo of containers. *[V.H. Young and L.A. Sawyer collection]*

Below: *London Fusilier* in January 1975. *[John Wiltshire collection]*

123

434. OCEAN ENVOY

L.R./I.M.O. Number 7221237
9,126g
6,068n
15,125d
Clark-Sulzer 5RND68
24.2.1972: Keel laid.
28.6.1972: Launched for Chittagong
Steamship Corporation Ltd.,
Chittagong, Pakistan.
11.9.1972: Completed. Pakistan
flag.

1974: Managers became Trans-
Oceanic Steamship Co. Ltd.,
Karachi, Pakistan.
1978: Owners restyled Pakistan
National Shipping Corporation,
Karachi.
1997: Sold to Dewan Shipping Lines
Ltd., Karachi and renamed DEWAN I.
20.3.1998: Laid up with surveys
overdue.
31.7.2002: Arrived Chittagong to be
broken up.

Above: *Ocean Envoy* with the Singapore skyline
in the background during September 1993.
[Simon Olsen, David Salisbury collection]

Below: The crosstree of *Dewan I* provides a
perch for seabirds in the Outer Anchorage at
Karachi on 23rd December 2000. She probably
went straight from here to Chittagong for
breaking up. *[Nigel Jones]*

435. LONDON CAVALIER

Name originally proposed LONDON
HALBERDIER
L.R./I.M.O. Number 7226287
9,210g
6,091n
15,139d
Hawthorn-Sulzer 5RND68
28.4.1972: Keel laid.
6.9.1972: Launched for London and
Overseas Freighters Ltd., London.
13.11.1972: Completed. British flag.
1979: Sold to Asian Mission
Corporation (Philippine Pacific
Ocean Lines Inc.), Manila,
Philippines and renamed ASIAN
LINER.

1980: Sold to Kanamaris Compania
Naviera S.A., Panama (Companhia
Portuguesa de Navegacao Ltda.
(COMPONAVE), Lisbon, Portugal)
for $5m and renamed SILAGA.
1985: Transferred to Diamond
Channel Shipping Corporation,
Panama (Companhia Portuguesa de
Navegacao Ltda. (COMPONAVE),
Lisbon).
1987: Sold to Olympos Shipping Co.
Ltd., Limassol, Cyprus (Anpo
Shipping Co. Ltd. (Anastasios G.
Politis), Piraeus, Greece) and
renamed SOCRATES.
5.6.2001: Arrived Alang for breaking
up by Indian breakers.
11.6.2001: Work began.

Top: *London Cavalier* in the delightful setting of
Otago Bay about 1974. *[Alwyn MacMillan,
David Salisbury collection]*

Bottom: As *Socrates* she arrives at Durban with
a cargo of timber about 1991. *[Trevor Jones,
David Salisbury collection]*

436. LONDON BOMBARDIER

Name originally proposed LONDON CARABINIER.
L.R./I.M.O. Number 7233761
9,210g
6,091n
15,139d
Hawthorn-Sulzer 5RND68
4.7.1972: Keel laid.
22.11.1972: Launched for London and Overseas Freighters Ltd., London.
12.1.1973: Completed. British flag.
1979: Sold to Eaton Maritime Corporation, Monrovia, Liberia (Helikon Shipping Enterprises Ltd., London) and renamed AKARNANIA under the Greek flag.
1986: Sold to Viking Traders Navigation Ltd., Limassol, Cyprus (Mayfair (Hellas) Co. Ltd., Piraeus, Greece) for $500,000 and renamed JUTE EXPRESS.
1995: Sold to Ioannis Shipping Ltd., Valletta, Malta (Euroferries S.A., Athens, Greece) and renamed IOANNIS I.
11.1996: Sold to Marchel Holdings Ltd., Piraeus under the Panama flag.
10.4.1997: Arrived at Alang to be scrapped by M.T. Shipbreakers.
11.5.1997: Demolition commenced.

Top: *London Bombardier* in the New Waterway. *[John Phillips, David Salisbury collection]*

Upper middle: *London Bombardier* on charter to Jebsen. *[V.H. Young and L.A. Sawyer collection]*

Lower middle: *Akarnania* at Singapore 18th June 1980. *[Nigel Jones]*

Bottom: *Jute Express* with a crumpled bow. *[V.H. Young and L.A. Sawyer collection]*

437. SANTA AMALIA

Names originally proposed
ARCADIAN FREEDOM and
SANTA CLIO.
L.R./I.M.O. Number 7304259
8,922g
6,199n
15,139d
Clark-Sulzer 5RND68
12.9.1972: Keel laid.
18.1.1973: Launched for Transportes
Surenos Armadora S.A., Panama,
(Colocotronis Ltd., London).
9.3.1973: Completed. Greek flag.
1974: Management transferred to
Colocotronis (Greece) S.A. (E.M.
Colocotronis), Piraeus, Greece.
1976: Sold to Castellana Shipping
Ltd., Monrovia, Liberia (Soutos
(Hellas) Maritime Corporation,
Piraeus) and renamed SAMOS
PROGRESS under the Greek flag.
1978: Transferred to Ionian
Endurance Marine Inc., Monrovia
(Soutos (Hellas) Maritime
Corporation, Piraeus) under the
Greek flag.
1980: Sold to Excel Maritime S.A.,
Panama (Evolution Maritime &
Enterprises S.A., Hong Kong) for
$6.1m and renamed FORTUNE
KING.
1983: Sold to TCT Compania
Naviera S.A., Panama (Golden
Navigation Co. Ltd., Hong Kong)
and renamed WORLD OCEANIC.
4.1986: Sold to Samta Petroleum
Private Ltd. (Samta Private Ltd.),
Singapore for $390,000 and renamed
HIN ANN.
1988: Transferred to Pride Shipping
Ltd., Valletta, Malta (Samta Shipping
Agencies Private Ltd., Singapore)
and renamed ASEAN PRIDE.
1990: Transferred to Asean Progress
Ltd. Valletta (Samta Shipping
Agencies Private Ltd., Singapore)

and renamed ASEAN PROGRESS.
1990: Sold to Silver Kris Maritime
Ltd., Valletta, Malta (Thai Shipping
and Chartering Co. Ltd., Bangkok,
Thailand) and renamed SILVER
KRIS.

1999: Sold to Honduran owners and
renamed HIE KHEAN.
7.2004: Still listed in 'Lloyd's
Register' but continued existence
must be in doubt as no movements
reported since December 1999.

Top: *Santa Amalia* bringing a deck cargo of US trucks into the New Waterway on 12th July 1975. *[John Wiltshire collection]*
Middle: *World Oceanic*, Hong Kong, November 1983. *[David Salisbury]*
Bottom: *Asean Progress*, Singapore, 23rd December 1989. *[Simon Olsen, David Salisbury collection]*

438. (CLUDEN (1)) TRANSVAAL

L.R./I.M.O. Number 7306348
9,089g
6,177n
15,180d
Hawthorn-Sulzer 5RND68
23.11.1972: Keel laid.
8.3.1972: Launched as CLUDEN for Matheson and Co. Ltd., London.
4.1973: Sold to DAL-Deutsche Afrika Linien G.m.b.H. & Co. (John T. Essberger), Hamburg, West Germany.
11.5.1973: Completed as TRANSVAAL.
1976: Management transferred to Transocean Liners (Proprietary) Ltd., Singapore and renamed MERLION under the Singapore flag.
1980: Sold to Hua Pao Maritime Inc., Monrovia, Liberia (Wah Tung Shipping Agency Co. Ltd., Hong Kong)(Far East Enterprising Corporation, Hong Kong) for $5m and renamed COLOSSUS under the Panama flag.
1988: Sold to Crystal Ships Management Inc., Monrovia (Treasure Maritime Ltd., Hong Kong) and renamed CRYSTAL under the St. Vincent and Grenadines flag.
1994: Sold to Ocean Crown Development Ltd. (North China Lines Ltd.), Hong Kong and renamed OCEAN CROWN under the St. Vincent and Grenadines flag.
1998: Management transferred to Hebei Ocean Shipping Co. (COSCO Hebei), Qinhuangdao, People's Republic of China.
2000: Renamed RICH ASCENT under the Cambodian flag.
2001: Renamed NEW MOON by Bestore Shipping Pte. Ltd., Cambodia under the Belize flag.
24.2.2003: Arrived Jiangyin, People's Republic of China to be broken up.

Top: *Cluden* was completed as *Transvaal* for German owners, for whom she was originally registered in Hamburg. The features of the Velle derrick installation are clearly seen in this photograph. The wide crosstrees were necessary to handle the topping and slewing motions and were connected to the hammerhead of the single boom. Each of the 10-ton derricks required three winches for its operation. *[Trevor Jones]*

Middle: Although *Transvaal* was owned by DAL-Deutsche Afrika Linien, she is seen here with the funnel of Arcadia Reederei. *[David Whiteside collection]*

Bottom: Transfer to Singapore management saw *Transvaal* renamed *Merlion*. Seen in the New Waterway during August 1979. *[David Salisbury]*

439. PANAGHIS VERGOTTIS

L.R./I.M.O. Number 7319591
8,953g
6,370n
15,139d
Sulzer Brothers, Winterthur 5RND68
1971: Ordered by M.A. Karageorgis S.A., Piraeus, Greece. Not proceeded with.
24.1.1973: Keel laid.
22.5.1973: Launched for Carlo Izo Shipping Co. Ltd., Monrovia, Liberia (Valiant Steamship Co. Ltd. (George Vergottis), London).
20.7.1973: Completed under the Greek flag.
1977: Managers became Valiant Shipping Co. Ltd. (George Vergottis), London.
1991: Sold to Mars Shipping Co. Ltd., Ta'Xbiex, Malta (Mycali Maritime Corp. S.A., Piraeus, Greece) and renamed VIRGINIA.
1995: Sold to Hong Yuen Maritime Ltd., Valletta, Malta (Hong Yuen Steamship Development Ltd., Singapore) and renamed HONG XIANG.
1999: Management transferred to Vibrant Sea Management Private Ltd., Singapore.
7.2004: Still listed in 'Lloyd's Register', flag unknown, but continued existence must be in doubt as no movements reported since November 1999 and her Maltese registration was cancelled in 1999.

Top: *Panaghis Vergottis.* [David Whiteside collection]
Middle: *Virginia* at Durban in 1993. [Trevor Jones, David Salisbury collection]
Bottom: *Hong Xiang,* Singapore, 27th June 1997. [Nigel Jones]

Top: *Stephanos Vergottis* after her launch on 18th July 1973. A lone shipyard worker stands atop her superstructure, from which flutters the Austin & Pickersgill flag, for until she completes her trials successfully she still formally belongs to the shipbuilder. *[Harold Appleyard]*

Middle: *Stephanos Vergottis* at Durban. *[Kevin Moore]*

Bottom: *Stephanos Vergottis*. *[David Whiteside collection]*

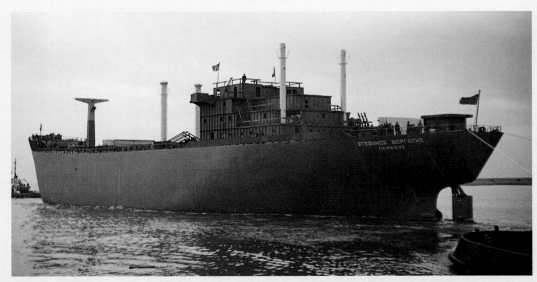

440. STEPHANOS VERGOTTIS

L.R./I.M.O. Number 7324170
8,953g
6,370n
15,139d
Clark-Sulzer 5RND68
1971: Ordered by M.A. Karageorgis S.A., Piraeus, Greece. Not proceeded with.
15.3.1973: Keel laid.
18.7.1973: Launched for Sterna Shipping Co. Ltd., Monrovia, Liberia (Valiant Steamship Co. Ltd. (George Vergottis), London.
28.9.1973: Completed. Greek flag.
1977: Managers became Valiant Shipping Co. Ltd. (George Vergottis), London).
1988: Sold to Shanghai Ocean Shipping Company (COSCO), Shanghai, People's Republic of China and renamed MIN JIANG.
1991: Transferred to Minsheng Shipping Co. Ltd., Chongqing,
Sichuan Province, People's Republic of China.
1998: Sold to Dalian Xinxing Shipping Co. Ltd., Dalian, People's Republic of China and renamed XIN XING I.
2004: Renamed XIN HE 2.
11.2004: Still listed in 'Lloyd's Register' as XIN XING I.

441. MARI

L.R./I.M.O. Number 7340679
8,925g
6,159n
15,251d
Hawthorn-Sulzer 5RND68
1971: Ordered by M.A. Karageorgis S.A., Piraeus, Greece. Not proceeded with.
24.5.1973: Keel laid.
15.10.1973: Launched for Buenaventura Armadora S.A., Panama (Bray Shipping Co. Ltd. (Basil E. Mavroleon), London.
8.2.1974: Completed. Greek flag.

Top: *Mari* in London docks. Owners were Bray Shipping Ltd., whose directors, Basil Elias Mavroleon and George E. Mavroleon, were first cousins of Basil M. Mavroleon of London and Overseas Freighters and of Austin & Pickersgill. *[Roy Kittle]*

Bottom: The former *Mari* as *Vali P*, approaching Heysham on 2nd May 1993. Her port anchor is partly lowered ready for dropping at the critical moment to take the way of the ship and assist her in turning in this restricted harbour. *[Paul Boot]*

1986: Sold to Valiper Shipping Co. Ltd., Limassol, Cyprus (Perosea Shipping Co. S.A., Piraeus) for $0.8m and renamed VALI P.
1997: Sold to Aloha Shipping Ltd., Valletta, Malta (Perosea Shipping Co. S.A., Piraeus) and renamed LUCKY WAY.
15.7.1999: Arrived Alang to be broken up by Ispat Traders.

442. WELSH TROUBADOUR

L.R./I.M.O. Number 7340681
9,201g
6,085n
15,180d
Clark-Sulzer 5RND68
1971: Ordered by M.A. Karageorgis S.A., Piraeus, Greece. Not proceeded with.
17.8.1973: Keel laid.
21.2.1974: Launched for Welsh Ore Carriers Ltd. (Gibbs & Co (Ship Management) Ltd.), Newport.
26.4.1974: Completed. British flag.
1978: Owners became Welsh Overseas Freighters Ltd.
1979: Sold to Peterhead Shipping Inc., Monrovia, Liberia (Establishment Abdul Latif Jameel, Jeddah, Saudi Arabia) (Acomarit Services Maritime S.A., Geneva, Switzerland, managers) and renamed WELSH JAY under the Panama flag.
1980: Transferred to Welsh Jay Shipping Ltd., Monrovia retaining the Panama flag.
1982: Management transferred to Jameel S.A.M., Monte Carlo.
1986: Sold to Maunland Navigation Inc., Manila, Phillipines (Vroon B.V., Breskens, Netherlands) and renamed SILAGO EXPRESS.
1995: Transferred to Northern Navira Inc., Monrovia (Vroon B.V., Breskens) and renamed NAVIRA EXPRESS under the Vanuatu flag.
1995: Management transferred to SBS Management A/S (Sven Sejersted Bodtker), Oslo, Norway.
1997: Transferred to February International Navigation Inc., Monrovia (Vroon B.V., Brekens), remaining under the Vanuatu flag.
1996: Ultimate owners become the Northern Shipholding Group A/S., Oslo, Norway, and management transferred to South Asia Ship Management (Private) Ltd., Karachi, Pakistan.
1997: Sold to Trojan Shipping Ltd., Tortola, British Virgin Islands and renamed RENA ONE under the flag of St. Vincent and the Grenadines.
4.9.1997: Arrived Calcutta for breaking up M.J. Scrap (Private) Ltd. having been sold for $166.50 per lightweight ton.
27.9.1997: Demolition commenced.
9.11.1997: Demolition completed.

Top: *Welsh Jay.* [Malcolm Cranfield collection]

Middle: *Silago Express* with a full deck cargo of military hardware, probably bound for the First Gulf War. The photograph also shows the extension pieces added to the derricks to enable them to be housed horizontally in the stowage crutches. [Roy Fenton collection]

Bottom: Still in Vroon ownership, but now renamed *Navira Express*, and displaying a slightly grazed forefoot. She has returned to her original home port, Newport, Monmouthshire on 31st March 1997. [Nigel Jones]

443. WATERLAND

L.R./I.M.O. Number 7341714
8,953g
6,460n
15,139d
Hawthorn-Sulzer 5RND68
1973: Ordered by Quincy Chuang, Hong Kong, and immediately resold to the Hong Kong Barge Company, Hong Kong.
23.10.1973: Keel laid.
26.4.1974: Launched for N.V. tot Voorzetting van de Koninklijke

Hollandsche Lloyd, Amsterdam, Netherlands.
20.6.1974: Completed. Netherlands flag.
1982: Renamed NEDLLOYD WATERLAND.
1983: Renamed WATERLAND.
1983: Sold to Redestos Shipping Co. Ltd., Limassol, Cyprus (Government of Cuba, Havana, Cuba) and renamed REDESTOS.
1994: Management transferred to Naviera Poseidon, Havana.
1.9.1998: Arrived Haiphong for

Top: *Waterland* had a unique arrangement of cargo gear, with a pair of kingposts abaft the number 4 hatch, but not the extra pair some SD14s had between numbers 2 and 3. On the New Waterway, 1st July 1981. *[Les Ring, Nigel Jones collection]*

Bottom: The Cuban *Redestos* on an autumnal Mersey, 28th October 1987. *[Paul Boot]*

demolition by Pha Rung Shipyard, having been sold for $183 per lightweight ton.
9.10.1998: Demolition completed.

Top: A possibly unique colour photograph of *Strathdare,* which was sold on her maiden voyage. P&O chose Strath 'D' names for their six vessels to signify 'SD14'. A distinctive feature of these ships was the large paired windows in the superstructure front. Only *Strathdare* and *Strathdevon* had rails, the later examples had fully-plated bulwarks. *Strathdare* has a black hull: later P&O SD14s had the corn colour. *[Turners (Photography) Ltd;, P&O Archives]*

Bottom: *City of Exeter*, Ellerman's sole SD14. *[John Lingwood collection]*

Opposite top: *Phoevos* on the New Waterway. *[Trevor Jones]*

Opposite middle: *Safina-e-Barkat*. *[David Whiteside collection]*

Opposite bottom: *Nour* in the Alfred Basin, Birkenhead Docks. *[Paul Boot]*

CITY OF EXETER

444.
STRATHDARE
L.R./I.M.O. Number
7341726
9,214g
6,264n
14,850d
Hawthorn-Sulzer 5RND68
1973: Ordered by Quincy
Chuang, Hong Kong.
27.2.1974: Keel laid.
4.7.1974: Launched for
Peninsular & Oriental
Steam Navigation
Company (P.&O. General
Cargo Division), London.
7.10.1974: Completed.
British flag.
27.12.1974: Sold whilst on
maiden voyage to Ellerman
Lines Ltd. (Ellerman City
Lines Ltd.), London.
1975: Renamed CITY OF
EXETER.
1980: Sold to Monodora
Shipping Corporation,
Monrovia, Liberia
('Granicos' Shipping
Corporation S.A., Piraeus,
Greece (Lyras Brothers
Ltd., London)) for $6m
and renamed PHOEVOS
under the Greek flag.
1982: Sold to the Islamic
Investment Shipping
Company One S.A.,
Panama (Pan-Islamic
Steamship Co. Ltd.,
Karachi, Pakistan) and
renamed SAFINA-E-
BARKAT.
1985: Management
transferred to Marlborough
Shipping Co. Ltd. (G.P., J.
and P.G. Margaronis),
London) and renamed
NOUR.
1988: Management
transferred to Fairwind
Enterprises Ltd. (Trevor
Fairhurst), London.
1995: Sold to Garter
Marine Ltd., Limassol,
Cyprus (Bonyad Marine
Services Inc., Athens,
Greece) and renamed
ZENITH.
1999: Sold to Third
Element Enterprises
Shipping Ltd., Nicosia,
Cyprus (Suter Shipping and
Trading S.A., Piraeus) and
renamed NIKOLAOS S.
23.12.1999: Arrived at
Haldia, India and reported
to have been broken up,
with flag withdrawn in
October 2000. However,
'Lloyd's Register'
continued to list the vessel
in April 2004.

445. SEA TRADER

L.R./I.M.O. Number 7341738
8,915g
6,177n
15,241d
Hawthorn-Sulzer 5RND68
30.4.1974: Keel laid.
16.9.1974: Launched for Allseas
Chartering Corporation Ltd.
Monrovia (Glafki Shipping Company
S.A. (A.Alafouzas) Athens, Greece).
7.11.1974: Completed. Greek flag.
1978: Sold to Jade Compania
Maritima S.A., Panama (Tyana
Compania Maritima S.A. (Thomas A.
Demseris), Piraeus, Greece) and

renamed JADE under the Greek flag.
1981: Managers became Fereniki
Shipping and Trading Co. S.A.
(Thomas A. Demseris), Piraeus.
1987: Sold to Northern Trader Co.
Ltd., Gzira, Malta (Sea World
Management and Trading Inc.
(Constantinos Dedopoulos), Athens)
and renamed CLEOPATRA.
1990: Sold to Branjo Shipping S.A.,
Panama (Neptun Denizcilik Ltd.
Sirketi, Istanbul, Turkey) and
renamed N. MARMARA.
1991: Sold to Jordan Shipping S.A.,
Panama (Brightest Star Maritime
Corporation, Piraeus) and renamed
DIGNITY.

18.11.1992: Grounded in position
37.41 north by 24.04 east during a
voyage from Odessa to Vietnam with
general cargo including cotton.
4.12.1992: Refloated and
subsequently towed to Piraeus.
27.2.1993: Arrived in Piraeus for
repairs and subsequently detained
and laid up.
2.11.1994: Sold at auction to Cross
Holding S.A., Monrovia, Liberia (M.B.
Moundreas Shipping Co. S.A.,
Piraeus) and renamed ANASTASIA C.
1994: Sold for breaking up to Dortec
Gemi Sokum Ticaret A.S, Turkey.
16.4.1995: Arrived Aliaga in tow.

Top: *Jade* in Sea
Reach, River
Thames during
June 1983 heading
for Silvertown with
a cargo of sugar for
the Tate and Lyle
refinery. *[David
Salisbury]*

Right: *Anastasia C*
being broken up at
Aliaga, Turkey.
*[Selim San, John
Lingwood
collection]*

446. STRATHDEVON

L.R./I.M.O. Number 7341740
9,214g
6,264n
14,850d
Clark-Sulzer 5RND68
1973: Ordered by Quincy Chuang, Hong Kong.
*1973:*Sold.
8.7.1974: Keel laid.
31.10.1974: Launched for Peninsular & Oriental Steam Navigation Company (P.& O. General Cargo Division), London.
24.1.1975: Completed. British flag.
16.12.1981: Sold to Empresa de Navegacion Mambisa, Havana, Cuba and renamed DONATO MARMOL.

1988: Sold to Black Swan Shipping Co. Ltd., Limassol, Cyprus (Naviera Poseidon S.A., Havana, Cuba) and renamed MAGISTER.
1997: Sold to Globe Trade Shipping Corporation, Monrovia, Liberia (Alva Investments Corporation, London) (Austin Navigation Inc., Harrow, managers) and renamed SARAH I under the St. Vincent and Grenadines flag.
1998: Management transferred to Sany Shipping (Private) Ltd., Singapore.
2000: Transferred to Orient Isle Ltd., British Virgin Islands (Sany Shipping (Private) Ltd., Singapore) and renamed PAVONIS under the St.

Top: *Strathdevon* in the Thames, 5th July 1979. Austin & Pickersgill decided that a spare propeller should be left off the basic specification. When owners such as P&O decided to carry one it was usually stowed on the poop house top. *[Roy Kittle]*

Bottom: The Cuban *Donato Marmol* in the St. Lawrence, 14th April 1986. *[René Beauchamp, David Salisbury collection]*

Vincent and Grenadines flag
2002: Management transferred to Prominent Shipping Services Ltd., Chittagong, Bangladesh.
7.2004: Still listed in 'Lloyd's Register'.

447. MARSHA

L.R./I.M.O. Number 7341752
9,042g
6,274n
15,261d
Clark-Sulzer 5RND68
19.9.1974: Keel laid.
10.1.1975: Launched for Hammond Shipping Inc., Monrovia, Liberia (Quincy Chuang, Hong Kong), (Hong Kong Shipping Agencies Ltd., Hong Kong, managers).
7.3.1975: Completed. Liberian flag.
1977: Sold with owning company to P.S. Li and Co. Ltd. (United Venture Management Inc., managers), Hong Kong.
1979: Transferred to Pacific Grand Carriers Corporation (P.S. Li and Co. Ltd.) (United Fair Agencies Ltd., managers), Hong Kong.
1985: Sold to Ultra Ocean S.A., Buenos Aires, Argentine for $2m

and renamed AMADEO.
1990: Sold to Stable Maritime Inc., Monrovia, Liberia (Ravenscroft Shipping Inc., Miami, Florida, USA) (Wallem Shipmanagement Ltd., Hong Kong, managers) and renamed STAR LIGHT.
1991: Sold to Maxi Shipping Ltd., Valletta, Malta (Brightest Star Maritime Corporation, Piraeus, Greece) and renamed TRUST.
1992: Transferred to Costa Norte Shipping Co. Ltd., Limassol, Cyprus (Brightest Star Maritime Corporation, Piraeus) and renamed WEST COAST.
1993: Sold to Carmetio Shipping Enterprises Ltd., Limassol, Cyprus (Dimko International Co. S.A. (Dimitrios Kondilos), Athens, Greece) and renamed RIVER BREEZE.
17.9.1995: Engine room and

Top: *Marsha* exhibiting a non-too-straight boot topping. *[David Whiteside collection]*

Bottom: *Amadeo* at Durban. *[Trevor Jones, David Salisbury collection]*

accommodation severely damaged by fire whilst anchored off Gibraltar whilst on a voyage from Piraeus to Morocco in ballast. The fire was brought under control the same day, but the vessel was declared a constructive total loss.
1996: Sold to Baptista & Irmaos Ltda. for breaking up.
25.1.1996: Arrived Lisbon.
11.3.1996: Work commenced.

448. SILVER CLOUD

L.R./I.M.O. Number 7341764
8,981g
6,160n
15,260d
Hawthorn-Sulzer 5RND68
1973: Ordered by Eton Shipping Ltd., Monrovia, Liberia (Hong Kong Barge Company, Hong Kong), as an SD14 cargo vessel. Contract was later changed to an SD15 design but later reverted to SD14.
1973: Sold.
4.11.1974: Keel laid.
25.2.1975: Launched for Silver Cloud Shipping Co. S.A., Panama (Stavros A. Daifas S.A., Piraeus, Greece).
9.5.1975: Completed. Greek flag.
1988: Sold to Gidafor Co. S.A., Monrovia (Abdul Rahmann Osman, Syria) (Seama International Shipping Ltd. (V.N. Mavreas), London, managers) and renamed OSMAN under the Panama flag.
1990: Sold to Leona Shipping Ltd., Valletta, Malta (Brightest Star Maritime Corporation, Piraeus) and renamed UNITY.
1994: Sold to Cantor Holdings Ltd., Panama and renamed ODEGETRIA under the Panamanian flag.
1995: Reported renamed UNIT.

Top: *Silver Cloud. [Ships in Focus collection]*

Bottom: *Unity* at Durban. *[Trevor Jones, David Salisbury collection]*

1995: Sold to Row Navigation Co. Ltd., Valletta, Malta (Thalkat Shipping S.A., Piraeus) and renamed ANDY.
1997: Sold to Naval Gent Maritime Ltd., Athens, Greece (Nicolakis Shipping S.A., Piraeus) and renamed NAVAL GENT under the Maltese flag.
2003: Transferred to Panama flag.
7.2004: Still listed in 'Lloyd's Register'.

449. **LINDENHALL**

L.R./I.M.O. Number 7341788
9,065g
6,420n
15,150d
Hawthorn-Sulzer 5RND68
1973: Ordered by Foklin Shipping Ltd. Monrovia, Liberia (Hong Kong Barge Company, Hong Kong).
12.1.1975: Keel laid.
23.4.1975: Launched for the West Hartlepool Steam Navigation Co. Ltd., Hartlepool.
1.7.1975: Completed. British flag.
1982: Transferred to Bush Hill Shipping Ltd., Hong Kong (West Hartlepool Steam Navigation Co. Ltd., Hartlepool) and renamed CARLOW HILL, remaining registered at Hartlepool.
1985: Sold to Larry Shipping Ltd., Port Vila, Vanuatu (Vroon B.V., Breskens, Netherlands) under the Philippines flag.
1985: Transferred to Prosperidad Shipping Inc., Manila, Phillipines (Vroon B.V., Breskens) and renamed SULU EXPRESS. The name BELGIAN EXPRESS had been chosen but was not acceptable to the registration authorities.
1996: Sold to Northern Danyal Inc., Monrovia (SBS Management A/S (Sven Sejersted Bodtker), Oslo, Norway) and renamed DANYAL EXPRESS under the Vanuatu flag.
1997: Sold for breaking up for $163 per lightweight ton.
18.8.1997: Arrived Chittagong for breaking up by K.S.M. Steel Re-Rolling Mills.
21.9.1997: Work commenced.

Top: *Lindenhall* in the New Waterway, 12th July 1975. *[Roy Kittle]*
Bottom: As *Carlow Hill* she retained Hartlepool registration, although nominally owned in Hong Kong. Seen at Singapore on 15th February 1983. *[Nigel Jones]*

450. (MAISI)
1 CONGRESSO DEL PARTIDO

L.R./I.M.O. Number 7341776
9,328g
6,165n
15,215d
Hawthorn-Sulzer 5RND68
1973: Ordered by Centa Shipping Ltd., Monrovia, Liberia (Hong Kong Barge Company, Hong Kong), as an SD14 cargo ship. Contract changed to SD15 design, then reverted to SD14.
1974: Sold.
3.3.1975. Keel laid.
24.6.1975: Launched as MAISI for

Empresa Navegacion Mambisa, Havana, Cuba.
8.1975: Name changed to 1 CONGRESO DEL PARTIDO.
5.9.1975: Completed. Cuban flag.
1995: Transferred to Naviera Poseidon, Havana.
31.5.1995: Detained at Lattakia, Syria.
1996: Sold to State Shipping Co. of North Korea, Pyongyang, North Korea and renamed SIN HEUNG I.
1998: Transferred to Korea Buhung Shipping Co., Pyongyang, North Korea and renamed KUWOLSAN.
9.6.1999: Detained at Kandla, India reportedly under arrest for carrying arms during Pakistan War.

Top: *Maisi* never sailed under this name but quickly became *1 Congreso del Partido*, as seen at Liverpool on 1st March 1986. *[Paul Boot]*
Bottom: Officially named *Sin Heung I* in North Korean ownership, her name was actually spelt *Sin Hung I* on her stern when photographed in Singapore Roads on 27th June 1997. *[Nigel Jones]*

2000: Transferred to Haigumgang Shipping Co. (Chinpo Shipping Co.), Hamgyongnam-do, North Korea and renamed RIMYONGSU.
2000: Transferred to Sungrisan Shipping Co., Pyongyang, North Korea and renamed SUNGRISAN 9.
5.1.2004: Arrived Jiangyin, Jiangsu Province, People's Republic of China for breaking up.

451. (BELIC) MONCADA

L.R./I.M.O. Number 7341790
9,328g
6,165n
15,215d
Hawthorn-Sulzer 5RND68
1973: Ordered by Eason Shipping Ltd., Monrovia, Liberia (Hong Kong Barge Company, Hong Kong).
1974: Sold.

28.4.1975: Keel laid.
4.9.1975: Launched as BELIC for Empresa Navegacion Mambisa, Havana, Cuba.
10.1975: Renamed MONCADA.
7.11.1975: Completed. Cuban flag.
1989: Transferred to Severn Shipping Co. Ltd., Valletta, Malta (Government of Cuba, Havana, Cuba) and renamed SEVERN.
1995: Management transferred to

Pan Pacific Shipping and Trading S.A., Hong Kong.
28.10.1996: Arrived Colombo and subsequently placed under arrest.
1997: Sold to Pride of the South Shipping Co. Ltd. Inc., Colombo, Sri Lanka and renamed PRIDE OF THE SOUTH under the Panama flag.
30.11.2003: Arrived Mumbai for demolition.
8.12.2003: Work began

452. CARLOS MANUEL DE CESPEDES

L.R./I.M.O. Number 7341805
9,327g
6,164n
15,215d
Hawthorn-Sulzer 5RND68
1973: Ordered by Komfort Shipping Ltd., Monrovia, Liberia (Hong Kong Barge Company, Hong Kong).
26.6.1975: Keel laid.
3.11.1975: Launched for Empresa Navegacion Mambisa, Havana, Cuba.
23.1.1976: Completed. Cuban flag.
1989: Transferred to Avon Shipping Co. Ltd., Valletta, Malta (Government of Cuba, Havana) and renamed AVON.
1994: Managers became Naviera Poseidon (Government of Cuba),

Havana.
1998: Sold to Alba Shipping Co., Panama (Adecon Shipping Inc., Mississauga, Ontario, Canada) and renamed CANADIAN PIONEER.
About 11.12.98: Anchored off Apapa/Lagos and offered for sale by Bangladeshi interests. Bought for scrap but tow proved uneconomical.
7.2004: Still listed by 'Lloyd's Register'.

453. IGNACIO AGRAMONTE

L.R./I.M.O. Number 7341817
9,327g
6,164n
15,215d
Hawthorn-Sulzer 5RND68
1973: Ordered by Cenford Shipping Ltd., Monrovia, Liberia (Hong Kong

Barge Company, Hong Kong).
7.9.1975: Keel laid.
19.12.1975: Launched for Empresa Navegacion Mambisa (Government of Cuba), Havana, Cuba.
4.3.1976: Completed. Cuban flag
1994: Managers became Naviera Poseidon (Government of Cuba), Havana.
5.9.1994: Detained at Lattakia.
1995: Sold to Clove Shipping Co. Ltd., Valletta, Malta (European Seaways Inc. (Nikolaos and Epaminondas Arcoumanis), Athens, Greece) and renamed IOANNIS A.
1997: Sold to Turnstone Ltd., Valletta, Malta (Seabirds Management Inc., Piraeus, Greece) and renamed TURNSTONE.
11.1.2001: Arrived at Alang for demolition.
21.1.2001: Work began.

Opposite top: Although a Cuban Government subsidiary, the owners of *Severn* have their own distinctive funnel colours incorporating a Maltese cross. Photographed off Singapore, 21st March 1993. *[Simon Olsen, David Salisbury collection]*

Opposite bottom: *Carlos Manuel de Cespedes* makes a smoky arrival at Liverpool on 8th March 1986. *[Paul Boot]*

Top: *Ignacio Agramonte* wears the usual Cuban funnel colours, with the sugar cane knife device. *[Louis Bosschaart, Ian Farquhar collection]*

Bottom: It is unusual for ships to find further owners after service with Cuba, but here a run-down *Turnstone* is seen on the Kiel Canal in the colours of Seabirds Management Inc. *[Holger Zimmerman, David Whiteside collection]*

454. **INDUSTRIA**
L.R./I.M.O. Number 7393365
9,345g
6,245n
14,850d
Clark-Sulzer 5RND68
5.11.1975: Keel laid.
27.2.1976: Launched for Metcalfe Shipping Co. Ltd. (Metcalfe, Son and Company), Hartlepool.
10.5.1976: Completed. British flag.
1978: Sold to Bangladesh Shipping Corporation, Dacca for £3.025m and renamed BANGLAR BAANI.

8.2.1982: Collided with the United States turbo-electric bulk carrier POTOMAC (13,558/1945) in the Gulf of Mexico in position 24.04 north by 84.30 west whilst on voyage from Chalna, Bangladesh to New York with wood pulp and general cargo which included crepe paper and frozen frogs legs. Sustained severe damage and the majority of her crew abandoned ship when she began taking in water. Remained afloat and taken in tow by American tug ROBIN X (198/1975).
13.2.1982: Arrived Tampa for

Top: *Industria* at Cape Town. Note the square section fabricated mast. *[Ian Shiffman, Roy Kittle collection]*

Bottom: *Banglaar Baani* on the New Waterway. *[David Salisbury]*

examination and repairs.
4.5.1982: Sailed for Baltimore to resume trading.
14.9.1996: Arrived at Chittagong for demolition.
10.1996: Work began.

455. STRATHDIRK

L.R./I.M.O. Number 7341829
9,230g
6,103n
14,850d
Clark-Sulzer 5RND68
1973: Contract signed.
23.12.1975: Keel laid.
28.4.1976: Launched for Peninsular and Oriental Steam Navigation Company (P.& O. General Cargo Division), London.
27.7.1976: Completed. British flag.
4.12.1981: Sold to Empresa Navegacion Mambisa (Government of Cuba), Havana, Cuba and renamed BARTOLOME MASO.
1988: Transferred to Chartway Shipping Co. Ltd., Limassol, Cyprus (Empresa de Navegacion Mambisa (Government of Cuba), Havana) and renamed OLEBRATT.
1994: Management transferred to Naviera Poseidon (Government of Cuba), Havana.
1996: Management transferred to Naviera Petrocost (Government of Cuba), Havana.
1997: Reported renamed GAEA.
1997: Sold to Nomar Shipping S.A.,

Top: *Strathdirk* and other later P&O SD14s had fully plated bulwarks, in contrast to the earlier pair which had rails. *[David Whiteside collection]*

Bottom: *Dawn* at Durban. *[Trevor Jones]*

Monrovia, Liberia (OIA Maritime Co. S.A., Athens, Greece) and renamed DAWN under the Panama flag.
2002: Sold to Balanced Holdings Ltd., Monrovia, Liberia (Dido Shipping Co. Ltd., Piraeus, Greece).
23.5.2002: Arrived at Aliaga for scrapping by Yazici Demir Celik A.S, Turkey.

145

456. **STRATHDOON**

L.R./I.M.O. Number 7431831
9,230g
6,103n
14,850d
Clark-Sulzer 5RND68
1973: Contract signed.
8.3.1976: Keel laid.
12.7.1976: Launched for Peninsular and Oriental Steam Navigation Company (P.& O. General Cargo Division), London.
29.10.1976: Completed. British flag.
1987: Sold to Bettina Shipping Co. Ltd., Valletta, Malta (Empresa Navegacion Mambisa (Government of Cuba), Havana, Cuba) and renamed EMERALD ISLANDS.
1994: Management transferred to Nippon Caribbean Shipping Co. Ltd., Tokyo, Japan (Government of Cuba, Havana).
1996: Management transferred to Empresa Navegacion Mambisa (Government of Cuba), Havana.
1997: Renamed WAVEL.
1997: Sold to Skimmer Ltd., Malta (Seabirds Management Inc., Piraeus) and renamed SKIMMER, under the Panamanian flag.
11.9.2002: Arrived Gadani Beach to be broken up.

457. STRATHDUNS

L.R./I.M.O. Number 7341843
9,230g
6,103n
14,850d
Clark-Sulzer 5RND68
1973: Contract signed.
4.5.1976: Keel laid.
7.10.1976: Launched for Peninsular and Oriental Steam Navigation Company (P & O General Cargo Division), London.
19.1.1977: Completed.
11.11.1981: Sold to Biman Shipping Co. S.A., Panama (Nippon Caribbean Shipping Co., Tokyo, Japan, operated by Empresa Navegacion Mambisa, Havana, Cuba), and renamed RUBY ISLANDS under the Maltese flag.
1987: Sold to Golden Comet Navigation Co. Ltd., Panama (Nippon Caribbean Shipping Co., Tokyo, Japan, operated by Empresa Navegacion Mambisa, Havana, Cuba) under the Maltese flag.
1990: Sold to Alaminos Shipping Co. Ltd., Limassol, Cyprus (Naviera Poseidon, Havana) and renamed ALAMINOS.
1998: Renamed IRINA under the Belize flag.
2000: Renamed ENOS under the St.Vincent and Grenadines flag.
13.3.2001: Arrived at Chittagong to be broken up, having been sold for $195 per lightweight ton.
8.4.2001: Work began.

Opposite top: *Strathdoon.* [V.H. Young and L.A. Sawyer collection]
Opposite middle: *Emerald Islands* with another version of the Cuban funnel and a pipe added to her exhaust. Singapore, March 1984. [Roy Kittle, David Salisbury collection]
Opposite bottom: *Skimmer* in Piraeus Roads, 27th December 1998. [Nigel Jones]

Top: *Strathduns* at London, October 1977. [David Salisbury]
Middle: *Ruby Islands*, New Waterway, 7th May 1982. [Paul Boot]
Bottom: Far from the Cuban sun, *Alaminos* wears Naviera Poseidon colours on a cold St. Lawrence Seaway, 27th December 1996. [Marc Piché, David Salisbury collection]

458. STRATHDYCE

L.R./I.M.O. Number 7341855
9,230g
6,103n
14,850d
Clark-Sulzer 5RND68

1973: Contract signed.
16.7.1976: Keel laid.
7.12.1976: Launched for Peninsular and Oriental Steam Navigation Company (P & O General Cargo Division), London.
17.3.1977: Completed.
26.10.1979: Sold to Prekookeanska Plovidba, Bar, Yugoslavia and renamed KOMOVI.
1992: Sold to Bar Overseas Shipping Ltd. (Regal Shipmanagement Ltd.), Valletta, Malta and renamed MONTE.
1997: Owners became Domino Shipping Co. Ltd. (Regal Shipmanagement Ltd.), Valletta, Malta.
1999: Management transferred to Prekookeanska Plovidba, Bar, Yugoslavia.
7.2004: Still listed in 'Lloyd's Register', although no movements have been reported since March 2001, and she is believed to have been broken up in China.

Top: *Strathdyce* passes Erith on the River Thames, July 1977. *[David Salisbury]*

Middle: *Komovi* gingerly approaches the Langton Entrance to Liverpool Docks, July 1987. *[Paul Boot]*

Bottom: Transferred to the Maltese flag, *Monte* retains her Yugoslavian funnel colours. *[Roy Kittle, David Salisbury collection]*

459. KATERINA DRACOPOULOS

L.R./I.M.O. Number 7422764
8,750g
6,440n
14,950d
Hawthorn-Sulzer 5RND68
1974: Contract signed.
11.10.1976: Keel laid.
Name originally chosen was
KATERINA DRACOPOULOS
21.2.1977: Launched for Pine Co.
Ltd., Monrovia, Liberia (Empros
Lines Shipping Company Special
S.A. (George Dracopoulos), Piraeus,
Greece) as KATERINA
DRACOPOULOU.
25.5.1977: Completed as
KATERINA DRACOPOULOS.
Greek flag.
1993: Sold to Delavar Shipping
Co. Ltd., Limassol, Cyprus
(Evangelos P. Nomikos
Corporation, Piraeus, Greece) and
renamed DANGOTE STAR.
1994: Renamed PETRA STAR.
1996: Management transferred to
Moss Marine Management S.A.,
Piraeus, operated by Southern
Steamships (London) Ltd., London
and renamed CHIAN STAR.

Top: *Katerina Dracopoulos*, a typically smart
Dracopoulos ship, passes Terneuzen on the Scheldt
in April 1990. *[David Salisbury]*

Bottom: *Skua* at Durban showing little change after
two decades of service. *[Trevor Jones, David
Salisbury collection]*

1999: Sold to Demart Shipping Co. Ltd.,
Cyprus (Seabirds Management Inc.,
Piraeus) and renamed SKUA.
2002: Sold to TDD Shipbreakers for
$144 per lightweight ton.
24.5.2002: Arrived at Alang.
29.5.2002: Work began.

460. **DUNELMIA (2)**

*The second SD14 with this name; see
Southwick yard number 871*
L.R./I.M.O. Number 7422776
9,346g
6,254n
14,840d
Hawthorn-Sulzer 5RND68
1974: Contract signed.
9.12.1976: Keel laid.
4.5.1977: Launched for Metcalfe
Shipping Co. Ltd. (Metcalfe, Son and
Co.), Hartlepool.
18.7.1977: Completed. British flag.
1979: Vessel and owning company

acquired by Houlder Brothers Ltd.
(Furness Withy and Co. Ltd.
managers), London for £4.26m.
1980: Sold to New Panda Navigation
S.A., Panama (Sin Chiao Shipping
(Private) Ltd., Singapore) for $9.15m
and renamed NEW PANDA.
1985: Sold to Cafung Navigation
S.A., Panama (Wah Tung Shipping
Agency Co. Ltd., Hong Kong) and
renamed TRADE FORTUNE.
1988: Managers became Parakou
Shipping Ltd., Hong Kong and
renamed TRADE FAIR.
1994: Sold to Halldor Shipping Co.

Ltd. (Thoresen and Co. (Bangkok)
Ltd.), Bangkok, Thailand (Arne
Teigen, Oslo, Norway) and renamed
HALLDOR.
9.4.2002: Beached at Tapsakae,
Thailand for breaking up

Top: *Dunelmia* (2) could be distinguished from
her earlier sister of the same name by the very
heavy square-sectioned foremast which
carried a 100-ton derrick, the largest fitted to
an SD14. *[Michael D.J. Lennon, John
Lingwood collection]*
Bottom: *New Panda* passes under Lion's Gate
Bridge, Vancouver on 11th March 1983. *[Don
Brown]*

461. CAPETAN MARKOS

L.R./I.M.O. Number 7422788
8,746g
6,441n
15,000d
Hawthorn-Sulzer 5RND68
1974: Contract signed.
23.2.1977: Keel laid.
1.7.1977: Launched for Johnal Shipping Corporation, Monrovia, Liberia (Glafki Shipping Company S.A. (A. Alafouzos), Athens, Greece).

7.10.1977: Completed, Greek flag.
1980: Sold to Caly Navigation S.A., Panama (Far East Enterprising Co. (H.K.) Ltd., Hong Kong) for $9.3m and renamed CALY.
1983: Managers became Wah Tung Shipping Agency Co. Ltd., Hong Kong.
1994: Sold to Hermes Shipping Co. Ltd. (Thoresen & Co. (Bangkok) Ltd.), Bangkok, Thailand (Arne Teigen, Oslo, Norway) and renamed HERMES III under the Panama flag.
1995: Renamed HERMES under the Thai flag.

Top: In Singapore Roads, 11th August 1979, a lighter floats away to give a clear view of *Capetan Markos*. The Alafouzos ships were in the nominal ownership of companies with titles formed from the names of family members, for instance Johnal from John Alafouzas. *[V.H. Young, Roy Kittle collection]*

Bottom: *Hermes* in the same location. *[V.H. Young, Roy Kittle collection]*

7.2004: Still listed in 'Lloyd's Register' and reported trading in September 2004.

462. SEA LION

L.R./I.M.O. Number 7422790
8,746g
6,441n
15,000d
Hawthorn-Sulzer 5RND68
1974: Contract signed.
6.5.1977: Keel laid.
27.9.1977: Launched for Themal Shipping Corporation, Monrovia, Liberia (Glafki Shipping Company S.A. (A. Alafouzos), Athens, Greece).
10.1.1978: Completed. Greek flag.
1982: Sold to Guangzhou Ocean Shipping Shipping Company (COSCO), Guangzhou, People's Republic of China and renamed NAN JIANG.
1999: Renamed JIN FU.
Prior to 2004: Renamed DONG FA.
7.2004: Still listed in 'Lloyd's Register' as NAN JIANG.

Top: *Sea Lion* in the calm waters of Sharjah, 28th February 1980. *[Roy Kittle]*

Middle: *Sea Lion* again in her native Alafouzos colours on the New Waterway. *[John Phillips, David Salisbury collection]*

Bottom: *Nan Jiang* at Singapore in July 1987. *[L.A. Sawyer, Roy Kittle collection]*

463. MORVIKEN

L.R./I.M.O. Number 7422805
9,117g
6,354n
14,950d
Clark-Sulzer 5RND68
1974: Contract signed.
4.7.1977: Keel laid.
9.1.1978: Launched for Wallem, Steckmest & Co. A.S., Bergen, Norway.
14.4.1978: Completed.
1982: Sold to Guangzhou Ocean Shipping Company (COSCO), Guangzhou, People's Republic of China and renamed RONG JIANG.
1999: Sold to Dalian Zhong Hai Hang Shipping Co., Dalian, People's Republic of China and renamed HAI JI SHUN.
7.2004: Still listed in 'Lloyd's Register', although continued existence must be in doubt as no movements reported since February 1999.

Top: *Morviken* in the New Waterway. The last two SD14s from South Dock had a pole mast forward, in this case carrying a crows nest. The wheelhouse has been extended, and note also the additional boat carried on the poop deckhouse. Who said all SD14s looked alike? *[John Phillips, David Salisbury collection]*

Bottom: *Rong Jiang* in the Kiel Canal. *[Holger Zimmerman, David Whiteside collection]*

Top: *Australind* was the last vessel to be launched from the South Dock Shipyard and the premises were then closed. Staff were transferred to the new shipbuilding complex under construction at Southwick. A new numbering system was introduced covering all new contracts based on adding together the last ship number at South Dock (464), and the current last number in use at Southwick (912) to give 1376. The next new contract was therefore numbered 1377. All subsequent A&P vessels were built at Southwick. *Australind* was also the last vessel built for the Australind Steam Navigation Co. Ltd. which was later closed down by its parent P & O Group. *[George Garwood, David Salisbury collection]*

Bottom: The light pole mast forward can be seen on *Maximo Gomez* in the St. Lawrence, 22nd December 1982. Note the gash on her hull. *[René Beauchamp, David Salisbury collection]*

464. AUSTRALIND

L.R./I.M.O. Number 7422817
9,006g
6,421n
15,150d
Clark-Sulzer 5RND68
1974: Contract signed by Wallem, Steckmest & Co. A.S., Bergen, Norway.
10.1976: Sold.
3.10.1977: Keel laid.
23.3.1978: Launched for Australind Steam Shipping Co. Ltd. (Trinder, Anderson and Co. Ltd.), London.
29.6.1978: Completed. British flag.
6.1980: Sold to Empresa Navegacion Mambisa (Government of Cuba), Havana, Cuba and renamed MAXIMO GOMEZ.
1995: Sold to Pan Pacific Shipping and Trading S.A., Hong Kong (Government of Cuba, Havana), remaining under the Cuban flag.
1997: Sold to Erodios Ltd., Valletta, Malta (Laruse S.A., Piraeus, Greece) and renamed ERODIOS.
2002: Sold for $600,000 and renamed NANKING under the South Korean and later the Jordanian flag.
7.2004: Still listed in 'Lloyd's Register'

Top: *Erodios.* Note the addition of a generator house abaft the funnel. *[Russell Priest]*

Bottom: *Nanking* at Mumbai, 17th March 2003 registered at Onsan, South Korea. Her new owner is believed to be Cuba. *[Nigel Jones]*

Vessels built by Hellenic Shipyards Company, Skaramanga, Greece

1051. (HELLENIC RENAISSANCE) KOSTANTIS YEMELOS

L.R./I.M.O. Number 6824965
9,084g
6,386n
15,349d
Sulzer 5RD68
6.4.1968: Keel laid.
3.8.1968: Launched for Spyros Coumantaros, Piraeus, Greece. Sold whilst fitting out.
7.12.1968: Completed for Cordial Shipping Co., Monrovia, Liberia (Yemelos Brothers General Enter-prises S.A., Piraeus) as KOSTANTIS YEMELOS. Greek flag.
1981: Sold to Alexion Maritime Corporation, Monrovia (Macedonia Shipping Co. Ltd. (Ion Dadakaridis), London) and renamed ALEXION HOPE under the Greek flag.
23.10.1982: Damaged when fire broke out in engine room whilst lying at Sharjah Anchorage during a voyage from Bourgas, Bulgaria to Bandar Khomeini, Iran.
30.11.1982: Dragged anchor for 1.5 miles after being struck in heavy weather at 04.30 hours by the Panamanian motor vessel EASTERN GUARDIAN (11,912/1957).

6.12.1982: Surveyed at Sharjah and subsequently anchored six miles off port.
17.2.1983: Left in tow of tug NAFEER for Bandar Abbas.
12.10.1985: Lying derelict in position 27.13 north by 51.48 east.
8.3.1986: Reported to have sunk in shallow water.

Top: *Kostantis Yemelos.* The Greek-built SD14s generally conformed to the basic specification, but all had winch houses. Photographed in English Bay, Vancouver, 14th June 1974. *[V.H. Young and L.A. Sawyer collection]*

Bottom: *Alexion Hope. [David Whitseside collection]*

156

1052. DORA PAPALIOS

L.R./I.M.O. Number 6901983
9,072g
6,370n
15,363d
Sulzer 5RD68

1967: Option taken out by Spyros Coumantaros, Piraeus, Greece.
3.1968: Taken over by Aegis Shipping Co. Ltd. (N.D. Papalios), Piraeus. This contract had been under negotiation with Bartram and Sons Ltd. but by mutual agreement following completion of licensing agreement was placed with Hellenic Shipyards in order to get their participation in the building programme under way.
3.8.1968: Keel laid.
9.11.1968: Launched for Codros Shipping Co., Monrovia, Liberia (Aegis Shipping Co. Ltd. (N.D. Papalios), Piraeus).
6.3.1969: Completed. Greek flag.
1975: Transferred to Intermar Transport Ltd., Limassol, Cyprus (Aegis Shipping Co. Ltd. (N.D. Papalios), Piraeus).
1976: Transferred to Duiker Shipping Corporation, Monrovia (Aegis

Shipping Co. Ltd. (N.D. Papalios), Piraeus) under the Greek flag.
28.8.1982: Laid up at Eleusis.
1985: Sold to Zebrina Shipping Ltd., Nicosia, Cyprus (Stylianos Markakis, Piraeus) for $425,000 and renamed ZEBRINA.
1986: Sold to Anupama Steel Ltd.,

Dora Papalios laid up at Piraeus 2nd October 1984. *[Nigel Jones]*

Mangalore, India, for $96 per light ton.
11.7.1986: Arrived Mangalore and demolition commenced.

1054. NEA HELLAS

L.R./I.M.O. Number 6909959
9,241g
6,370n
15,379d
Sulzer 5RD68

1967: Option taken out by Spyros Coumantaros, Piraeus.
3.1968: Taken over by Aegis Shipping Co. Ltd. (N.D. Papalios), Piraeus, Greece).
9.11.1968: Keel laid.
8.2.1969: Launched for Nea Hellas Shipping Co. Ltd., Famagusta, Cyprus

(Aegis Shipping Co. Ltd. (N.D. Papalios), Piraeus).
16.5.1969: Completed. Cyprus flag.
1976: Transferred to Topi Shipping Corporation, Monrovia, Liberia (Aegis Shipping Co. Ltd. (N.D. Papalios), Piraeus) and renamed AEGIS FREEDOM under the Greek flag.
1985: Placed under the Panama flag.
1985: Sold to Sybil Navigation Ltd., Limassol, Cyprus (Starfield Maritime Management Ltd., Geneva, Switzerland) for $400,000 together with 1056 and 1061 and renamed SYBIL I.

Nea Hellas as *Aegis Freedom*. *[David Whiteside collection]*

27.10.1985: Wrecked approximately one mile off Southwest Passage Lighthouse, Mississippi River in position 28.54 north by 89.26 west after dragging her anchor during Typhoon 'Juan'. Vessel keeled over and was abandoned by her crew, one of whom was lost. Declared a constructive total loss.

1055. **MISS PAPALIOS**

L.R./I.M.O. Number 6917138
9,241g
6,370n
15,379d
Sulzer 5RD68
8.2.1969: Keel laid.
26.4.1969: Launched for Aktor Shipping Co. Ltd., Famagusta, Cyprus (Aegis Shipping Co. Ltd. (N.D. Papalios), Piraeus, Greece).
18.7.1969: Completed. Cyprus flag.
2.1.1976: Abandoned after grounding on Bombay Reef, Paracel Islands, South China Sea, in position 16.03 north by 112.28 east in severe weather during a voyage from Tientsin, China to Karachi. Her hull was badly cracked and in danger of breaking up.
Previous 9.3.1976: Refloated and towed to Whampoa, China. Declared a constructive total loss and sold to local shipbreakers.

1056. **AEGIS FAME**

L.R./I.M.O. Number 6923412
9,241g
6,370n
15,480d
Sulzer 5RD68
26.4.1969: Keel laid.
12.7.1969: Launched for Marvaliente Compania Naviera S.A., Panama (Aegis Shipping Co. Ltd. (N.D. Papalios), Piraeus, Greece).
11.10.1969: Completed for Fame Shipping Co. Ltd., Famagusta, Cyprus (Aegis Shipping Co. Ltd. (N.D. Papalios), Piraeus). Greek flag.
1985: Sold to Interlaken Shipping Co. Ltd., Limassol, Cyprus (Starfield Maritime Management Ltd., Geneva, Switzerland) for $400,000 together with yard numbers 1054 and 1061 and renamed INTERLAKEN.
1986: Sold to Tong San S. de R.L., Taipei, Taiwan and renamed TONG SAN under the Honduran flag.
1987: Sold to Ging Ya Metal Enterprises Ltd.
5.2.1987: Arrived Kaohsiung, Taiwan for breaking up.

Opposite top: During her relatively short career, *Miss Papalios* avoided the attentions of most colour photographers. *[Fotoflite incorporating Skyfotos]*

Opposite bottom: *Aegis Fame* at Singapore in February 1980. *[Don Brown, David Salisbury collection]*

Top: *Aegis Fame* under Swiss control as *Interlaken* at Durban. *[Trevor Jones]*

Middle: *Aegis Banner* in the New Waterway in August 1978, on charter to Cuba. *[David Salisbury]*

Bottom: *Lafina*, the former *Aegis Banner*, at Singapore, 18th March 1986. *[Roy Kittle]*

1057. **AEGIS BANNER**
L.R./I.M.O. Number 6930142
9,025g
6,377n
15,480d
Sulzer 5RD68
12.7.1969: Keel laid.
20.9.1969: Launched for Marorgulu Compania Naviera S.A., Panama (Aegis Shipping Co. Ltd. (N.D. Papalios), Piraeus, Greece). Greek flag.
12.12.1969: Completed for Banner Shipping Co. Ltd., Famagusta, Cyprus (Aegis Shipping Co. Ltd. (N.D. Papalios), Piraeus.
1985: Placed under Panama flag.
1985: Sold to Lafina Shipping Ltd., Nicosia, Cyprus (Stylianos Markakis, Piraeus) for $500,000 and renamed LAFINA.
1986: Sold to Taher and Co. Ltd., Chittagong, Bangladesh for $99 per lightweight ton for breaking up.
15.9.1986: Arrived Sitakunda Beach, Chittagong.
20.9.1986: Work commenced.

1059. FROSSO K

L.R./I.M.O. Number 7004548
9,069g
6,310n
15,379d
Sulzer 5RD68

20.9.1969: Keel laid.
29.11.1969: Launched for St. Ioannis
Shipping Corporation, Monrovia,
Liberia (Mariners Shipping Agency
S.A. (G. Kefalas), Piraeus, Greece).
12.2.1970: Completed. Greek flag.
31.3.1981: Stranded four miles west
south west of Malmo, Sweden in
position 56.36 north by 12.52 east
during a voyage from Norfolk,
Virginia, USA to Szczecin, Poland.
5.4.1981: Refloated and towed to
Szczecin.
2.11.1981: Reported in tow in
position 49.45 north by 172.42 west
following a serious engine room fire
during a voyage from Japan to
Vancouver.
15.11.1981: Arrived Vancouver with
tug escort.
1987: Sold to Karida Shipping Co.
Ltd., Limassol, Cyprus (Blue Flag
Navigation Ltd., Piraeus) and
renamed ROKER PARK.
1990: Transferred to Park Shipping
Co. Ltd., Valletta, Malta (Blue Flag
Navigation Ltd., Piraeus).
1991: Sold to Mamer Shipping Ltd.,
Valletta (Alco Shipping Co.
(Alexandros Coutroubis), Piraeus)
and renamed MAMER.
Previous to 17.2.1992: Generators
burnt out whilst berthed at
Cienfuegos, Cuba loading a cargo of
raw sugar for the Black Sea.
22.2.1992: Towed to Rio Haina,
Dominican Republic and some
repairs effected.
29.2.1992: Moved to Puerto Viejo,
Dominican Republic.
About 20.9.1992: Cargo transhipped.
6.7.1993: Towed to Santo Domingo,
Dominican Republic.
1994: Sold to Procesadora de
Metales del Caribe, Santo Domingo,

and renamed AUSTIN STAR.
9.2.1995: Sailed from Puerto
Viejo, Dominican Republic,
bound for Cartegena, Columbia,
having been sold to Societa
Industrial de Productos. Reported to have reverted to
MAMER for this voyage.
23.2.1995: Demolition began.

Top: *Frosso K* off New York, July 1979.
*[Trevor Leverton, David Salisbury
collection]*
Middle: A well-laden *Frosso K*. *[V.H.
Young and L.A. Sawyer collection]*
Left: Names associated with Sunderland
were used by Blue Flag Navigation
whose Nik. Koros had been educated in
the town. Ironically, *Roker Park* was
built, not on the Wear, but in Greece.
Seen loading potash on Teesside with a
rather rusty blue flag as a bow crest.
[Nigel Cutts]
Opposite top: *Maria K*. *[V.H. Young and
L.A. Sawyer collection]*
Opposite bottom: *Sea Nymph* at anchor
off Singapore, 23rd January 1988.
[Simon Olsen, David Salisbury collection]

1060. **MARIA K**

L.R./I.M.O. Number 7006065
9,069g
6,310n
15,379d
Sulzer 5RD68
29.11.1969: Keel laid.
5.2.1970: Launched for Frosso
Shipping Company, Monrovia,
Liberia (Mariners Shipping Agency
S.A. (G. Kefalas), Piraeus, Greece).
13.6.1970: Completed. Greek flag.
1986: Sold to Sea Nymph Maritime
S.A., Panama (K.Y.C. Line (S)
(Private) Ltd., Singapore) and
renamed SEA NYMPH.
1988: Sold to Lorentzen Rederi A/S
(Fridtjof Lorentzen), Oslo, Norway
and renamed MARACANA I under
the Panama flag.
1988: Sold to Tropical Navigation
Inc., Panama .

1989: Sold to Sea Freight Carrier
Corporation Inc., Panama (John
McRink and Co. Ltd., Hong Kong)
and renamed LADY VICKY.
1990: Sold to Holister Inc., Panama
(Parakou Shipping Ltd., Hong Kong)
and renamed ERRIA INGE.
About 7.4.1990: Departed Bedi,
India and unreported until arriving in
India some time later, and believed to
have sailed for North Korea or
Vietnam under illegal control.
Prior to 11.1.1991: Sighted at
Bangkok, Thailand as PALU III.
1991: Sold to Chinese breakers as
ERRIA INGE.
25.12.1992: Arrived Hungpu, China
for demolition. When the vessel was
broken up a number of corpses were
found concealed in her hull and on
12th December 1993 a report in the
'Daily Telegraph' alleged a vessel

named HAI SIN, breaking up at
Canton, had on board 10 badly
burned and decomposing bodies,
found in a disused refrigerated
storeroom. Links were made by
investigators to crew members reported missing 12 months previously
following a fire on board the Liberian
tanker NAGASAKI SPIRIT (52,787/
1989) which had collided with a
container ship off Singapore. These
men had been seen leaving in a
lifeboat which had then become
engulfed in flames. It was concluded
that the bodies had been taken from
the sea by HAI SIN and placed in the
refrigerated store. It later transpired
that HAI SIN was actually ERRIA
INGE, reported stolen and missing a
year before, and owned by Australian
Eric Boas. No satisfactory confirmatory
report has been seen.

1061. **AEGIS TRADE**

L.R./I.M.O. Number 7016058
9,025g
6,481n
15,364d
Sulzer 5RD68
5.2.1970: Keel laid.
4.4.1970: Launched for Coronet
Shipping Co., Panama (Aegis
Shipping Co. Ltd. (N.D. Papalios),

Piraeus, Greece).
13.6.1970: Completed. Greek flag.
1985: Sold to Titisee Navigation Co.
Ltd., Panama (Starfield Maritime
Management Ltd., Geneva, Switzerland) for $525,000 together with yard
numbers 1054 and 1056 and renamed
TITISEE under the Cyprus flag.
1986: Sold to Pacific Enterprises for
$104.50 per lightweight ton for

breaking up at Gadani Beach, Pakistan.
14.11.1986: Arrived.
23.11.1986: Demolition commenced.

Top: *Aegis Trade* at Cape Town. *[V.H. Young and
L.A. Sawyer collection]*

Bottom: *Aegis Trade* as *Titisee* under Swiss
control. *[David Whiteside collection]*

162

1062. RINOULA

L.R./I.M.O. Number 7020619
9,069g
6,392n
15,065d
H. Cegielski-Sulzer 5RD68
4.4.1970: Keel laid.
23.5.1970: Launched for Compania
Naviera Syra S.A., Panama (Lemos
and Pateras Ltd., London).
4.8.1970: Completed. Greek flag.
1981: Sold to Sugar and Molasses
Charters Inc., Monrovia, Liberia
(Overseas Shipping Co., Piraeus,
Greece) and renamed UNITY under
the Greek flag.
1982: Renamed UNITY I.
1984: Sold to Alvena Shipping Co.
Ltd., Limassol, Cyprus (Polar Star
Maritime Co. Ltd. (Vas Maltezos),
Piraeus) and renamed NAYA.
1985: Management transferred to
Mayfair (Hellas) Co. Ltd. (Vas
Maltezos), Athens.
1993: Principal of Mayfair (Hellas)
Co. Ltd. becomes Stamatios
Liatsikas.
1994: Sold to Bantam Shipping Co.
Ltd., Monrovia, Liberia (Cometas
Shipping Co. Ltd., Mariupol, Ukraine)
and renamed SUNLIGHT under the St.
Vincent and Grenadines flag.
1996: Management transferred to
Four Seasons Ship Management Ltd.,
Mariupol.
20.2.1997: Arrived at Alang to be
broken up by Abichal Shipbreakers.
10.3.1997: Demolition commenced.

Bottom: *Naya* at Durban. *[Trevor Jones, David Salisbury collection]*

Top: *Rinoula* at Cape Town. *[V.H. Young and L.A. Sawyer collection]*

Middle: *Unity I* on 22nd April 1982. *[René Beauchamp, David Salisbury collection]*

1063. JOHN MICHALOS

L.R./I.M.O. Number 7025308
9,074g
6,396n
15,327d
H. Cegielski-Sulzer 5RD68
23.5.1970: Keel laid.
18.5.1970: Launched for N.G.
Livanos Maritime Co. S.A., Piraeus,
Greece.
24.7.1970: Completed. Greek flag.
1987: Sold to Sea Trade and
Construction Ltd., Dhaka, Bangladesh

and renamed SEA ADVENTURER.
1993: Sold to Government of the
People's Republic of North Korea,
Pyongyang, North Korea and
renamed SAM HAE.
1997: Transferred to Korea Pongsu
Shipping Co. Ltd. (Government of the
People's Republic of North Korea),
Pyongyang and renamed KU RYONG.
5.2004: Renamed SAM HAI 1.
7.2004: Still listed in 'Lloyd's
Register'.

Top: *John Michalos.* Note the light tie beam
between the kingposts, a feature repeated on
several later Skaramanga SD14s, and the
gently-rounded funnel casing. *[V.H. Young and
L.A. Sawyer collection]*

Bottom: The Bangladesh-owned *Sea Adventurer*
at Singapore in April 1988. *[Simon Olsen,
David Salisbury collection]*

1064. SCAPWIND

L.R./I.M.O. Number 7029756
9,077g
6,394n
15,379d
H. Cegielski-Sulzer 5RD68
18.7.1970: Keel laid.
12.9.1970: Launched for Palanka
Shipping Corporation S.A.,
Monrovia, Liberia (Circe Shipping
Enterprises Ltd. (G.Z. Lanaras and Ion
Paraschis), Athens, Greece).
18.11.1970: Completed. Greek flag.
1983: Management transferred to
Alpha Managing and Financing Inc.
(G.D. Daispyros), Athens.
1984: Management transferred to
Vernicos Maritime Co. S.A. (C.C., D.
and N.A. Vernicos), Piraeus).
1989: Sold to Zamora Navigation Co.
Ltd., Limassol, Cyprus (Ancora
Investment Trust Inc., Piraeus) and
renamed MARINER.
1993: Transferred to
Panmediterranean
Shipping Co. Ltd.,
Valletta, Malta
(Ancora Investment
Trust Inc., Piraeus).
Prior to 2002: Sold
and renamed WAN
CHANG under the
Chinese flag.
2004: Renamed LI JIA.
7.2004: Still listed by
'Lloyd's Register'.

Top: *Scapwind* in the New
Waterway, 24th August
1987. *[Rowley Weeks,
David Salisbury collection]*
Middle: *Scapwind*
approaching Liverpool, also in
August 1987. *[Paul Boot]*
Bottom: *Mariner* at
Montreal, 10th July 1991.
*[René Beauchamp, Roy
Kittle collection]*

1065. ROSARIO

L.R./I.M.O. Number 7037868
9,077g
6,394n
15,379d
H. Cegielski-Sulzer 5RD68
12.9.1970: Keel laid.
21.11.1970: Launched for International
Shipping Ltd., Monrovia, Liberia
(Lemuria Shipping Corporation (Jan
Weise), New York, USA) (Lumber and
Shipping Corporation S.A., managers).
22.1.1971: Completed. Greek flag.
1972: Management transferred to
Lanauta Ltd., Piraeus, Greece.
1973: Owners reported as Lemuria
Shipping Corporation (Spyros
Tsilimparis), New York, USA
(Lanauta Ltd., Piraeus, managers).
1974: Management transferred to
Lanauta Shipping E.P.E. (Spyros
Tsilimparis), Athens, Greece.
1984: Sold to Radian Sun Navigation
S.A., Panama (G.Th. Sigalas,
Piraeus) and renamed SAN JOHN
under the Greek flag.
1986: Management transferred to
Trade Fortune Inc. (G.Th. Sigalas
and G.N. Tattos), Piraeus.
1988: Sold to Evansville Overseas
Inc., Panama (Ship Management
Division, Holbud Ltd., London) and
renamed AL RAZIQU.
19.7.1992: Reported to be leaking
during a voyage from Bangkok to
Mombasa.
29.7.1992: Arrived Mombasa under
escort and after discharge was given

permission to sail to Alang for
demolition.
1.8.1992: Anchored off port and later
resold to Pakistani shipbreakers.
18.9.1992: Sailed Alang for Karachi
but resold to Sara Maritime Ltd.
(Delta One International), Panama,
renamed DELTA III under the St.
Vincent and Grenadines flag and drydocked for repairs at Dubai.
1993: Sold to Galaxy Shipping Ltd.,
Dubai, United Arab Emirates and
renamed CHALLENGE under the St.
Vincent and Grenadines flag.
2.8.1993: Sprang a leak and developed
a heavy list whilst at outer anchorage,
New Mangalore, India, whilst on a

Top: *Rosario* on Lake Ontario in November 1978.
Note the 'TS' monogram on the bow for Spyros
Tsilimparis. *[David Kohl, David Salisbury
collection]*

Middle: *Al Raziqu* at Durban in Holbud colours.
This is another SD14 with tie bars between its
kingposts. *[Trevor Jones, David Salisbury
collection]*

voyage from Kandla to Luanda,
Angola with a cargo of sugar, soap
and rice. Subsequently keeled over
whilst being towed to shallow water
and sank in position 12.54.08 north
by 74.46.01 east. Three crew
members were lost.

1066. **NIKI**

L.R./I.M.O. Number 7046900
9,075g
6,394n
15,379d
H. Cegielski-Sulzer 5RD68
21.11.1970: Keel laid.
30.1.1971: Launched for Omala
Shipping Co. S.A., Panama (N.E.
Neophytos, Piraeus, Greece).
7.4.1971: Completed. Greek flag.
1982: Reported to have been renamed NIKI II.
1983: Sold to Pilar Shipping S.A.,
Panama and later St. Helier, Jersey
(Sablestar Ltd., London, agents) and
renamed PILARMAST under the
Panama flag.
1984: Management transferred to
S.L. Sethia Liners Ltd., London.
1986: Transferred to Maritz Shipping
S.A., Panama (S.L. Sethia Liners Ltd.,
London) and renamed MARITZ STAR.
1987: Management transferred to
Nerofleet Ltd., London.
1992: Sold to Korea Tonghae Shipping Co. (Government of the People's
Republic of North Korea), Pyongyang
and renamed PYONG CHON.

1996: Transferred to Sehae Shipping
Private Co. Ltd. (Korea Tonghae
Shipping Co.), Pyongyang.
22.8.1997: Arrived at Alang to be
broken up by Priyank Steel, having
been sold for $177.5 per lightweight
ton. Work began the same day.

Top: *Niki* on the New Waterway, August 1976,
with Mitsui's orange funnel. Her king posts are
closer together than usual. *[David Salisbury]*

Middle: *Pilarmast. [David Whiteside collection]*

Bottom: *Pyong Chon. [Russell Priest, Trevor
Jones collection]*

167

1067.
KALLIOPI YEMELOS
L.R./I.M.O. Number 7041182
9,074g
6,388n
15,327d
H. Cegielski-Sulzer 5RD68
12.10.1970: Keel laid.
12.12.1970: Launched for Komar General Enterprises S.A., Panama (Yemelos Brothers General Enterprises S.A., Piraeus, Greece).

15.2.1971: Completed. Managers Chios Navigation Co. Ltd. (I.C. and D.C. Caroussis and N.A. Pittas), London. Greek flag.
1973: Management transferred to Yemelos Brothers General Enterprises S.A., Piraeus, Greece).
1982: Sold to Black King Shipping Corporation, Monrovia, Liberia (Inter Shipping Management Ltd. (D.A. Lemos and P.G. Papantoniou), London) (Macedonia Shipping Co. Ltd., London, managers) and

Top: *Kalliopi Yemelos* at Hong Kong in November 1980. Note the blue spiral painted on the ensign staff. *[David Salisbury]*

Bottom: *Toxotis* at Vancouver, 23rd March 1974. *[Don Brown]*

renamed LITSION PRIDE.
9.8.1982: Sunk off Khor Musa, Iran after being struck by Iraqi missiles during a voyage from Dunkirk to Bandar Khomeni with a cargo of sugar. All crew members saved.

1068. TOXOTIS

L.R./I.M.O. Number 7052210
9,082g
6,385n
5,327d
H. Cegielski-Sulzer 5RD68
12.12.1970: Keel laid.
27.2.1971: Launched for Panamic Shipping Co. S.A., Panama. (Tsavliris Shipping Ltd., London).

6.5.1971: Completed. Greek flag.
1987: Sold to Hamilton Maritime Co. Ltd., Limassol, Cyprus (Vernicos Maritime Co. Ltd. (C.D. and N.A. Vernicos), Piraeus) and renamed TOXA.
1994: Sold to Millenium Maritime Ltd., Valletta, Malta (Ray Shipping Enterprises, Karachi, Pakistan) and renamed HARMONY SKY.

1995: Sold to Jaryan Maritime Ltd., Isle of Man (Senyar Maritime Establishment, Dubai, United Arab Emirates) and renamed TOPAZ under the Belize flag.
21.6.1997: Arrived at Alang, India for scrapping by Senyar Maritime Establishment.
4.12.1997: Work commenced.

Above and below: *Toxa*, still in Tsavliris funnel colours, in St. Lawrence ice, 12th December 1989. *[Marc Piché, Roy Kittle and David Salisbury collections]*

1069. TAXIARCHIS

L.R./I.M.O. Number 7108942
9,078g
6,389n
15,327d
H. Cegielski-Sulzer 5RD68
27.2.1971: Keel laid.
8.5.1971: Launched for Campeon
Navegacion S.A., Panama (Kronos
Shipping Co. Ltd. (D.G. and M.G.
Lemos), London).
5.7.1971: Completed. Greek flag.
1982: Sold to St. Mary Maritime Co.
S.A., Panama (Marship Corporation,
Piraeus, Greece) and renamed
ATROPOS.
1984: Managers became Marship
Services Inc., Piraeus.
2.8.1986: Arrived Gadani Beach,
Pakistan for breaking up having been
sold for $94.50 per lightweight ton.

Opposite: Three views of *Taxiarchis*. Note how the tie beams have become standard on the basic model from Skaramanga. *[David Whiteside collection; David Kohl, David Salisbury collection; V.H. Young and L.A. Sawyer collection]*
Top: *Neotis* off San Francisco. *[George Lamuth, David Salisbury collection]*
Bottom: Seen at Vancouver in July 1989, with her name shortened to *Neos*, and ostensibly sold but still wearing the Tsavliris funnel colours with which she was launched. *[Don Brown, David Salisbury collection]*

1070. **NEOTIS**

L.R./I.M.O. Number: 7114977
9,082g
6,385n
15,327d
H. Cegielski-Sulzer 5RD68
8.5.1971: Keel laid.
17.7.1971: Launched for Panbalco Shipping Co. S.A., Panama (Tsavliris Shipping Ltd., London).

4.10.1971: Completed. Greek flag.
1987: Sold to Coralsand Navigation Co. Ltd., Limassol, Cyprus (Vernicos Maritime Co. Ltd. (C.D. and N.A. Vernicos), Piraeus, Greece) and renamed NEOS.
4.11.1994: Arrived at Alang for scrapping by Mahavir Inductomelt (Private) Ltd.
4.12.1994: Demolition commenced.

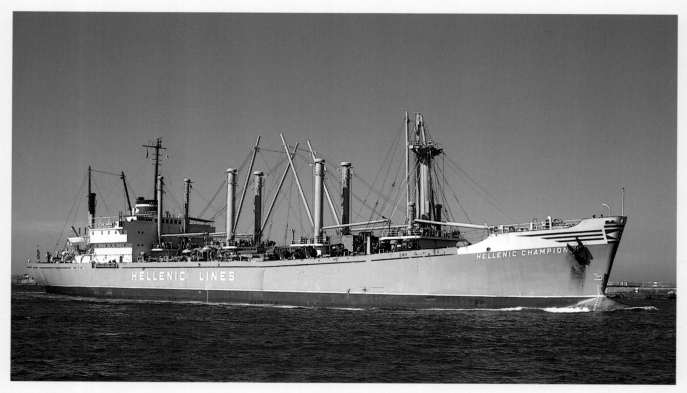

1071. HELLENIC CHAMPION

L.R./I.M.O. Number 7117242
8,987/5,881g
6,497/3,611n
15,037/12,701d
MAN R9V 52/55
5.6.1971: Keel laid.
21.8.1971: Launched for Hellenic Lines Ltd., London and later Piraeus (P.G. Callimanopoulos, Piraeus, Greece).
18.12.1971: Completed. Greek flag.
23.12.1988: Laid up at Piraeus when owner filed for bankruptcy.

1984: Reported renamed C. CHAMPION.
1984: Sold to Lynx Trading Corporation, Monrovia, Liberia (Forum Maritime S.A. (St. Katounis), Piraeus) (International Sugar Transport Inc., London, managers) and renamed ATLANTIC LEADER under the Panama flag.
5.1986: Sold to Borsha Shipping Co. S.A., Panama (Mamoni Shipping Co. Ltd. (S. Bose), Calcutta, India) and renamed BIPASHA.
1990: Placed under Maltese flag.
2.4.1991: Hull damaged in collision with the Isle of Man-registered bulk carrier BROOMPARK (18,189/1982)

Top: *Hellenic Champion* at Durban on 1st March 1977. *[Peter Newton, Roy Kittle collection]*

Below: *Bipasha* at Singapore 29th April 1988, showing her bulbous bow. *[Alwyn MacMillan, Jim Prentice collection]*

in Chittagong Outer Anchorage. Cargo subsequently discharged at Mongla.
30.4.1991: Sustained further damage during cyclone and sold to breakers.
8.7.1991: Arrived Chittagong for breaking up by Rahim Steel Mills (Private) Ltd.

1072. HELLENIC CHALLENGER

L.R./I.M.O. Number 7122754
8,987/5,881g
6,497/3,711n
15,037/12,701d
MAN R9V 52/55
21.8.1971: Keel laid.
30.10.1971: Launched for Hellenic

Lines Ltd., London and later Piraeus (P.G. Callimanopoulos, Piraeus, Greece).
15.3.1972: Completed. Greek flag.
23.12.1988: Arrested after owner filed for bankruptcy.
1985: Sold by auction to Sally Shipping Ltd. S.A., Panama. (Universal Chartering Corporation of Greenwich, Connecticut, USA) for

$641,000 and renamed SARA D.
13.12.1985: Abandoned off Mersing, Malaysia, following an engine room fire whilst on a voyage from Inchon to India and Europe with a cargo of 12,000 tonnes of sugar. Later that day sank following a collision with the Chinese motor vessel WU MEN (9,672/1976) whilst anchored in position 02.16 north by 104.56 east.

Top: *Hellenic Challenger* at Durban. *[Trevor Jones, David Salisbury collection]*

Bottom: Seen again, this time at Capetown on 27th June 1977. Yard numbers 1071 to 1076 were the only major variation from the basic design of SD14 built at Skaramanga. As well as more extensive cargo gear, they had bulbous bows and a third deck to the superstructure which was extended outwards to provide passenger accommodation. Externally they were in some ways the Greek equivalents of the Sunderland-built *Belle Rose* and *Belle Isle*. *[Ian Shiffman, Roy Kittle collection]*

1073. HELLENIC CARRIER

L.R./I.M.O. Number: 7203687

	1983:
8,987/5,881g	9,993g
6,497/3,611n	8,115n
15,153/12,701d	18,924d

MAN R9V 52/55

30.10.1971: Keel laid.
8.1.1972: Launched for Hellenic Lines Ltd., London and later Piraeus (P.G. Callimanopoulos, Piraeus, Greece).
20.4.1972: Completed. Greek flag.
6.5.1981: Damaged in collision with the US barge carrier LASH

ATLANTICO (26,406/72) off Cape Henry in position 36.17 north by 75.34 west during a voyage from New Orleans to Karachi. Arrived Hampton Roads later that day. Later declared a constructive total loss.
1981: Sold to Atlantic Towing Inc. who rebuilt and lengthened hull by adding an 180 feet section and converting her to a chemical tanker. New dimensions: 164.65 (BB) x 20.45 x 8.916 metres
1983: Returned to service for Atlantic Co. Ltd. Partnership, Wilmington, Delaware, USA (Allied Towing Corporation, Norfolk, Virginia, USA) as SEA VENTURE.

Top: *Hellenic Carrier* at Cape Town. The widened third deck of the superstructure is very apparent here. *[Ian Shiffman, David Salisbury collection]*

1986: Ultimate owner became Waterways Transportation and Trading Co., Minneapolis, Minnesota, USA.
1987: Ultimate owners became Atlantic Tankships Inc., St Paul, Minnesota, USA.
1995: Owner became Atlantic Tankships Inc., Norfolk, Virginia, USA.
7.2004: Still listed in 'Lloyd's Register'.

Around 7.00am on 6th May 1981 *Hellenic Carrier*, en route from Savannah to Baltimore with a mixed cargo including chicken feed and timber, was in collision with Prudential Lines' barge carrier *LASH Atlantico* (26,406/1972) in dense fog about 35 miles south east of Cape Henry, North Carolina. Despite the conditions *LASH Atlantico* had been travelling at a reported speed of 18 knots and, as the subsequent Coast Guard hearing revealed, with defective radar. Her bow cut heavily into the starboard mid-ships side of *Hellenic Carrier* flooding number 3 hold and rupturing the fuel tanks. Both vessels remained afloat and *Hellenic Carrier* was successfully towed to Lambert Point Docks in Norfolk, Virginia, where she was subsequently declared a constructive total loss. Barely nine years old, she was bought by the local towing and

salvage company, Allied Towing Corporation, who saw her potential for a most unusual conversion. United States shipyards have a well established record for major ship surgery but there have been few instances where a dry cargo ship has undergone a transformation to tanker.

The reconstruction was undertaken at Hampton Roads where the damaged section of the hull between frames 85 - 118 (effectively the whole of number 3 hold and the after part of number 2) was cut away and a new 180-foot long section inserted, thus increasing her length by 71 feet. The main bulkeads between numbers 1/2 and 3/4 holds were retained but the 'tween decks throughout the main forward section were removed and the hull divided into seven tank sections, sub-compartmented by two continuous

longitudinal bulkheads running between the fore-peak and a new cofferdam bulkhead positioned 10 feet ahead of the original engine room bulkhead. The aft hold, number 5, was less altered to form the number 8 tank with only a new centre line bulkhead constructed and the 'tween deck retained. The hatchways were of course removed and the openings fully plated over. Above deck all the cargo gear and the deck houses were cut away and in their place a small hose-handling crane and continuous catwalk from the superstructure to the forecastle were provided. The superstructure block was partly rebuilt with a new wheelhouse set on top of the former navigation bridge structure which was converted into a cargo monitor room.

Despite the apparent lack of sophisticated cargo tank facilities the conversion has obviously been a success and 21 years later *Sea Venture* is still in service with Atlantic Tankships Inc., trading principally on the east coast of the United States.

Opposite bottom and this page left: *Sea Venture* was photographed at a snowy Portsmouth, New Hampshire on 3rd February 2003. *[William Schell]*
Below: General arrangement drawing reproduced courtesy of Atlantic Tankships Inc.

M/T "SEA VENTURE"

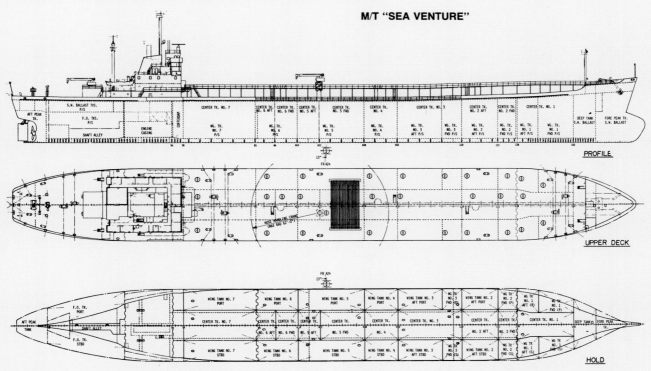

1074. HELLENIC IDEAL

L.R./I.M.O. Number 7208467
8,987/5,881g
6,497/3,611n
15,153/12,701d
MAN R9V 52/56
8.1.1972: Keel laid.
24.3.1972: Launched for Hellenic Lines Ltd., London and later Piraeus (P.G. Callimanopoulos, Piraeus, Greece).
24.6.1972: Completed. Greek flag.
1984: Sold to Eurolook Shipping Ltd., Limassol, Cyprus (Anangel Shipping Enterprises S.A. (A. Angelicoussis and G. Pateras),

Piraeus) (Adelfia Shipping Enterprises S.A., Piraeus, managers) and renamed TOLMI.
1988: Sold to Bulkship (Nigeria) Ltd., Apapa, Nigeria (Lorentzens Rederi Co. (Fridtjof Lorentzen), Oslo, Norway) and renamed INNA WAKILI.
1989: Sold to Anteus Marine Ltd., St. Julian's, Malta (Alfa Shipping Co. S. de R.L., Piraeus) and renamed TELEMACHOS.
1990: Managers became Ariston Management Co. Ltd., Piraeus.
1991: Sold to Mega Union Shipping Ltd., Valletta, Malta (Mega Trust Maritime S.A., Piraeus) and renamed

Top: *Hellenic Ideal* at Cape Town, 1st March 1977. *[Roy Kittle collection]*

Bottom: *Hellenic Navigator* at Durban. *[Trevor Jones, David Salisbury collection]*

MEGA UNION.
1993: Sold to Prudent International Shipping and Trading Ltd., Nassau, Bahamas (Fouladi General Trading Co., Dubai, United Arab Emirates) and renamed PRUDENT VOYAGER under the St. Vincent and Grenadines flag.
6.1.1996: Arrived Alang in tow for breaking up by Nagarseth Shipbreakers.

1075. HELLENIC NAVIGATOR

L.R./I.M.O. Number 7217913
8,987/5,881g
6,497/3,611n
15,153/12,701d
MAN R9V 52/56
24.3.1972: Keel laid.
27.5.1972: Launched for Hellenic Lines Ltd., London and later Piraeus (P.G. Callimanopoulos, Piraeus, Greece).
11.9.1972: Completed. Greek flag.
21.2.1981: Sustained damage forward when in collision with an oil field structure off Ras Al Khaafji

during a voyage from Houston to Karachi.
1984: Sold to Symbol Shipping Co. Ltd., Limassol and later Nicosia, Cyprus (Shipping and Commercial Corporation (M. Lambros), Piraeus) and renamed GIANNIS L.
1988: Sold to Korea Tonghae Shipping Co. (Government of the People's Republic of North Korea), Pyongyang, North Korea and re-named KUM GANG.
1996: Transferred to Sehae Shipping Private Co. Ltd. (Korea Tonghae Shipping Co. (Government of the People's Republic of North Korea), Pyongyang.

Top: *Giannis L* at Montreal, 17th October 1985. *[René Beauchamp, David Salisbury collection]*

Bottom: Under North Korean ownership as *Kum Gang*, the heavy lift derrick has gone from the foremast. *[Russell Priest]*

1999: Transferred to Tonghae Sonbak Co. Ltd. (Government of the People's Republic of North Korea), Pyongyang.
7.2004: Still listed by 'Lloyd's Register' but continued existence must be in doubt as no movements reported since February 2000.

1076. GRIGORIOS C. IV

L.R./I.M.O. Number 7224643
8,987/5,880g
6,497/3,611n
15,153/12,701d
MAN R9V 52/56
27.5.1972: Keel laid.
5.8.1972: Launched for Hellenic
Lines Ltd., London and later Piraeus
(P.G. Callimanopoulos, Piraeus,
Greece).
20.12.1972: Completed. Greek flag.
12.10.1979: Engine room and
accommodation gutted by fire whilst
on a voyage from New Orleans to
Limassol.
25.10.1979: Arrived Piraeus under
tow for repairs.
1984: Sold to Venture Overseas S.A.,
Panama (Alma Maritime Co. S.A.
(Igidoros Tsangaris), Piraeus) and
renamed TIMIOS STAVROS.
1988: Sold to Spacetop Navigation
Ltd., Nicosia, Cyprus (Ilios Shipping
Co. S.A. (C.P. Eliopoulos), Piraeus)
and renamed SAINT ANDREAS.

1989: Sold to Taurange Shipping
Inc., Panama (Atlas Shipping Lines
Ltd. (Sanaullah Chowdhury),
Chittagong, Bangladesh) and renamed SAFAR.
5.11.1998: Arrived Chittagong for
breaking up by Habib Steels Ltd.

Top: *Gregorios C. IV* puts into Cape Town with a
deck cargo of buses. *[V.H. Young and L.A.
Sawyer collection]*
Middle: *Saint Andreas* at Singapore, 21st
November 1989. *[V.H. Young, Roy Kittle
collection]*
Bottom: *Timios Stavros. [David Hunt collection]*

1077. **SCAPBREEZE**

L.R./I.M.O. Number 7118014
9,085g
6,283n
15,315d
Cegielski-Sulzer 5RD68
17.7.1971: Keel laid.
11.9.1971: Launched for Enka
Shipping Corporation, Monrovia,
Liberia (Circe Shipping Enterprises
Ltd. (G.Z. Lanaris and Ion Paraschis),
Piraeus, Greece).
1.12.1971: Completed. Greek flag.
1983: Sold to Southern Victor
Navigation Co. Ltd., Limassol,
Cyprus (Vernicos Maritime Co. S.A,
Piraeus) and renamed BREEZE.
22.12.1983: Bombed and set on fire
by an Iraqi aircraft in Khor Musa
during a voyage in convoy from
Antwerp to Bandar Khomeni with
14,400 tonnes of sugar in bags.
Subsequently ran aground in Bushire
Roads. The master and one crew
member were killed.

Top: *Grigorios C. IV* as *Safar* at Singapore, 18th
November 1995. *[Simon Olsen, Roy Kittle
collection]*

Above: *Scapbreeze* with a full deck cargo. *[David
Whiteside collection]*

Below: Seen again at Singapore, 12th April
1980. *[V.H. Young, Roy Kittle collection]*

1106. REA

L.R./I.M.O. Number 7104714
9,025g
6,473n
15,315d
Cegielski-Sulzer 5RD68
30.1.1971: Keel laid.
3.4.1971: Launched for Claudio
Shipping and Investment Inc.,
Panama (Franco Shipping Co. Ltd.
(P.J. Caias and G.C. Mavroyalis),
Athens, Greece).
15.6.1971: Completed. Greek flag.
1979: Management transferred to
Tabac Corporation (N.A. and G.A.
Frangistas), Athens.
1988: Sold to Brea Shipping Corporation,
Monrovia, Liberia (Singa Ship
Management Private Ltd. (Ole
Hegland), Singapore) and renamed
BREA under the Panama flag.
1989: Management transferred to B.
and H. Management Ltd. (Arvid
Bergvall and Michael Hudner),
Hamilton, Bermuda.
1991: Renamed REA.
1991: Sold to Cardinal Maritime Co.
S.A., Panama. It was intended to
rename the ship IOAN, but this was
not carried out.
1995: Sold to Nelson Navigation
Inc., Panama (Technical Marine
Planning (Overseas) Ltd., Piraeus)
and renamed MARE.
1997: Sold to Trans Asia Shipping
Ltd. S.A., Belize (East West Marine
Private Ltd., Dhaka, Bangladesh) and
renamed SEA BIRD.
1999: Renamed SEA BIRD I.
1999: Renamed SEA TIGER and
transferred to Honduran flag.
2000: Renamed NORTH STAR II.

Top: *Rea. [David Salisbury]*

19.10.2000: Arrived Chittagong for
breaking up.

Middle: At Singapore displaying Frangistas funnel
colours. *[Trevor Jones, David Salisbury
collection]*

Bottom: The addition of a letter B makes her
Brea, seen entering the Kiel Canal at Holtenau.
[Holger Zimmerman, David Whiteside collection]

1107. DESPINA

L.R./I.M.O. Number 7110335
9,085g
6,284n
15,216d
Cegielski-Sulzer 5RD68
3.4.1971: Keel laid.
5.6.1971: Launched for Gulliver
Shipping Co. Ltd., Monrovia,
Liberia (Franco Shipping Co. Ltd.
(P.J. Caias and G.C. Mavroyalis),
Athens, Greece).
10.8.1971: Completed. Greek flag.
1979: Management transferred to
Tabac Corporation (N.A. and G.A.

Frangistas), Athens.
1987: Sold to Brookfield Shipping
Co. Ltd., Panama (Canopus Shipping
S.A. (Andreas and George Kyrtatas),
Athens) and renamed HARMONY I.
1988: Sold to Government of the
People's Republic of North Korea,
Pyongyang, North Korea and re-
named KYONG SONG.
1996: Transferred to Sehae Shipping
Private Co. Ltd. (Korea Tonghae
Shipping Co.) (Government of the
People's Republic of North Korea),
Pyongyang.
1999: Transferred to Taedonggang

Top: *Despina. [V.H. Young and L.A. Sawyer collection]*

Bottom: In North Korean ownership, *Kyong Song* still looks cared for at Singapore in November 1989. *[V.H. Young, Roy Kittle collection]*

Sonbok Co. Ltd., Nampo, North
Korea (Government of the People's
Republic of North Korea,
Pyongyang).
2002: Sold to Chinese breakers for
$150 per lightweight ton.
11.11.2002: Arrived Zhuhai.

Vessels built by Companhia Comercio e Navegacao (CCN), Rio de Janeiro

031. SERRA VERDE

L.R./I.M.O. Number 7218204
9,112g
6,244n
15,241d
Mecapesa-MAN K6Z70/120E
2.1972: Keel laid.
22.5.1972: Launched for Empresa de Navegacao Alianca S.A., Rio de Janeiro, Brazil.
2.1.1973: Completed. Brazilian flag.
1983: Sold to Seapine Maritime Inc. (Compania Maritima Elica S.A. (D. Kondylios), Piraeus, Greece) and renamed ELIZABETH.
1988: Transferred to Polytrans Shipping Co. Ltd., Limassol, Cyprus (Compania Maritima Elica S.A. (D. Kondylios), Piraeus) and renamed ELIZABETH K.
1991: Sold to Mega Luck Shipping Ltd., Valletta, Malta (Mega Trust Maritime S.A., Piraeus) and renamed MEGA LUCK.
1992: Transferred to Mogli Shipping Co. Ltd., Malta (Mega Trust Maritime S.A., Piraeus) and renamed MOGLI.
1994: Sold to Lavender Services Inc., Monrovia, Liberia (Threemar Maritime Corporation S.A., Piraeus) and renamed AMANECIDA.
1995: Placed under Honduras flag.
1996: Sold to Zalcosea Marine Inc., Panama (Seatime Shipping Private Ltd., Singapore) and renamed ZALCOSEA II under the St. Vincent and the Grenadines flag
1996: Transferred to Jahan Shipping Inc., Belize City, Belize (Seatime Shipping Private Ltd., Singapore) and renamed JAHAN.
27.12.1996: Reported sunk about 680 miles from Capetown in position

Top: *Serra Verde* in the New Waterway, 24th May 1976. *[Paul Boot]*
Middle: *Elizabeth K. [Holger Zimmerman, David Whiteside collection]*
Bottom: *Mogli* at Montreal, 22nd July 1992. *[René Beauchamp, Roy Kittle collection]*

32.45 south by 00.045 east whilst on a voyage from Brazil to Iraq with a cargo of sugar. Although the crew of 28 abandoned ship, searches failed to find them. It is believed that a Ghanaian crime syndicate had taken over the ship.
6.1.1997: Vessel arrived at Tema under name of ZALCOSEA II.

Placed under arrest by naval authorities with heavy financial penalties proposed by South African Government for time wasted on abortive search.
1998: An attempted auction at Accra attracted no interest.
16.11.1999: Declared a constructive total loss.

032. SERRA DOURADA

L.R./I.M.O. Number 7224617
9,112g
6,244n
15,241d
Mecapesa-MAN K6Z70/120E
22.5.1972: Keel laid.
14.7.1972: Launched for Empresa de Navegacao Alianca S.A., Rio de Janeiro, Brazil.
23.3.1973: Completed. Brazilian flag.
1983: Sold to Naviera Universal S.A., Lima, Peru and renamed UNIMAR.
18.4.1985: Towed into Los Angeles by tug PETER FOSS after a fire in the engine room.
1985: Transferred to Naviera Universal S.A., Panama (Naviera Universal S.A., Lima, Peru) and renamed MARE.
30.1.1988: Attacked by Iranian gunboats in error during a voyage to Bushire, Iran. Fire ensued and she was abandoned by her crew. Taken in tow for Dubai.
4.2.1988: Anchored in position 25.16 north by 54.59 east where she subsequently sank. Smit-Tak, who were in charge of salvage operations, were ordered to remove wreck as it was considered a danger to shipping. Hulk removed by cutting into eight sections and lifting pieces from sea bed on to a barge by crane SMIT CYCLONE, and transporting to Ajman, UAE, for breaking up.
24.4.1991: Work completed.

Top: *Serra Dourada* at Cardiff in 1981. *[Bob Allen]*

Middle: An earlier shot of *Serra Dourada* at North Woolwich on the Thames in September 1980. *[David Salisbury]*

Bottom: The Peruvian-owned *Unimar* at Durban. *[Trevor Jones]*

Vessels below with dual tonnages have a 'tween deck in number 5 hold and are thus eligible to have tonnage mark assigned.

033. **RODRIGO TORREALBA**

L.R./I.M.O. Number: 7226407
9,112/5,813g
6,244/2,927n
14,992d
Mecapesa-MAN K6Z70/120E
14.7.1972: Keel laid.
6.9.1972: Launched for Companhia Paulista de Comercio Maritimo (Wilfried Penha Borges), Rio de Janeiro, Brazil.
22.5.1973: Completed. Brazilian flag.
10.2.1980: Holed when grounded on a reef in position 21.40 north by 38.49 east whilst on a voyage from Santos to Jeddah.
11.1.1981: Towed in and, although declared a constructive total loss, later repaired.
1981: Sold to Sulcis Shipping Corporation, Monrovia, Liberia (Titan Shipping and Brokerage Ltd. (M.H. Ghertsos, J.P. and N.F. Papanicolaou), London) and renamed FEDORA under the Greek flag.
1985: Sold to Naviera Centromar S.A., Panama (Naviera Universal S.A., Lima, Peru) and renamed UNISELVA.
1988: Ship and company registered in Netherlands Antilles.
1994: Sold to Focus Point International Inc. (Unimarine Shipping Lines Inc.), Cebu, Philippines and renamed ASIA PROSPERITY under the Belize flag.

6.4.1995: Arrived at Kolkata, India
8.1995: Demolition began by Jain Udyog.
30.12.1995: Demolition complete.

034. **LLOYDBRAS**

L.R./I.M.O. Number 7232951
9,112/5,813g
6,244/2,927n
14,992/12,211d
Mecapesa-MAN K6Z70/120E
Ordered by Companhia Paulista de Comercio Maritimo (Wilfried Penha Borges), Rio de Janeiro, Brazil.
6.9.1972: Keel laid. Sold during building.
17.11.1972: Launched for Companhia de Navegacao Lloyd Brasileiro, Rio de Janeiro.
17.7.1973: Completed. Brazilian flag.

1988: Sold to Transatlantic Glory S.A., Panama (Good Faith Shipping Co. S.A. (Nikolaos Frangos and Nicholas G. Moundreas), Piraeus, Greece) and renamed BRASILIA.
28.12.1988: Fire in accommodation whilst at San Juan, Puerto Rico during a voyage from Paranagua to the USA with a cargo of steel and lumber. Fire extinguished. Later declared a constructive total loss, but repaired.
1989: Transferred to Geranos Shipping Co. Ltd., Valletta, Malta (Good Faith Shipping Co. S.A. (Nikolaos Frangos and Nicholas G. Moundreas), Piraeus, Greece) and renamed KAVO GERANOS.
23.2.2000: Arrived Mumbai for demolition.

Opposite top: *Uniselva* at Durban before her registration was changed from Panama to Netherlands Antilles. *[Trevor Jones, David Salisbury collection]*
Opposite middle: *Uniselva* damaged and beached, apparently for breaking. Nevertheless, she traded further as *Asia Prosperity* before being broken up. *[V.H. Young and L.A. Sawyer collection]*
Top: *Lloydbras* arriving Cape Town. *[Trevor Jones]*
Middle: *Kavo Geranos*. *[V.H. Young and L.A. Sawyer collection]*
Middle: *L/L Chile* at Guayaquil. *[Markus Berger]*

035. (PRINCESA ISABEL) L/L CHILE

L.R./I.M.O. Number: 7304584
8,681/5,597g
5,813/2,729n
14,609d
Mecapesa-MAN K6Z70/120E
17.11.1972: Keel laid.
26.1.1973: Launched for Neptunia Sociedade de Navegacao Ltda., Sao Paulo, Brazil.
Sold whilst fitting out.
17.9.1973: Completed for Lloyd-Libra Navegacao S.A., Rio de Janeiro, Brazil as L/L CHILE.
30.3.1987: Laid up at Rio de Janeiro.
1990: Sold to Race Shipping Inc., Monrovia, Liberia (Momentum Marine Services (Panama) S.A.), renamed ALEXANDRA.
19.10.1991: Fire in engine room whilst effecting repairs afloat at Governador Island, Rio de Janeiro, and subsequently laid up.
1993: Transferred to Seacross Shipping Co., Monrovia, Liberia (Commander Maritime Corporation, Piraeus, Greece).
Previous to 31.12.2000: Arrived Niteroi, Brazil for demolition.

036. **L/L PERU**

L.R./I.M.O. Number 7315739
8,681/5,597g
5,813/2,729n
14,611d
Mecapesa-MAN K6Z70/120E
Ordered by Neptunia Sociedade de
Navegacao Ltda., Sao Paulo, Brazil.
26.1.1973: Keel laid. Sold whilst
building.
27.4.1973: Launched for Lloyd-
Libra Navegacao S.A., Rio de
Janeiro.
5.11.1973: Completed. Brazilian flag.
17.4.1983: Laid up at Rio de Janeiro
until 1987.
29.8.1987: Laid up again at Rio de
Janeiro.
1990: Sold to Fulvia Shipping S.A.,
Panama (Good Faith Shipping Co.
S.A. (Nikolaos Frangos and Nicholas
G. Moundreas), Piraeus, Greece) and
renamed FULVIA.
1999: Sold to Franser Shipping S.A.,
Piraeus.
15.11.2000: Arrived Mumbai for
demolition.
23.11. 2000: Work began.

037. **L/L EQUADOR**

L.R./I.M.O. Number 7324534
8,681/5,597g
5,813/2,729n
14,611/11,613d
Mecapesa-MAN K6Z70/120E
Ordered by Neptunia Sociedade de
Navegacao Ltda., Sao Paulo, Brazil.
27.4.1973: Keel laid. Sold during
building.
9.7.1973: Launched for Lloyd-Libra
Navegacao S.A., Rio de Janeiro,
Brazil.
26.12.1973: Completed. Brazilian flag.
Owners may later have been recorded as Companhia de Navegacao
Maritima Netumar (LOLISA), Rio

de Janeiro.
29.1.1983: Laid up at Rio de Janeiro.
24.10.1985: Resumed trading.
1.8.1990: Laid up at Rio de Janeiro.
1991: Sold to Mega Trust Maritime
S.A., Piraeus, Greece and renamed
MEGA BREEZE under the Malta flag.
1992: Transferred to Mega Breeze
Shipping Ltd., Valletta, Malta (Mega
Trust Maritime S.A., Piraeus) and
renamed AKELA.
1995: Sold to Zalco Shipping and
Marketing Private Ltd., Panama
(Seatime Shipping (Private) Ltd.,
Singapore) and renamed ZALCO

Top: *L/L Peru* as *Fulvia* at Cap St. Michel, St.
Lawrence 18th October 1991. *[Marc Piché,
David Salisbury collection]*

PIONEER.
9.11.1995: Grounded at mouth of
River Mahanadi after losing an
anchor, in position 20.06 north by 86
28.74 east, 25 km from Paradip,
India. Subsequently declared a
constructive total loss.
16.4.1997: Reported still aground
with an 11 degree list to port.
23.11.2000: Broken up in
Bangladesh.

Opposite middle: *L/L Equador* at Colon. It was some time before Austin & Pickersgill fitted winch houses as standard features, but CCN included them on all their vessels. *[Marcus Berger]*

Opposite bottom: *Akela.* Note how the superstructure is extended behind the funnel. Other photographs reveal this is an open-backed structure. *[David Whiteside collection]*

Top: *Serra Azul* off Penarth, 2nd April 1981. *[Bob Allen]*

Middle: *Link Target* in Langton Dock, Liverpool in July 1987. *[Paul Boot]*

038. **SERRA AZUL**

L.R./I.M.O. Number 7329027
9,112g
6,244n
15,241d
Mecapesa-MAN K6Z70/120E
9.7.1973: Keel laid.
28.8.1973: Launched for Empresa de Navegacao Alianca S.A. (Companhia Armadora Brasileira), Rio de Janeiro, Brazil.
1.3.1974: Completed. Brazilian flag.
1983: Sold to Senator Maritime Inc., Monrovia, Liberia (Overlink Maritime Inc., Piraeus, Greece) and renamed LINK TARGET.
1988: Sold to Oceanreign Marine Ltd., Limassol, Cyprus (Vergos Marine Management S.A. (Michael Vergos), Piraeus, Greece).
1991: Sold to Kapitan Shipping Ltd., Valletta, Malta (Technical Marine Planning (Overseas) Ltd., Piraeus) and renamed LINK.
1994: Transferred to Elinka Shipping Ltd., Valletta, Malta (Technical Marine Planning (Overseas) Ltd., Piraeus) and renamed ELINKA.
1996: Sold to Intermed Navigation S.A., Monrovia, Liberia (Mare Nostrum S.A. (Nicholas Manos and Ioannis Chrisovelonis), Piraeus) under the Panama flag.
3.9.1998: Assisted by Argentine Coastguard after losing engine power and flooding of number 1 hold when 72 miles south east of Comodoro Rivadavia on a voyage from Santos to Callao with 14,000 tonnes of sugar. Reported arrested by local agents in respect of expenses.
2000: Sold to Multiport Overseas Co. Inc., Piraeus and renamed CELINE under the Panama flag.
Prior to 11.5.2001: Reported engine break down off River Plate and entered Alpha Zone Anchorage, Montevideo.
14.5.2001: Taken in tow for Surabaya by St. Vincents and Grenadines registered tug SAL-VAGE LEADER (907/1976). She was on passage from Argentina to Surabaya with sugar having been laid up for two years at San Antonia Este, Gulf of Matias, Argentina.
7.2001: After discharge of cargo at Surabaya, repairs considered uneconomical and sold to Bangladesh breakers.
23.11.2001: Sailed for Chittagong to be broken up.

039. SERRA BRANCA

L.R./I.M.O. Number 7333705
9,112g
6,244n
15,261d
Mecapesa-MAN K6Z70/120E
28.8.1973: Keel laid.
16.10.1973: Launched for Empresa de Navegacao Alianca S.A. (Companhia Armadora Brasileira), Rio de Janeiro, Brazil.
26.7.1974: Completed. Brazilian flag.
1983: Sold to Matatag Shipping

Corporation, Manila, Philippines (Vroon B.V., Breskens, Netherlands) and renamed SERRA.
1988: Transferred to Matatag Shipping Corporation (Philippine Pacific Ocean Lines Inc.), Manila, Philippines (Vroon B.V., Breskens, operators).
1989: Operators became Dalex Shipping Co. S.A., Piraeus, Greece.
2.1.1995: Damaged when fire broke out in engine room whilst bunkering at anchor in Teneriffe Roads during a

voyage from Casablanca to Recife in ballast. Later declared constructive total loss but repaired.
1995: Sold to Anixis Shipping Co. Ltd., Valletta, Malta (Epaminondas G. Logothetis (Karlog Shipping Co. Ltd.), Piraeus) and renamed ANIXIS.
1997: Sold to Flamingo Maritime Ltd., Valletta, Malta (Laruse S.A., Piraeus) and renamed FLAMINGO A.
3.10.2002: Arrived at Alang for breaking up.
10.10.2002: Work began.

Top: An empty *Serra Branca* in the New Waterway, 10th July 1976. *[John Wiltshire collection]*

Right: *Anixis* at Durban. *[Trevor Jones, David Salisbury collection]*

092. LLOYD LIVERPOOL

L.R./I.M.O. Number 7357816
9,111/5,812g
6,243/2,926n
15,421/12,213d
Mecapesa-MAN K6Z70/120E
16.10.1973: Keel laid.
7.12.1973: Launched for Companhia de Navegacao Lloyd Brasileiro, Rio de Janeiro, Brazil.
26.7.1974: Completed. Brazilian flag.
1988: Sold to Altis Shipping Co., Valletta, Malta (George Kalafatis, Lisbon, Portugal) for $1.8m and renamed ARIAN.
1991: Sold to Commodore Navigation Ltd., Valletta, Malta (Technical Marine Planning (Overseas) Ltd., Piraeus, Greece) and renamed BORA BORA I.
1992: Sold to Dancing Shipping Co. Ltd., Valletta, Malta (Alexandra Marine Management Co., Piraeus, Greece) and renamed DANCING SISTER.
1997: Sold to Aelsteel Shipping Ltd., Valletta, Malta (Infretra Shipping Inc. (D.N. Papadopoulos), Piraeus) and renamed THETIS.
5.5.1997: Sustained main engine problems in position 03.41 north by 02.35 south after leaving Bata, Equatorial Guinea with a cargo of bagged rice. Attempts to start engine failed.
15.5.1997: Towed to Abidjan by the Saint Vincent and Grenadines registered tug IROKO (197/1965).
22.8.1998: Arrived Port Said.

27.5.2003: Caught fire whilst under arrest in the Great Bitter Lake, Suez Canal. Suez Canal Authority tugs extinguished blaze.
7.2004: Still listed in 'Lloyd's Register'.

Top: *Lloyd Liverpool* at Vancouver in February 1979. *[Don Brown, David Salisbury collection]*
Middle: *Arian* passing Walsoorden in July 1989. *[David Salisbury]*
Bottom: *Dancing Sister* in the Mersey, 8th October 1994. Note the extension to the exhaust pipe. *[Nigel Jones]*

093. LLOYD HAMBURGO

L.R./I.M.O. Number 7357828
9,111/5,812g
6,243/2,926n
14,688/12,213d
Mecapesa-MAN K6Z70/120E
7.12.1973: Keel laid.
8.2.1974: Launched for Companhia de Navegacao Lloyd Brasileiro, Rio de Janeiro, Brazil.
26.9.1974: Completed. Brazilian flag.
1985: Laid up at Rio de Janeiro until 1988.
1988: Sold to Ballina Navigation Co. Inc., Limassol, Cyprus (Anpo Shipping Co. Ltd. (Anastasios G. Politis), Piraeus, Greece) and renamed ICARUS.
Previous to 30.8.1998: Arrived Eleusis.
8.10.1999: Laid up.
2001: Sold to Indian breakers for $150 per lightweight ton.
3.11.2001: Arrived Sachana, India for demolition.

094. (REGINA) REGINA CELI

L.R./I.M.O. number 7357830
9,111g
6,100n
15,139d
Mecapesa-MAN K6Z/120E
8.2.1974: Keel laid.
9.4.1974: Launched for Linhas Brasileiras de Navegacao Ltda., Rio de Janeiro, Brazil.
7.11.1974: Completed for Companhia Maritima Ltda. (Linhas Brasileiras de Navegacao Ltda., Rio

Above: *Lloyd Hamburgo* inward bound for Rotterdam on 22nd May 1976. *[Paul Boot]*

Below: As *Icarus* at Durban about 1990, the 24-year old ship looks very smart, although it has lost some of the generous array of whip aerials which she carried under Brazilian ownership. Note the bow crest of owner Anastasios Politis. *[Trevor Jones, David Salisbury collection]*

de Janeiro, Brazil) as REGINA CELI. Brazilian flag.
1988: Transferred to Linhas Brasileiras de Navegacao Ltda., Rio de Janeiro, Brazil.
1991: Sold to Mega Rio Shipping Ltd., Valletta, Malta (Mega Trust Maritime S.A., Piraeus Greece) and renamed MEGA RIO.
1993: Sold to King Louis Shipping Co. Ltd., Valletta, Malta and renamed BAGHEERA.
29.4.1993: Fire and explosion in engine room 40 miles off

Novorossisk, Russia whilst outward bound in the Sea of Azov on a voyage from Mariupol to India with a cargo of fertiliser.
1.5.1993: Fire extinguished but engine room flooded. Towed initially to Istanbul.
10.5.1993: Arrived Piraeus. Declared a constructive total loss. Sold to Ege Celik Endustrisi A.S. for breaking up.
17.2.1994: Left Piraeus under tow.
10.3.1994: Demolition commenced at Aliaga.

095. **LLOYD ROTTERDAM**

L.R./I.M.O. Number 7357842
9,111/5,812g
6,243/2,926n
14,688/12,213d
Mecapesa-MAN K6Z70/120E
9.4.1974: Keel laid.
29.5.1974: Launched for Companhia de Navegacao Lloyd Brasileiro, Rio de Janeiro, Brazil.
6.12.1974: Completed. Brazilian flag.
1983: Sold to Northwest Trading Ltd., Monrovia, Liberia (Panmar Trading Ltd. S.A. (M. Macris), Piraeus) and renamed CAPTAIN GEORGE L under the Greek flag.
1984: Sold to Meteora Trading Ltd., Monrovia, Liberia (Ocean Marine Industries Ltd., Piraeus, Greece) and renamed EVELYN under the Panama flag.
24.11.1986: Grounded 12 miles west south west of Ilha de Orango in position 10.56 north by 16.22 west during a voyage from Beira, Mozambique to Lisbon with a cargo of sugar.
27.11.1986: Abandoned by crew

Top: *Bagheera,* ex-*Regina Celi*, berthed at Piraeus on 22nd June 1993 shortly after the engine room fire which led to her scrapping. The combination of green hull, hatch sides and masts is unusual. *[Nigel Jones]*

Bottom: A very smart *Lloyd Rotterdam* leaves the port after which she was named in July 1977. *[David Salisbury]*

after engine room flooded. Subsequently declared a constructive total loss and abandoned.

096. LLOYD ANTUERPIA

L.R./I.M.O. Number 7357854
9,111/5,812g
6,243/2,926n
14,688/12,213d
Mecapesa-MAN K6Z70/120E
1.6.1974: Keel laid.
12.7.1974: Launched for Companhia de Navegacao Lloyd Brasileiro, Rio de Janeiro, Brazil.
26.3.1975: Completed. Brazilian flag.
28.4.1982: Reported aground in the vicinity of English Bank, Recife and refloated undamaged same day.
1983: Sold to Cape Rio Shipping Ltd., Monrovia, Liberia (Ocean Marine Industries Ltd., Piraeus, Greece) and renamed RIO under the Greek flag.
1986: Reported sold to Meteora Trading Ltd. (Ocean Marine Industries Ltd., Piraeus) and renamed ORION VI under the Panama flag.
1986: Sold to Octagon Shipping Ltd., Limassol, Cyprus (Velos (London) Ltd., London) and renamed SEA PASSION.
9.1.1987: Ran aground at Lattakina.
1988: Sold to Roula Shipping and Trading Co. (Private) Ltd. (Ocean Carriers Ltd., Colombo, Sri Lanka) and renamed FAWAZ.
1989: Sold to Eastern Discovery S.A., Panama (Ritz Marine S.A., Piraeus).
5.12.1995: Detained at Syros whilst bunker supplier sought payment of outstanding account.
1996: Sold and renamed BUZZARD I under the Panama flag.
1996: Sold to Heras World Shipping S.A., Amman, Jordan and renamed CARIBOU under the Panama flag.
10.8.1997: Arrived Chittagong for demolition by K.S.M. Steel Rerolling Mills.
26.8.1997: Demolition began.

Opposite page: *Lloyd Antuerpia* is seen twice, firstly on the Thames at Erith in July 1976 when barely a year old, and in Dutch waters on 5th September 1978, with her boot topping needing attention. *[David Salisbury; John Wiltshire collection]*

This page top: *Lloyd Antuerpia* as *Fawaz*, the fifth of the seven names she was eventually to carry, in the Suez Canal on 19th June 1995. *[Nigel Jones]*

This page bottom: In contrast, *Semiramis* spent almost all her active life under only one name. Although sold after her grounding in 1989, she spent much of the rest of her life laid up and damaged. She was photographed at Houston about 1982. Note the addition of permanent, rather than canvas, awnings over the bridge wings. *[Harry Stott, David Salisbury collection]*

097. **SEMIRAMIS**
L.R./I.M.O. Number 7357866
9,112g
6,226n
14,572d
Mecapesa-MAN K6Z70/120E
6.1974: Keel laid.
30.7.1974: Launched for Linhas Brasileiras de Navegacao Ltda., Rio de Janeiro, Brazil.
15.5.1975: Completed. Brazilian flag.
7.4.1989: Grounded on Mandel Luis Reef, near Sao Luis, Brazil, following a serious fire during a voyage from Belem to Santos.

18.4.1989: Refloated and taken in tow to Fortaleza, Brazil, for examination. Declared a constructive total loss, but sold for further trading.
1990: Sold to Omnium Shipping S.A., Monrovia, Liberia (Momentum Marine Services S.A., Piraeus, Greece) and renamed ELINA.
25.7.1990: Damaged by fire at Las Palmas.
14.7.1995: Still in port unrepaired and appeared abandoned.
9.1996: Aground Vori Bay, Andros after breaking free from tugs whilst bound from Las Palmas to Aliaga for demolition.
9.1998: Still aground and breaking up.

101. SANTA ISABELLA

L.R./I.M.O. Number 7357907
9,314g
6,181n
14,800d
Mecapesa-MAN K6Z70/120E
5.1975: Keel laid.
24.6.1975: Launched for Cosmos Shipping and Trading Corporation, Monrovia, Liberia (Rudolf A. Oetker (Hamburg Sudamerikanische D.G. Eggert & Amsinck), Hamburg, West Germany).
5.2.1976: Completed for Cosmos Shipping and Trading Corporation, Monrovia (Nautconsult Shipping Co. Ltd., London). Singapore flag.
1977: Transferred to Santa Isabella Maritima S.A., Panama (Nautconsult

Shipping Co. Ltd., London).
1982: Sold to Star Defence Shipping, Monrovia (Companhia Nacional de Navegacao, Lisbon, Portugal) and renamed NACIONAL SETUBAL under the Panama flag.
May subsequently have been named NUNO GONCALVES.
1988: Sold to Evaco Overseas Inc., Panama (Companhia de Tranportes Maritima Ltda. (COMTRAMAR), Lisbon and renamed FATIMA C.
1988: Sold to Citadel Shipping Inc., Panama (Craftcope Ltd., Isleworth, Middlesex) and renamed FATIMA under the Bahamas flag.
1990: Sold to Korea Daesong Shipping Co. Inc. (Korea Daesong Trading Corporation) Pyongyang,

Top: *Santa Isabella* in the New Waterway, August 1976. The arrangement of guard rails at the top of the derrick posts was changed for this and subsequent vessels, probably because of the inclusion in the posts of mechanical hold ventilation fans. *[G. Garwood, David Salisbury collection]*

North Korea and renamed SAE BYOL.
1998: Transferred to Dong Myong Shipping Co. (Government of North Korea), Pyongyang and renamed DONG MYONG.
25.4.2001: Arrived Chittagong for breaking up. There are reports of her carrying the names AB ROK GANG and ORIENT STAR in 1997 and 1998.

Opposite bottom: Like the British SD14s, those first built by CCN had open side rails extending from forecastle to superstructure, whilst some later examples had fully-plated bulwarks. The latter were an optional extra, as examples of both variants were built in parallel. CCN introduced its own variation, with plated bulwarks alongside number 1 hatch, changing to rails running through to the usual break point ahead of the superstructure. Painted white, the plates are apparent in this photograph of the *Nacional Setubal* entering Birkenhead Docks on 20th April 1986. *[Paul Boot]*

Top: *Santa Ursula* in the Welland Canal. *[David Kohl, David Salisbury collection]*

Bottom: *Leiria* at Durban. *[Trevor Jones, David Salisbury collection]*

102. **SANTA URSULA**

L.R./I.M.O. Number 7357919
9,314g
6,181n
14,900d
Mecapesa-MAN K6Z70/120E
7.1975: Keel laid.
12.8.1975: Launched for Cosmos Shipping and Trading Corporation, Monrovia, Liberia (Rudolf A. Oetker (Hamburg Sudamerikanische D.G. Eggert & Amsinck), Hamburg).
23.4.1976: Completed for Santa Ursula Maritima S.A., Panama (Nautconsult Shipping Co. Ltd., London). Singapore flag.
1982: Sold to Lady Margaret Maritime Corporation, Monrovia (CTM -

Companhia Portuguesa de Transportes Maritimos E.P., Lisbon, Portugal) and renamed LEIRIA.
1986: Managers became Portline S.a.r.l., Lisbon and renamed FRANCISCO ARRUDA.
1987: Sold to East Port Maritime Inc., Panama (Companhia de Transportes Maritimas Ltda. (COMTRAMAR), Lisbon) and renamed PEDRO C.
1991: Sold to Seamajor Shipping Co. Ltd., Limassol, Cyprus (Anpo Shipping Co. Ltd. (Anastasios G. Politis), Piraeus, Greece) and renamed ACHILLES.
28.5.2001: Arrived at Chittagong from Durban to be broken up.

103. SANTA INES

L.R./I.M.O. Number 7357921
9,158/5,988g
6,507/3,482n
14,899d
Mecapesa-MAN K6Z70/120E
13.8.1975: Keel laid.
26.9.1975: Launched for Cosmos Shipping and Trading Corporation, Monrovia, Liberia (Rudolf A. Oetker (Hamburg Sudamerikanische D.G. Eggert & Amsinck), Hamburg, West Germany).
26.8.1976: Completed for Cosmos Shipping and Trading Corporation, Monrovia (Nautconsult Shipping Co. Ltd., London). Singapore flag.
1977: Transferred to Santa Ines Maritima S.A., Panama (Nautconsult Shipping Co. Ltd., London).
1982: Sold to Edward Man Shipping Private Ltd. (Scotspore Shipmanagement Private Ltd.), Singapore. The name EDWARD MAN was proposed, but instead she was renamed ARAFURA SEA.
1983: Sold to Arafura Sea Shipping (Private) Ltd. (Denholm Shipmanagement (Singapore) Private Ltd.), Singapore.
1985: Sold to Rosilena Ltd., Gibraltar (Shipping Management S.A.M. (Vlasov Group), Monte Carlo) and renamed CATALAN BAY.
1986: Owners became Catalan Bay Ltd., Gibraltar (Shipping Management S.A.M. (Vlasov Group), Monte Carlo).
1987: Sold to Dauntless Shipping Co. Ltd., Limassol, Cyprus (Haltree Enterprises Ltd., Hounslow) and renamed CATALAN.
1991: Transferred to Spartan Shipping Ltd., Valletta, Malta (Haltree Enterprises Ltd., Hounslow) and renamed ALAN.
1994: Managers became Unipak

Top: From *Santa Ines* onwards, many of the CCN SD14s had enhanced cargo gear, often including the newly-introduced twin crane. Mounted on an individual pedestal, each crane could operate individually or, linked with its partner, give up to twice the safe working load. By rotating the

Shipping and Trading (Private) Ltd., Karachi, Pakistan.
5.4.1998: Arrived Chittagong for breaking up by Shah Amanat Shipbreakers.
6.4.1998: Work began.

pedestal, the cranes could serve adjacent hatchways, either independently or in tandem. *Santa Ines* also carries extra derricks at the superstructure front, with platforms for the winches, and the foremast has been replaced with a pair of derrick posts. She is anchored off Vancouver in June 1981. *[Don Brown, David Salisbury collection]*

Middle: *Arafura Sea* at Durban. *[Trevor Jones, David Salisbury collection]*

Bottom: A weary-looking *Catalan* at Durban. *[Trevor Jones, David Salisbury collection]*

104. SANTA TERESA

L.R./I.M.O. Number 7357933
9,158g
6,508n
14,900d
Mecapesa-MAN K6Z70/120E
29.9.1975: Keel laid.
14.11.1975: Launched for Cosmos Shipping and Trading Corporation, Monrovia, Liberia (Rudolf A. Oetker (Hamburg Sudamerikanische D.G. Eggert & Amsinck), Hamburg, West Germany).
1.10.1976: Completed for Santa Teresa Maritima S.A., Panama (Nautconsult Shipping Co. Ltd., London). Singapore flag.
1982: Sold to Frederick Man Shipping (Private) Ltd. (Scotspore Shipmanagement Private Ltd.), Singapore. The name FREDERICK MAN was proposed, but instead she was renamed BANDA SEA.

1983: Transferred to Banda Sea Shipping (Private) Ltd. (Denholm Ship Management (Singapore) Private Ltd., Singapore.
1985: Sold to New Delhi Trading Ltd., Gibraltar (Shipping Management S.A.M. (Vlasov Group), Monte Carlo) and renamed ROSIA BAY.
1987: Sold to Dulce Panama S.A., Panama (Transocean Shipping Ltd., Hong Kong) and renamed KURI.
1989: Managers became Seama International Shipping Ltd. (V.N. Mavreas), London.
1993: Sold to Evadia Navigation Co. Ltd., Limassol, Cyprus (Aster Maritime Inc., Piraeus) and renamed LITSA.
30.1.1999: Fire in engine room off Senegal in position 12.57 north by 17.44 west whilst on a voyage from Tema to Las Palmas in ballast. Fire spread and crew left vessel. Towed to Dakar Roads by local trawler with

Top: The positioning of the cargo gear for *Santa Teresa* and her sister *Santa Ines* shows that the arrangement of hatchways was modified in this pair. Number 2 hatch was increased to 19 metres from a typical 12 metres, and the length of number 3 reduced in proportion. These modifications reflected the arrangement of the holds below the 'tween decks, with number 2 hold considerably longer than number 3, 30 metres compared with 8.5 metres. The deck cranes were, presumably, fitted immediately above the bulkhead between numbers 2 and 3 holds, which in these vessels extended through the 'tween decks. *Santa Teresa* is seen on the New Waterway in July 1980 with her pilot ladder in position. *[David Salisbury]*

Bottom: *Kuri* at Durban in the early 1990s. *[Trevor Jones, David Salisbury collection]*

owner declaring vessel fit only for demolition.
6.3.2001: Arrived Aliaga in tow for scrapping by Iksa Metal Ltd.

105. CERESIO

L.R./I.M.O. Number 7357945
9,302g
6,362n
14,800d
Mecapesa-MAN K6Z70/120E
14.11.1975: Keel laid.
11.2.1976: Launched for Suramarin
S.A., Panama (H.H. Thyssen,
Bornemisza, West Germany) (Suisse-
Outremar Reederei A.G., Basle,
Switzerland).
23.11.1976: Completed for Suramarin
S.A., Panama (Nautconsult Shipping
Co. Ltd., London). Liberian flag.
1983: Sold to Freedom Shipping
Corporation S.A., Panama
(Pergamos Shipping Co. Ltd. (A.K.
Antoniou), London) and renamed
FREEDOM A.S.
1989: Sold to Kingsford Lines III,
Valletta, Malta (Norbulk Shipping
Agencies Ltd., London) and renamed
FREEDOM.
1991: Sold to Astro Gold Shipping
Co. Ltd., Limassol, Cyprus
(Pergamos Shipping Co. S.A.,
Piraeus, Greece) and renamed
ASTRON.
1997: Sold to Paradny Shipping Co.
Ltd., Limassol, Cyprus and renamed
ALTAIR.
28.5.1997: Arrived Mauritius
Anchorage with a vertical crack
about 95cms long in the port shell
plating of number 3 hold whilst
inward bound on a voyage from
Vietnam to the west coast of Africa
with 12,000 tonnes of rice. The
crack was partially repaired but
vessel arrested by cargo owners on
account of delay and cargo was
subsequently transhipped. Crew later

left vessel leaving master to await
instructions from owner who was
believed to have gone bankrupt.
Vessel had no classification certificates
and was considered unseaworthy and
not permitted to sail until repaired.
Director of Shipping later reported to
have taken possession.
1998: Sold to Mauritian owners and
renamed MSZ-1.
1998: Sold to Rebecca Shipping
Corporation, Monrovia, Liberia
(Communications and Commerce
International Private Ltd., Karachi,
Pakistan) for onward sale for breaking up and renamed REAL PEARL
under the St. Vincent and the
Grenadines flag.
1998: Sold to L'Eastern Overseas,
Palm Crest Beach, Karachi for
demolition.
28.3.1998: Vessel expected to arrive

Top: *Ceresio* saw a return to a more basic
specification. She is seen off Cuxhaven in June
1979 in the colours of the Thyssen Group. *[David
Salisbury]*

Middle: *Freedom A.S.* at Durban. *[Trevor Jones,
David Salisbury collection]*

Karachi under tow of the Russian tug
EPRON (1,085/1983) where she was
to remain outside port limits whilst
awaiting main engine repairs.
1999: Reported in service and
renamed ALTAIR.
2.2001: Deleted from 'Lloyds
Register' as existence in doubt.

106. **ARACAJU**

L.R./I.M.O. Number 7357957
9,314g
6,181n
14,797d
Mecapesa-Man K6Z70/120E
19.1.1976: Keel laid.
6.5.1976: Launched for Tierramarin S.A., Panama (Rudolf A. Oetker (Hamburg Sudamerikanische D.G. Eggert & Amsinck)), Hamburg West Germany).
28.12.1976: Completed for Cosmos Shipping and Trading Corporation, Monrovia, Liberia (Nautconsult Shipping Co. Ltd., London). Singapore flag.
1983: Sold to Peerless Shipping Corporation, Monrovia (Companhia Nacional de Navegacao S.a.r.l, Lisbon, Portugal) and renamed

NACIONAL SAGRES under the Panama flag.
1986: Managers became Portline S.a.r.l., Lisbon and renamed AFONSO DOMINGUES.
1987: Sold to Lire Shipping Inc., Panama (Companhia de Transportes Maritimos Ltda. (COMTRAMAR), Lisbon) and renamed DIANA C.
1989: Sold to Avila Shipping Co., Panama (Lusonautis - Companhia de Navegacao S.A., Lisbon) and renamed LUSO ANA.
1992: Sold to Biscia Shipping Co. Ltd., Limassol, Cyprus (Pateras Management Inc., Piraeus, Greece) and renamed GELI P.
6.7.1993: Collided with oil platform ASHRAFI WHP-1 in the Gulf of Suez in position 27.48 north by 33.43.01 east whilst on a voyage from Constantza to

Manila with steel products. Damage sustained to bow and forepeak and holed in number 1 hold.
11.7.1993: Towed to Hurghada and detained by port authorities. Temporary repairs effected.
17.8.1993: Towed to Suez and later arrested.
1998: Sold to Al Farouk Trading and Importing Co. Egypt for breaking up with work carried out at Suez during 1998.

Top: *Aracaju.* The short pole masts at the break of the forecastle are used to handle the man-landing beam used to swing a member of the crew ashore to handle mooring ropes whilst transiting the St. Lawrence Seaway. *[Kevin Moore]*

Bottom: *Nacional Sagres* in the New Waterway, July 1985. *[David Salisbury]*

107. ANGOL

L.R./I.M.O. Number 7411325

	1986
8,981g	11,047g
5,304n	6,170n
14,664d	17,834d

Mecapesa-MAN K6Z70/120E

31.5.1977: Keel laid.
5.8.1977: Launched for Compania Chilena de Navegacion Interoceanica S.A., Valparaiso, Chile.
30.3.1978: Completed. Chilean flag.
7.4.1986: Arrived Flensburg to be lengthened and converted into a semi-containership by Flensburger Schiffbau-Gesellschaft G.m.b.H.

New dimensions: 167.65 x 20.45 x 8.867 metres.
1992: Sold to East Coast Marine Co. Ltd., Limassol, Cyprus (Kypros Lines S.A. (Andreas Yiannoulou), Athens, Greece) and renamed CITY OF AKAKI.
1993: Managers became Cyprus Sea Lines S.A., Athens.
1997: Transferred to Richmond Shipping Co. Ltd. Limassol, Cyprus (Cyprus Maritime Co. Ltd., Athens) and renamed DON AKAKI.
1999: Renamed LA EXPRESS.
30.1.2001: Arrived Chittagong having been sold to breakers for $184 per lightweight ton.

Top: Seen at Durban, *Angol* has a combination of conventional deck cranes and mast cranes. With the latter the whole of the mast structure rotates to allow cargo working at either of the adjacent holds. The jibs can be positioned to serve the hatches separately or in tandem. These mast cranes were to be a standard feature on the Prinasas. *[Trevor Jones, David Salisbury collection]*

Bottom: As *City of Akaki* after lengthening and the addition of a further crane. The new style derricks are seen more clearly in this view. The forward mast has been replaced by a lighter structure to carry the navigation light which is needed following lengthening. *[Trevor Jones]*

108. ANAKENA

L.R./I.M.O. Number 7411337

	1988
9,314g	11,046
6,180n	6,709n
14,664d	17,659d

Mecapesa-MAN K6Z70/120E

9.8.1977: Keel laid.

11.10.1977: Launched for Compania Chilena de Navegacion Interoceanica S.A., Valparaiso, Chile.

17.7.1978: Completed. Chilean flag.

18.6.1988: Arrived at Ulsan, South Korea to be lengthened and converted into a semi-containership by Hyundai Mipo Dockyard Co. Ltd. New dimensions: 167.65 x 20.45 x 8.489 metres.

1992: Sold to West Coast Marine Co. Ltd., Limassol, Cyprus (Kypros Lines S.A. (Andreas Yiannoulou),

Athens, Greece) and renamed NATALI H.

1993: Managers became Cyprus Sea Lines S.A., Athens.

1996: Renamed GLOBAL NATALI.

26.10.1996: Abandoned by her crew north of the Seychelles in position 02.36 south by 53.39 east, after fire broke out in a hold containing cotton during a voyage from Mumbai, Sharjah and Durban to Brazil with a cargo including cotton, rice, chemicals and firecrackers.

29.10.1996: Fire extinguished, but engine room, accommodation and number 7 hold destroyed. Crew safe.

31.10.1996: Towed to Port Victoria and placed under arrest, but released 5.9.1997. Declared a constructive total loss.

18.12.1997: Left Port Victoria in tow

Top: A sister to *Angol*, *Anakena* was photographed at Durban prior to her 1988 rebuild. The masts have been turned so that jibs can serve all four hatches. *[Trevor Jones, David Salisbury collection]*

Bottom: In rebuilt form, *Global Natali* transits the Suez Canal on 29th May 1996, just months before a fire ended her career. This and other photographs show that, despite several renamings and sale from Chilean to Greek owners, she retained the same funnel colours throughout her career, probably because she was chartered back to her original owners. *[Nigel Jones]*

of Russian tug KAPITAN BEKLEMISHEV (1,160/1985) for shipbreakers at Mumbai under the name GLOBE.

28.1.1998: Arrived to be broken up by R.K. Engineering.

27.3.1998: Work commenced.

121. **LLOYD GENOVA**

L.R./I.M.O. Number 7433127
9,112g
6,226n
14,572d
Mecapesa-MAN K6Z70/120E
4.3.1976: Keel laid.
21.6.1976: Launched for Companhia
de Navegacao Lloyd Brasileiro, Rio
de Janeiro, Brazil.
15.3.1977: Completed. Brazilian
flag.
22.9.1978: Grounded near Salina
Cruz in position 16.10 north by 94.56
west during a voyage from Paranagua
to Vancouver.
4.10.1978: Refloated.
1989: Sold to Sea-Key Shipping Co.
Ltd., Limassol, Cyprus (Anpo
Shipping Co. Ltd. (Anastasios G.

Politis), Piraeus, Greece) and renamed PHAETHON.
13.6.1999: Dragged anchor in
Chittagong Outer Anchorage coming
into contact with the Cypriot motor

vessel SHANNON (9,100/1976). Some
flooding and cargo damage reported.
Subsequently resumed trading.
1.4.2001: Arrived Chittagong to be
broken up.

123. **RIO CONQUISTA**

L.R./I.M.O. Number 7433149
8,994g
6,243n
14,604d
Mecapesa-MAN K6Z70/120E
3.6.1978: Keel laid.
18.8.1978: Launched for Companhia
de Navegacao Maritima Netumar
(LOLISA), Rio de Janeiro, Brazil.
28.12.1978: Completed. Brazilian flag.
1979: Sold to Linhas Maritimas de
Angola U.E.E (The People's Republic of Angola), Luanda, Angola and
renamed EBO.
26.12.1993: Arrived Lisbon and
placed under arrest.
9.12.1999: Reported still in port and
under arrest, but now renamed
KIANDA.
11.2001: Reported renamed LISA
under the Cyprus flag.
13.6.2002: Reported renamed LISA
L under the Panama flag.
2003: Sold to Kassab Intershipping
LLC, Ajman, United Arab Emirates
under the Mongolian flag.
7.2004: Still listed in 'Lloyd's
Register'.

Opposite top: As *Lloyd Genova* is helped to turn on 10th May 1982 her smoky exhaust contrasts strongly with the clear mountain sky over Vancouver, demonstrating why she later received an extension to her exhaust pipe. Despite ownership by a liner company, she represents a reversion to a more basic specification. *[Don Brown, Davd Salisbury collection]*

Opposite middle: *Phaethon* passes Terneuzen on the Scheldt in March 1991. *[Bernard Morton, David Salisbury collection]*

Opposite bottom: *Ebo.* Note the wide winch platforms and the massive heavy-lift derrick, rated at 80 tons. *[David Whiteside collection]*

Top: Despite reportedly being renamed, *Ebo* still carries her old name in October 2000 whilst lying alongside *Hoji Ya Henda* in the Irmaos & Batista scrap yard at Lisbon. *[Trevor Jones]*

Middle: *L/L Colombia. [Marcus Berger]*

Bottom: *Amity Union* on the Kiel Canal. *[Holger Zimmerman, David Whiteside collection]*

125. **L/L COLUMBIA**

L.R./I.M.O. Number 7433141
9,112g
6,244n
14,900d
Mecapesa-MAN K6Z70/120E
Ordered by Lloyd-Libra Navegacao
S.A., Rio de Janeiro, Brazil.
20.3.1978: Keel laid.
19.5.1978: Launched for Companhia
de Navegacao Maritima Netumar
(LOLISA), Rio de Janeiro.
26.1.1979: Completed. Brazilian flag..
1995: Sold to Geranium Marine Ltd.
(Bonyad Marine Services Inc.),
Athens, Greece and renamed
PROCYON under the
Cyprus flag.
1996: Transferred to
Everlasting Amity
Sendirian Berhad, Kuala
Lumpur, Malaysia (Seabon
Holding Corporation,
Athens, Greece) and
renamed AMITY UNION.
1997: Managers deleted.
15.10.1997: Detained at
Tema.
1999: Sold to Atlantic
Ruby (M) Sendirian
Berhad, Kuala Lumpur
(Seabon Holding Corpora-
tion, Athens, Greece) and
renamed LANTIC RUBY.
16.5.2000: Sold by judicial
sale at Antwerp to Bolivian
owners and renamed
MILACKU.
10.2.2001: Arrived at
Alang for breaking up,
having been sold for $167
per lightweight ton.

127. LLOYD MARSELHA

L.R./I.M.O. Number 7433153
9,112g
6,243n
15,088d
Mecapesa-MAN K6Z70/120E
10.5.1976: Keel laid.
3.9.1976: Launched for Companhia de Navegacao Lloyd Brasileiro, Rio de Janeiro, Brazil.
28.4.1977: Completed. Brazilian flag.
1989: Sold to Lux Lily Shipping Corporation, Monrovia, Liberia (Colonial Marine Industrial Inc., Savannah, Georgia, USA) for $3.3m and renamed LUX LILY under the Vanuatu flag.
1990: Sold to Sunkissed Marine Co. Ltd., Limassol, Cyprus (Hamburg Maritime Agencies G.m.b.H., Hamburg, West Germany) and renamed KAPPA MARY.
1990: Management transferred to Lexmar Corporation, Greenwich, Connecticut, USA.
1991: Management transferred to Michael K. Kritikakis Group of Companies Salvage and Towage, Piraeus, Greece.
1992: Renamed PA MAR.
28.5.1993: Damaged propeller and tail shaft whilst in the Red Sea whilst on a voyage Piraeus to China.
7.7.1993: Arrived Colombo Roads for inspection.
3.8.1993: Arrived Singapore.
12.9.1993: Departed for Shantou, China.
3.11.1993: Arrived at Shantou and placed under arrest.
1995: Sold to Shanghai Agricultural Industry and Commerce Corporation and Hai Tong Shipping Co., Shanghai, People's Republic of China and renamed NONG GONG SHAN 8.
15.5.2002: Class withdrawn at owner's request. Subsequently renamed YANG YUAN and JING REN under the Chinese flag.
7.2004: Still listed in 'Lloyd's Register' as NONG GONG SHAN 8, but no movements reported since March 2002.

This page top: *Lloyd Marselha* on the New Waterway in July 1984. *[David Salisbury]*

Left: *Kappa Mary*. *[David Whiteside collection]*

Opposite page top: *Monte Cristo* on the New Waterway. She introduced yet another set of cargo gear, with four cranes forward. *[Rowley Weeks, David Salisbury collection]*

Opposite page middle: *Edward R.* *[V.H. Young and L.A. Sawyer collection]*

Opposite page bottom: Even approaching 20 years of age, SD14s could still find employment in the liner trades: *NZOL Jaya* at Durban about 1998. *[Trevor Jones, David Salisbury collection]*

129. **MONTE CRISTO**

L.R./I.M.O. Number 7433165
8,680g
5,812n
14,940d
Mecapesa-MAN K6Z70/120E
21.8.1978: Keel laid.
27.10.1978: Launched for
Empresa de Navegacao Alianca
S.A. (Companhia Armadora
Brasileira), Rio de Janeiro,
Brazil.
27.8.1979: Completed. Brazilian flag.
1986: Transferred to
Transnave Navegacao S.A.,
Rio de Janeiro.
1989: Reported in course of
transfer to M.I.T. Transportes
Maritimos Internacionales
Ltda, Rio de Janeiro and to be
renamed M.I.T. SAO PAULO,
but this did not take place.
1993: Sold to Bristol S.A.,
Monrovia, Liberia (Stylianos
Markakis, Piraeus, Greece) and
renamed BRISTOL under the
St. Vincent and Grenadines flag.
1994: Sold to Eddyship S.A.,
Panama (Great Circle Shipping
Agency Ltd., Bangkok, Thailand) and renamed EDWARD R.
1997: Renamed NZOL JAYA
whilst on charter to New
Zealand Orient Line.
1999: Renamed EDWARD R on
completion of charter.
2001: Management transferred
to Precious Shipping Public Co.
Ltd., Panama.
25.10.2001: Arrived Gadani
Beach for breaking up.

130. **MONTE ALTO**

L.R./I.M.O. Number 7433177
8,680g
5,812n
14,328d
Mecapesa-MAN K6Z70/120E
30.10.1978: Keel laid.
27.12.1978: Launched for Empresa de Navegacao Alianca S.A. (Companhia Armadora Brasileira), Rio de Janeiro, Brazil.
19.11.1979: Completed. Brazilian flag.
9.6.1983: Collided in fog with the Norwegian motor vessel MOLUND (489/1959) whilst on voyage from Helsinki to Vismar. MOLUND sank about 13 miles off Utklippan Light with the loss of six of the crew of eight.
1986: Transferred to Transnave Navegacao S.A., Rio de Janeiro.
1989: Reported in course of transfer to M.I.T. Transportes Maritimos Internacionales Ltda, Rio de Janeiro and to be be renamed M.I.T. BRASILIA, but this did not take place.
22.11.1989: Sailed Santos for Iraq but suffered engine trouble.
26.1.1990: Anchored off Durban. Owners in financial difficulties.
7.9.1990: Taken into port and berthed with a view to sale by Judicial Public Auction.
22.3.1991: Sold to Palm Companhia Naviera S.A., Panama (Transcontinental Maritime and Trading S.A., Piraeus, Greece) and renamed REGENT under the Bahamas flag.
1992: Management transferred to Target Marine S.A. (A. Poulman and L. Papazis), Piraeus, Greece.
1997: Renamed NZOL SURYA whilst on charter to New Zealand Orient Line under the Liberian flag.
1998: Sold to Arma Shipping S.A., Nassau, Bahamas (Sacks Maritime S.A., Piraeus) and renamed IRIS.
1999: Management transferred to Target Marine S.A. (A. Poulman and L. Papazis), Piraeus.
19.5.2000: In collision at Tanjung Perak with Indonesian patrol vessel PULAO RATAWO which sank with the loss of one member of the crew of 54. Damage to IRIS was slight.

2000: Sold to Shinhan Capitol Co. Ltd. (Woochang C. and A. Co. Ltd.), Seoul, South Korea.
2002: Sold to Sea Fortune Shipping Co. Ltd., Hong Kong (Dalian Haiching Shipping Co. Ltd., Dalian, People's Republic of China) and renamed FORTUNE SEA under the Panama flag.
7.2004: Still listed in 'Lloyd's Register'.

131. **MONTE PASCOAL**

L.R./I.M.O. Number 7433189
8,680g
5,812n
14,328d
Mecapesa-MAN K6Z70/120E
15.1.1979: Keel laid.
30.3.1979: Launched for Empresa de Navegacao Alianca S.A. (Companhia Armadora Brasileira), Rio de Janeiro,

Top: *Monte Alto* in the New Waterway, 13th May 1982. *[Paul Boot]*
Middle: *NZOL Surya. [Russell Priest]*
Bottom: *Iris. [Russell Priest]*

Brazil.
20.12.1979: Completed. Brazilian flag.
1986: Transferred to Transnave Navegacao S.A., Rio de Janeiro.
Prior to 13.5.1989: Laid up at Rio de Janeiro, remaining for seven years.
1989: Reported in course of transfer to M.I.T. Transportes Maritimos Internacionales Ltda., Rio de Janeiro but this did not take place.
1996: Sold to Nicole Marine Trading Inc., Panama (Olivine Ltd. Ship Management, Dublin, Ireland) remaining laid up under the Brazilian flag.
Previous to 28.2.2001: Delivered to breakers at Niteroi having been laid up there since before 11.1.1999.

141. ANISIO BORGES

L.R./I.M.O. Number
7433191
8,203g
6,214n
14,443d
Mecapesa-MAN
K6Z70/120E
22.4.1982: Keel laid.
6.7.1982: Launched for Companhia Paulista de Comercio Maritimo (Wilfred Penha Borges), Rio de Janeiro, Brazil.
2.2.1983: Completed. Brazilian flag. (The 200th SD14 launch and completion).
1984: Sold to Companhia Maritime Nacional Ltda. (Linhas Brasileiras de Navegacao (LIBRA)), Rio de Janeiro and renamed NACIONAL SANTOS.
1996: Sold to Tilton Oceanic Corporation, Monrovia, Liberia (Cathcart Shipping Ltd., London) and renamed VILMA under the Bahamas flag.
1999: Management transferred to H. Glahr & Co. G.m.b.H. and Co., K.G., Bremen, Germany.
23.11.1999: Main engine damaged and towed to Saint Anna Bay.
2000: Sold at Curacao to Khari Shipping Co. Ltd., Cyprus (Pacific and Atlantic Corporation (Alex Giannakopoulos), Piraeus, Greece) and renamed ORIENTAL KIKU under the Bahamas flag.
9.8.2002: Main engine breakdown 100 miles south south east of Pylos.
13.9.2002: Arrived Piraeus in tow of Tsavliris tug MEGAS ALEXANDROS (638/1974).
26.8.2002: Sailed Piraeus.
7.2004: Still listed in 'Lloyd's Register'.

Top: Monte Pascoal at North Woolwich on the Thames in March 1981 showing much detail, including the cranked Suez Canal davit right on the forecastle head which replaced the more usual radial type in SD14s built elsewhere. Note also the signal mast on the forecastle carrying the forward navigation lights. *[David Salisbury]*

Middle: *Monte Pascoal* at Niteroi on 30th April 2001 as she is gradually demolished. *[John Sins, Nigel Jones collection]*

Bottom: *Oriental Kiku*, the former *Anisio Borges* with yet another variation in cargo gear. *[Russell Priest]*

143. LEONOR

L.R./I.M.O. Number 7433206
8,203g
6,190n
14,290d
Mecapesa-MAN K6Z 70/120E
Ordered by Companhia de Navegacao Maritima Netumar (LOLISA), Rio de Janeiro.

22.4.1982: Keel laid.

14.4.1983: Launched. Vessel then lay at builder's yard unfinished.

29.6.1988: Completed for Westbrook Maritime and Trading Inc, Monrovia, Liberia (Valiant Shipping Co. (London) Ltd., London) retaining intended name LEONOR. Greek flag. Because of the delay, this and yard number 160 were the last two SD14s to be completed, 20 years after the first delivery.

1989: Sold to Far Tweendeckers A/S (Sverre Farstad & Co. A/S), Aalesund, Norway and renamed FAR SUEZ.

1992: Sold to Haven Maritime Inc., Monrovia, Liberia (Unicorn Lines Proprietary Ltd., Durban, South Africa) (Sverre Farstad & Co. A/S, Aalesund, managers) and renamed FRONTIER under the flag of St. Vincent and the Grenadines.

1994: Sold to Areca Maritime Co. Ltd., Limassol, Cyprus (Pacific and Atlantic Corporation (Alex Giannakopoulos), Piraeus) and renamed BLUE FRONTIER.

1995: Transferred to Savelin Shipping Co. Ltd., Cyprus (Pacific and Atlantic Corporation (Alex Giannakopoulos), Piraeus) and renamed SAINT SPIRIDONAS.

1996: Renamed STAVROFOROS.

1999: Renamed EXPRESS SHANGHAI.

2000: Transferred to Marine Glory Shipping Co. Ltd., Cyprus (Pacific and Atlantic Corporation (Alex Giannakopoulos), Piraeus) and renamed ORIENTAL SPIRIT.

2002: Sold to Arroz Shipping and

Trading Ltd., Saint Vincent and Grenadines (H.A.R.T. Shipping Corporation, Piraeus) and renamed GOLDEN PRIDE under the Comoros flag.

2002: Sold to Stone Maritime Inc., Panama (Larus S.A., Piraeus) and renamed NAMA.

7.2004: Still listed in 'Lloyd's Register'.

Top: *Leonor* passes Walsoorden on the Scheldt in July 1989. Cargo gear has changed again, with goal posts forward and a heavy lift derrick on the conventional main mast. Note also the large selection of navigation lights on the bridge signal mast. *[David Salisbury]*
Middle: *Frontier. [Trevor Jones, David Salisbury collection]*
Bottom: As *Express Shanghai* she has gained yet another crane between holds 2 and 3. *[David Whiteside collection]*

145. LLOYD ARGENTINA

L.R./I.M.O. No. 7433218
8,680g
6,100n
15,022d
Mecapesa-MAN K6Z 70/120E
4.8.1980: Keel laid.
10.10.80: Launched for Companhia de Navegacao Lloyd Brasileiro, Rio de Janeiro, Brazil.
6.6.1981: Completed. Brazilian flag.
1989: Sold to Transportes Maritimos Internacionales Ltda., Rio de Janeiro and renamed MIT RIO DE JANEIRO.
1990: Sold at Durban by tender to Aegean Sea S.A., Panama (Seaways Shipping Enterprises Ltd., Piraeus, Greece) for $4.8m and renamed STELLA F.
1997: Renamed STALLION I.
1997: Sold to Transpacific Eternity S.A., Panama (Franser Shipping S.A. (Angela Frangos and Dion Seretakos), Piraeus, Greece) and renamed ANTARES III.
2002: Sold to Lady Shipping S.A., Panama (Maritime Enterprises Management S.A., Piraeus) and renamed LADY STEEL.
9.2004: Renamed GASPARD.
9.2004: Still in service.

Top: *Lloyd Argentina*, outbound down the Fraser River. She has yet another variation of cargo gear, conventional derricks at the foremast and two cranes. *[Don Brown]*
Middle: *Lady Steel* enters the Mersey on 18th October 2003. She may well prove to have been the last SD14 to visit the UK. *[Nigel Bowker]*
Bottom: *Gaspard*, recently renamed, at Durban 29th September 2004. *[Trevor Jones]*

147. BIANCA

L.R./I.M.O. Number 7433220
8,680/5,175g
5,812/2,729n
14,328d
Mecapesa-MAN K6Z70/120E
Possible intended name
MONTE CASTELLO.
13.10.1980: Keel laid.
12.12.1980: Launched for
Empresa de Navegacao
Alianca S.A. (Companhia
Armadora Brasileira), Rio de
Janeiro, Brazil.
17.8.1981: Completed.
Brazilian flag.
1996: Sold to Kerslake
Investments Inc., Panama
(Acomarit Services Maritimes
S.A., Geneva, Switzerland)
(Acomarit (UK) Ltd., Glas-
gow, managers) and renamed
HANSA under the Liberian
flag.
1997: Transferred to Hansa
Shipping Ltd., Isle of Man
(Acomarit Services Maritimes
S.A., Geneva, Switzerland)
(Acomarit (UK) Ltd., Glas-
gow, managers) under the
Liberian flag.
1998: Sold to Evagelia
Shipping Co. Ltd., Valletta,
Malta (Pitiousa Shipping
S.A., Athens, Greece) and
renamed EVAGELIA.
2000: Renamed
SAFMARINE EVAGELIA
whilst on charter to
Safmarine for SAFWAF
service.
7.2004: Still listed in 'Lloyd's
Register'.

Top: *Bianca* approaches the locks at Antwerp, April 1986. *[David Salisbury]*
Middle: *Evagelia* at Durban, after conversion to a partial container ship. Container supports have been added along the deck and her exhaust pipe extended. A deck has been added to the superstructure, and the bridge rebuilt. *[Trevor Jones, David Salisbury collection]*
Bottom: *Safmarine Evagelia* at Durban in 2001. *[Trevor Jones, David Salisbury collection]*

Top: *Lloyd Mexico* was a repeat of *Lloyd Argentina*, but has been painted in a different style, with the upper part of masts and derricks, plus the signal mast, in black. Note also the red derrick blocks, presumably painted this colour as a safety feature. Photographed passing Walsoorden on the Scheldt in April 1990. *[David Salisbury]*

Bottom: A rather weary-looking *Esperanza III* at Durban. *[Trevor Jones]*

149. LLOYD MEXICO

L.R./I.M.O. Number 7433232
9,111g
6,244n
14,627d
Mecapesa-MAN K6Z70/120E
13.12.1980: Keel laid.
13.2.1981: Launched for Companhia de Navegacao Lloyd Brasileiro, Rio de Janeiro, Brazil.
3.11.1981: Completed. Brazilian flag.
1992: Sold to Efessos Shipping S.A., Panama (Marine Challenger S.A., Piraeus, Greece) and renamed ESPERANZA III.
22.8.1997: Ran aground on Prongs Reef, off Colaba in Mumbai port area, India, in position 18.52 north by 72.49 east in heavy seas, after dragging her anchor whilst on a voyage from Ilichevsk to Kandla with a cargo of steel plates, paper and asbestos. Smit-Tak salvage team engaged for salvage. Much cargo damaged, leakage of oil from bunkers, water in engine room and in holds number 1 to 4.
11.1.1998: After 5,750 tonnes of cargo had been discharged, refloated and towed into Mumbai.
15.2.1998: Delivered to Vidham Enterprises, Mumbai for demolition.
7.3.1998: Demolition commenced.

151. ANA LUISA

L.R./I.M.O. Number 7433244
8,680/5,597g
5,813/2,729n
14,328/11,842d
Mecapesa-MAN K6Z70/120E
Possible intended name MONTE BELLO.
16.2.1981: Keel laid.
30.4.1981: Launched for Empresa de Navegacao Alianca S.A. (Companhia Armadora Brasileira), Rio de Janeiro, Brazil.
4.12.1981: Completed. Brazilian flag.
1996: Sold to Seapar Navegacao Maritima Ltda., Rio de Janeiro, Brazil and renamed ESPERANCA IV.
1997: Sold to Pitiousa Maritime Co. Ltd., Limassol, Cyprus (Pitiousa Shipping S.A., Athens, Greece) and renamed MEROULA.
22.10.1999: Grounded at Buoy 45 while at anchor in Banana Roads, Matadi, whilst bound for Matadi from South African ports with 8,000 tonnes of general cargo containers and bagged salt.

12.11.1999: Refloated undamaged by tug/supply vessels RED DOVE (1991/ 1,147, Saint Vincent) and TERRY TIDE (1983/264, USA).
2000: Renamed SAFMARINE MEROULA whilst on charter to Safmarine for SAFWAF service.
7.2004: Still listed in 'Lloyd's Register'.

152. LLOYD HOUSTON

L.R./I.M.O. Number 7433256
9,112g
6,244n
14,347d
Mecapesa-MAN K6Z70/120E
4.5.1981: Keel laid.
3.7.1981: Launched for Companhia de Navegacao Lloyd Brasileiro, Rio de Janeiro, Brazil.
29.12.1981: Completed. Brazilian flag.
4.5.1990: Laid up at Rio de Janeiro.
1993: Sold to King's Port Shipping Co. Ltd., Limassol, Cyprus (Anpo Shipping Co. Ltd. (Anastasios G. Politis), Piraeus, Greece) and renamed ARISTOTELES.
2002: Sold to Jaipur Ltd. (Five Seas Shipping Establishment), Sharjah, United Arab Emirates and renamed JAIPUR under the Panama flag.
7.2004: Still listed by 'Lloyd's Register'.

153. L/L BRASIL

L.R./I.M.O. Number 7433268
9,112g
8,244n
14,800d
Mecapesa-MAN K6Z70/120E
Ordered by Lloyd-Libra Navegacao
S.A., Rio de Janeiro, Brazil.
6.7.1981: Keel laid.
28.8.1981: Launched for Lloyd-
Libra Navegacao S.A., Rio de
Janeiro.
2.4.1982: Completed. Brazilian flag.
1995: Sold to Arikana Shipping Co.,
Nicosia, Cyprus (Pacific and Atlantic
Corporation (Alex Giannakopoulos),
Piraeus, Greece) and renamed
SAINT NECTARIOS.
1999: Renamed EXPRESS
SEMINOLE.
2000: Sold to Long Feng Shipping,
S.A., Panama (Shandong Province

Yantai International Marine Shipping
Co., Shandong, People's Republic of
China) and renamed LONG FENG.
2002: Sold to North Korea and
renamed RA NAM.
7.2004: Still listed by 'Lloyd's
Register'.

Top: *Lloyd Houston* as *Aristoteles* in Piraeus
Roads. *[Nigel Jones]*

Middle: *L/L Brasil. [Markus Berger]*

Bottom: *Express Seminole* in the Suez Canal.
[Trevor Jones]

156. RODRIGO

L.R./I.M.O. Number 7433270
8,203g
6,214n
14,443d
Mecapesa-MAN K6Z70/120E
15.2.1982: Keel laid.
16.4.1982: Launched for Companhia
Paulista de Comercio Maritimo
(Wilfred Penha Borges), Rio de
Janeiro, Brazil.
13.1.1983: Completed. Brazilian flag.
1984: Sold to Companhia Maritima
Nacional Ltda. (Linhas Brasileiras de
Navegacao (LIBRA)), Rio de Janeiro
and renamed NACIONAL RIO.

1996: Renamed LIBRA RIO.
1998: Sold to Meanrose Shipping
Co. Ltd., Limassol, Cyprus (Pacific
and Atlantic Corporation (Alex
Giannakopoulos), Piraeus, Greece)
and renamed SAINT ANTONIOS.
19.5.1999: Engine failure in position
28.28 north by 163.22 east.
26.5.1999: Taken in tow to
Yokohama.
1999: Renamed ORIENTAL
CROWN
2000: Renamed EXPRESS ORIENT.
2001: Sold to New Lily Shipping Co.
Ltd, Cyprus and renamed ORIENTAL
PEACE.

Top: The former *Rodrigo* as *Libra Rio* in the
Houston Ship Canal, 20th September 1997. She
carries yet another variation of cargo gear: Velle-
type swinging derricks with masts reminiscent
of the later British SD14s. *[Nigel Jones]*

12.9.2002: Arrived Abidjan in tow
after engine room flooded. Repaired
and returned to service.
12.5.2003: Left Abidjan bound in
tow to Dubai for repairs.
2004: Sold to Veesham Shipping
Inc., Dubai (Mato Trading LLC,
Sharjah) under the Panamanian flag.
9.2004: Still listed by 'Lloyd's
Register'.

157. ALESSANDRA

L.R./I.M.O. Number 7433282
Mecapesa-MAN K6Z70/120E
8,680/5,597g
5,813/2,729n
14,279d
At some stage vessel was modified to carry 500TEU; tonnages 8,975g 6,308n 12,803d
Possible intended name MONTE FORMOSA.
7.7.1982: Keel laid.
8.9.1982: Launched for Empresa de Navegacao Alianca S.A., Rio de Janeiro, Brazil.
13.1.1983: Completed. Brazilian flag.
1994: Sold to Van Dyk Shipping Corporation, Monrovia, Liberia (Maritime Services Aleuropa G.m.b.H., Hamburg, Germany) and renamed NOBILITY.
1995: Sold to Bandwith Shipping Corporation, Monrovia, Liberia (Egon Oldendorff, Lübeck, Germany) and renamed JOBST OLDENDORFF.
2001: Managers became Oldendorff Carriers G.m.b.H. and Co., Lübeck.
2002: Sold to Ribena Navigation Co. Ltd., Cyprus (Pitiousa Shipping S.A.,

Piraeus) and renamed SAFMARINE CONGO whilst on Safmarine SAFWAF service.
7.2004: Still listed by 'Lloyd's Register'.

158. LLOYD VENEZUELA

L.R./I.M.O. Number 7433294
9,111g
6,243n
14,347d
Mecapesa-MAN K6Z70/120E
3.11.1982: Launched for Companhia de Navegacao Lloyd Brasileiro, Rio de Janeiro, Brazil.
28.4.1983: Completed. Brazilian flag.
1989: Sold to Lux Rose Shipping Corporation, Monrovia, Liberia (Colonial Marine Industries Inc., Savannah, Georgia, USA) and renamed LUX ROSE under the Vanuatu flag.
1990: Sold to Rose Navigation S.A., Monrovia (Hamburg Maritime Agencies G.m.b.H., Hamburg, Germany) and renamed ROSE under the

Vanuatu flag.
1991: Transferred to Berezan Shipping Co. Ltd., Limassol, Cyprus (Hamburg Maritime Agencies G.m.b.H., Hamburg).
1992: Managers became Globe Trade and Transport Inc., Piraeus, Greece.
1996: Sold to Nirmala Shipping Co. Ltd., Limassol (Pacific and Atlantic Corporation (Alex Giannakopoulos), Piraeus) and renamed SAINT IOANNIS.
1999: Renamed EXPRESS SANTIAGO.
2000: Sold to Sheng Hwa Shipping Co. Ltd. S.A., Panama (China Yantai Shipping Co. Ltd.), (Yantai Marine Shipping Co., Yantai, Shandong Province, People's Republic of China) and renamed LONG XIANG.
2001: Transferred to the Hong Kong flag.
2003: Transferred to Tong Hua Shipping Co. (Yantai Marine Shipping Co., Yantai).
7.2004: Still listed by 'Lloyd's Register'.

159. RENATA

L.R./I.M.O. Number 7433309
8.,680/5,597g
5,812/2,729n
14,279d
Mecapesa-MAN K6Z70/120E
Possible intended name MONTE
CLARO.
8.9.1982: Keel laid.
22.12.1982: Launched for Empresa
de Navegacao Alianca S.A., Rio de
Janeiro, Brazil.
30.5.1983: Completed. Brazilian flag.
1994: Sold to Hasco-Ahlers Interna-

tional Inc., Panama (Hasco-Ahlers
Shipping Co. S.A., Luxembourg) and
renamed FU SHAN. The name
INTEGRITY was reported, but not
confirmed.
1997: Sold to Manaslu Shipping Co.
Ltd., Nicosia, Cyprus (Shanghai Hai
Hua Shipping Co. Ltd., Shanghai,
People's Republic of China) and
renamed MANASLU.
9.2004: Sold to Aurelia Reederei
Eugen Friederich G.m.b.H.
Schiffahrtsges & Co. K.G., Bremen,
Germany and renamed SAFMARINE

Top: *Renata* passing Walsoorden on the
Scheldt in April 1985. She has only cranes
forward of the superstructure in common
with other deliveries to Naviera Alianca.
[David Salisbury]

Bottom: *Tucurui* was a sister to *Leonor*. She
was one of a number of SD14s to become
part of the fleet of George Vergottis. *[David
Salisbury collection]*

NAMIBE.
10.2004: Still listed by 'Lloyd's
Register'.

160. TUCURUI

L.R./I.M.O. Number 7802976
8,203g
6,190n
14,290d
Mecapesa-MAN K6Z70/120E
Ordered by Companhia de
Navegacao Maritima Netumar
(LOLISA), Rio de Janeiro, Brazil.
8.11.1982: Keel laid.
22.12.1983: Launched. Then lay
uncompleted at builder's yard.
22.6.1988: Completed for Gorham
Shipping S.A., Monrovia, Liberia
(Valiant Shipping Co. (London) Ltd.)
retaining intended name TUCURUI.
Greek flag.

Because of the delay, this and yard
number 143 were the last two SD14s
to be completed, 20 years after the
first delivery.
15.12.1989: Sold to Far
Tweendeckers A/S (Sverre Farstad &
Co. A/S), Aalesund, Norway and
renamed FAR STAR.
1992: Sold to Seawave Marine Inc.,
St. Vincent and the Grenadines
(Unicorn Lines (Proprietary) Ltd.,
Durban, South Africa) (Sverre
Farstad & Co. A/S, Aalesund,
managers) and renamed HORIZON.
1994: Sold to Arango Marine Co.
Ltd., Limassol, Cyprus (Pacific and
Atlantic Corporation (Alex

Giannakopoulos), Piraeus) and
renamed BLUE HORIZON.
1995: Sold to Jordan National
Shipping Lines, Amman, Jordan and
renamed JORDAN II under the
Panama flag.
1996: Transferred to Islamic Solidarity
Jordan Inc. (Jordan National Shipping Lines), Amman.
2004: Sold to Ever Success International
Ltd., Hong Kong (China Communications Import/Export Corporation,
Beijing, People's Republic of China)
and placed under the St. Vincent and
Grenadines flag.
7.2004: Still listed by 'Lloyd's
Register'.

Top: Seen at Durban soon after her sale to become *Far Star*, her livery has changed little.
[Trevor Jones, David Salisbury collection]

Middle: Unicorn Lines' *Horizon* at Durban. She has gained a container crane.
[Trevor Jones]

Bottom: As *Blue Horizon* at Vancouver, June 1995.
[Don Brown, David Salisbury collection]

Vessels built by Robb Caledon Shipbuilders Ltd., Dundee

D568. SALTA

L.R./I.M.O. Number 7405986
8,948g
6,099n
15,170d
Doxford 67J4
1973: Contract placed by Empresa Lineas Maritimas Argentinas (ELMA), Buenos Aires, Argentina as part of a package negotiated by consultants A & P Appledore Ltd., which involved a total of nine vessels, three to be built by Robb Caledon and six by Astilleros

Fabricas Navales del Estado, Argentine (q.v).
4.6.1975: Keel laid.
9.6.1976: Launched.
20.1.1977: Completed. Argentine flag.
1996: Sold to Container and Bulk Ltd., Valletta, Malta (P. and P. Shipping Co. (Hellas) S.A. (N.J. Papazoglou), Piraeus, Greece) and renamed SEA DUKE.
8.2.2001: Arrived at Chittagong for breaking up, having been sold for $190 per lightweight ton.

Top: *Salta* passes Vlissingen outward bound from the Scheldt in July 1985. The Robb Caledon SD14s, and those built under licence in Argentina, differed considerably from the basic Sunderland model. Accommodation was enlarged for a complement of 49, and fully air-conditioned. Number 5 hold now had a 'tween deck, and number 4 'tween deck had 45,000 cubic feet of rerigerated space. The number 3 hold deep tank was adapted to carry vegetable oils. *[David Salisbury]*

Bottom: As *Sea Duke*, the ship is seen again in the Scheldt, this time passing Walsoorden on 24th July 1998. *[David Salisbury]*

D569. **JUJUY II**

L.R./I.M.O. Number 7405998
9,234g
6,577n
14,982d
Doxford 67J4
1973: Contract placed as for SALTA.
3.3.1976: Keel laid.
17.3.1977: Launched for Empresa
Lineas Maritimas Argentinas
(ELMA), Buenos Aires, Argentina.
29.8.1977: Completed. Argentine flag.
1992: Sold to Paisley Maritime Inc.,
Monrovia, Liberia (Sharpur Maritime

(Private) Ltd., Karachi, Pakistan) and
renamed QAMAR under the Panama
flag.
1997: Sold to Marzan Shipping Ltd.,
Malta (Bengal Shipping Line Ltd.,
Chittagong, Bangladesh) and renamed AL MARZAN.
2000: Sold to Ocean Maritime
Management Co. Ltd., Pyongyang,
North Korea and renamed JA
GANG.
7.2004: Still listed by 'Lloyd's
Register'.

Top: *Jujuy II* at Durban. A total of 138 TEUs could be carried, 92 stowed under decks. To handle these containers, 22-ton Velle swinging derricks were fitted. *[Trevor Jones, David Salisbury collection]*

Bottom: *Al Marzan* at Durban. *[Trevor Jones, David Salisbury collection]*

D570. **TUCUMAN**

L.R./I.M.O. Number 7406007
8,922g
6,144n
14,930d
Doxford 67J4
1973: Contract placed as for
SALTA.
22.3.1977: Keel laid.
21.1.1978: Launched for Empresa
Lineas Maritimas Argentinas

(ELMA), Buenos Aires, Argentina.
30.5.1978: Completed. Argentine flag.
1992: Sold to Rizan Maritime Ltd.,
Monrovia, Liberia (Shahpur Maritime
(Private) Ltd., Karachi, Pakistan) and
renamed MUZAFFAR AZZIZ under
the Panama flag.
2000: Sold to Dominave S.A.,
Panama and renamed OREOZILI.
3.4.2001: Sold by the Admiralty
Marshall at Gibraltar to Intertrade

Top: *Tucuman* in the Kiel Canal. *[Holger
Zimmerman, David Whiteside collection]*

Bottom: *Almirante Storni* off Calshot in the
Solent during the early 1980s. *[Alan
Stansbridge, David Salisbury collection]*

Lines S.A., Panama and renamed
AZIZ.
4.8.2001: Arrived Alang for demolition.

Vessels built by Astilleros Fabricas Navales del Estado, Ensenada

47. ALMIRANTE STORNI

L.R./I.M.O. Number 7411868
8,924g
6,057n
14,930d.
Doxford 67J4
1973: Contract placed as for Robb Caledon vessels (q.v.).
3.1977: Keel laid.
18.6.1977: Launched for Empresa Lineas Maritimas Argentinas (ELMA), Buenos Aires, Argentina.
10.1978: Completed. Argentine flag.
1992: Sold to Compania Naviera Discovery S.A., Panama (Bonyad Marine Services Inc., Athens, Greece) and renamed JANBAZ 1.
1993: Transferred to Bounty Marine Ltd., Cyprus (Bonyad Marine Services Inc., Athens).
1995: Transferred to Abode Marine Ltd., Cyprus.
1997: Managers became Seabon Holding Corporation, Athens.
2000: Sold to J. and I. Shipping Co. Ltd., St. Vincent and Grenadines (Ocean Marine Shipping L.L.C, Dubai, United Arab Emirates) and renamed ADREKNI.
7.2004: Still listed by 'Lloyd's Register'.

Top and middle: At Vancouver on 1st January 1991, containers dominate the cargo of *Almirante Storni,* the name is in white and the signal mast has been reinforced. *[Don Brown]*
Bottom: *Janbaz I* at Durban. *[Trevor Jones, David Salisbury collection]*

48. (NEUQUEN)
NEUQUEN II

L.R./I.M.O. Number 7411870
8,924g
6,057n
14,930d
Doxford 67J4
1973: Contract placed as for
ALMIRANTE STORNI.
29.8.1977: Keel laid.
10.3.1978: Launched as NEUQUEN
for Empresa Lineas Maritimas
Argentinas (ELMA), Buenos Aires,
Argentina.
2.1979: Completed as NEUQUEN II.
Argentine flag.
1992: Sold to Interfreed Maritime
Co. Ltd., Limassol, Cyprus (John J.
Rigos Marine Enterprises S.A,
Piraeus) and renamed
PANORMITIS.
1999: Sold to Korea Moran Shipping
Co. (Government of the People's
Republic of Korea), Pyongyang, North
Korea and renamed MOKRAN I.
2001: Renamed EUN BONG.
7.2004: Still listed by 'Lloyd's
Register', although there are reports
that she became a total loss in 2002.

Top: *Neuquen II* at Vancouver, 29th July
1986. *[Don Brown, David Salisbury
collection]*

Middle: *Panormitis* cautiously approaches
Heysham, 2nd November 1996. *[Paul Boot]*

Bottom: *Panormitis* again, this time at
Durban about 1992. *[Trevor Jones, David
Salisbury collection]*

49. **LIBERATADOR GENERAL JOSE DE SAN MARTIN**

L.R./I.M.O. Number 7411882
8,922g
6,144n
14,930d
Doxford 67J4
1973: Contract placed as for ALMIRANTE STORNI.
8.4.1978: Keel laid.
26.9.1978: Launched for Empresa Lineas Maritimas Argentinas (ELMA), Buenos Aires, Argentina.
8.1979: Completed. Argentine flag.
23.1.1991: Grounded off Puerto Plata during a voyage from Buenos Aires to Houston.
30.1.1991: Refloated.
1994: Sold to Prudence International

Shipping S.A., Panama (Eternity Shipping Agencies Ltd. (C.F. Lyu), Hong Kong) and renamed PRUDENT CHALLENGER under the St. Vincent and Grenadines flag.
1995: Sold to Maryland Maritime Services Private Ltd., Bombay, India under the St. Vincent and Grenadines flag.
1996: Sold to Prudent International Shipping and Trading Ltd., Nassau, Bahamas (Fouladi General Trading Co., Dubai, United Arab Emirates) under the St. Vincent and Grenadines flag.
4.10.1997: Collided with the Qatar tanker JIWANAT QATAR (25,800/ 1991) in Chittagong Roads and suffered minor damage.
1999: Sold to Tomini Shipping Co. Ltd., Gibraltar (Alpina Ship Management APS, Naestved, Denmark) and renamed

PACIFIC CHALLENGER under the St. Vincent and Grenadines flag.
2001: Transferred to United Ocean Shipping Co. Ltd., St. Vincent and Grenadines (Alpina Ship Management APS, Naestved, Denmark) and renamed UNITED TRADER.
8.7.2003: Arrived at Alang to be broken up by Ashit Services.
12.7.2003: Work began.

Top: Carrying the longest name of any SD14, *Liberatador General Jose de San Martin* at Vancouver in June 1988 with hatches open. The AFNE-built vessels incorporated much British equipment, notably the Doxford engine. *[Don Brown, David Salisbury collection]*

Bottom: *Pacific Challenger,* Mumbai, New Year's Day 2000. *[Nigel Jones]*

50. DR. ATILIO MALVAGNI

L.R./I.M.O. Number 7411894
8,924g
6,057n
14,930d
Doxford 67J4
1973: Contract placed as for
ALMIRANTE STORNI.
23.10.1978: Keel laid.
19.1.1979: Launched for Empresa
Lineas Maritimas Argentinas
(ELMA), Buenos Aires, Argentina.
13.6.1980: Completed. Argentine flag.
14.10.1989: Damaged in collision
with a Government-owned dredger
about seven miles off Buenos Aires
when outward bound for north
European ports.
1991: Sold to Obtain Shipping Co.
Ltd., Nicosia, Cyprus (John J. Rigos
Marine Enterprises S.A., Piraeus,
Greece) and renamed PLANITIS.
1995: Sold to Petassos Navigation
Co. Ltd., Valletta, Malta (Dalex
Shipping Co. Ltd. (G. Dalacouras),
Piraeus) and renamed ASTIVI.
1996: Sold to Modest Maritime Co.
Ltd., Nicosia (Rota Shipping S.A.,
Piraeus) and renamed
PLATYTERA.
4.4.1996: Reported broken down
about 500 miles south east of
Durban with fuel system problems.
10.4.1996: Towed into Port Elizabeth by tug WOLRAAD
WOLTEMADE (2,918/1976).
19.4.1996: Sailed after repairs.
2002: Sold to Congo Development
SPRL, Kinshasa (Kashin Co. Ltd.)
and renamed SHINKAI MARU
under the Cambodia flag.
8.6.2002: Engine problems 12 miles south
of Cape Agulhas. Taken in tow by the
tug WOLRAAD WOLTEMADE
(2,918/1976).
11.6.2002: Arrived Capetown and

subsequently detained.
6.5.2003: Sold by judicial sale and
renamed SHINKAI under the
Mongolian flag
4.9.2003: Arrived Alang to be
broken up by Nagarseth
Shipbreakers.
9.9.2003: Work commenced.

Top: *Dr. Atilio Malvagni* in the New Waterway,
July 1983. *[David Salisbury]*

Middle: As *Planitis* at Durban about 1993, her
signal mast has additional supports. *[Trevor
Jones, David Salisbury collection]*

Bottom: *Presidente Ramon S. Castillo* in the
New Waterway about 1981. *[Rowley Weeks,
David Salisbury collection]*

51. PRESIDENTE RAMON S. CASTILLO

L.R./I.M.O. Number 7411909
8,924g
6,057n
14,930d
Doxford 67J4
1973: Contract placed as for ALMIRANTE STORNI.
1979: Keel laid.
16.8.1979: Launched for Empresa Lineas Maritimas Argentinas (ELMA), Buenos Aires, Argentina.
13.6.1980: Completed. Argentine flag.
1995: Sold to Co-operativa de Trabajo Manuel Belgrano Ltda. (Co-operativa de Trabajo Maritima Argentina) (Argocean S.A., managers), Buenos Aires, Argentina.
7.2004: Still listed by 'Lloyd's Register', although continued existence must be in doubt, as no movements reported since June 1996.

52. (GENERAL BELGRANO) GENERAL MANUEL BELGRANO

L.R./I.M.O. Number 7411911
8,924g
6,057n
14,930d
Doxford 67J4
1973: Contract placed as for ALMIRANTE STORNI.
17.9.1979: Keel laid.
30.5.1980: Launched for Empresa Lineas Maritimas Argentinas (ELMA), Buenos Aires, Argentina.
25.4.1981: Completed as GENERAL MANUEL BELGRANO. Argentine flag.
1995: Sold to Co-operativa de Trabajo Manuel Belgrano Ltda. (Co-operativa de Trabajo Maritima Argentina) (Argocean S.A., managers), Buenos Aires, Argentina.
25.3.1997: Reported under arrest at Conakry, Guinea after discharge of cargo.
1998: Sold to Three Oceans Ltd., Cayman Islands and renamed ALYSSA under the St. Vincent and Grenadines flag.
12.4.2003: Sold to Hans Global Ltd., Sharjah.
2.7.2003: Renamed PARVATI under the Mongolian flag.
29.6.2003: Arrived Alang to be broken up by Hans Global Ltd.

Middle: *General Manuel Belgrano* at Vancouver on 13th November 1985. Note the container fittings on the deck and hatch covers. *[Don Brown, David Salisbury collection]*

Bottom: In Singapore Roads ten years later on 30th December 1995, ownership and livery have changed but not the name *General Manuel Belgrano*. *[Nigel Jones]*

Vessels built by Smith's Dock Ltd., South Bank, Middlesbrough

Smith's Dock's involvement with the SD14 programme followed nationalisation in 1977, and the decision to incorporate the yard into the Merchant Shipbuilding Division of British Shipbuilders along with Austin & Pickersgill. In 1981, Austin & Pickersgill had a reasonable order book and Smith's were short of work, so contracts for two SD14s which Austin & Pickersgill were then negotiating with the Carrian Group, Hong Kong, were transferred to South Bank as numbers 1349 and 1350. Except for the engines, these vessels were repeats of four built at Southwick for World Wide Shipping, and of number 1426 recently ordered by Wah Kwong at Southwick, except that heavy-lift derricks were not fitted. In the event, Carrian Group went into liquidation leaving Smiths with two vessels in the last stages of fitting out. When completed they were laid-up until a deal was worked out with Cuba. The ships were of the SD14 Fourth Series and British Shipbuilders then decided to adopt this configuration as a successor to the SD14, calling it the SD King 15 Class, more in line with what had always been the SD14's true deadweight capacity of about 15,000 tons. Four more vessels of this design were built at Smith's Dock in another deal with Cuba, but no more orders were received. Discounting the two vessels whose delivery was delayed in Brazil, number 1360 thus became the last SD14/SD15 to be completed.

1349. (CARRIANNA LILAC) LILAC ISLANDS

L.R./I.M.O. Number 8120727
8,976g
6,237n
15,175d
Clark-Hawthorn Sulzer 5RLB56
8.1981: Contract placed by Carrian Group.
3.11.1981: Keel laid.
6.5.1982: Launched for Carrian Shipping Ltd., Hong Kong.
10.11.1982: Vessel completed trials and laid up following liquidation of Carrian Group.
1983: Handed over to Valletta Shipping Corporation, Panama (Grand Marine Holdings Ltd., Hong Kong) and renamed LILAC ISLANDS, demise chartered to Empresa Navegacion Mambisa (Government of Cuba), Havana, Cuba. Original plan was to rename her VALLETTA.
1988: Involvement of Grand Marine Holdings Ltd. ceases, operator continues to be Empresa Navegacion Mambisa, Havana.
1994: Management transferred to Naviera Poseidon, Havana, operator continues to be Empresa Navegacion Mambisa, Havana.
2000: Transferred to Battersea Maritime Co. S.A., Panama (Naviera Poseidon, Havana), operator continues to be Empresa Navegacion Mambisa, Havana.
2004: Sold to associates of Aqua Azur Shipmanagement B.V., Netherlands and renamed ALDONA.
7.2004: Still listed in 'Lloyd's Register'.

Top *Carrianna Lilac* on trials, 10th October 1983. *[Michael Green]*

Middle: *Lilac Islands* in superb external condition on the New Waterway. *[V.H. Young and L.A. Sawyer]*

Bottom: *Lilac Islands* on the Kiel Canal. *[Holger Zimmerman, David Whiteside collection]*

226

1350. (CARRIANNA LOTUS) LOTUS ISLANDS

L.R./I.M.O. Number 8120739
8,976g
6,237n
15,175d
Clark-Hawthorn Sulzer 5RLB56
8.1981: Contract placed by Carrian Group.
21.12.1981: Keel laid.
16.9.1982: Launched for Carrian Shipping Ltd., Hong Kong.

21.1.1983: Vessel completed trials and laid up following liquidation of Carrian Group.
1983: Handed over to Wadena Shipping Corporation, Monrovia, Liberia (Grand Marine Holdings Ltd., Hong Kong) and renamed LOTUS ISLANDS under the Panama flag, demise chartered to Empresa Navegacion Mambisa (Government of Cuba), Havana, Cuba. Original plan was to rename vessel WADENA.
1988: Involvement of Grand Marine

Holdings Ltd. ceases, operator continues to be Empresa Navegacion Mambisa, Havana.
1994: Management transferred to Naviera Poseidon, Havana, operator continues to be Empresa Navegacion Mambisa, Havana.
2000: Transferred to Rearlake Shipping Co. Inc, Panama (Naviera Poseidon, Havana), operator continues to be Empresa Navegacion Mambisa, Havana.
7.2004: Still listed in 'Lloyd's Register'.

Top: *Carrianna Lotus* immediately after launch on 16th September 1972. *[Michael Green]*

Middle: *Carrianna Lotus* on trials, 10th January 1983. *[Michael Green]*

Bottom: An exceptionally deep-laden *Lotus Islands* in the St. Lawrence, August 1989 still wearing Carrian funnel colours. *[Marc Piché, David Salisbury collection]*

227

1357. SOUTH ISLANDS
L.R./I.M.O. Number 8500965
8,996g
6,239n
15,147d
Clark-Hawthorn Sulzer 5RLB56
4.1985: Keel laid.

30.10.1985: Launched.
20.3.1986: Completed for South Islands Shipping Co. Ltd., Limassol, Cyprus (Empresa Navegacion Mambisa (Government of Cuba), Havana).
1994: Management transferred to Naviera Poseidon (Government of

Cuba), Havana.
2000: Sold to Vietnam Sea Transport and Chartering Co. (VITRANSCHART), Ho Chi Minh City, Vietnam and renamed PHUONG DONG 3.
7.2004: Still listed in 'Lloyd's Register'.

1358. WEST ISLANDS
L.R./I.M.O. Number 8500977
8,995g
6,239n
15,136d
Clark-Hawthorn Sulzer 5RLB56
6.1985: Keel laid.
25.3.1986: Launched.
10.7.1986: Completed for West Islands Shipping Co. Ltd., Limassol, Cyprus (Empresa

Navegacion Mambisa (Government of Cuba), Havana).
1994: Management transferred to Naviera Poseidon (Government of Cuba), Havana.
2000: Sold to Vietnam Sea Transport and Chartering Co. (VITRANSCHART), Ho Chi Minh City and renamed PHUONG DONG 1.
7.2004: Still listed in 'Lloyd's Register'.

Top: *South Islands.* The catwalk, just visible below the bridge windows, is to facilitate cleaning. *[Roy Fenton collection]*

Middle: The completed *West Islands* is manouevred in the Tees. The short length of bulwark amidships gave a measure of protection to the air pipes which served as pressure release valves in the event of overfilling the deep tanks in the floodable number 3 hold. *[Michael Green]*

Top: *West Islands*, now wearing green, in Singapore roads, 24th June 1998. The stern anchor is part of the package of extra fittings for ships expected to navigate the St. Lawrence Seaway. *[Nigel Jones]*

Middle: *West Islands* as *Phuong Dong 1*. *[Russell Priest]*

Bottom: *East Islands* passes Walsoorden on the Scheldt in April 1987. This class had six of its ten dericks uprated to lift 15 tons. *[David Salisbury]*

1359. **EAST ISLANDS**
L.R./I.M.O. Number 8500989
8,996g
6,239n
15,120d
Clark-Hawthorn Sulzer 5RLB56
3.5.1985: Keel laid.

23.6.1986: Launched.
11.1986: Completed for East Islands Shipping Co. Ltd., Limassol, Cyprus (Empresa Navegacion Mambisa (Government of Cuba), Havana).
1994: Management transferred to Naviera Poseidon (Government of Cuba), Havana.

2000: Sold to Vietnam Sea Transport and Chartering Co. (VITRANSCHART), Ho Chi Minh City, Vietnam and renamed PHUONG DONG 2.
7.2004: Still listed in 'Lloyd's Register'.

1360. NORTH ISLANDS

L.R./I.M.O. Number 8500991
8,996g
6,239n
15,120d
Clark-Hawthorn Sulzer 5RLB56
22.11.1985: Keel laid.
15.10.1986: Launched.
12.2.1987: Completed for North
Islands Shipping Co. Ltd., Limassol,
Cyprus (Empresa Navegacion
Mambisa (Government of Cuba),
Havana).

1994: Management transferred to
Naviera Poseidon (Government of
Cuba), Havana.
7.9.1997: Lost propeller and ran
aground off the coast of Llollea, near
San Antonio, Chile, whilst on a
voyage from San Antonio to Panco
with a cargo of fertiliser. The bow
section filled with water and vessel
broke in two. Chilean Navy helicop-
ters took off crew of 28 men and two
women. Later reported broken up.

This page top: *North Islands*, the last launch
from the South Bank shipyard, 15th October
1986. *[Michael Green]*

This page bottom: *North Islands* in the River
Mersey 11th September 1987. *[Paul Boot]*

Opposite: *North Islands* broken in two off the
coast of Chile in September 1997. Titan
Salvage succeeeded in removing bunker and
lubricating oil from the wrecked ship. *[Titan
Salvage]*

PRINASA-121s built by Companhia Comercio e Navegacao (CCN), Rio de Janeiro

098. AMALIA

L.R./I.M.O. Number 7357878
11,373/8,583g
6,281/4,545n
14,566/11,674d
Mecapesa-MAN K7SZ70/125
1973: Ordered.
26.9.1974: Keel laid.
6.12.1974: Launched for Companhia de Navegacao Maritima Netumar, Rio de Janeiro, Brazil as AMALIA.
24.9.1975: Completed. Brazilian flag.

1989: Sold to Brugge Marine Co. Ltd., Nicosia, Cyprus (Blue Flag Navigation Ltd., Piraeus, Greece) and renamed SUNDERLAND SPIRIT.
1994: Sold to Hainan Hua Tong Shipping Co. Ltd., Hainan Island, People's Republic of China and renamed YONG TONG.
1997: Sold to breakers in the People's Republic of China for $130 per lightweight ton.

Top: First Prinasa-121, *Amalia*. The 60-ton Stülcken derrick could be swung between the two masts to serve two adjacent hatches. The remaining cargo gear had a more modest lifting capacity, with 16 derricks rated at just 5 tons. *[Dave Kohl, David Salisbury collection]*

Bottom: *Sunderland Spirit* photographed at Durban about 1992. The name is to be applauded, even if the ship was actually built many thousands of miles from the River Wear. *[Trevor Jones, David Salisbury collection]*

099. CAIÇARA

L.R./I.M.O Number 7357880
11,373/8,583g
6,281/4,545n
14,566/11,373d
Mecapesa-MAN K7SZ70/125
1973: Ordered.
6.12.1974: Keel laid.
28.2.1975: Launched for Companhia de Navegacao Maritima Netumar, Rio de Janeiro, Brazil as CAIÇARA.

19.11.1975: Completed. Brazilian flag.
1989: Sold to Olfron Marine Co. Ltd., Nicosia, Cyprus (Blue Flag Navigation Ltd., Piraeus, Greece) and renamed SUNDERLAND ENDEAVOUR.
1994: Sold to Pan Asia Ocean Glory Shipping Inc., Hong Kong and renamed GOLDEN FUTURE under the Panama flag.

Top: *Caiçara* with a crumpled stem. *[Dave Kohl, David Salisbury collection]*

Bottom: *Sunderland Endeavour. [Trevor Jones David Salisbury collection]*

7.2004: Still listed in 'Lloyd's Register', but continued existence must be in doubt as no movements reported since July 1997.

100. JOANA

L.R./I.M.O. Number 7357892
11,373/8,583g
6,281/4,545n
14,587/12,054d
Mecapesa-MAN K7SZ70/125
1973: Ordered.
1.3.1975: Keel laid.
5.5.1975: Launched for Companhia de Navegacao Maritima Netumar, Rio de Janeiro, Brazil as JOANA.
2.8.1976: Completed. Brazilian flag.
8.9.1989: Sold to Vendome Marine Co. Ltd., Nicosia, Cyprus (Blue Flag Navigation Ltd., Piraeus, Greece) and renamed SUNDERLAND CRAFTSMAN.
1994: Sold to Rectagi Private Ltd. (Jaya-JK Shipping Private Ltd.), Singapore and renamed PANGLIMA.
1995: Management transferred to Jaya Shipment Private Ltd., Singapore.
9.1.2000: Arrived at Alang for breaking up, having been sold for $150 per lightweight ton.

Top: *Joana* in the St. Lawrence Seaway, 28th July 1979. *[René Beauchamp, David Salisbury collection]*

Bottom: *Joana as Panglima.* Note the straight-line sheer of the Prinasas. *[Nigel Jones]*

Opposite top: Seen at Durban about 1989, *Celina Torrealba* had a much reduced cargo gear. *[Trevor Jones, David Salisbury collection]*

Opposite middle: *City of Durham. [Trevor Jones, David Salisbury collection]*

Opposite bottom: *Sea Lady 1*, also at Durban about 1995. *[Trevor Jones, David Salisbury collection]*

115. CELINA TORREALBA

L.R./I.M.O. Number 7432862
11,372/8,583g
6,281/4,545n
14,281/12,247d
Mecapesa-MAN K6SZ70/125A
1974: Ordered.
28.9.1976: Launched for Companhia Paulista de Comercio Maritimo Wilfried Penha Borges), Rio de Janeiro, Brazil as CELINA TORREALBA.
8.1977: Completed. Brazilian flag.
1991: Sold to Negro Shipping Co. Ltd., Nicosia, Cyprus (Blue Flag Navigation Ltd., Piraeus, Greece) and renamed CITY OF DURHAM.
1994: Sold to Sea Bell Maritime Ltd., Valletta, Malta (Aquarian Shell Marine Inc., Athens, Greece) and renamed SEA LADY 1.
1996: Sold to Oasis Maritime Ltd.,

Valletta (Harmony Shipping LLC, Dubai, United Arab Republic) and renamed HARMONY WAVE.
21.9.1998: Arrived at Alang for

breaking up by Annapurna Ship-breaking Company, having been sold for $127 per lightweight ton. Demolition began the same day.

117. FROTAKOBE

L.R./I.M.O. Number 7432874
11,373/8,585g
6,267/4,962n
14,659/12,100d
Mecapesa-MAN K6SZ70/125A
1974: Ordered.
5.1977: Launched for Frota Oceanica Brasiliera S.A., Rio de Janeiro, Brazil as FROTAKOBE.

18.1.1978: Completed. Brazilian flag.
16.1.1986: Seriously damaged by an engine room fire whilst lying at the yard of Estaleiro Maua S.A., Rio de Janeiro. Later declared a constructive total loss.
1.6.1986: Demolition begun by Industrias Reunidas Caneco S.A., Rio de Janeiro.
30.6.1986: Demolition completed.

Top: *Frotakobe* at Durban with its mast cranes deployed to good effect. *[Trevor Jones]*
Bottom: *Lloyd Mandu* was one of just two Prinasas with basic conventional cargo gear. *[Holger Zimmerman, David Whiteside collection]*
Opposite page top: *Frotamanila.* Her cargo gear comprised eight 40-ton twin cranes. Along with *Frotakobe* and *Frotasingapore,* she spent several years on charter to Oldendorff. *[Roy Kittle, David Salisbury collection]*
Opposite page middle: *Bel Azur.* *[Russell Priest]*
Opposite page bottom: *Saint Pavlos.* *[Alastair Paterson, David Salisbury collection]*

119. **LLOYD MANDU**

L.R./I.M.O. Number 7432886
11,373/8,585g
6,267/4,962n
14,550/11,674d
Mecapesa-MAN K6SZ70/125A
1974: Ordered.
1.3.1978: Launched for Companhia de Navegacao Lloyd Brasiliera S.A., Rio de Janeiro, Brazil as LLOYD MANDU.
15.3.1979: Completed. Brazilian flag.
1993: Sold to Memory Navigation Co. Ltd., Limassol, Cyprus (Anpo Shipping Co. Ltd. (Anastasios G. Politis), Piraeus, Greece) and renamed PROMETHEUS.
24.10.1994: Damaged by fire in the engine room whilst lying at Apapa following arrival from Imbituta. One member of the crew was killed. Towed to Piraeus.
6.2.1995: Sailed for Iraklion.
10.2.2001: Arrived Chittagong for breaking up, having been sold for $182 per lightweight ton

132. **FROTAMANILA**

L.R./I.M.O. Number 7432898
11,373/8,586g
6,267/4,962n
14,65/12,100d
Mecapesa-MAN K6SZ70/125A
1974: Ordered.
20.7.1979: Launched for Frota Oceanica Brasiliera S.A., Rio de Janeiro, Brazil as FROTAMANILA.
28.3.1980: Completed. Brazilian flag.
1995: Sold to Lubeca Marine Management (HK) Ltd., Hong Kong and renamed BEL AZUR.
1996: Transferred to Mauritius Steam Navigation Co. Ltd., Rogers and Co. Ltd. and Indian Ocean Bulk Carriers Ltd. (Rogers and Co. Ltd.),

Port Louis, Mauritius.
1998: Sold to Borelly Shipping Co. Ltd., Limassol, Cyprus (Pacific and Atlantic Corporation (Alex Giannakopoulos), Piraeus) and renamed SAINT PAVLOS.

2000: Sold to Long Fu Shipping S.A., Panama (China Yantai Shipping Co. Ltd., Hong Kong) and renamed LONG FU.
7.2004: Still listed in 'Lloyd's Register'.

134. **FROTADURBAN**

L.R./I.M.O. Number 7432903
11,373/8,586g
6,267/4,962n
14,550/12,100d
Mecapesa-MAN K6SZ70/125A
1974: Ordered.
26.10.1979: Launched for Frota
Oceanica Brasiliera S.A., Rio de
Janeiro, Brazil as FROTADURBAN.
11.8.1980: Completed. Brazilian flag.
1995: Sold to Lubeca Marine
Management (HK) Ltd., Hong Kong.
1997: Transferred to Capricorn

Steamship Co. Ltd., Port Louis,
Mauritius (Oldendorff Asia Private
Ltd., Singapore, managers).
1997: Renamed EDWARD
OLDENDORFF.
1998: Renamed SECIL SERAYA.
3.2.1999: Renamed EDWARD
OLDENDORFF.
2000: Sold to Amartrans International
Private Ltd. (Intercontinental Maritime Private Ltd.), Singapore and
renamed AMAR.
7.2004: Still listed in 'Lloyd's
Register'.

Top: *Frotadurban* carries seven crane derricks.
[Trevor Jones, David Salisbury collection]

Bottom: *Edward Oldendorff* at Durban, extending
the connection between Oldendorff and A&P
designed vessels. *[Trevor Jones, David Salisbury collection]*

Opposite top: *Nicia.* Her outfit features a mast
crane similar to that fitted to some CCN
SD14s. *[Trevor Jones, David Salisbury collection]*

Opposite bottom: *Lloyd Tupiara*, another with
conventional gear. *[David Salisbury]*

135. NICIA

L.R./I.M.O. Number 7432915
11,373/8,586g
6,297/4,546n
14,650/12,100d
Mecapesa-MAN K6SZ70/125A
1974: Ordered.
6.2.1980: Launched for Companhia Paulista de Comercio Maritimo (Wilfried Penha Borges), Rio de Janeiro, Brazil as NICIA.
9.1980: Completed. Brazilian flag.
1995: Sold to Unilago Shipping N.V., Willemstad, Curacoa, Netherlands Antilles (Naviera Universal S.A., Lima, Peru) and renamed UNILAGO.
13.12.1997: Arrived Balboa in tow of the tug GERONIMO (144/1959) after breaking down off the Pacific coast of Costa Rica.
29.12.1997: Sailed for Callao after repairs.
26.6.1998: Arrived Alang to be broken up by Alang Shipbreakers Private Ltd., having been sold for $124 per lightweight ton. Work commenced the same day.

137. LLOYD TUPIARA

L.R./I.M.O. Number 7432927
11,373/8,585g
6,267/4,962n
14,199/12,100d
Mecapesa-MAN K6SZ70/125A
1974: Ordered.
7.5.1980: Launched for Companhia de Navegacao Lloyd Brasiliera S.A., Rio de Janeiro, Brazil as LLOYD TUPIARA.
11.2.1980: Completed. Brazilian flag.
1989: Sold to Seacross Navigation Co. Ltd., Limassol, Cyprus (Anpo Shipping Co. Ltd. (Anastasios G. Politis), Piraeus, Greece) and renamed ANTEOS.
23.11.1993: Stranded near Buoy 83A in the River Scheldt with rudder damage whilst on a voyage from Antwerp to Tripoli.
24.11.1993: Refloated and taken into Flushing Roads.
1998: Management transferred to Aurora Shipping S.A. (Aldebaran Shipping Ltd.), Athens.
7.2.2001: Arrived at Alang to be broken up, having been sold for $179 per lightweight ton.

139. LLOYD ALEGRETE

L.R./I.M.O. Number 7432939
11,373/8,585g
6,267/4,962n
14,650/12,100d
Mecapesa-MAN K6SZ70/125A
1974: Ordered.
31.7.1980: Launched for Companhia de Navegacao Lloyd Brasiliera S.A., Rio de Janeiro, Brazil as LLOYD ALEGRETE.
17.12.1981: Completed. Brazilian flag.
1992: Sold to Marine Challenger S.A., Piraeus, Greece and renamed CHALLENGER IV under the Panama flag.
1997: Transferred to Marine Challenger S.A., Panama (Franser Shipping S.A. (Angela Frangos and Dion Seretakos), Piraeus).
14.8.2001: Arrived at Chittagong to be broken up, having been sold for $161 per lightweight ton.
10.9.2001: Demolition commenced.

Top: *Lloyd Alegrete.* [David Salisbury]

Middle and bottom: *Lloyd Bahia* anchored in Guanabara Bay, Rio de Janeiro on 24th March 2000. She was sold for scrap soon afterwards. [Nigel Jones]

154. LLOYD BAHIA

L.R./I.M.O. Number 7432941
11,372/8,585g
6,267/4,962n
14,166/12,100d
Mecapesa-MAN K6SZ70/125A
1974: Ordered.
9.11.1981: Launched for Companhia de Navegacao Lloyd Brasiliera S.A., Rio de Janeiro, Brazil as LLOYD BAHIA.
30.7.1982: Completed. Brazilian flag.
28.5.1993: Arrived at Rio de Janeiro and laid up.
2.7.2003: Arrived at Alang to be broken up by Dempo.
3.7.2003: Work began.

155. FROTASINGAPORE

L.R./I.M.O. Number 7432953
Mecapesa-MAN K6SZ70/125A
11,372/8,585g
6,267n
14,600d
1974: Ordered.
12.2.1982: Launched for Frota Oceanica Brasiliera S.A., Rio de Janeiro, Brazil as FROTASINGAPORE.
7.10.1982: Completed. Brazilian flag.
1995: Sold to Lubeca Marine Management (HK) Ltd., Port Louis, Mauritius.
1996: Transferred to Mauritius Steam Navigation Co. Ltd., Rogers and Co. Ltd. and Indian Ocean Bulk Carriers Ltd. (Rogers and Co. Ltd.), Port Louis, Mauritius.
1997: Renamed BEL AIR.
1998: Calvados Shipping Co. Ltd., Limassol, Cyprus (Pacific and Atlantic Corporation, (Alex Giannakopoulos), Piraeus, Greece) and renamed SAINT MARKOS
2000: Sold and renamed ORIENTAL HONOUR.
2001: Renamed GREEN.
2002: Renamed JAT NA MU.
7.2004: Still listed in 'Lloyd's Register'.

Middle: *Frotasingapore* at Durban. *[Trevor Jones, David Salisbury collection]*

Bottom: *Jat Na Mu* at Singapore, 31st March 2002. *[Nigel Jones]*

Appendix 1: General information

Prior to the 1930s, most general cargo vessels were built to a single-deck design with forecastle and poop, and either a long or short bridge erection. The new designs which were presented after the depression years which followed, however, were almost all two-decked vessels, variously described as complete superstructure or shelter deck types, featuring continuous upper and second decks about 7ft 6ins apart, which together formed a 'tween deck. Most of these designs complied with regulations then in force which, principally, exempted most of this 'tween deck from tonnage measurement under certain conditions, thus reducing gross and net tonnage, but carried the penalty of reduced draught (since freeboard was measured from the lower deck) and, consequently, deadweight. They were designated open shelter deck vessels, and were perceived as the most economical type then available for general trading. Poop, bridge and forecastle erections were then often added above the basic structure.

With maximum deadweight, rather than reduced gross and net tonnages, considered more appropriate for wartime operation, the conditions governing the open shelter deck option which allowed tonnage exemption for the 'tween decks, were not adopted for most Second World War newbuilding tramp ship designs (including the 'Liberty'), and during this period ships were delivered as closed shelter deckers, sometimes described as full scantling vessels. In this design freeboard was measured from the upper deck and the increased draught allowed some 2,000 tons more cargo to be carried than was possible in the open condition. After the war, interest in the open shelter deck design revived, but, increasingly, the suitability of the closed variant in the rapidly changing trading patterns of the day saw that type begin to dominate the market.

In line with this trend, the SD14 was designed as a full scantling, closed shelter deck vessel, with an upper deck serving as the strength and freeboard deck, a second deck in numbers 1, 2. 3 and 4 holds only, and a forecastle. The fact that the second deck did not extend into number 5 hold, and was, therefore, not continuous throughout the vessel, meant that the basic SD14 could not operate in an open shelter deck configuration. However, the six vessels designed independently by Hellenic Shipyards for Hellenic Lines, and nine SD14s built by CCN for operation by Brazilian liner companies, were fitted with a second deck in number 5 hold and, by complying with other necessary regulations, these were completed with the arrangements in place for a relatively simple conversion to be made which allowed them to sail in either the open or closed shelter deck mode, to suit the owner's requirements, depending on current trading conditions. The nine modified vessels built by Robb Caledon and AFNE also had a 'tween deck in number 5 hold, but were completed simply as closed shelter deckers, without this facility for change.

Coincident with the development of the SD14 design, these outdated and somewhat controversial regulations governing the open/closed shelter deck options were actually under review by international authorities. They were eventually replaced by simpler rules, still aimed at allowing tonnage exemption for the 'tween deck space, but making that exemption dependent upon the application of a pre-determined tonnage mark. This second loadline marking, comprising a horizontal line surmounted by a downward-pointing equilateral triangle, positioned aft of the usual load line disc, indicates the reduced draught to which the vessel may load in order to claim tonnage reductions. As before, that benefit carries the penalty of reduced deadweight. Those vessels having the facility to convert from open to closed shelter deck, or which complied with the new tonnage mark rules, can be identified in the ship histories by having dual gross, net and deadweight tonnages recorded.

From the earliest days of steam propulsion, ship design had favoured an engines-midships configuration, with longitudinal strength and trim considerations restricting the more economical layout provided by positioning the engine room at the aft end in smaller vessels, and, although there were always exceptions, it was only in the early nineteen-fifties that improvements in structural design made it possible to successfully develop single-deck (or the basically similar raised quarter-deck) vessels larger than the typical Thames 4,500 tons deadweight collier. Now, of course, any thought of an upper size limit to the single-decker has virtually disappeared.

The main advantage of moving the machinery space aft was to utilise for carrying cargo the almost full-cube midship space, hitherto lost in most cargo vessels to the main engine and machinery installation. This could then be repositioned in what had previously been a less advantageous cargo hold restricted by the shape of the aft body hull form, and by a shaft tunnel highly susceptible to cargo handling damage. Whilst the machinery right-aft layout was readily accepted by bulk carrier and tanker operators, its adoption for general cargo carriers was a slower process and, although some vessels were built with this arrangement, a more popular configuration for this class of ship became the three-quarter aft design, and, with this popularity increasing, Austin & Pickersgill opted to develop that format for the SD14 design.

MAIN PARTICULARS

Main particulars
The following details apply to the First, Second and Third Series SD14s. The changes applicable to Fourth Series vessels are also noted. Where ship dimensions have been modified subsequent to delivery, the changes are recorded within the history of that ship. Deadweights, gross and net tonnages varied from ship to ship and are, therefore, quoted within each ship history.

The SD14 was designed to imperial measurements, before the full adoption of the metric system in the UK. A calculated metric equivalent is shown.

Length, overall	462' 6"	140.97m
Length, B.P	440' 2"	134.16m
Breadth, moulded	67' 0"	20.42m
Depth, moulded		
to upper deck	38' 6"	11.73m
to second deck	28' 6"	8.69m
Load draught	29' 0"	8.84m

As designed, LBP was 440' 0" and load draught 28' 6"; changes to the freeboard rules referred to in the text and made before the first vessel was completed, increased draught to 29' 0" and added 2" to the length between perpendiculars.

The Hellenic Shipyards liner-type SD14 incorporated a bulbous bow resulting in the following change:

Length, overall	469' 3"	143.03m

The Fourth Series SD14 dimensions were changed as a result of the modified hull form, as follows:

Length, overall	472.44 feet	144.00m
Length, BP	451.11 feet	137.50m
Breadth, moulded	67.00 feet	20.42m
Depth, moulded		
to upper deck	38.55 feet	11.75m
to second deck	28.54feet	8.70m
Load draught	29.10feet	8.87m

Main engines
The following types of main engine have been used in the SD14. The specific unit fitted to each vessel is indicated in the relevant ship history.

Sulzer 5RD68
Five-cylinder, vertical, single-acting, two-stroke, direct injection, reversible diesel engine of crosshead construction, fitted with two exhaust gas turbo-chargers.

Cylinder bore	680mm
Piston stroke	1,250mm
Bhp (max. continuous)	5,500 @ 135revs/min
Bhp (service)	4,950 @ 130revs/min

Sulzer 6RD68
General particulars as for 5RD68 but with one extra cylinder.

Bhp (max. continuous)	7,200 @ 135revs/min
Bhp (service)	6,500 @ 130revs/min

Sulzer 5RND68
General particulars as for 5RD68 but with one exhaust gas turbo-charger. The engine design was uprated to produce:

Bhp (max. continuous)	7,500 @ 137revs/min
Bhp (service)	6,750 @ 132.5revs/min

Sulzer 4RND68M

General particulars as for 5RND68 but with four cylinders, uprated to produce:

Bhp (max. continuous)	7,600 (metric) @ 150revs/min
Bhp (service)	6,840 (metric) @ 145revs/min

Sulzer 5RLB56

General design as for other Sulzer engines with five cylinders and one exhaust gas turbo-charger.

Cylinder bore	560mm
Piston stroke	1,150mm
Bhp (max. continuous)	7,500 (metric) @ 170revs/min
Bhp (service)	6,750 (metric)

Sulzer 5RTA48

This engine was proposed for the final version of the SD14, designated the SDKing15 by British Shipbuilders, but no ships of this design were built.
General design as 5RLB56.

Cylinder bore	480mm
Piston stroke	1,400mm
Bhp (max. continuous)	7,400 (metric) @ 154revs/min
Bhp (service)	6,660 (metric) @ 149revs/min

MAN K6Z70/120E (fitted to SD14s built by CCN)

Six-cylinder, vertical, single-acting, two-stroke, reversible diesel engine of crosshead construction. Fitted with two exhaust gas turbo-chargers.

Cylinder bore	700mm
Piston stroke	1,200mm
Bhp (max. continuous)	8,400 @ 140revs/min

MAN R9V52/55 (fitted to liner type SD14s built by Hellenic Shipyards)

Nine-cylinder, in line, single-acting, four-stroke, reversible diesel engine working through reduction gearing.

Cylinder bore	520mm
Piston stroke	550mm
Bhp (max. continuous)	8,220 @ 410/144revs/min

Doxford 67J4 (fitted to vessels built by Robb Caledon and AFNE)

Four-cylinder, vertical, single-acting, two-stroke, opposed-piston, reversible diesel engine of crosshead construction. Fitted with one exhaust gas turbo-charger.

Cylinder bore	670mm
Piston stroke	2,140mm (combined)
Bhp (max. continuous)	9,000 @ 127revs/min
Bhp (service)	8,000 @ 124revs/min

The following types of main engine were used in the SD15 (A & P), SD18 and CCN Prinasa-121 designs, as indicated in the relevant ship history.

Doxford 76J4 (fitted to SD15 *Armadale*, A & P hull 866)

Four-cylinder, vertical, single-acting, two-stroke, opposed-piston, reversible diesel engine of crosshead construction. Fitted with one exhaust gas turbo-charger.

Cylinder bore	760mm
Piston stroke	2,180mm (combined)
Bhp (max. continuous)	10,000 @ 119revs/min
Bhp (service)	8,415 @ 113revs/min

Sulzer 6RND68

As designed, the basic specification of the SD15 (A & P) included this main engine. However, the above Doxford engine was offered as an alternative and fitted in *Armadale* at the owner's request.
Six-cylinder, vertical, single-acting, two-stroke, direct injection, reversible diesel engine of crosshead construction, fitted with one exhaust gas turbo-charger.

Cylinder bore	680mm
Piston stroke	1,250mm
Bhp (max. continuous)	9,900 @ 150revs/min
Bhp (service)	8,415 @ 143revs/min

Sulzer 6RND68M (fitted to SD18 design)

General particulars as for 6RND68 (above) but uprated to produce:

Bhp (max. continuous)	11,400 @ 150revs/min
Bhp (service)	9,690

MAN K7SZ70/125 (fitted to first three CCN Prinasa-121 vessels)

General particulars as for K6Z70/120E (above).

Cylinder bore	700mm
Piston stroke	1,250mm
Bhp (max. continuous)	11,550

MAN K6SZ70/125A (fitted to remainder of the CCN Prinasa-121 vessels)

General particulars as for K7SZ70/125A (above).

Cylinder bore	700mm
Piston stroke	1,250mm
Bhp (max. continuous)	11,400

Engine builders

The following manufacturers supplied the main engines listed above, to SD14, SD15, SD18 (A & P) and Prinasa-121 designs:

Vickers Ltd., Barrow-in-Furness, UK
*Hawthorn Leslie (Engineers) Ltd. Newcastle-upon-Tyne, UK
*George Clark & NEM Ltd., Wallsend, UK
Scott's Engineering Co. Ltd., Port Glasgow, UK
Sulzer Brothers, Winterthur, Switzerland
H. Cegielski, Poznan, Poland
Mecanica Pesada S.A. (Mecapesa), San Paulo, Brazil
Maschinenfabrik Augsberg-Nurnberg A.G. (MAN), Augsberg, Germany
Doxford Engines Ltd., Sunderland, UK.

*These two companies later amalgamated within British Shipbuilders and traded as:
Clark-Hawthorn Ltd., Wallsend, UK and later:
Clark-Kincaid Ltd., Wallsend and Greenock, UK)

Appendix 2: Outline hull and machinery specification of a standard SD14

This is a lightly edited version of the original specification issued by Austin & Pickersgill.

DESIGN

1. DIMENSIONS

Length overall	462' 6"
Length B.P.	440' 0"
Breadth mid.	67' 0"
Depth mid to upper deck	38' 6"
Height of 'tween decks at side, amidships	10' 0"
Height of forecastle	7' 6"
Height of deckhouses	7' 6"
Sheer forward	9' 0"
Sheer aft	nil
Camber (straight line)	18"
Load draft, mean	28' 6"

2. TONNAGES (approximate)

Deadweight:		
	cargo	12,866
	oil fuel	969
	diesel oil	111
	fresh water	126
	lub. oil	38
	stores, crew, etc.	55
	spare gear	35
	Total	14,200

N.B. Oil capacities in the above table are at 98% full

Gross tonnage	8,800
Net tonnage	6,100

3. CAPACITIES
Total grain capacity incl. hatches: cu. ft.766,000
                                           cu. ft./ton 59.7
Total water ballast 3,323 tons = 26% cargo d.w.

4. SPEED AND POWER
Speed in service under average fair weather conditions to be 14 knots, on a power of 4,950 BHP at the main engine, consuming about 19½ tons oil fuel per day (main engine only) at 130 r.p.m. This is equivalent to 90% of the maximum continuous rating of the engine.

5. CLASSIFICATION AND SURVEY
Lloyds + 100A1 + L.M.C.
British Board of Trade
Suez and Panama Navigation Rules.

6. GENERAL ARRANGEMENT
Full scantling type. 5 holds (number 3 floodable).
'Tween decks in numbers 1, 2, 3 and 4 compartments.
Machinery and accommodation spaces between numbers 4 and 5 holds.
Deep transom stern.

7. CARGO SPACES
Tank top increased in lieu of ceiling.
No cargo battens.
Flush steel pontoon hatch covers on second deck.
Watertight steel single-pull hatch covers on weatherdeck, wire operated by ship's winches.
Structural steelwork as required to comply with Grain Loading Regulations, and fittings, wires, etc., provided for shifting boards or feeders.
Shifting boards and feeders not supplied.
Designed to sail loaded with deep tank empty.

8. CARGO GEAR
2 x 5-ton S.W.L. derricks to each cargo hatch (10 in all).
1 x 3-ton electric winch to each derrick, each with wire compressor and 6" bollard for topping derricks.
All winches to have Ward-Leonard control.
Vessel to have a foremast stiffened for future fitting of 25- or 30-ton derrick and 2 pairs of hexagonal-shaped derrick posts. All unstayed.
Windlass and 5-ton warping winch to be provided for mooring.

9. STERNFRAME AND RUDDER
Sternframe of cast steel.
Rudder of cast steel, with mild steel plating forming streamlined section, 'Simplex' pattern.
Forged steel backpost and stock, horizontal coupling.

10. DOUBLE BOTTOM
Cellular sub-division transversely into port, starboard and centre tanks.
Oil fuel in number 3 double bottom tank port and starboard and centre forward of engine room.
Number 2 centre double bottom tank to be generally considered as a water ballast tank, but provision to be made for use as an oil fuel tank, if required.
Raised tank top in machinery space to suit main engine and shaft height.
Lubricating oil drain tank below main engine, with diesel oil at sides.
Tank top straight out to sides, with drain wells.

11. CONSTRUCTION
All welded, fabricated. Riveted gunwale bar.
Transverse side frame, longitudinal deck beams.

12. DEEP TANK
No centre division. Large single plate bolted flush hatch cover.
Water ballast or dry cargo. No heating coils. No cargo battens.

13. DECKHOUSES
All steel, swedged on sides. Steel entrance doors. No skylights.
14" sidelights in officers' accommodation.
12" sidelights in crew accommodation.
No deadlights to be fitted. Steel protection plates to be arranged at lower tier house front.
Fixed windows in wheelhouse. No sidelights in washplaces or toilets.

Steel ladders both inside and outside.
Bitumastic lightweight deck covering on exposed decks over accommodation.

14. ACCOMMODATION
European, as follows:

captain	1
pilot	1
deck officers	4
chief engineer	1
second engineer	1
junior engineers	6
petty officers	3
caterers	4
seamen	6
engineroom hands	4
	31

All in single rooms. Bulkheads, painted. Class 'B' type where required by Rule.
No ceilings. Vinyl tiles on deck, except upper deck passages and wheelhouse, where composition to be laid. Quarry tiles in galley. Vinyl sheet in toilets. Steel furniture to be used as extensively as possible. Canvas awnings over accommodation spaces.

15. GALLEY
Oil-fired drip-feed range.
Electric bread prover.
Electric steaming oven.
Electric Bain Marie, serving into crews' messroom.
Electric 10 gallon hot water boiler.
Galvanised steel dresser with stainless steel sink bowl and cupboards.
Equipment generally to be stove enamelled finish.

16. PANTRY
Electric hotpress.
Electric 3 gallon hot water boiler.
Hardwood furniture.
Stainless steel sink.

17. DUTY MESS
Stainless steel sink unit.
Table and seat for 3 persons.

18. DOMESTIC STORES
Cold chambers insulated with fibreglass, galvanised steel or plywood sheathed and floor of cork slabs with granolithic cement, fitted with wood gratings, galvanised shelves and fittings.
Capacity approximately as follows:

meat room	650 cu.ft.
vegetable room	500 cu.ft.
handling room	300 cu.ft.

Refrigerating machinery to be air-cooled Freon type.
Dry store adjoining, fitted with bins, shelving and gratings.

19. INSULATION
Casings adjoining machinery and boilers etc., to be insulated as required by Board of Trade.
Vent trunking, hot water piping, steam piping to be lagged.

20. HEATING AND VENTILATION
Low pressure supply, steam heated and centrally controlled.
Punkah louvres to all rooms. Natural exhaust.
Mechanical exhaust from galley and dry store.

21. WATER SERVICES
Domestic hot and cold services on pressure feed system.
Hot water through steam heated storage calorifier.
Cooled drinking water from tank in cold stores.

22. BILGE AND BALLAST
Bore as per Lloyds' rules.
Mild steel with flexible couplings led through double bottom wing tanks.
Strum boxes on all suctions.
No pipes in cargo holds.
Independent valve boxes for bilge and ballast lines.

23. HEATING COILS
1½" heavy gauge solid drawn black tube in H.O. double bottom tanks. 1¼ sq. ft./ton.

24. WASHDECK LINES
Extending fore and aft along deck at hatch, one side with brass hose connections.

25. FIRE EXTINGUISHING
Hand extinguishers throughout accommodation, chemical type as B.O.T. requirements with smoke helmet apparatus, electric drill, safety lamps and hatchets.
No fire extinguishing in cargo spaces.
CO_2 installation in engineroom.
Diesel driven emergency fire pump, fitted outside machinery space.

26. STEERING GEAR
Two ram type, electric hydraulic 2 power units, each comprising electric motor, driving variable delivery pump.
Telemotor control from wheelhouse with combined auto-pilot console.
Local mechanical control handwheel on steering gear.

27. WINDLASS
Electric 70/58 h.p. slip ring motor, drum control.
$2\frac{1}{8}$" special steel cable.
17 tons at 26 feet minimum at cable lifters.
5½ tons at 118 feet minimum at warp ends.
Lever bowstoppers.

28. LIFE-SAVING
1 x fibreglass 24' 0" oared lifeboat.
1 x fibreglass 24' 0" motor lifeboat.
Gravity-type davits.
2 x hand winches with 1 electric portable hoisting unit.
1 x 16-man inflatable life-rafts.

29. LADDERS
1 x 22' 0" long aluminium accommodation ladder with curved fixed steps.
8' 0" long extension with flat fixed steps.
Fixed platform and hand winch port and starboard.
1 x 30' 0" long regulation shore gangway.

30. EQUIPMENT
Anchors and cables as Rule.
Reflector type dry card compass with spare bowl available for use as auxiliary compass.
Cherub log.
8 lever clocks.
Barometer.
Rudder indicator.
1 clear-view screen.
Norwegian foghorn.
Megaphone.
1 set electric signal lamps.
1 set oil signal lamps.
Loud hailer.
Telephones, bridge-engine room/forecastle/aft.
Gyro compass and auto pilot.

31. SPARE GEAR
Lloyds' Long Voyage and equipment makers' standard.

32. PAINTING
Outside shell to be shotblasted and prime coated prior to delivery of steel.
Bottom shell:
    1 coat primer and 1 coat anti-corrosive prior to launch.
    1 coat tropical anti-fouling at drydocking.
Boot topping:
    1 coat undercoat and 1 coat boot topping prior to launch.
    1 coat boot.topping at drydocking
Topsides:
    1 coat undercoat and 1 coat gloss paint prior to launch.
    1 coat gloss paint at drydocking.
Stern areas:
    2 coats anti-galvanic composition.
Superstructures:
    2 coats primer.
    1 coat undercoat.
    2 coats marine enamel.
Cargo spaces:
    1 coat red oxide.
    1 coat metallic paint.
Chain locker:
    bituminous solution and enamel.
Water ballast tanks:
    cement wash.
Oil fuel tanks:
    bare steel.
Steel decks and tank top:
    bare steel.

33. ELECTRICAL
For alternators and switchboard, see Machinery Specification.
Incandescent lighting in officers', engineers' and crew's accommodation, messrooms, passageways, galley, pantry, engine room, washplaces, wheel-house, store rooms, weatherdeck lighting and portables.
500 watt derrick post floodlights.
5 sets cargo clusters with 2 connections per hatch.
Lifeboat and gangway floodlights.
Navigation and signal mast lights.
Morse lamp, Aldis lamp and connections.
4 x 30 kva 440/220 volt transformers for lighting.
2 x 24 volt batteries and charging board for L.P. circuits.
Crew alarm bell system.
Bells from hospital, dining saloon, refrigeration chambers and engine room.
200 amp shore connection.
Wiring only for owners' supply items:
W/T, D/F and auto alarm.
Radar.
Echo sounder.
All cables, butyl insulated, P.C.P. type 660 or 250 volt grade according to Rule.

34. STORES
Vessel to be equipped as required for Construction Rules.
Owners to provide:
    all consumable stores, oils, paints, etc
    navigational aids
    photographs
    cutlery
    crockery
    bedding and napery
    medical supplies
    books
    charts
    deck and cabin stores
    galley stores and utensils
    stationery
    flags
    lifeboat provisions, charts, first aid kit and radio
    model.

35. COMPLETION
To be built to requirements of rules and regulations of Lloyd's and B.O.T. as in force at date of building agreement.
To be drydocked in Sunderland for 3 tides.
Delivered off River Wear after satisfactory sea trials.
Guarantee period 6 months.

36. SUMMARY OF CAPACITIES

Cargo spaces	Frames	Cubic feet (grain)
No. 1 hold	138-169	84,900
No. 2 hold	99-138	158,900
No. 3 hold	84-99	61,300
No. 4 hold	54-84	121,500
No. 5 hold	4-37	103,700
TOTAL HOLDS		530,000
No. 1 'tween decks	138-169	61,800
No. 2 & 3	84-138	115,500
No. 4	54-84	59,000
TOTAL 'TWEEN DECKS		236,300
TOTAL CARGO SPACES		**766,600**

OUTLINE SPECIFICATION OF MACHINERY

37. CLASSIFICATION
The machinery to be built and installed under the survey and to the requirements of Lloyd's Register of Shipping and Board of Trade where applicable.

38. GENERAL DESCRIPTION

The propelling machinery to be fitted three quarters aft in the vessel and to consist of a reversible single acting, two-stroke cycle, airless fuel/injection, turbo-charged Sulzer 5RD68 diesel engine.

No scavenge pumps or auxiliary blowers to be fitted. The cylinder jackets, cylinder covers, pistons and fuel valve nozzles to be freshwater cooled. The turbo-charger exhaust gas inlet and outlet casings to be cooled by freshwater from the jacket water circulating system and the air coolers to be cooled by seawater from the seawater circulating main.

Freshwater circulating, seawater cooling, forced lubrication and heavy fuel oil booster pumps to be independently driven.

The main engine to be arranged to operate on heavy fuel oil having a viscosity of up to 3,500 seconds Redwood No. 1 at 100°F. with alternative connections for changing over to diesel oil without delay.

Designation	Sulzer 5RD68
No. of cylinders	5
Cylinder bore	680mm.
Piston stroke	1,250mm.
B.H.P. (maximum continuous)	5,500
R.P.M.	135
Position of engine controls	Port side aft at starting platform level.
Electric supply	440 volts, 3-phase, 60-cycles.
No. of turbo-charges	2
Weight of exhaust gases at 5,500 B.H.P.	84,700 lb/hr.
Temperature of exhaust gases at 5,500 B.H.P.	635°F.
Diameter of exhaust pipe	39"
Maximum allowable back pressure in exhaust system	12" w.g.
Estimated fuel consumption based on a gross calorific value of 18,500 B.T.Us. per lb. at 5,500 B.H.P.:	19.5 tons per day.

This consumption is subject to a tolerance of +5% for variations in the quality of fuel oil and errors of observation.

39. BOILER

One vertical composite type boiler designed for a working pressure of 100 p.s.i. and having an evaporation of 2,250 lbs/hour from the exhaust gas side and 2,850 lbs/hour from the oil fired side.

To be complete with suitable oil burning equipment and all necessary mountings and fittings.

40. ELECTRIC GENERATING PLANT

Three diesel driven alternators to be installed, each designed for a maximum continuous output of 170 kW when running at a speed of 1,200 r.p.m. at 440 volts 3-phase 60-cycles, 0.8 power factor.

Each engine to have oil and water pumps and coolers mounted on engine.

41. AUXILIARY MACHINERY

Two starting air compressors, each capable of compressing 125 cubic feet of free air per minute to a pressure of 425 p.s.i.

One diesel driven emergency air compressor, capable of compressing 8 cubic feet of free air per minute to a pressure of 350 p.s.i.

Two jacket water circulating pumps, each capable of delivering 110 tons per hour at a pressure of 32 p.s.i.

Two piston water circulating pumps, each capable of delivering 50 tons per hour at a pressure of 64 p.s.i.

Two lubricating oil pumps, each capable of delivering 67 tons per hour at a pressure of 71 p.s.i.

Two fuel valve cooling water pumps, each capable of delivering 5 tons per hour at a pressure of 43 p.s.i.

One jacket water cooler, capable of cooling 110 tons of fresh water per hour from 154°F. to 131°F. when circulated with seawater at 90°F.

One lubricating oil cooler, capable of cooling 67 tons of lubricating oil per hour from 117°F. to 109.4°F. when circulated with seawater at 90°F.

One piston water cooler, capable of cooling 50 tons of freshwater per hour from 122°F. to 108°F. when circulated with seawater at 90°F.

One main seawater pump, capable of delivering 240 tons per hour at a pressure of 26 p.s.i.

One ballast and standby seawater circulating pump, capable of delivering 240 tons per hour at a pressure of 26 p.s.i.

Two general service, bilge and fire pumps, each capable of delivering 80/120 tons per hour against a head of 230/70 feet.

Two heavy oil booster pumps, each capable of delivering 4.5 tons per hour at a pressure of 142 p.s.i.

One heavy oil transfer pump, capable of delivering 20 tons per hour against a head of 100 feet.

One diesel oil transfer pump, capable of delivering 10 tons per hour against a head of 100 feet.

Two heavy fuel oil purifiers of suitable capacity and type.

Two steam heaters to work in conjunction with the heavy oil purifiers.

One diesel oil purifier of suitable capacity and type.

One lubricating oil purifier of suitable capacity and type.

One steam heater to work in conjunction with the lubricating oil purifier.

One 1½" bore purifier sludge pump.

One seawater evaporator having a capacity of 10 tons per day.

One freshwater distiller having a capacity of 2,000 gallons per day.

One drains cooler capable of dealing with about 3,000 lbs. of condensate per hour.

One boiler feed water filter tank of the gravitation type having a capacity of 600 gallons per hour.

Two boiler feed water pumps, each capable of delivering 600 gallons per hour.

One oily water separator of the manually operated type having a capacity of 25 tons per hour.

Two starting air storage tanks, each having a capacity of 265 cubic feet at a pressure of 425 p.s.i.

One auxiliary air storage tank, having a capacity of 23 cubic feet at a pressure of 350 p.s.i.

42. FUNNEL

To be of approved design and of ample dimensions to accommodate the main engine exhaust pipe, diesel alternator exhaust pipes and boiler uptakes.

43. SHAFTING

To be of solid forged ingot steel, turned all over and 1¼" larger in diameter in way of bearings. Shaft bearings to be of cast iron lined with white metal in the bottom halves and of the self-lubricating type with oil bath. The aftermost bearing to be lined with whitemetal in the top and bottom halves.

44. STERN TUBE

To be of cast iron, strongly proportioned and firmly secured to the stern frame by a steel nut.

Tube to be fitted with a long brass bush fitted with strips of lignum vitae or Tufnol so arranged that they can be withdrawn for renewal.

45. PROPELLER

To be of Nikalium with cast iron cone cover.

46. SEA VALVES

Sea valves of 3" bore and above to have bodies of fabricated mild steel and below 3" bore of gunmetal.

47. FIRE FIGHTING APPLIANCES

To be suitably arranged in the machinery spaces to comply with Survey requirements, including CO_2 installation.

48. ENGINE ROOM CRANE

One 5-ton S.W.L. single motor electric crane to be installed in the engineroom casings for lifting main engine parts.

49. VENTILATION

Four suitable ventilators, each fitted with a fan delivering 10,750 cubic feet of air per minute at a pressure of 1.5 inches w.g.

One 12" diameter extraction fan to be fitted for purifier space.

50. WORKSHOP

To be fitted with a 6½" centres lathe, 1¼" maximum capacity drilling machine and a double ended grinding machine with 10" x 1" wheels.

All machines driven by independent electric motors.

51. SPARE GEAR

To be supplied in accordance with Lloyd's requirements for ocean-going vessels.

52. OUTFIT

To include all necessary tools and equipment for overhauling and maintaining the machinery.

NOTE: Thermometers to be graduated in °F.
Pressure gauges to be calibrated in lbs/sq. in.
Fuel tanks to be calibrated in tons.
Lubricating oil tanks to be calibrated in gallons.

OPTIONAL EXTRAS

Items of outfit and equipment supplementary to the basis specification which may, if required, be supplied and fitted at extra cost to be quoted, as determined by makers' current prices.

1. 25 tons S.W.L. derrick at foremast serving number 2 hatch with 8-ton winches instead of 3-tons capacity, and all necessary running gear and equipment.
2. Heavy derrick as above, but having S.W.L. of 30-tons.
3. Two derricks of 10-tons S.W.L. at number 2 hatch, instead of 5-tons capacity, and operated by 5-ton winches.
4. 10-ton derricks, as above, but in association with heavy derrick as described in Items 1 and 2.
5. Two 10-ton derricks at number 4 hatch operated by 5-ton winches, and with derrick posts strengthened to suit.
6. 'Tween deck in number 5 hold with flush steel pontoon hatch covers.
7. Deck fittings to permit the carriage of timber cargoes.
8. Fitting 6" x 2" whitewood cargo battens throughout holds and 'tween decks (excluding floodable hold).
9. Supplying timber feeders and shifting boards as required by Grain Loading Rules, in addition to fittings as specified.
10. Fitting watertight flat in fore peak tank below main deck to form fore fore peak store.
11. Equipping vessel for the navigation of the St. Lawrence Seaway with the following items:
   (a) Fitting cable lifter to existing 5-ton warping winch and supplying bow stopper, 27½ cwt. stern anchor, 60 fathoms 1 3/8"steel cable, chain locker and hawsepipe.
   (b) Man landing boom at break of forecastle port and starboard.
   (c) Navigation lighting in accordance with Canadian Lighting Regulations.
   (d) Sewage disposal plant ejecting by ship's compressed air supply.
   (e) Fitting four at 5-ton cargo winches in place of four at 3-ton, suitable for mooring duties, in pairs forward and aft in association with four universal fairleads and four roller fairleads on deck for leads.
   (f) One welded half round 4" x 2" fender on shell port and starboard about 200' 0" long amidships and steel hoods over shipside discharges.
12. Installing a system of CO_2 fire extinguishing throughout cargo spaces, in addition to specified system for engine room. Smoke detection included.
13. Fitting portable steel heating coils in number 3 floodable hold with a heating surface of 1½ sq ft. per ton suitable for the carriage of edible oil cargoes. (Cargo pumps **not** included.)
14. Revising accommodation and all associated equipment for the carriage of a crew of 38 persons, instead of 31.
15. All bulkheads throughout crew spaces to be plastic faced instead of painted. (Basis ship accommodation.)
16. Air conditioning all accommodation spaces in place of the existing heating and ventilation.
17. Providing 24" x 18" windows in officers' and engineers' accommodation instead of 14" sidelights. (Basis ship accommodation.)
18. Fluorescent lighting instead of incandescent.
   (a) throughout accommodation.
   (b) in engine room.
19. One additional clear view screen in wheelhouse.
20. Additional aluminium accommodation ladder.
21. Standby air cooled-refrigeration unit.
22. Supplying and fitting navigational aids and nautical instruments.
   (a) Radar   (i) AEI 'Escort'.
                    (ii) Marconi 'Raymarc'.
                    (iii) K.H. Type 14/12.
   (b) Echo sounder: Marconi 'Seamare'.
   (c) Direction finder: Marconi 'Lodestone 1V'.
   (d) Radio transmitter and receiver, auto alarm, battery and charging equipment: Marconi.
   (e) Portable lifeboat radio: Marconi 'Survivor'.
   (f) VHF transmitter/receiver: Marconi 'Argonaut'.
   (g) Broadcast equipment: Marconi (10 speakers).
   (h) Internal telephones, captain/bridge/chief engineer/engine room.
   (i) Electric log: Walkers Commodore.
   (j) Stress finder: Kelvin Hughes.
   (k) Stability indicator: Kelvin Hughes (Ralston).
   (1) Flags (40).
   (m) Chronometer: Mercer.
   (n) Electric clock system with eight clocks (Kelvin Hughes), in place of specified mechanical clocks.
23. Spare cylinder liner.
24. Separate oil-fired and waste heat boilers instead of composite boiler.
25. Spare tail shaft.
26. Spare propeller:
   (a) cast iron
   (b) manganese bronze.
27. Whitemetal lined stern tube instead of lignum vitae.
28. Slower speed generating sets (600-720 R.P.M.).
29. Self-cleaning purifiers instead of standard type.
30. Additional standby purifier.
31. Fresh water generator instead of evaporator and distiller, with chlorination plant.
32. Bridge control of main engine.

NOTE: By adopting all or several of these items, other aspects of the design or specification may be affected, i.e. deadweight, size of alternators, equipment numeral.

Appendix 3: Shipyard cost comparisons

This table shows a comparison of hull and machinery costs prepared by other UK builders against the Austin & Pickersgill specification and plan, September 1966.

Costs quoted exclude profit margins, and other additional items normally included in the selling prices of newbuildings, such as commissions and levies.

Austin & Pickersgill Ltd.	£880,060
Bartram & Sons Ltd.	£955,750
Caledon Shipbuilding & Engineering Co. Ltd.	£977,030
Burntisland Shipbuilding Co. Ltd.	£977,440
John Readhead & Sons Ltd.	£1,013,501
Doxford & Sunderland Shipbuilding & Engineering Co. Ltd.	£1,014,000
Hawthorn Leslie (Shipbuilders) Ltd.	£1,035,690
Lithgows Ltd.	£1,041,000
Scotts Shipbuilding & Engineering Co. Ltd.	£1,074,000
Associated Shipbuilders Ltd. (Swan Hunter).	£1,092,010
Vickers Ltd.	£1,130,424
Cammell Laird.	£1,159,315
Harland & Wolff Ltd.	£1,178,215
John Brown (Clydebank) Ltd.	£1,342,500

General arrangement drawing of South Dock yard number 450, *1 Congreso del Partido*

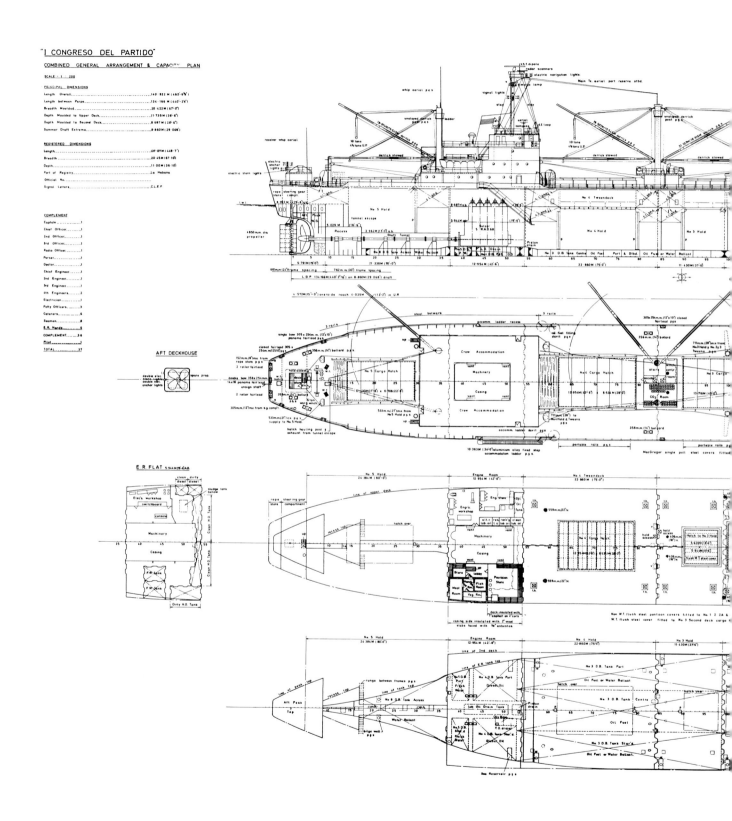

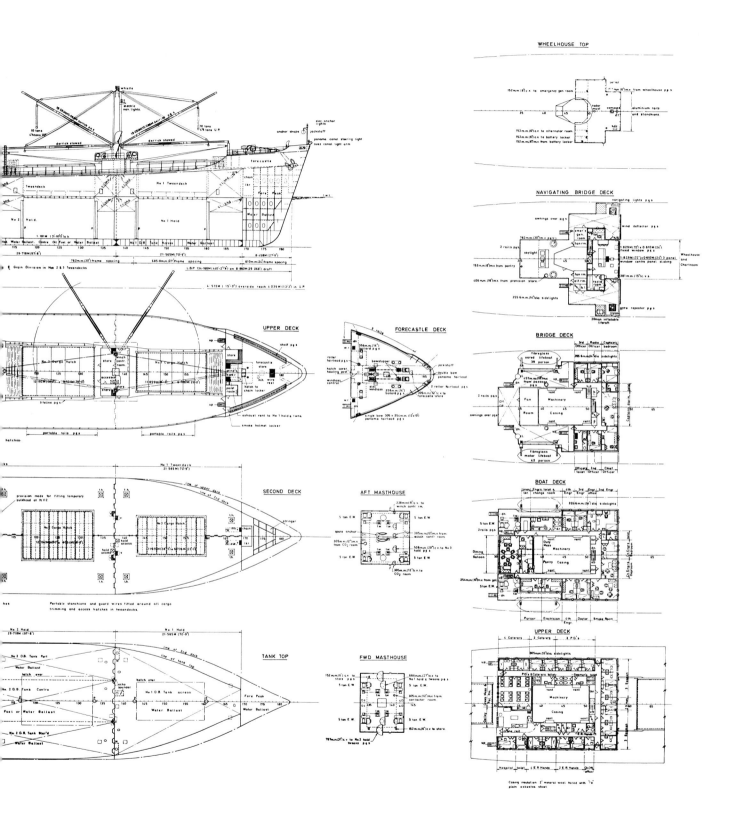

Appendix 4: SD14 price increases, 1968-1983

As the SD14 building programme gathered momentum, it was decided that it was good policy not to accept orders on an extended delivery basis and, wherever possible, completion dates no more than 18/24 months ahead from tender date were offered. New cost estimates were, therefore, prepared at about 6-monthly intervals for a tranche of perhaps five newbuildings, calculated to suit the newly specified forward delivery date. Although many enquiries and subsequent orders resulted from direct contacts with owners, most emanated from specialist ship sale and purchase brokers. Some of these worked with specific owner-clients who preferred to do business via a third-party, rather than doing the 'leg-work' themselves, but perhaps more were freelance operators who kept themselves up-to-date with details of the latest Austin & Pickersgill offer, which they then circulated around the shipping offices, hoping to persuade owners that buying an SD14 was a good idea! In both cases their reward was a commission, usually pitched about 1% of the selling price but, exceptionally, considerably higher.

As demand for the SD14 increased, the basis price naturally also increased. However, it has also to be remembered that most of the vessels were built during a period of monetary inflation outside the control of the shipbuilder. In addition, as noted in the text, improvements were regularly made to the design, and these reasons also contributed to basis price increases, some quite dramatic. The following table gives an approximate indication of that price as calculated for particular delivery dates. The amounts shown are for ships built to the basic specification and plan applying at the date quoted. In many cases owners asked for certain extras from the builder's standard list, or of their own choice, to be included in the contract price, together, perhaps, with an allowance for any changes which might be made during building, and for other items and charges likely to be incurred. This meant that an approximate purchase price could be finalised at an early stage of negotiations, allowing owners to arrange finance and credit facilities, covering virtually the entire cost of their vessel before contract signing. These additional items are not shown in the amounts quoted.

Delivery date	Basis price (£)	Delivery date	Basis price (£)
Early 1968	915,000	Early 1975	1,850,000
Early 1969	940,000	End 1976	2,285,000,
Mid 1969	1,075,000	Early 1977	2,285,000
Early 1971	1,100,000	Early 1978	4,650,000
Mid 1971	1,150,000	End 1978	4,625,000
End 1971	1,200,000	Early 1979	4,900,000
Early 1972	1,200,000	End 1979	5,150,000
Mid 1972	1,325,000	Early 1980	5,150,000
End 1972	1,395,000	Mid 1980	4,950,000
Mid 1973	1,395,000	End 1980	5,000,000
End 1973	1,875,000	Early 1981	5,000,000
Early 1974	1,650,000	Mid 1982	5,975,000
End 1974	1,750,000	End 1982	6,225,000

Appendix 5: Representative financial data

The variations in the price paid per ship by the respective owners, shown as selling price in the table, not only reflects the periodic increases in basis price as indicated in Appendix 4, but also takes into account the cost of any owners extras which might have been included in that particular contract. Extras negotiated after contract signing would normally be the subject of a separate account, settled by a cash on completion. The main purpose of the table is to show the profits made per ship by Austin & Pickersgill (A&P) and Bartram (B) over the period under review. Unfortunately, similar detailed results are not available for subsequent years, but they did continue at this highly satisfactory level for quite some time into the future.

Ship no.	Shipyard	Date	Building cost (£)	Profit (£)	Selling price (£)
852	A & P	1968	836,000	90,000	926,000
410	B	1968	921,000	80,000	1,001,000
856	A & P	1969	903,000	113,000	1,016,000
415	B	1969	1,062,000	168,000	1,230,000
859	A & P	1969	888,000	147,000	1,035,000
419	B	1969	1,081,000	171,000	1,252,000
862	A & P	1969	986,000	180,000	1,166,000
424	B	1970	1,445,000	86,000	1,531,000
869	A & P	1971	1,176,000	159,000	1,335,000
429	B	1971	1,257,000	163,000	1,420,000
872	A & P	1971	1,399,000	251,000	1,650,000
431	B	1972	1,271,000	160,000	1,431,000
878	A & P	1972	1,355,000	225,000	1,580,000
432	B	1972	1,289,000	187,000	1,476,000
879	A & P	1972	1,321,000	206,000	1,526,000
879	A & P	1972	1,321,000		

Appendix 6: Annual summary of SD14s built, lost and broken up

The construction date is taken to be the year the ship entered service. In some instances this differs from the year completed, for instance CCN yard numbers 143 and 160 which were launched in 1983 but entered service only in 1988.

A 'loss' is recorded only when the ship has been sunk, grounded or been scuttled. Other constructive total losses where the ship has subsequently been delivered to and demolished at a breaker's yard are included in the 'Broken up' column. For example, *An Tai* (Bartram yard number 432) and *Her Loong* (Bartram yard number 433) both suffered severe damage and

were subsequently broken up. *An Tai*, which sank at her berth at Port Klang and was later raised in sections that were cut up locally, is listed as a 'loss'; whereas *Her Loong*, gutted by fire at Hamburg and then towed to breakers in Spain, is deemed to have been broken up.

The summary of the number of ships in service at the end of each year has been shown only up to the completion of the last two examples in 1988. Thereafter, doubts about the existence of an increasing number of ships preclude an accurate assessment of this figure.

Year	A&P South-wick	South Dock	Hellenic	CCN	Robb Caledon	AFNE	Smith's Dock	Annual total built	Losses	Broken up	In service at year end
1968	4	4	1					9			9
1969	5	5	5					15			24
1970	1	6	6					13			38
1971	7	5	10					22	1		58
1972	7	5	5					17			75
1973	7	5		7				19			94
1974	7	5		6				18			112
1975	1	6		2				9			121
1976	2	5		6				13		1	133
1977	1	5		2	2			10			143
1978	6	3		3	1	1		14			157
1979	8			4		2		14			171
1980	9					2		11			182
1981	2			5		1		8			190
1982	4			1			1	6	1		195
1983				5			1	6		2	199
1984	1							1			200
1985									2	1	197
1986							3	3	3	7	190
1987							1	1	1	3	187
1988				2				2		1	188
1989									1	1	See note
1990									1		
1991									2	2	
1992										3	
1993									2	3	
1994										7	
1995										5	
1996									2	7	
1997									2	11	
1998										8	
1999									2	9	
2000										8	
2001									1	20	
2002										10	
2003									1	6	
2004									1	2	
Total	72	54	27	43	3	6	6	211	25	115	

Appendix 7: Major operators

Listed here are companies, groups or governments operating three or more SD14s, and the names of their SD14s with the page number of their entry in the yard lists. Note that the number of names listed under each operator is not always a guide to how many ships were operated, as charters and transfers meant that an individual ship might be renamed several times whilst essentially under one owner.

D. & G. Agoudimos and J. Meletis (Flandermar Shipping Co. S.A.), Piraeus
Agia Efymia	38
Agios Gerassinos	112
Nissos Keffalonia	40

A. Alafouzas (Glafki Shipping Company S.A.), Piraeus
Aegira	78
Athanassia	64
Lesvos	64
Capetan Giannis	105
Capetan Manolis	107
Capetan Markos	151
Sea Hawk	80
Sea Trader	136

Navegacao Alianca S.A., Rio de Janeiro
Alessandra	215
Ana Luisa	212
Bianca	210
Monte Alto	206
Monte Cristo	205
Monte Pascoal	206
Renata	216
Serra Azul	187
Serra Branca	188
Serra Dourada	183
Serra Verde	182

Linhas Maritimas de Angola U.E.E., Luanda
Ebo	202
Hoji ya Henda	72
Kifangondo	80
Lundoge	78

Australind Steam Shipping Co. Ltd. (Trinder, Anderson and Co. Ltd.), London
Ajana	71
Armadale	39
Arrino	69
Australind	155

Blue Flag Navigation Ltd. (Nik. Koros), Piraeus
City of Durham	235
Roker Park	160
Sunderland Craftsman	234
Sunderland Endeavour	233
Sunderland Spirit	232

Bonyad Marine Services Inc, Athens/Seabon Holding Corporation, Athens
Amity Union	202
Janbaz 1	221
Konarak	48
Lantic Union	202
Panda Faget	61
Procyon	202
Zenith	135

Wilfried Penha Borges (Companhia Paulista de Comercio Maritima), Rio de Janeiro
Anisio Borges	207
Celina Torrealba	235
Nicia	239
Rodrigo	214
Rodrigo Torrealba	184

Brightest Star Maritime Corporation, Piraeus
Trust	138

Unity	139
West Coast	138

P.G. Callimanopoulos (Hellenic Lines Ltd.), Piraeus
Grigorios C. IV	178
Hellenic Carrier	174
Hellenic Challenger	173
Hellenic Champion	172
Hellenic Ideal	176
Hellenic Navigator	177

People's Republic of China
An Dong Jiang	82
An Fu Jiang	84
An Lu Jiang	74
An Sai Jiang	75
An Yang Jiang	81
Chao Yang	102
Dong Fang 66	92
Eastern Bright	93
Ever Bright	84
Floating Mountain	65
Fortunate Star	84
Fortune Sea	206
Hai Ji Shun	153
Hanbonn Brother	93
Hanbonn Concord	83
Hun Jiang	96
Jin Fu	152
Join Cheung	56
Lian Feng	118
Lian Nong	92
Ling Hai 18	73
Long Feng	213
Long Fu	237
Long Xiang	215
Manaslu	216
Mandarin Ocean	119
Mei Jiang	73
Merrytrans	119
Min Jiang	131
Nan Jiang	152
Nong Gong Shan 8	204
Ocean Join	84
Pangani	89
Ping Jiang	79
Qing Jiang	77
Rich Ascent	128
Rong Jiang	153
She De	118
Shun Yi	88
Shun Yuan 6	93
Xi Run	88
Xin Hai Teng	110
Yong Tong	232
Yu Jia	75
Yuan Guang	43
Yuan Jiang	98
Yue Yang	48

Colocotronis Ltd., London
Juventus	55
Natal	52
Santa Amalia	127
Santa Artemis	120
Santa Clio	57
Santa Katerina	119
Santa Maja	120
Santa Vassiliki	118
Tanganyika	55
Togo	56

Government of Cuba, Havana
Alaminos	147
Avon	142
Bartolome Maso	145
Belic	142

Calixto Garcia	71
Carlos Manuel de Cespedes	142
Cedar Hill	51
Donato Marmol	137
East Islands	229
Emerald Islands	146
Gaea	145
Ignacio Agramonte	143
Lilac Islands	226
Lotus Islands	227
Magister	137
Maisi	141
Maximo Gomez	155
Nanking	155
North Islands	230
Odelis	103
Olebratt	145
Pamit C	70
Redestos	133
Rose Islands	103
Ruby Islands	147
Severn	142
South Islands	228
Star	51
Star I	51
Tephys	70
Wavel	146
West Islands	228
1 Congreso del Partido	141

Thomas A. Demseris, Piraeus
Jade	136
Jade II	94
Jade III	95

George Dracopoulos (Empros Lines), Piraeus
Anna Dracopoulos	65
Avance	65
Empros	76
Katerina Dracopoulos	149

Empresa Lineas Maritimas Argentinas, Buenos Aires
Almirante Storni	221
Dr. Atilio Malvagni	224
General Manuel Belgrano	225
Jujuy	219
Liberatador General Jose de Martin	223
Neuquen II	222
Presidente Ramon S. Castillo	225
Salta	218
Tucuman	220

John T. Essberger, Hamburg
Tibati	52
Topega	52
Transvaal	128

Nikolaos Frangos and Nicholas G. Moundreas (Good Faith Shipping Co. Ltd.), Piraeus
Antwerp	32
Brasilia	184
Fulvia	186
Good Dolphin	33
Good Lord	104
Good Patriot	32
Good Sun	104
Kavo Geranos	184
Liberator A	32
Lord Venkata	32
Mar Courrier	115
Princess	33

Wave Crest	104

Frota Oceanica Brasiliera S.A., Rio de Janeiro
Frotadurban	238
Frotakobe	236
Frotamanila	237
Frotasingapore	241

Alex Giannakopoulos (Pacific and Atlantic Corporation), Piraeus
Blue Frontier	208
Blue Horizon	217
Express Orient	214
Express Santiago	215
Express Seminole	213
Express Shanghai	208
Oriental Crown	214
Oriental Honour	241
Oriental Kiku	207
Oriental Spirit	208
Saint Antonios	214
Saint Ioannis	215
Saint Markos	241
Saint Nectarios	213
Saint Pavlos	237
Saint Spiridonas	208
Stavroforos	208

Gibbs and Co. (Shipmanagement) Ltd., Newport
Welsh Endeavour	59
Welsh Trident	58
Welsh Troubadour	132

S.C. Halkias, Piraeus
Juanita Halkias	109
Recalada Light	109
Texel Light	108
Sklerion	108

Hamburg Sudamerkinanische D.G., Hamburg
Aracaju	199
Santa Ines	196
Santa Isabella	194
Santa Teresa	197
Santa Ursula	195

Holbud Ltd., London
Aliadrakini	52
Al Hafizu	113
Al Raziqu	166
Al Johffa	120

Inftrutra G.m.b.H. & Co., O.H.G., Hamburg
Cosmokrat	47
Cosmonaut	46
Cosmopolit	48
Cosmostar	51
Durban Carrier	47

Lamport and Holt Ltd., Liverpool
Belloc	89
Boswell	88
Bronte	82
Browning	84

Larrinaga Steamship Co. Ltd., Liverpool
Miguel de Larrinaga	40
Ramon de Larrinaga	49
Rupert de Larrinaga	38

M.J. Lemos Co. Ltd., London
Ioannis	109
Prodromos	109
San George	41
Tiger Bay	57
Toros Bay	57

Linhas Brasileiras de Navegacoa Ltda., Rio de Janeiro
Regina	190
Regina Celi	190
Semiramis	193

Lloyd Brasileiro, Companhia de Navegacao, Rio de Janeiro
Lloydbras	184
Lloyd Alegrete	240
Lloyd Antuerpia	192
Lloyd Bahia	241
Lloyd Genova	202
Lloyd Hamburgo	190
Lloyd Houston	212
Lloyd Liverpool	189
Lloyd Mandu	237
Lloyd Marselha	204
Lloyd Mexico	211
Lloyd Rotterdam	191
Lloyd Tupiara	239

Lloyd Libra Navegacao Ltda., Sao Paolo
L/L Brasil	212
L/L Chile	185
L/L Columbia	203
L/L Peru	186
L/L Equador	186

London and Overseas Freighters Ltd., London
London Bombardier	126
London Cavalier	125
London Fusilier	123
London Grenadier	122

Vas Maltezos (Mayfair (Hellas) Ltd.), Piraeus
Jute Express	126
Naya	163
Teti	39

G.P., J. and P.G. Margaronis (Marlborough Shipping Co. Ltd.), London
Agios Markos	48
Belle	62
Nour	135

Matheson and Co. Ltd., London
Carrel	113
Cluden (1)	128
Cluden (2)	77
Collin	113

Mavroleon Brothers Ltd., London
Akri	31
Alioussa	35
Argolis	37
Avlaki	30
Carina	35
Ermioni	54
Janey	37
Nicola	30
Patricia M	60
Sacha	54
Syrie	31

John McRink and Co. Ltd., Hong Kong
Lady Aryette	50
Lady Trude	53
Lady Vicky	161

Mega Trust Maritime S.A., Piraeus
Akela	186
Mega Breeze	186
Mega Luck	182
Mega Rio	190
Mega Union	176

Metcalf, Son and Co., Hartlepool
Dunelmia (1)	44
Dunelmia (2)	150
Industria	144

M.I.T. Transportes Maritimos Internacionales Ltda., Rio de Janeiro
M.I.T. Rio de Janeiro	209
Monte Alto	206
Monte Cristo	205
Monte Pascoal	206

Nautconsult Shipping Co. Ltd., London
Aracaju	199
Babitonga	61
Ceresio	198
Santa Ines	196
Santa Isabella	194
Santa Teresa	197
Santa Ursula	195
Vermelha	61

Companhia de Navegacao Maritima Netumar, Rio de Janeiro
Amalia	232
Caiçara	233
Joana	234
L/L Columbia	203
Leonor	208
Rio Conquista	202
Tucurui	217

People's Republic of North Korea, Pyongyang
Dong Myong	194
Eun Bong	222
Hae Gum Gang	40
Hyang Ro Bong	102
Ja Gang	219
Jag Ganga	177
Jangdaesan	63
Ku Ryong	164
Kum Gang	177
Kuwolsan	141
Kyong Song	181
Mokran I	222
Ocean Ho	63
Pyong Chon	167
Ra Nam	213
Rimyongsu	141
Ryong Gang 2	93
Sae Byol	194
Sam Hae	164
Sam Hai 1	164
Sin Heung 1	141
Sungrisan 9	141

Egon Oldendorff, Lübeck
Catharine Oldendorff	68
Dorthe Oldendorff	45
Edward Oldendorff	238
Eibe Oldendorff	67
Fair Spirit	67
Future Hope	92
Globe Trader	93
Good Faith	90
Happy Chance	66
Hille Oldendorff	53
Hinrich Oldendorff	66
Imme Oldendorff	50
Impala	93
Jobst Oldendorff	215
Secil Kiaat	90
Secil Seraya	238
Splendid Fortune	68

P&O, London
Strathdare	135
Strathdevon	137
Strathdirk	145
Strathdoon	146
Strathduns	147
Strathdyce	148

Pakistan National Shipping Corporation, Karachi
Ayubia	98
Kaghan	97
Murree	96
Ocean Envoy	124

N.D. Papalios (Aegis Shipping Co. Ltd.), Piraeus
Aegis Banner	159
Aegis Fame	158
Aegis Freedom	157
Aegis Island	32
Aegis Trade	162
Aegis Venture	33
Degedo	32
Dora Papalios	157
George N. Papalios	104
Mimis N. Papalios	104
Miss Papalios	158
Nea Hellas	157
Venturer	33

Parakou Shipping Ltd., Hong Kong
Delight Glory	68
Trade Fair	99
Trade Fair	150

Anastasios G. Politis (Anpo Shipping Co. Ltd.), Piraeus
Achilles	195
Anteos	239
Aristoteles	212
Icarus	190
Phaethon	202
Prometheus	237
Socrates	125

Rogers and Co. Ltd., Port Louis
Bel Air	241
Bel Azur	237
Belle Isle	43
Belle Rose	62

Seabirds Management Inc., Piraeus
Cormorant	51
Gannet	64
Skimmer	146
Skua	149
Turnstone	143

Seabon Holding Corporation see Bonyad Marine Services Inc.

Starfield Maritime Management Ltd., Geneva
Interlaken	158
Sybil I	157
Titisee	162

Companhia de Transportes Maritimos Ltda., Lisbon
Diana C	199
Fatima C	194
Luso Ana	199
Pedro C	195

Thoresen and Co. (Bangkok) Ltd., Bangkok
Hai Ming	111
Hai Meng	114
Halldor	150
Hermes	151
Hermes III	151

NavieraUniversal, Lima
Mare	183
Unilago	239
Unimar	183
Uniselva	184

George Vergottis, London
Atheras	38
Atrotos	40
Jade Bay	49
Myrtos	112

Panaghis Vergottis 129
Sea Moon	112
Stephanos Vergottis	131
Vardiani	40
Vergray	38
Vergstar	40

Vernicos Maritime Co. S.A. (C.D. and N.A. Vernicos), Piraeus
Neos	171
Pigeon	37
Toxa	169

Government of the Socialist Republic of Vietnam, Ho Chi Minh City
Agate 1	58
Agate	58
Fareast	99
Luc-Nam	87
Quartz	59
Saigon 1	59
Saigon 2	58
Saigon 3	94
Saigon 5	95
Song Duong	78
Thai-Binh	81
To-Lich	88

N.J. Vlassopoulos Ltd., Piraeus
Ithaki	106
Maria	115
Moldova	117
Sklerion	107

Vroon B.V., Breskens
African Express	75
European Express	74
Navira Express	132
Samar Express	108
Scandinavian Express	95
Scotian Express	94
Seaway	95
Serra	188
Silago Express	132
Simara Express	122
Sulu Express	140

Wah Tung Shipping Agency Co. Ltd., Hong Kong
Caly	151
Colossus	128
Fareast Beauty	99
Her Loong	123
Trade Fortune	150

West Hartlepool Steam Navigation Co. Ltd., West Hartlepool
Ardenhall	44
Carlow Hill	140
Lindenhall	140

World Wide Shipping Ltd., Hong Kong
United Drive	101
United Effort	100
United Enterprise	99
United Spirit	102

Andreas Yiannoulou, Athens
City of Akaki	200
Don Akaki	200
Global Natali	201
La Express	200
Natali H	201

Yugoslavia (various owning companies)
Komovi	148
Monte	148
Piva	89
Rio B	89
Rumija	69

INDEX OF SHIPS

The following conventions are used: first in-service names in upper case; subsequent names in upper and lower; proposed names in brackets including names under which ship was launched but did not enter service which go in upper case; names of other ships mentioned (usually tugs or vessels involved in collisions) in italics.